YO
BA&!

5

KIYOHIKO AZUMA

CONTENTS

YOTSUBA&!
KIYOHIKO AZUMA

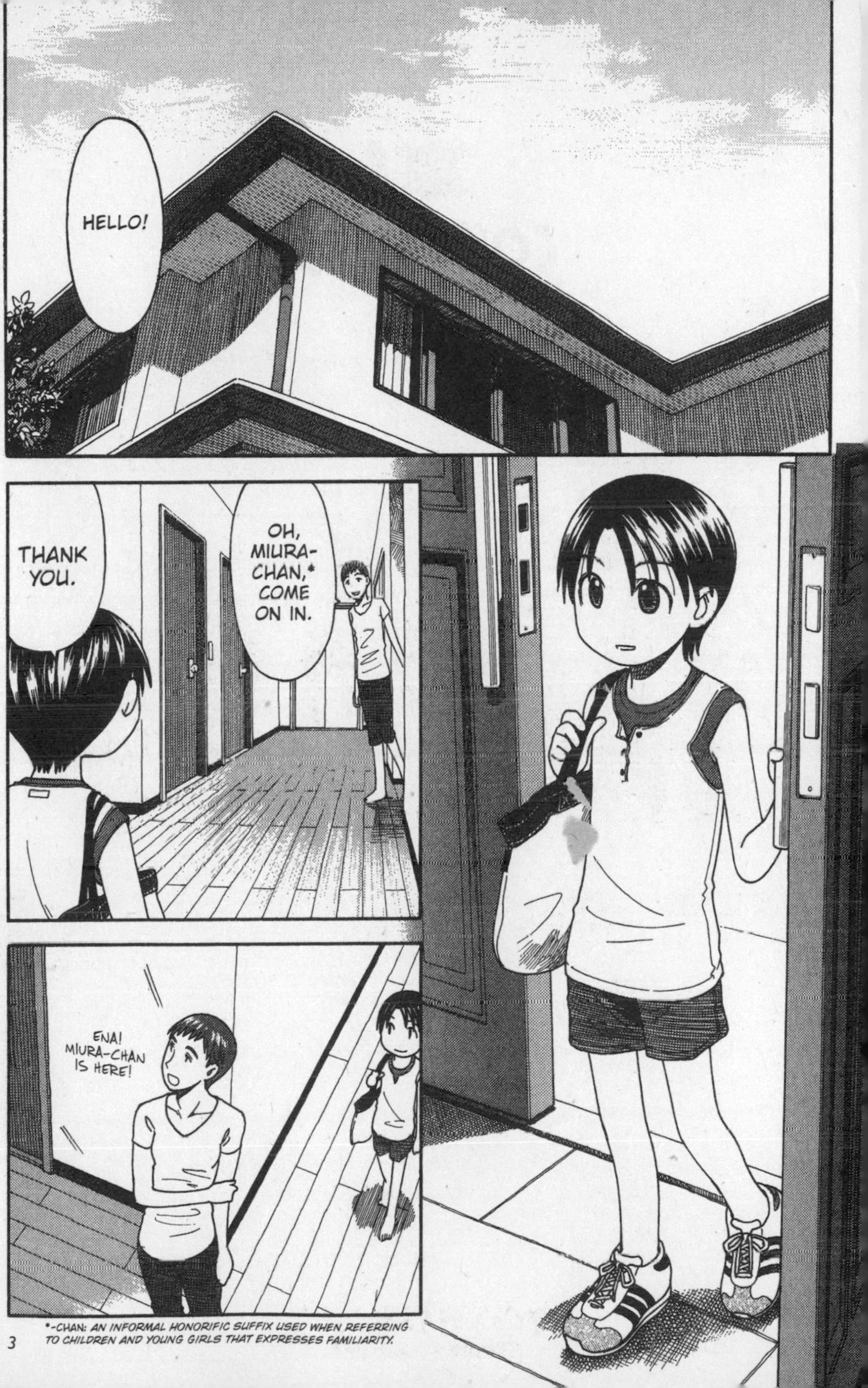
HELLO!
OH, MIURA-CHAN,* COME ON IN.
THANK YOU.
ENA! MIURA-CHAN IS HERE!

*-CHAN: AN INFORMAL HONORIFIC SUFFIX USED WHEN REFERRING TO CHILDREN AND YOUNG GIRLS THAT EXPRESSES FAMILIARITY.

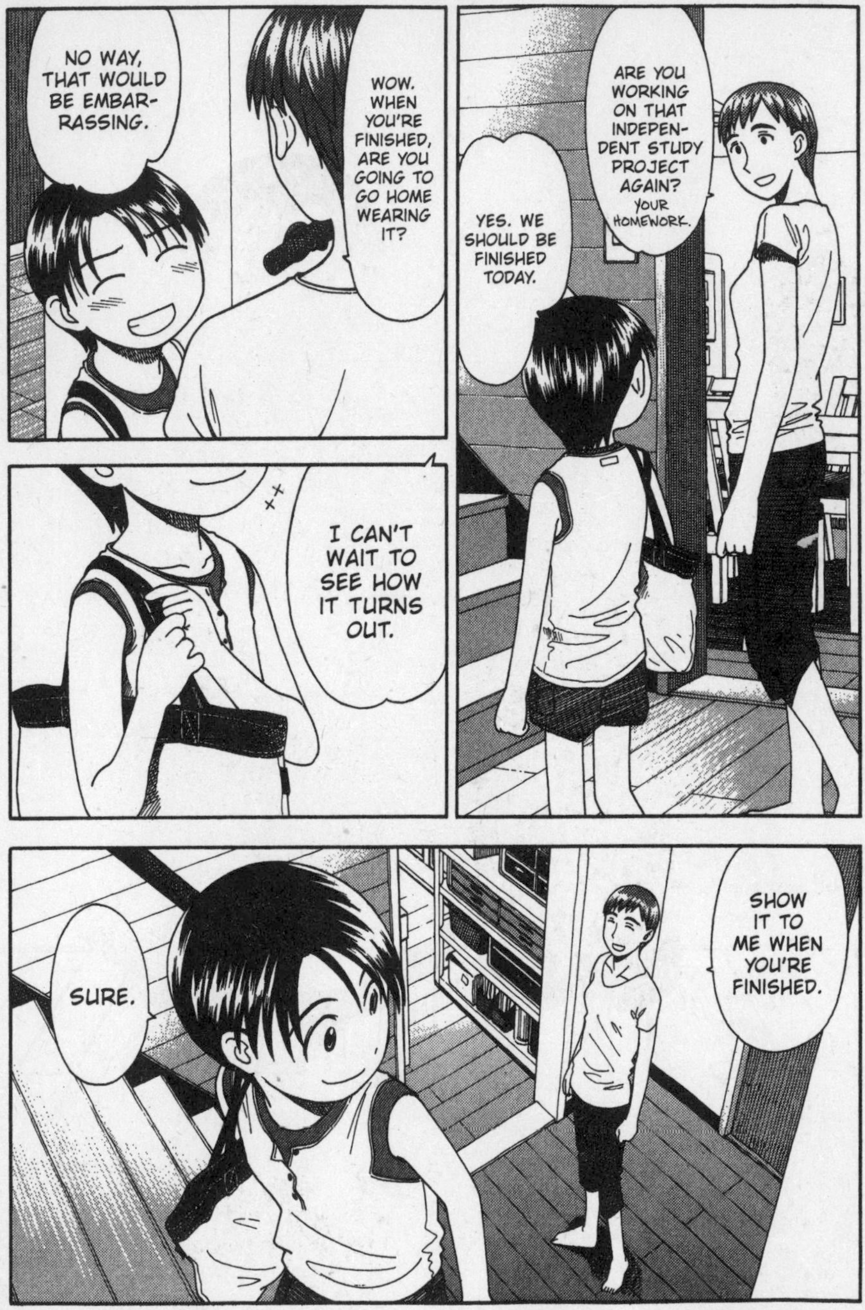
ARE YOU WORKING ON THAT INDEPENDENT STUDY PROJECT AGAIN?
YOUR HOMEWORK.
YES. WE SHOULD BE FINISHED TODAY.
WOW. WHEN YOU'RE FINISHED, ARE YOU GOING TO GO HOME WEARING IT?
NO WAY, THAT WOULD BE EMBARRASSING.
I CAN'T WAIT TO SEE HOW IT TURNS OUT.
SHOW IT TO ME WHEN YOU'RE FINISHED.
SURE.

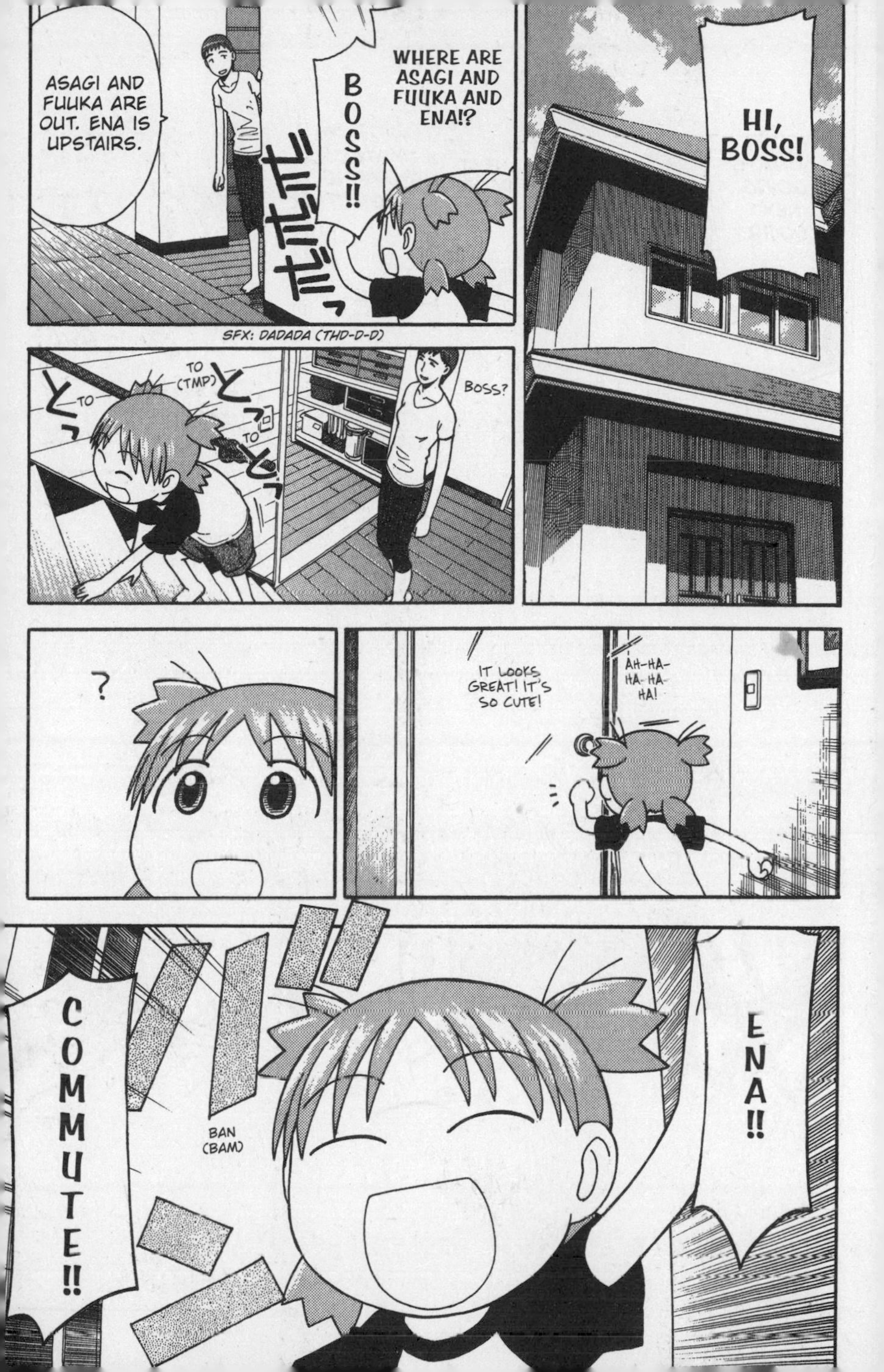
HI, BOSS!
BOSS!!
WHERE ARE ASAGI AND FUUKA AND ENA!?
ASAGI AND FUUKA ARE OUT. ENA IS UPSTAIRS.
SFX: DADADA (THD-D-D)
BOSS?
TO (TMP)
TO
TO
AH-HA-HA-HA-HA!
IT LOOKS GREAT! IT'S SO CUTE!
?
ENA!!
BAN (BAM)
COMMUTE!!

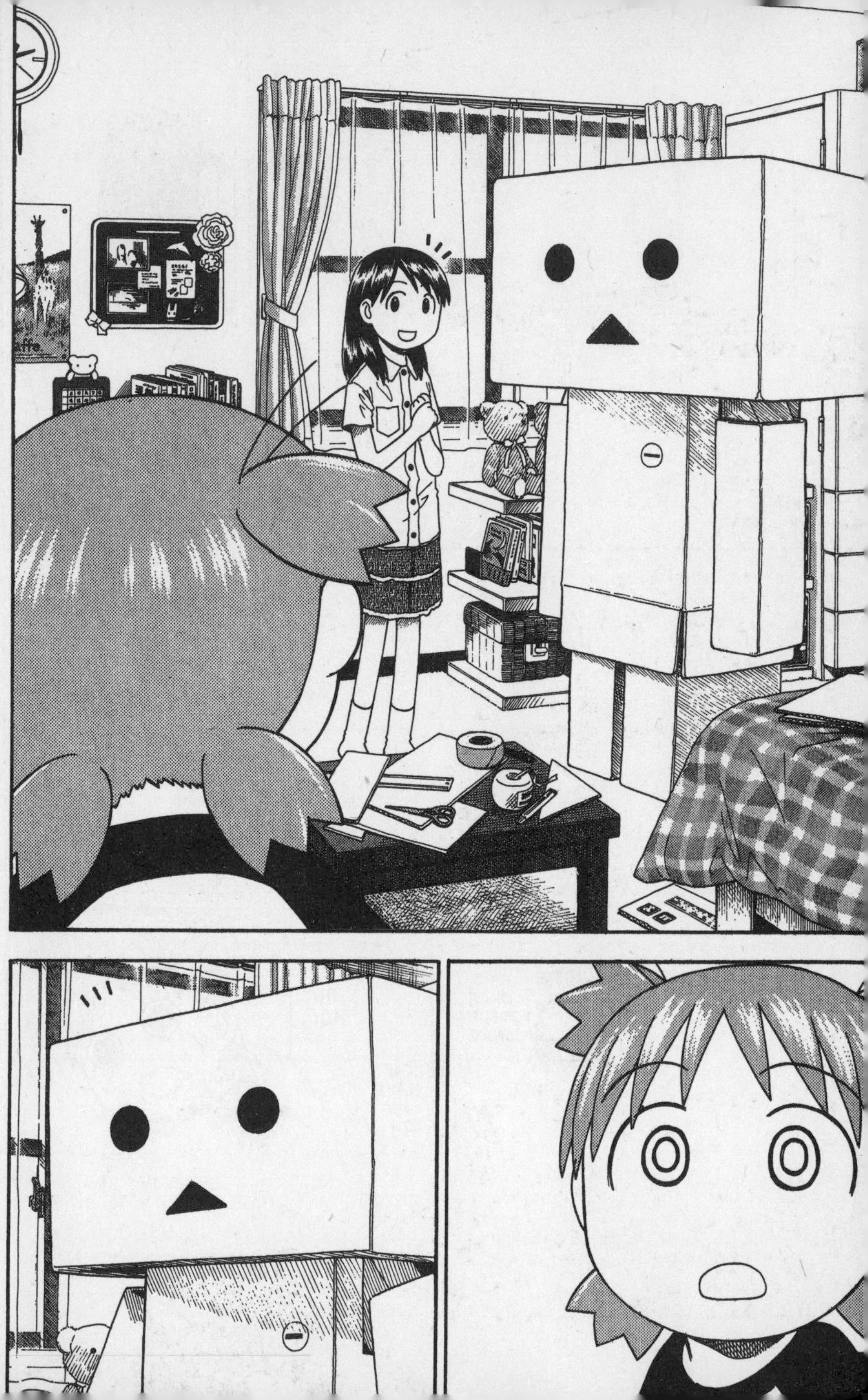

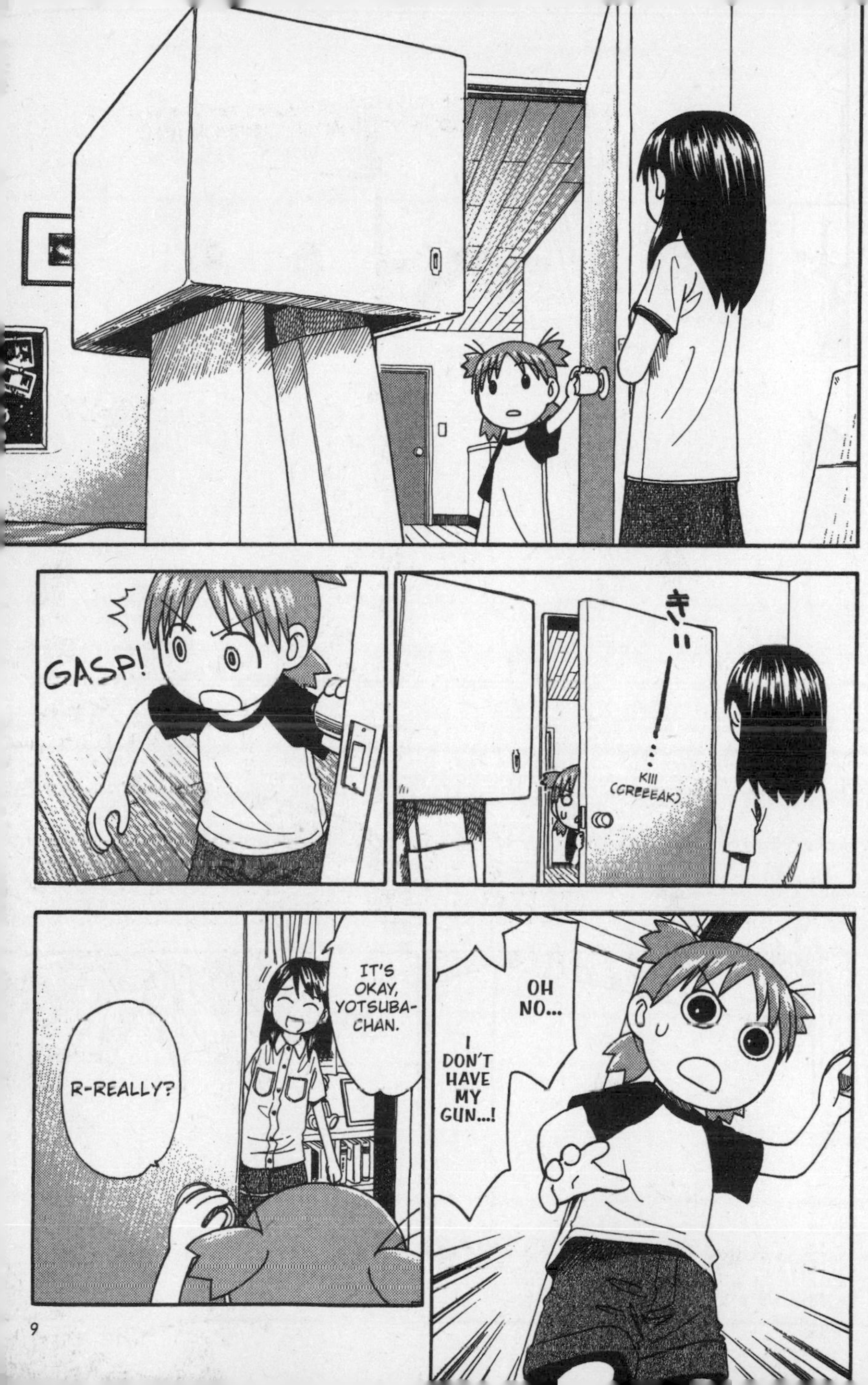
KIII (CREEEAK)
GASP!
OH NO...
I DON'T HAVE MY GUN...!
IT'S OKAY, YOTSUBA-CHAN.
R-REALLY?

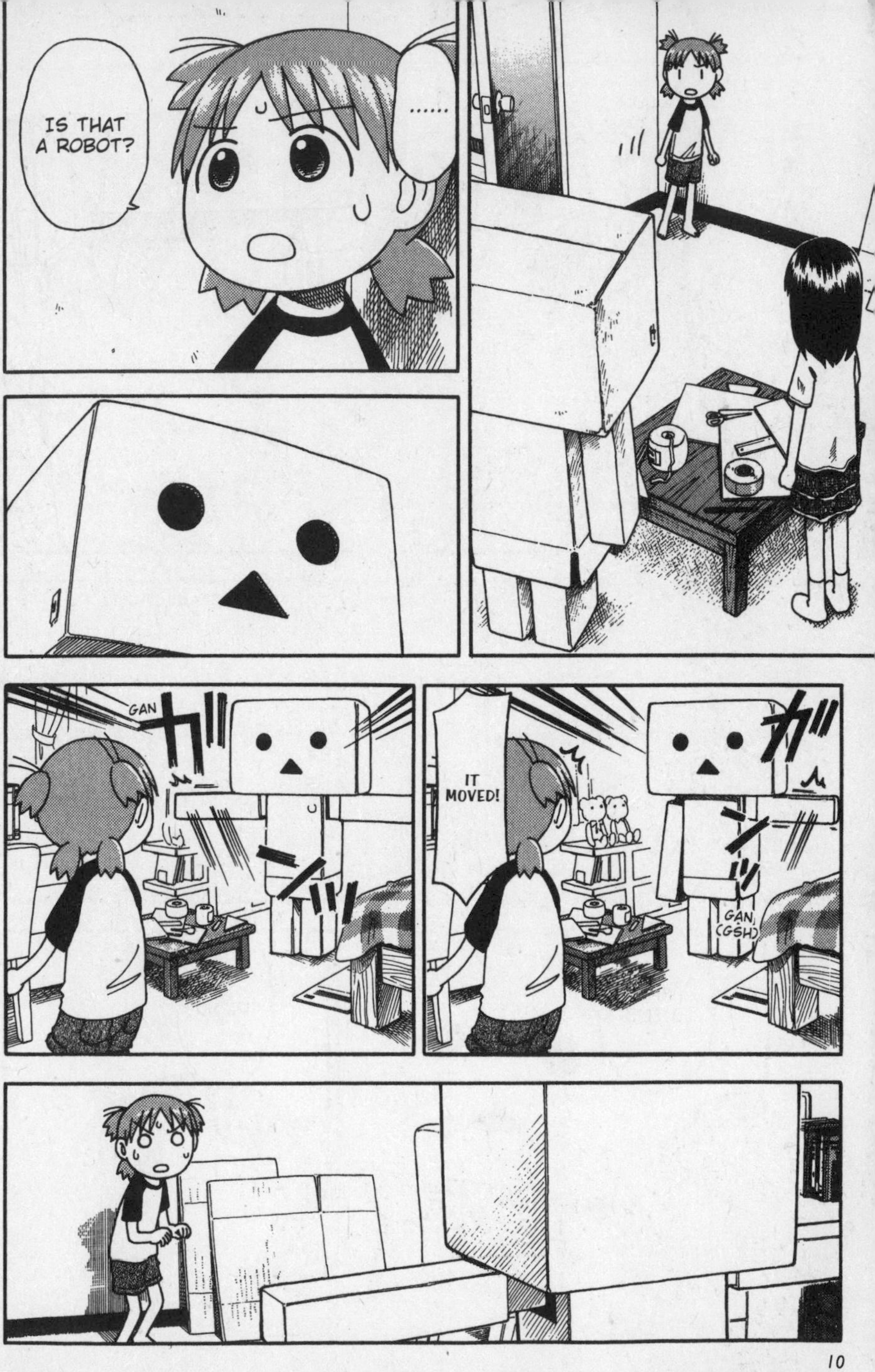
......
IS THAT A ROBOT?
IT MOVED!
GAN, (GSH)
GAN

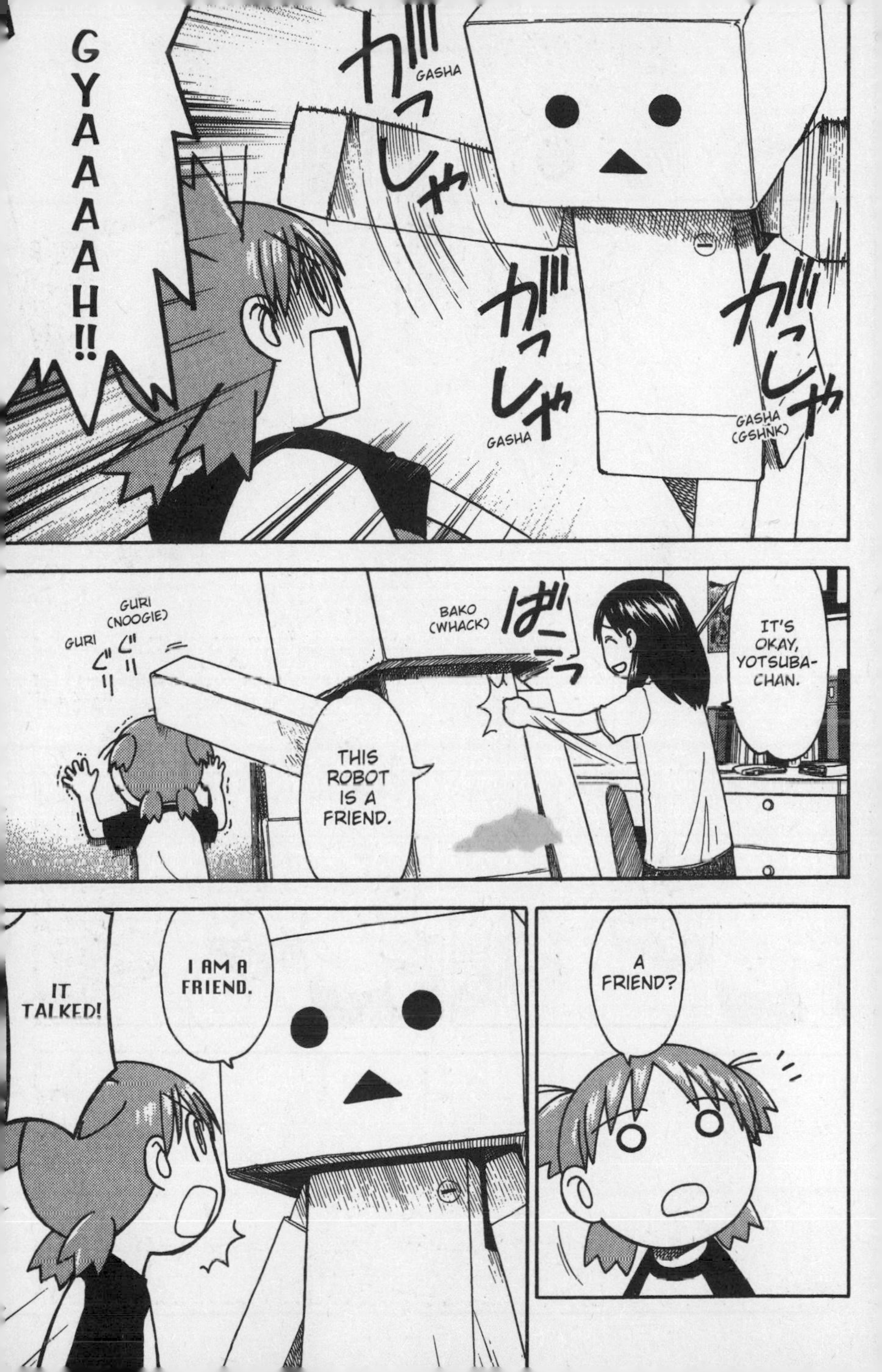
がっしゃ
GASHA
GASHA (GSHNK)
がっしゃ
GASHA
GYAAAAAH!!
IT'S OKAY, YOTSUBA-CHAN.
ばこっ
BAKO (WHACK)
THIS ROBOT IS A FRIEND.
ぐり
GURI (NOOGIE)
ぐり
GURI
A FRIEND?
I AM A FRIEND.
IT TALKED!

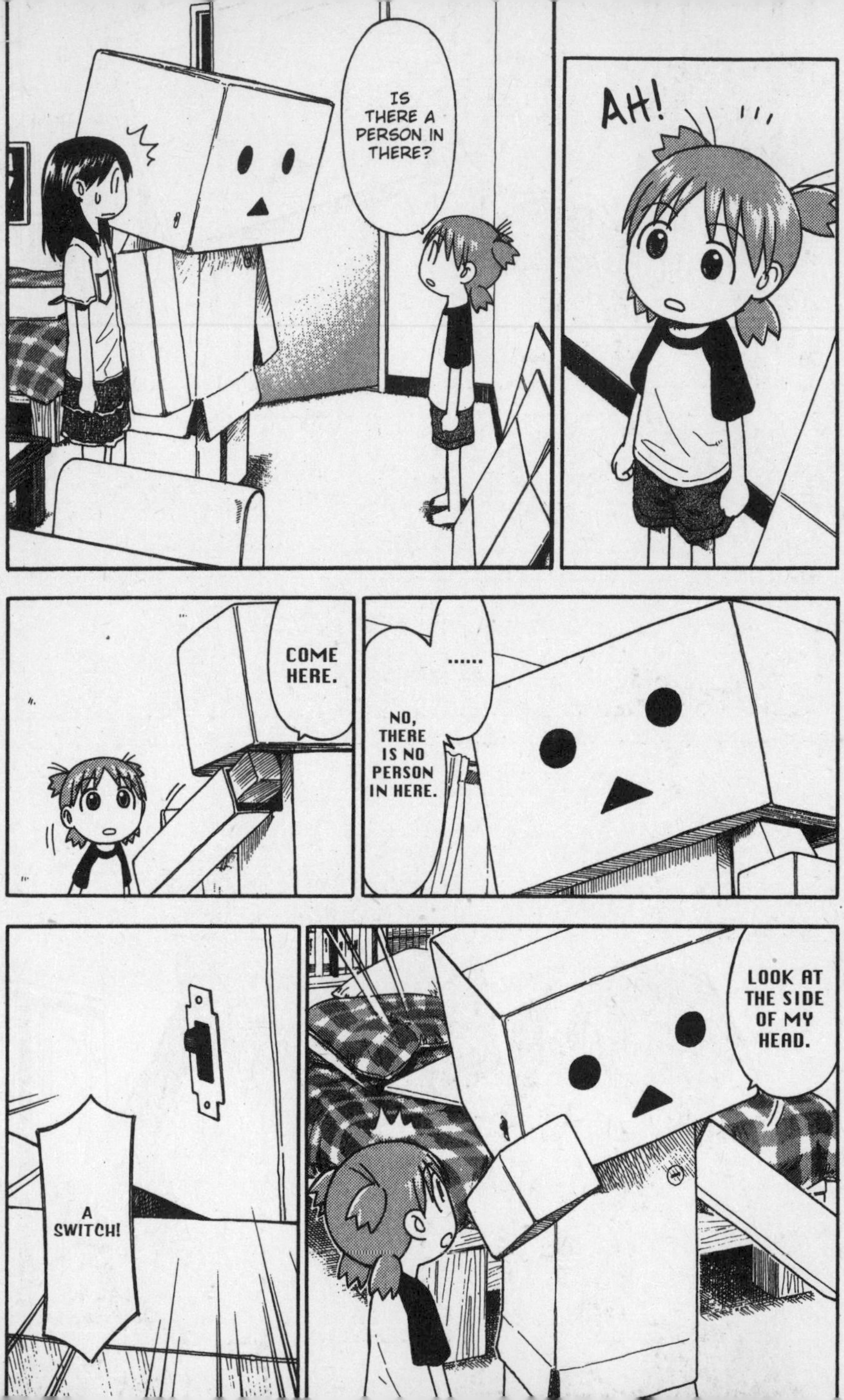
AH!
IS THERE A PERSON IN THERE?
......
NO, THERE IS NO PERSON IN HERE.
COME HERE.
LOOK AT THE SIDE OF MY HEAD.
A SWITCH!

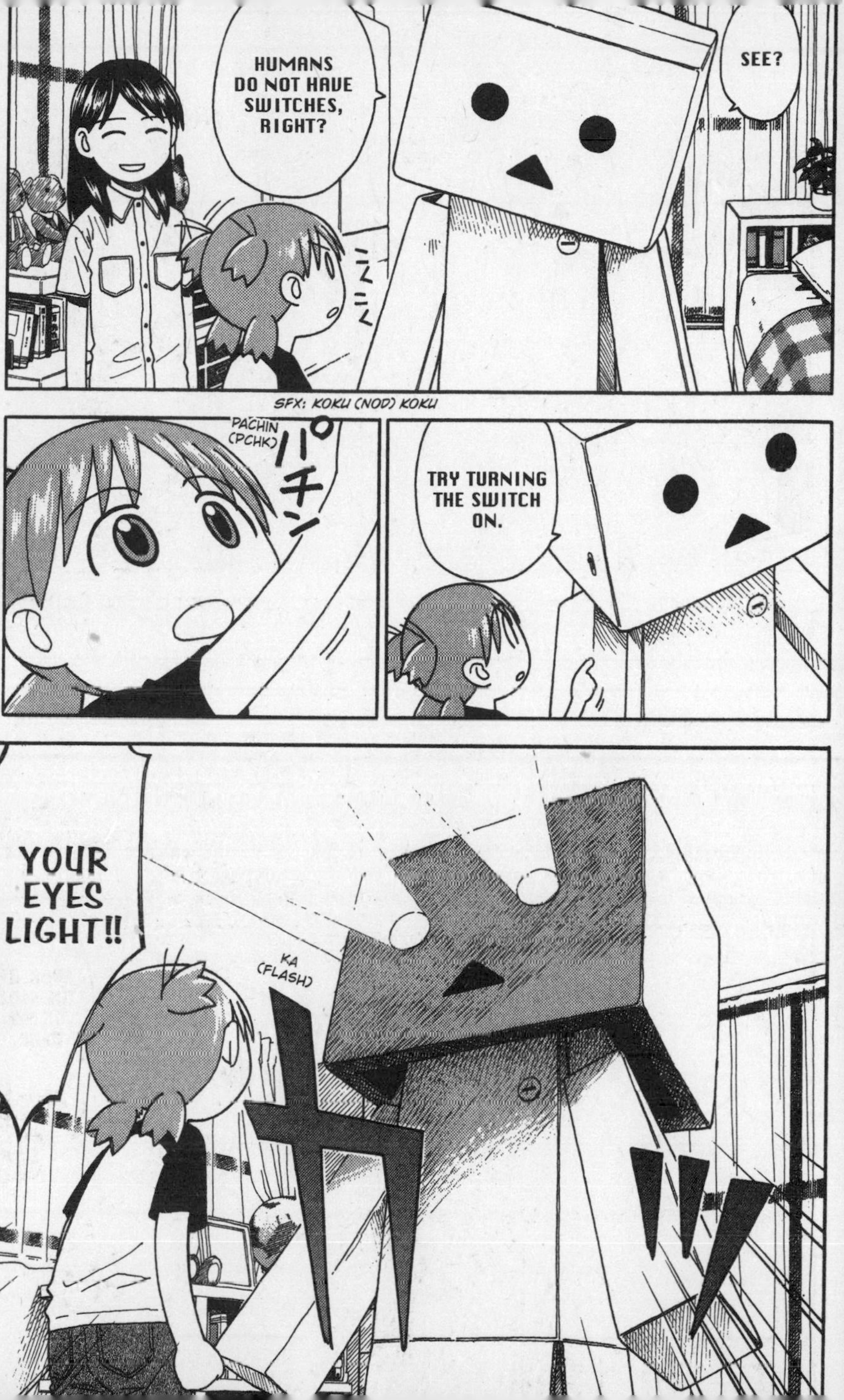
SEE?
HUMANS DO NOT HAVE SWITCHES, RIGHT?
SFX: KOKU (NOD) KOKU
TRY TURNING THE SWITCH ON.
パチン
PACHIN (PCHK)
YOUR EYES LIGHT!!
KA (FLASH)

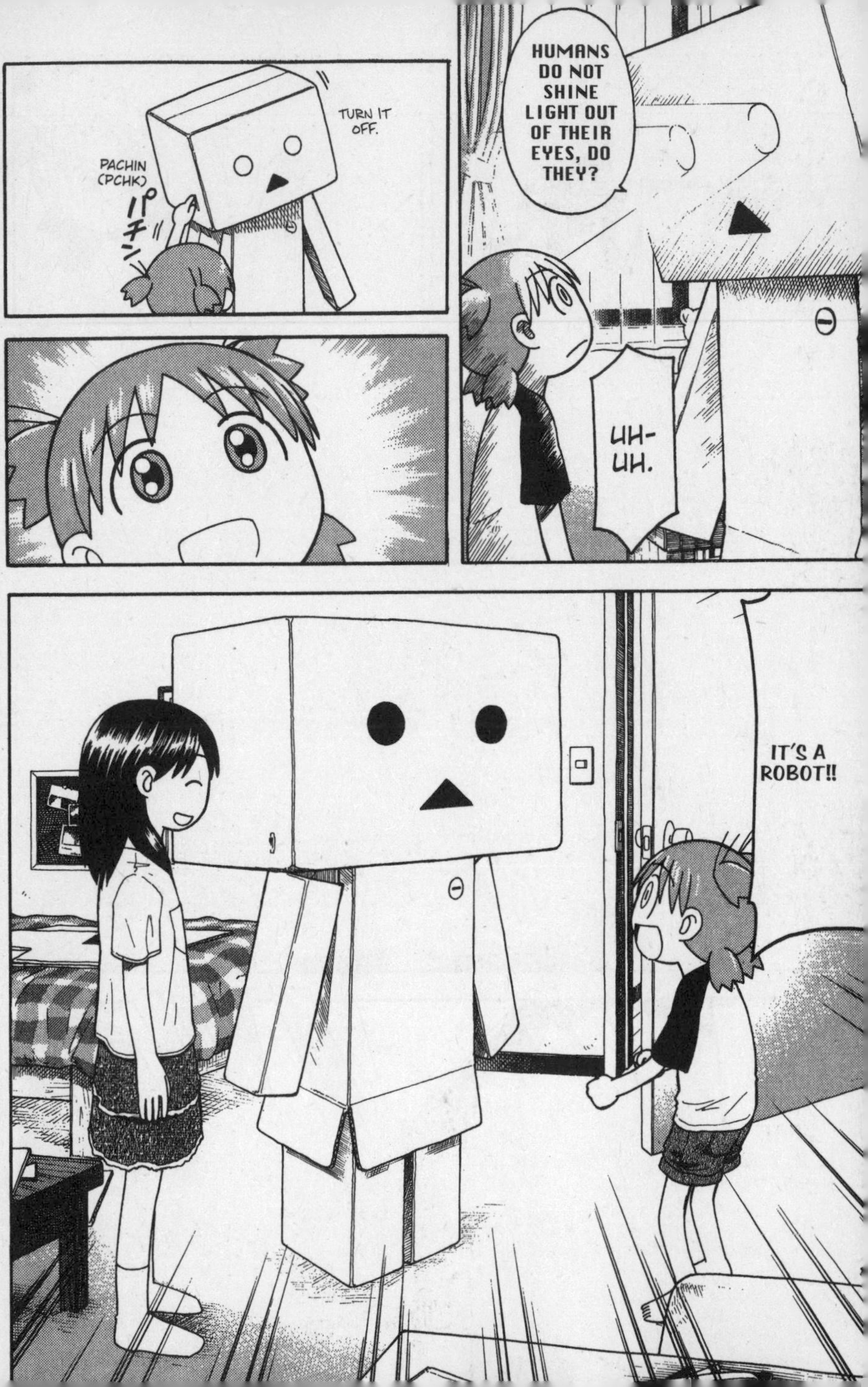
HUMANS DO NOT SHINE LIGHT OUT OF THEIR EYES, DO THEY?
UH-UH.
TURN IT OFF.
パチン
PACHIN (PCHK)
IT'S A ROBOT!!

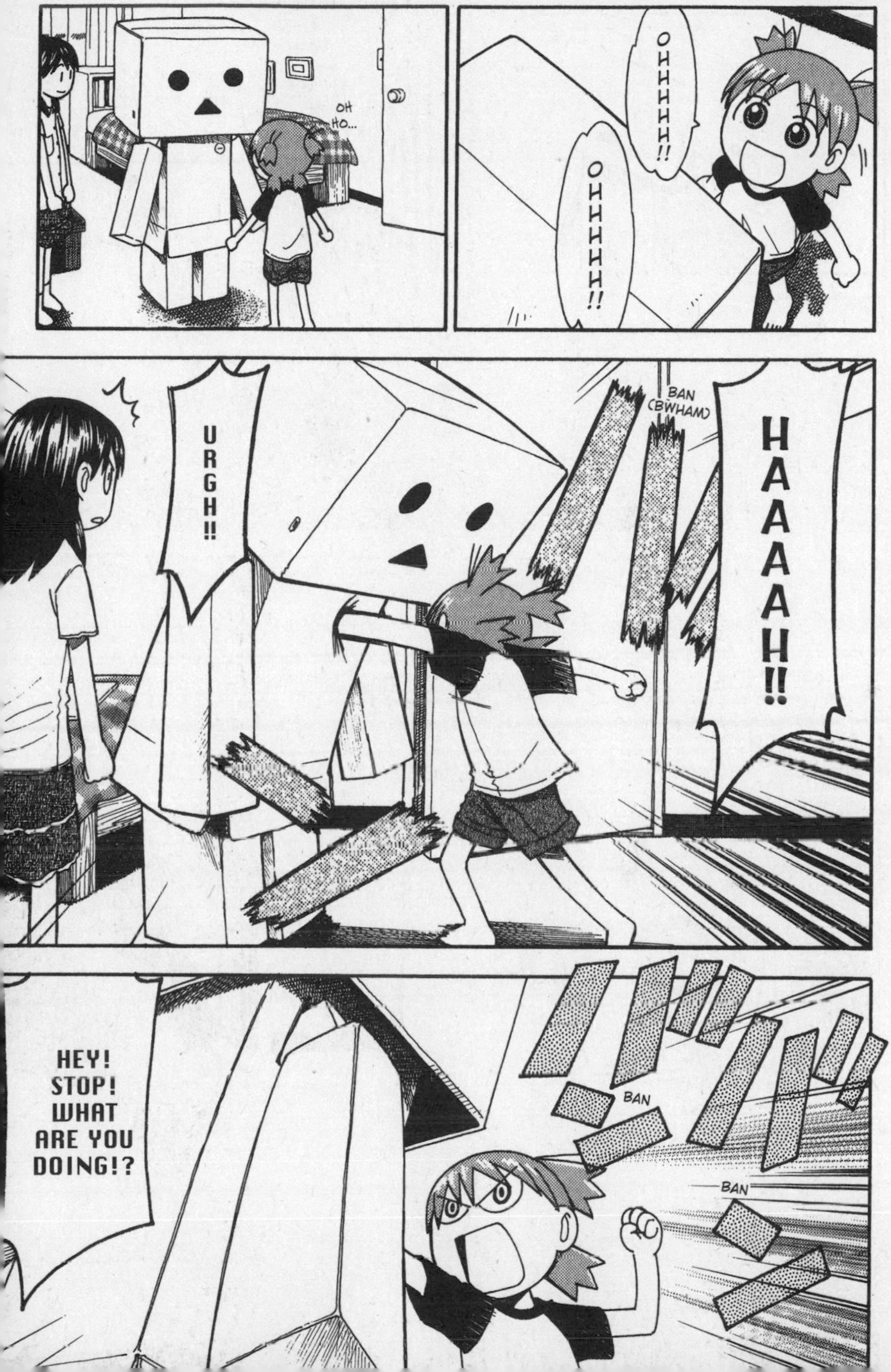
OHHHHH!!
OHHHHHH!!
OH HO...
HAAAAAH!!
BAN (BWHAM)
URGH!!
BAN
BAN
HEY! STOP! WHAT ARE YOU DOING!?

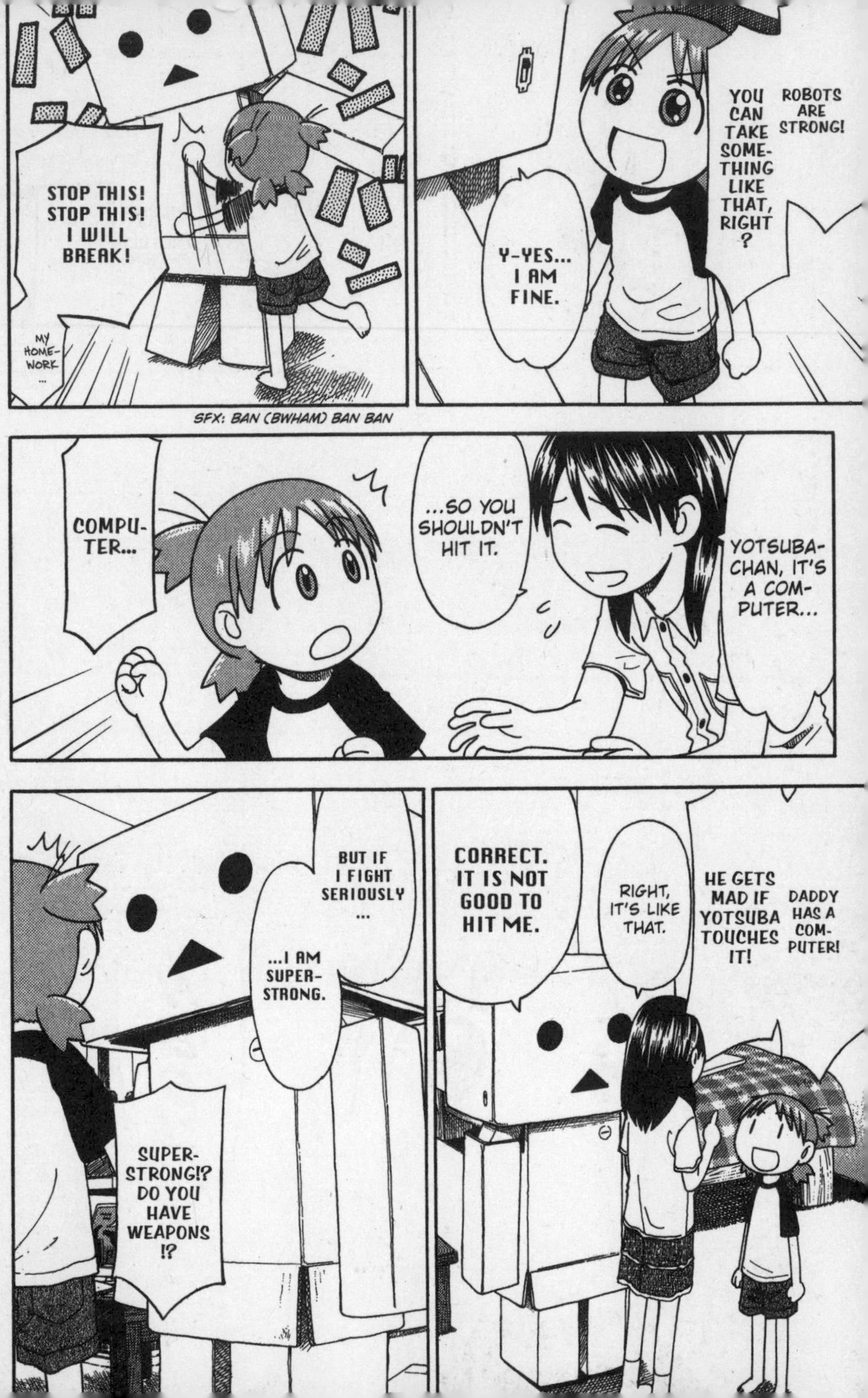
ROBOTS ARE STRONG!
YOU CAN TAKE SOMETHING LIKE THAT, RIGHT?
Y-YES... I AM FINE.
STOP THIS! STOP THIS! I WILL BREAK!
MY HOMEWORK...
SFX: BAN (BWHAM) BAN BAN
YOTSUBA-CHAN, IT'S A COMPUTER...
...SO YOU SHOULDN'T HIT IT.
COMPUTER...
DADDY HAS A COMPUTER!
HE GETS MAD IF YOTSUBA TOUCHES IT!
RIGHT, IT'S LIKE THAT.
CORRECT. IT IS NOT GOOD TO HIT ME.
BUT IF I FIGHT SERIOUSLY...
...I AM SUPER-STRONG.
SUPER-STRONG!? DO YOU HAVE WEAPONS!?

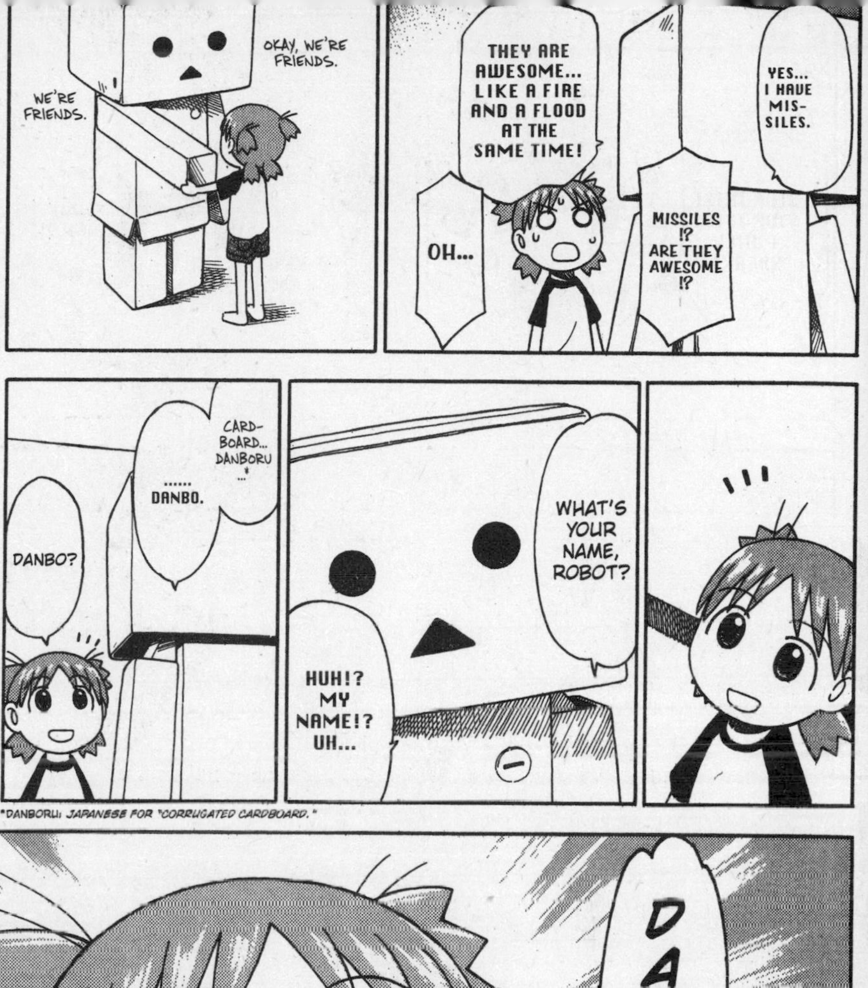
YES... I HAVE MIS-SILES.
MISSILES !? ARE THEY AWESOME !?
THEY ARE AWESOME... LIKE A FIRE AND A FLOOD AT THE SAME TIME!
OH...
OKAY, WE'RE FRIENDS.
WE'RE FRIENDS.
WHAT'S YOUR NAME, ROBOT?
HUH!? MY NAME!? UH...
CARD-BOARD... DANBORU* ...
...... DANBO.
DANBO?

*DANBORU: JAPANESE FOR "CORRUGATED CARDBOARD."

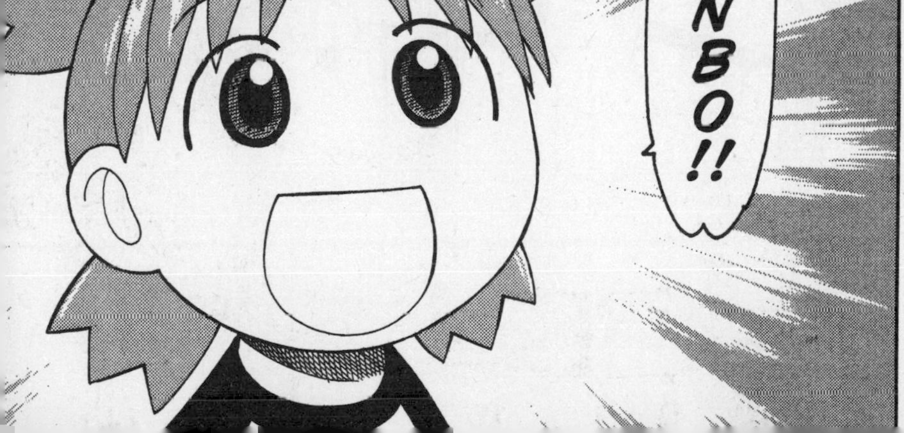
DANBO!!

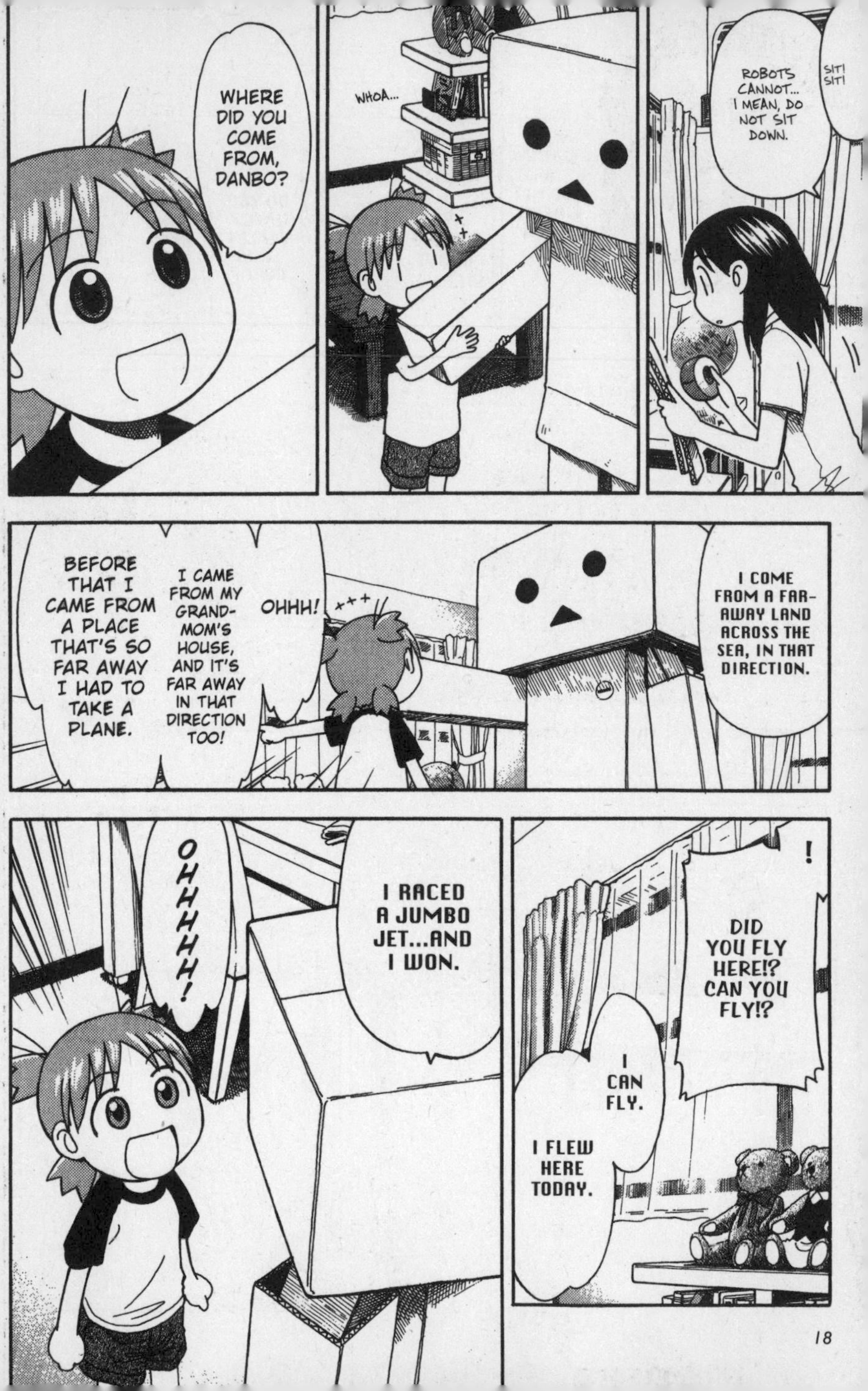
SIT! SIT!
ROBOTS CANNOT... I MEAN, DO NOT SIT DOWN.
WHOA...
WHERE DID YOU COME FROM, DANBO?
I COME FROM A FAR-AWAY LAND ACROSS THE SEA, IN THAT DIRECTION.
OHHH!
I CAME FROM MY GRAND-MOM'S HOUSE, AND IT'S FAR AWAY IN THAT DIRECTION TOO!
BEFORE THAT I CAME FROM A PLACE THAT'S SO FAR AWAY I HAD TO TAKE A PLANE.
!
DID YOU FLY HERE!? CAN YOU FLY!?
I CAN FLY.
I FLEW HERE TODAY.
I RACED A JUMBO JET...AND I WON.
OHHHHH!

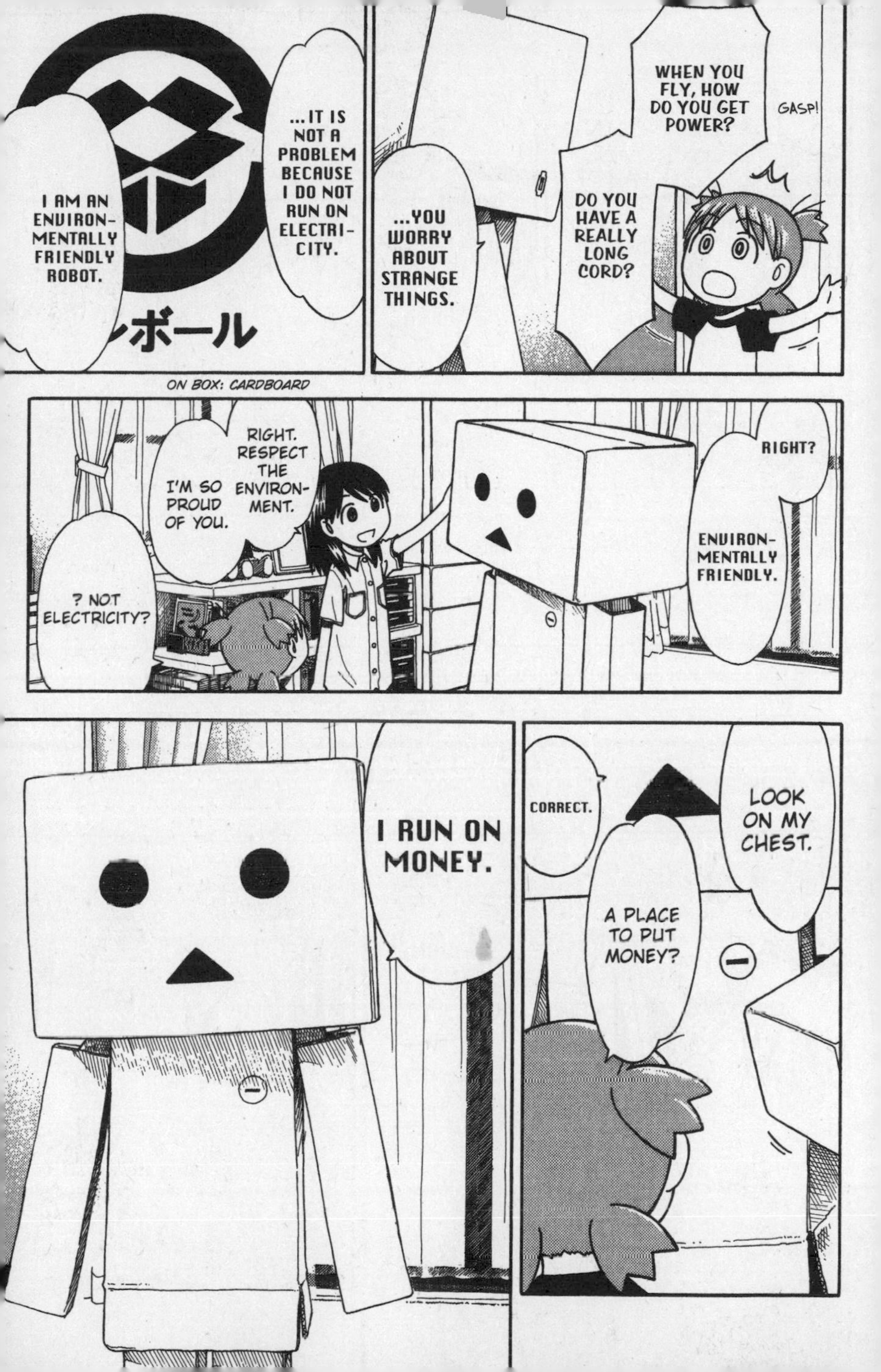
WHEN YOU FLY, HOW DO YOU GET POWER?
GASP!
DO YOU HAVE A REALLY LONG CORD?
...YOU WORRY ABOUT STRANGE THINGS.
...IT IS NOT A PROBLEM BECAUSE I DO NOT RUN ON ELECTRI-CITY.
I AM AN ENVIRON-MENTALLY FRIENDLY ROBOT.
ンボール
ON BOX: CARDBOARD
RIGHT?
ENVIRON-MENTALLY FRIENDLY.
RIGHT. RESPECT THE ENVIRON-MENT.
I'M SO PROUD OF YOU.
? NOT ELECTRICITY?
LOOK ON MY CHEST.
A PLACE TO PUT MONEY?
CORRECT.
I RUN ON MONEY.

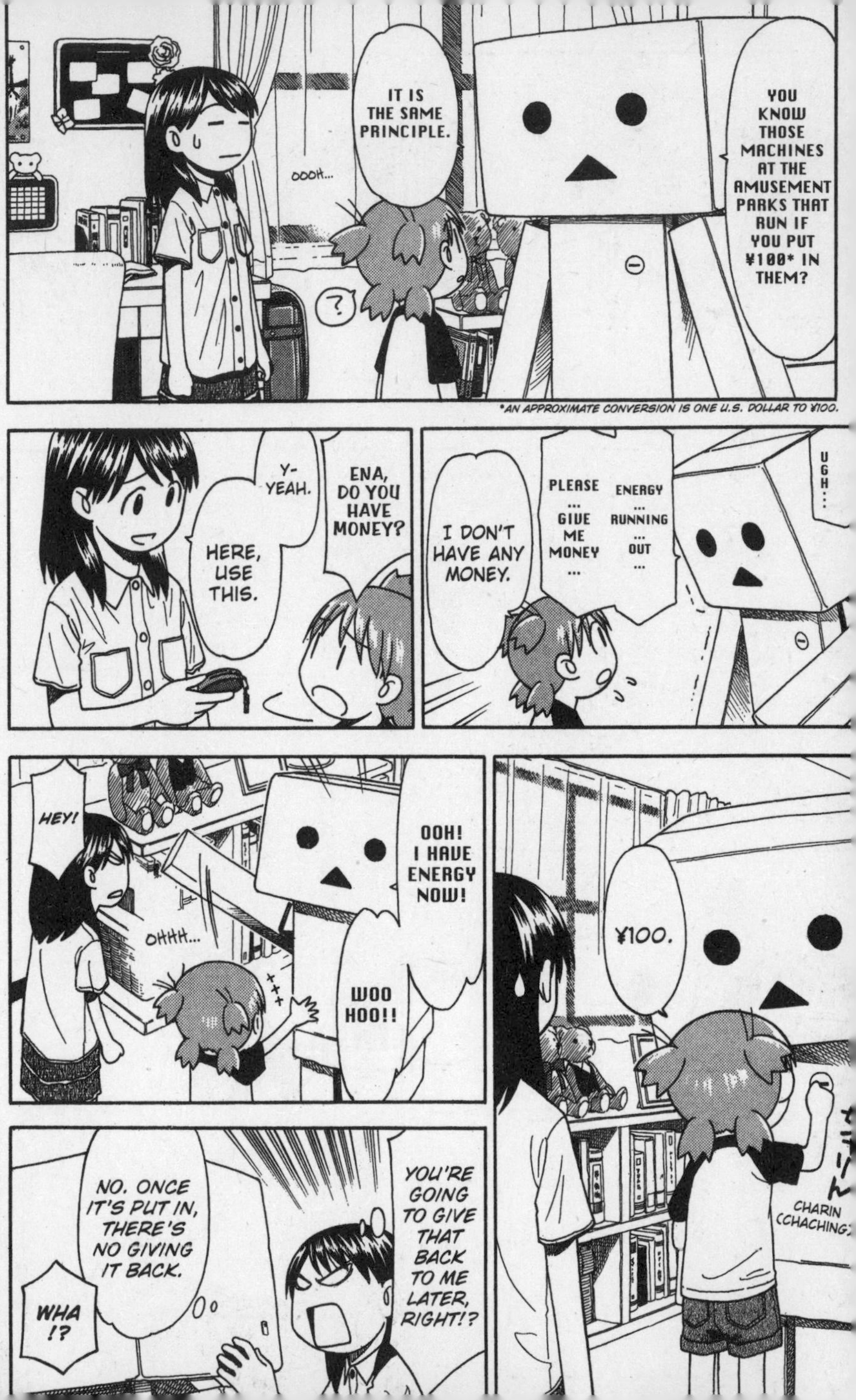
YOU KNOW THOSE MACHINES AT THE AMUSEMENT PARKS THAT RUN IF YOU PUT ¥100* IN THEM?
IT IS THE SAME PRINCIPLE.
OOOH...
?
UGH...
ENERGY ... RUNNING ... OUT ...
PLEASE ... GIVE ME MONEY ...
I DON'T HAVE ANY MONEY.
ENA, DO YOU HAVE MONEY?
Y- YEAH.
HERE, USE THIS.
¥100.
CHARIN (CHACHING)
OOH! I HAVE ENERGY NOW!
WOO HOO!!
OHHH...
HEY!
YOU'RE GOING TO GIVE THAT BACK TO ME LATER, RIGHT!?
NO. ONCE IT'S PUT IN, THERE'S NO GIVING IT BACK.
WHA !?

*AN APPROXIMATE CONVERSION IS ONE U.S. DOLLAR TO ¥100.

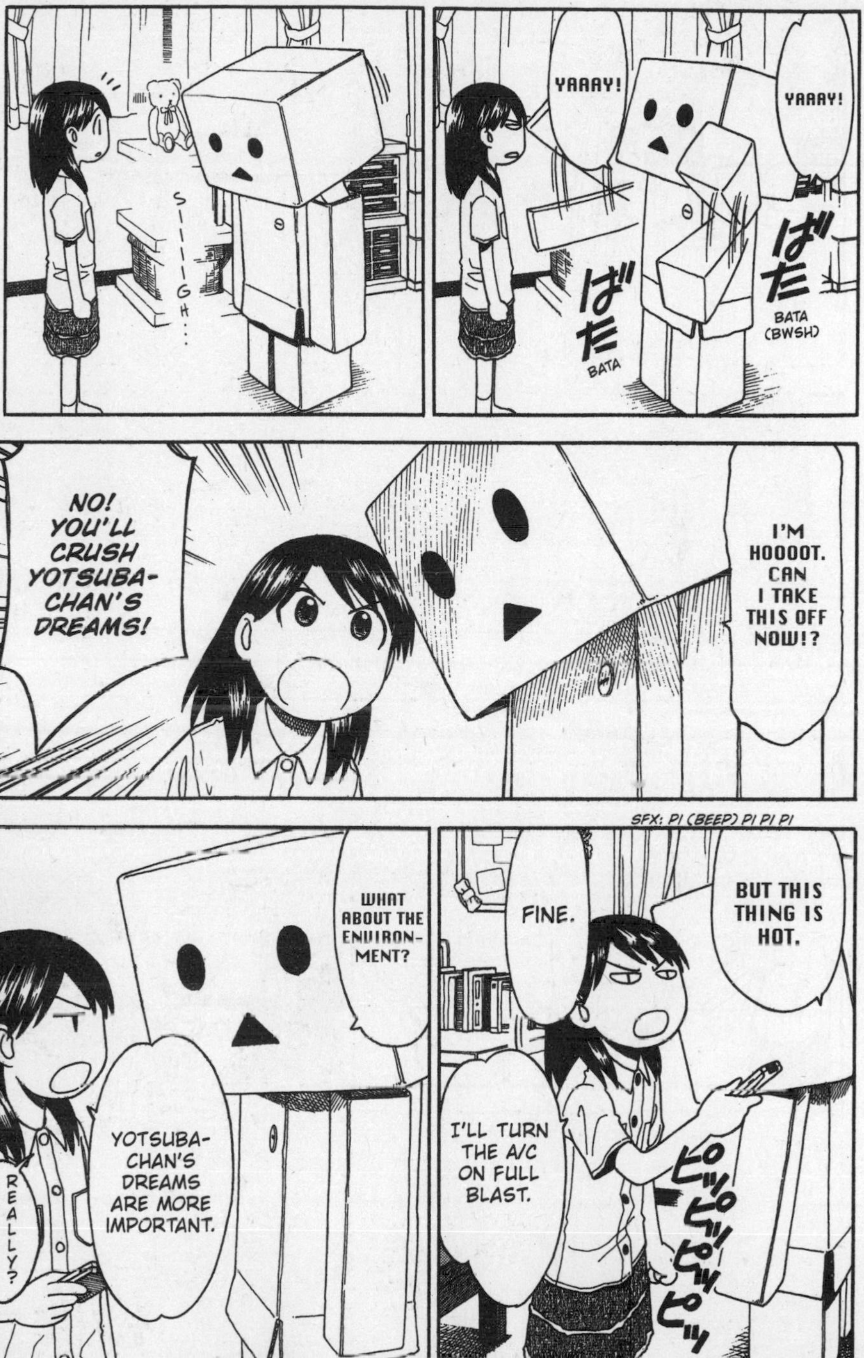
YAAAY!
ばた
BATA (BWSH)
YAAAY!
ばた
BATA
SI-I-I-GH...
I'M HOOOOT. CAN I TAKE THIS OFF NOW!?
NO! YOU'LL CRUSH YOTSUBA-CHAN'S DREAMS!
SFX: PI (BEEP) PI PI PI
BUT THIS THING IS HOT.
FINE.
I'LL TURN THE A/C ON FULL BLAST.
ピッピッピッピッピッ
WHAT ABOUT THE ENVIRONMENT?
YOTSUBA-CHAN'S DREAMS ARE MORE IMPORTANT.
REALLY?

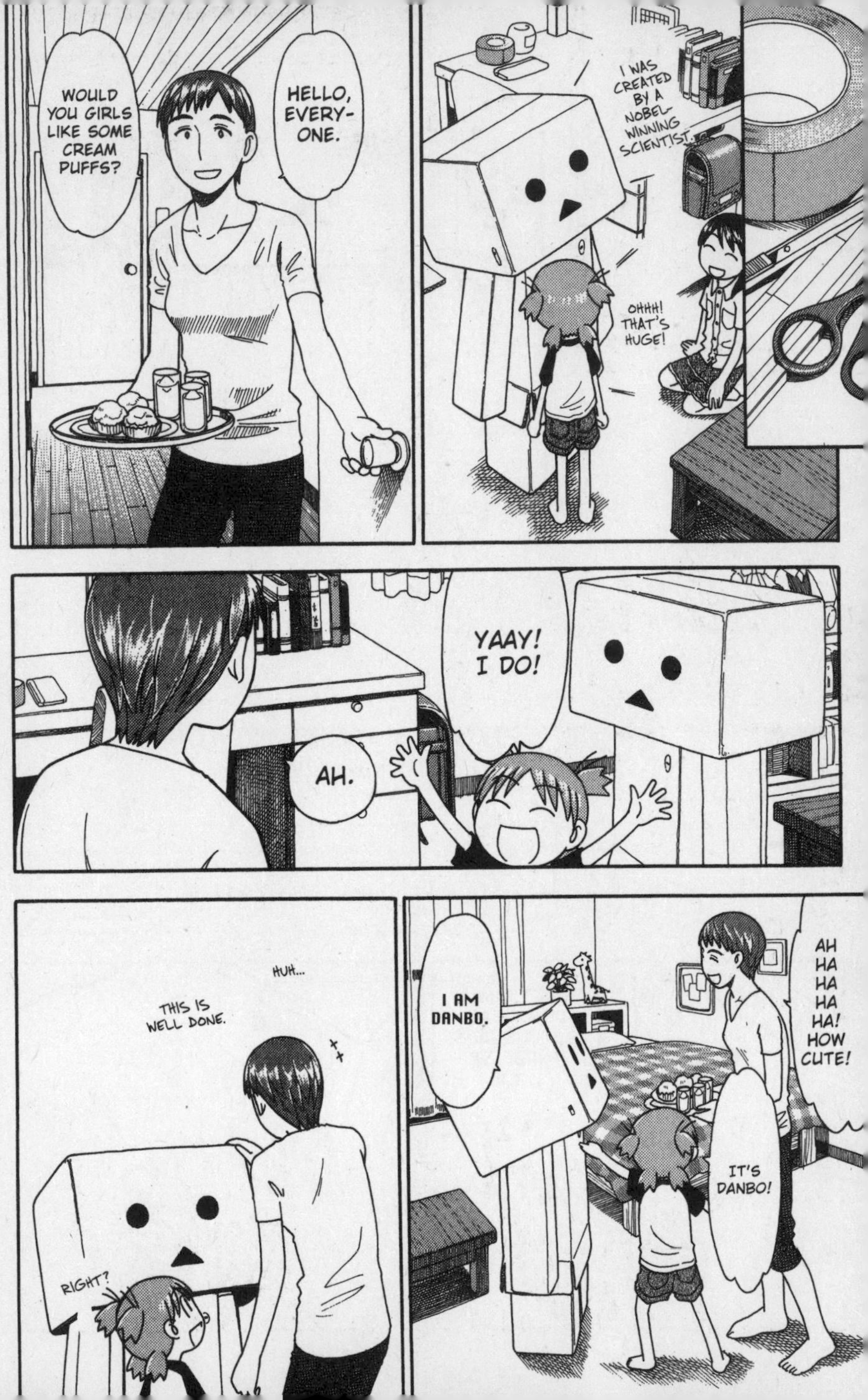
I WAS CREATED BY A NOBEL-WINNING SCIENTIST.
OHHH! THAT'S HUGE!
HELLO, EVERYONE.
WOULD YOU GIRLS LIKE SOME CREAM PUFFS?
YAAY! I DO!
AH.
AH HA HA HA HA! HOW CUTE!
I AM DANBO.
IT'S DANBO!
HUH...
THIS IS WELL DONE.
RIGHT?

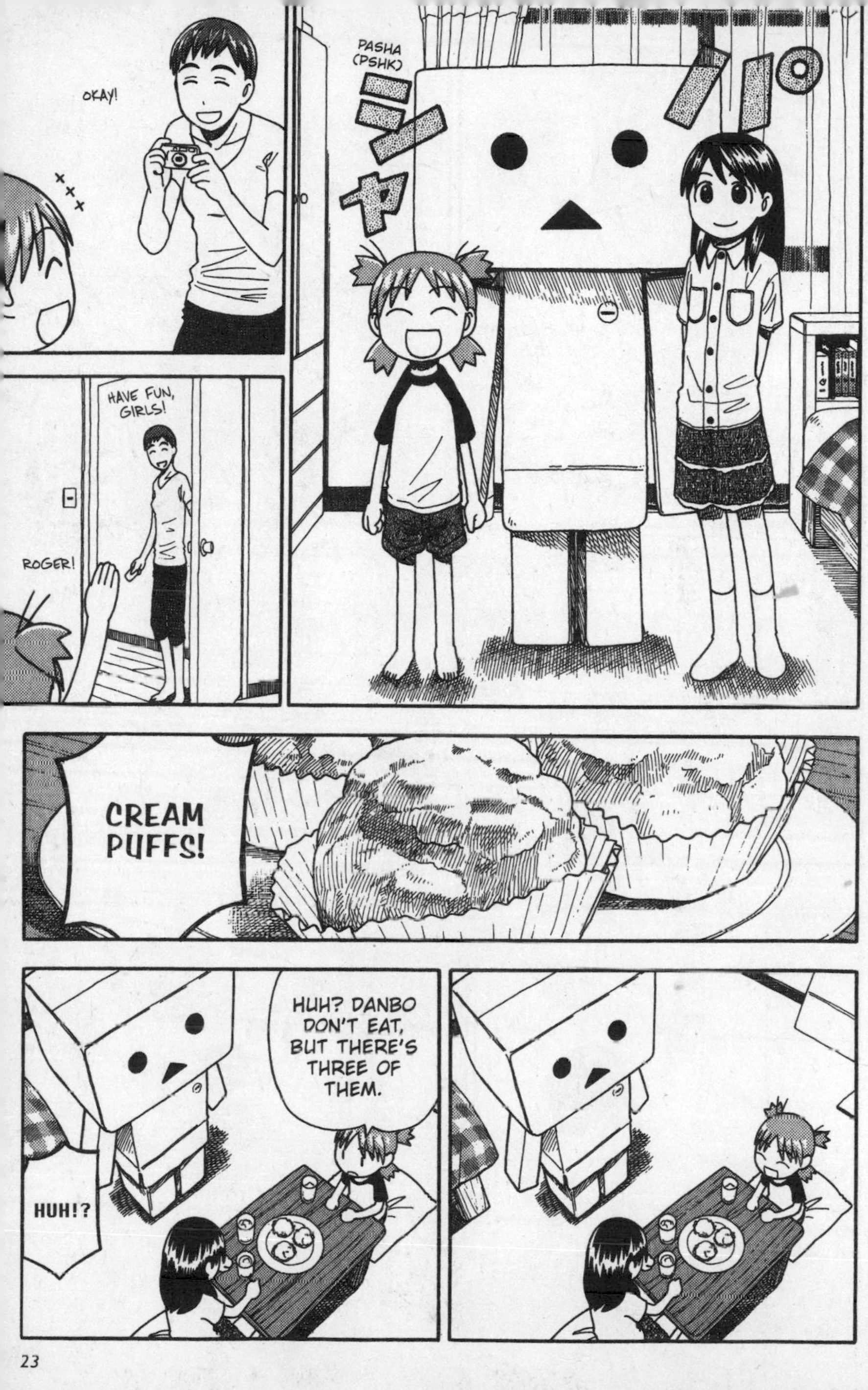
PASHA (PSHK)
OKAY!
HAVE FUN, GIRLS!
ROGER!
CREAM PUFFS!
HUH? DANBO DON'T EAT, BUT THERE'S THREE OF THEM.
HUH!?

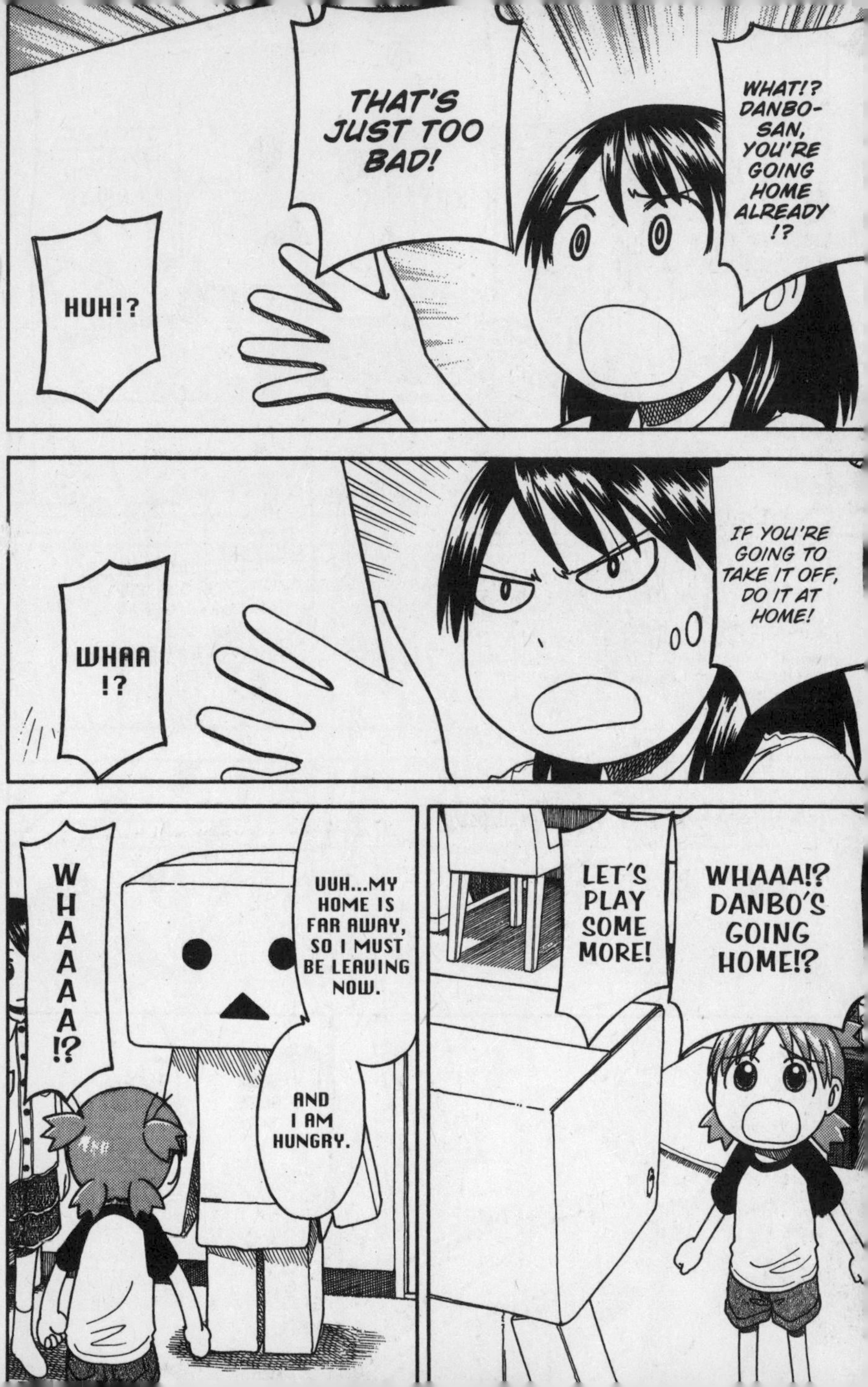
WHAT!? DANBO-SAN, YOU'RE GOING HOME ALREADY!?
THAT'S JUST TOO BAD!
HUH!?
IF YOU'RE GOING TO TAKE IT OFF, DO IT AT HOME!
WHAA!?
WHAAAA!? DANBO'S GOING HOME!?
LET'S PLAY SOME MORE!
UUH...MY HOME IS FAR AWAY, SO I MUST BE LEAVING NOW.
AND I AM HUNGRY.
WHAAAAA!?

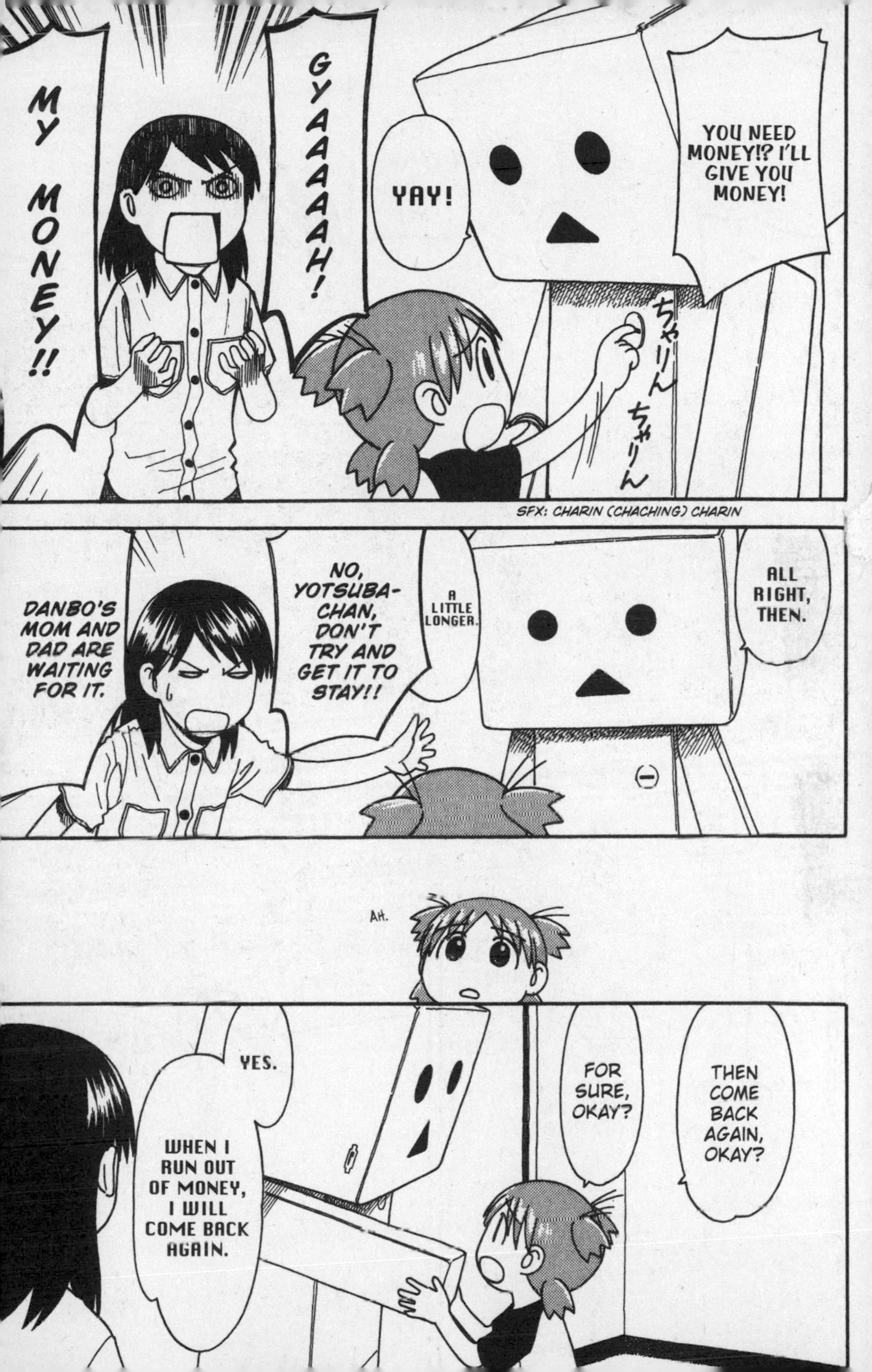
YOU NEED MONEY!? I'LL GIVE YOU MONEY!
YAY!
GYAAAAAAH!
MY MONEY!!
ちゃりん ちゃりん
SFX: CHARIN (CHACHING) CHARIN
ALL RIGHT, THEN.
A LITTLE LONGER.
NO, YOTSUBA-CHAN, DON'T TRY AND GET IT TO STAY!!
DANBO'S MOM AND DAD ARE WAITING FOR IT.
AH.
THEN COME BACK AGAIN, OKAY?
FOR SURE, OKAY?
YES.
WHEN I RUN OUT OF MONEY, I WILL COME BACK AGAIN.

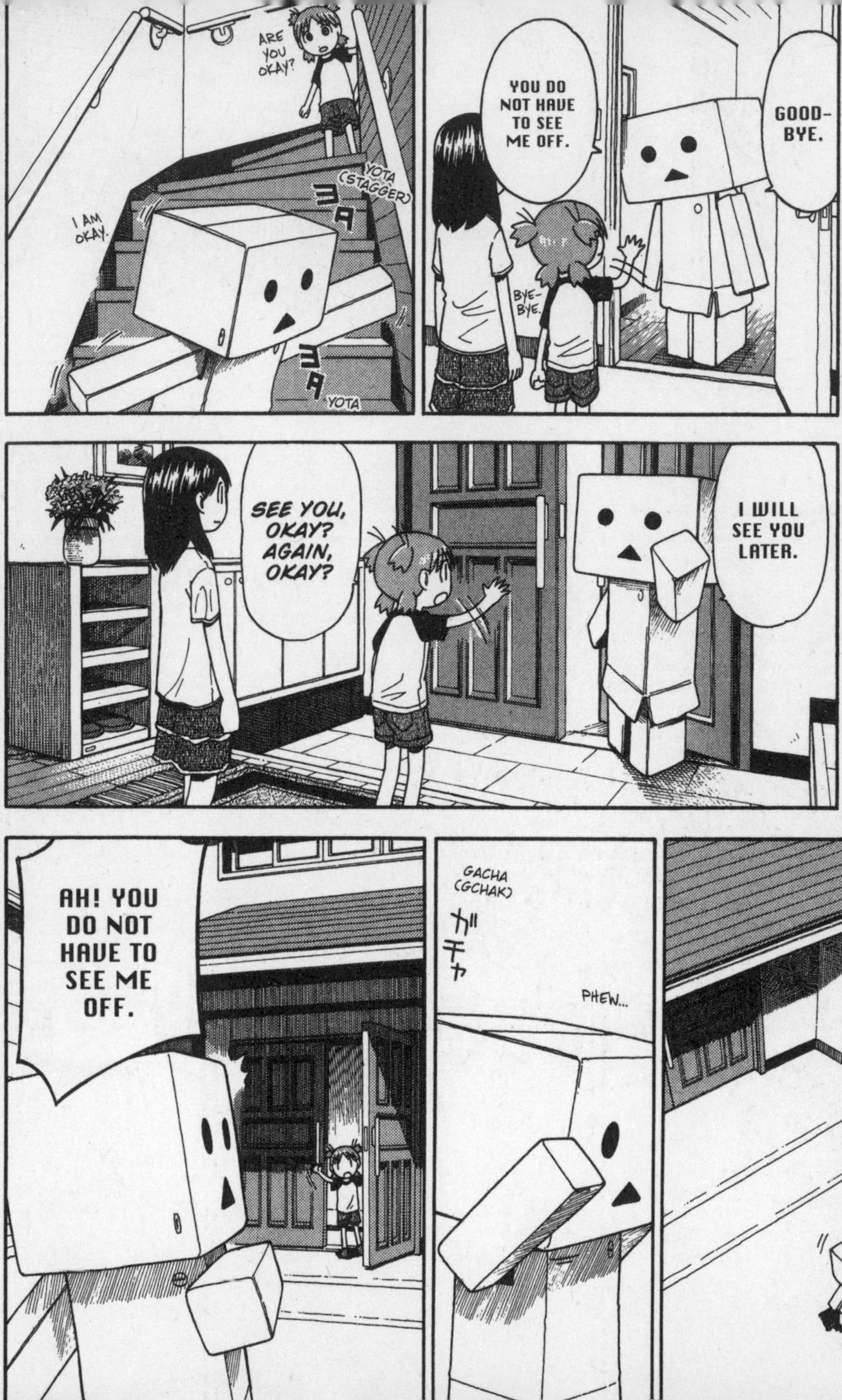
GOOD-BYE.
YOU DO NOT HAVE TO SEE ME OFF.
BYE-BYE.
ARE YOU OKAY?
ヨタ
YOTA (STAGGER)
I AM OKAY.
ヨタ
YOTA
I WILL SEE YOU LATER.
SEE YOU, OKAY? AGAIN, OKAY?
ガチャ
GACHA (GCHAK)
PHEW...
AH! YOU DO NOT HAVE TO SEE ME OFF.

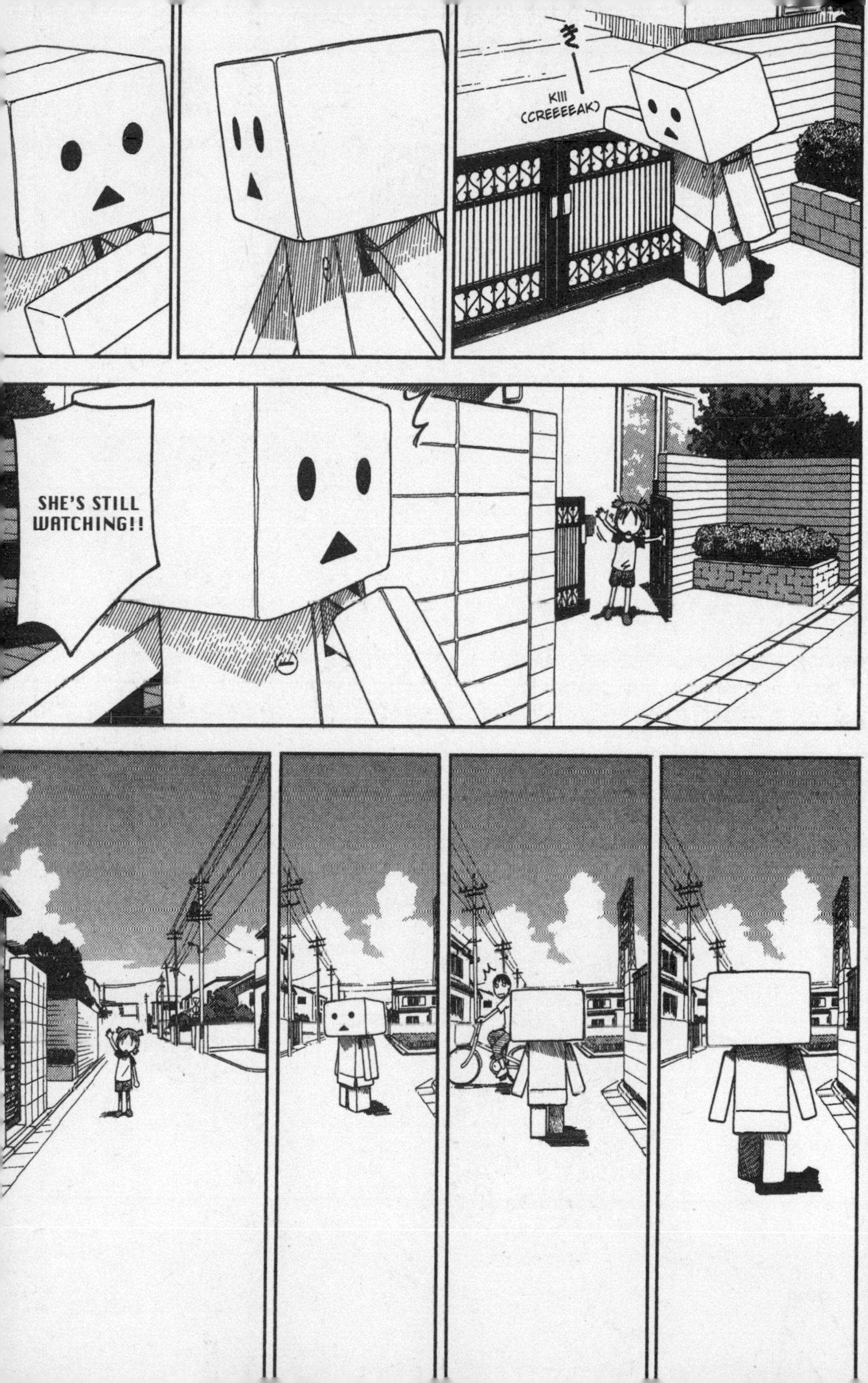
き
KIII
(CREEEEAK)
SHE'S STILL
WATCHING!!

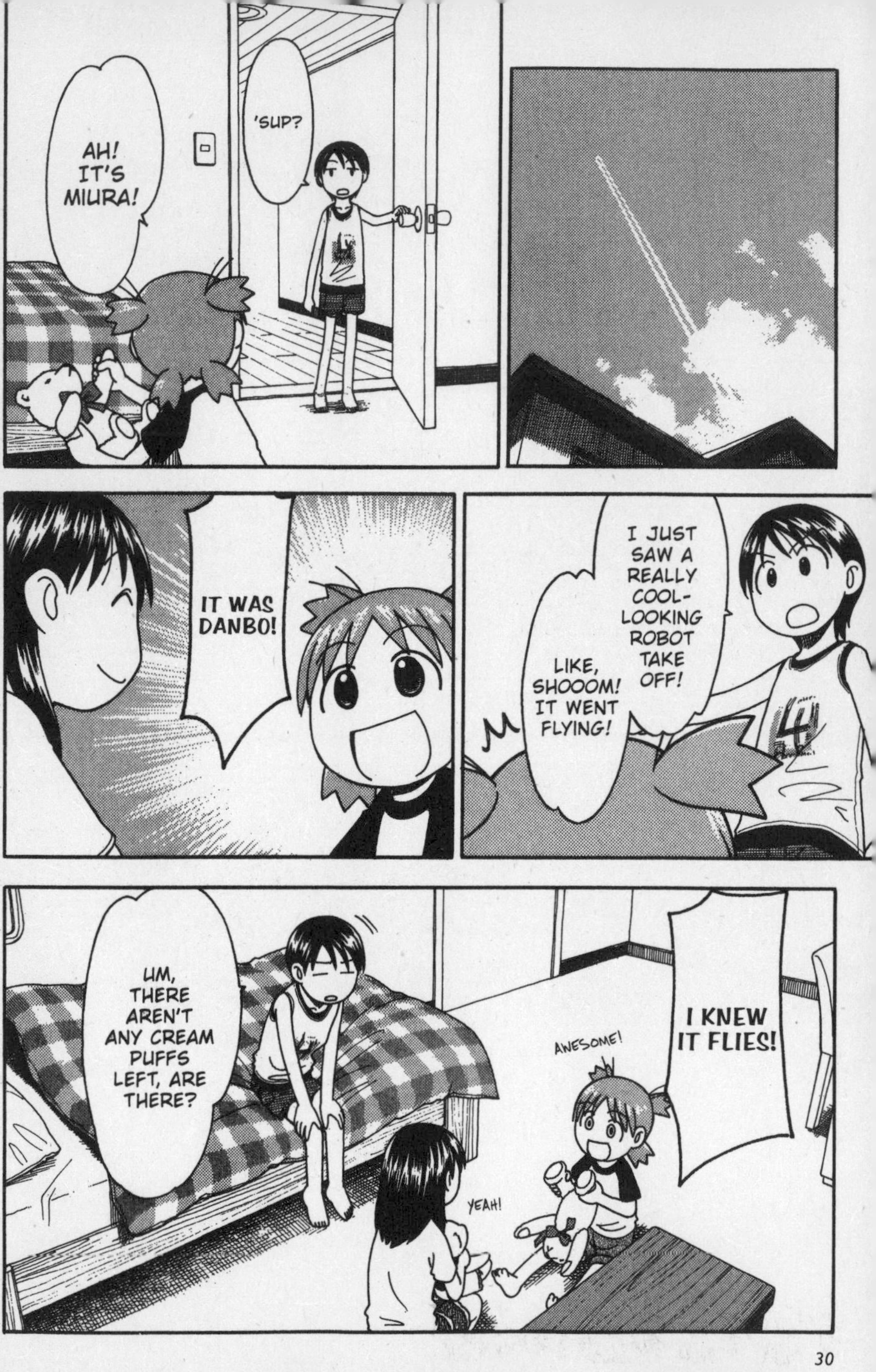
'SUP?
AH! IT'S MIURA!
I JUST SAW A REALLY COOL-LOOKING ROBOT TAKE OFF!
LIKE, SHOOOM! IT WENT FLYING!
IT WAS DANBO!
I KNEW IT FLIES!
AWESOME!
UM, THERE AREN'T ANY CREAM PUFFS LEFT, ARE THERE?
YEAH!

YOTSUBA&!

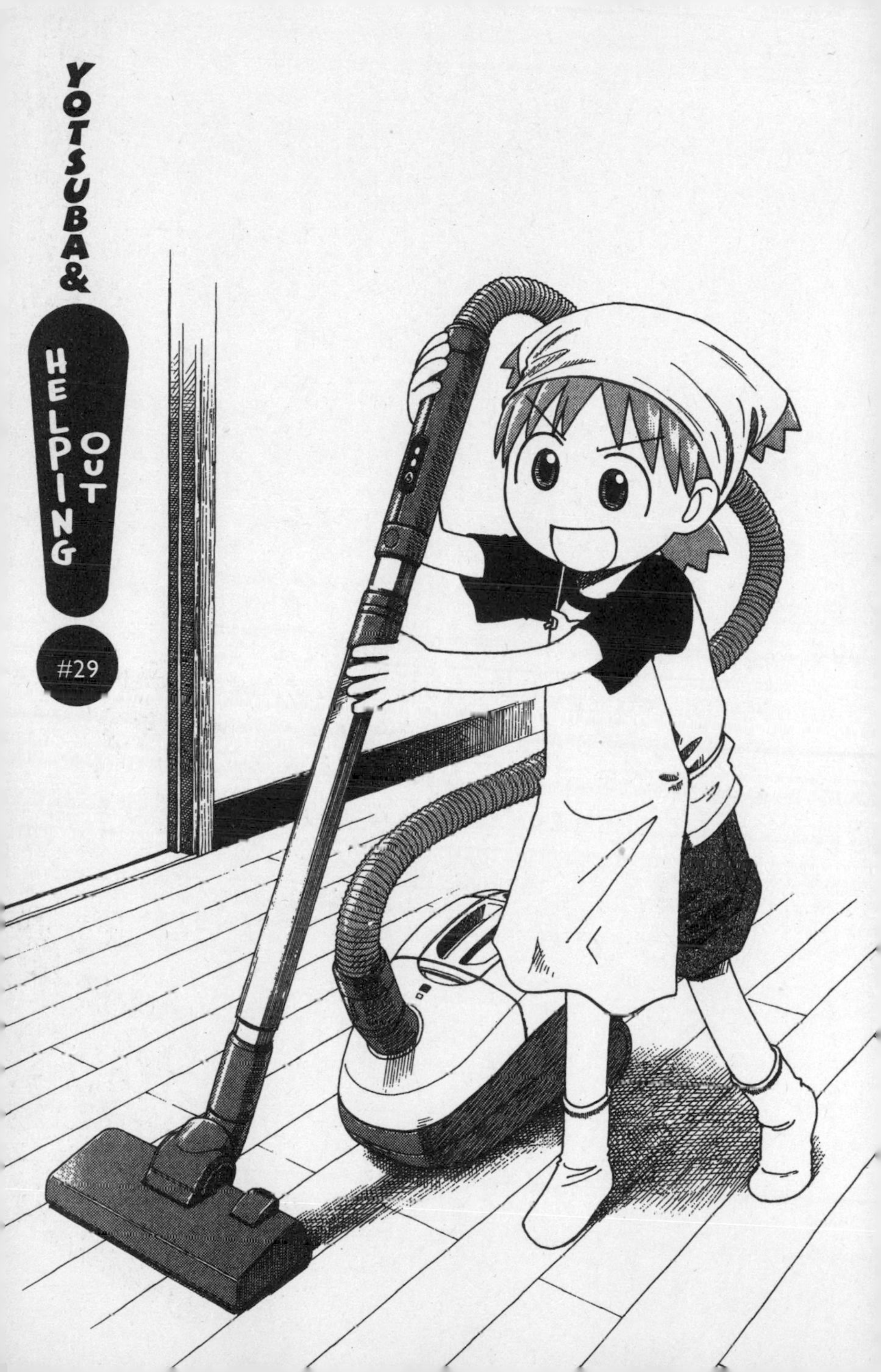
YOTSUBA&
HELPING OUT
#29

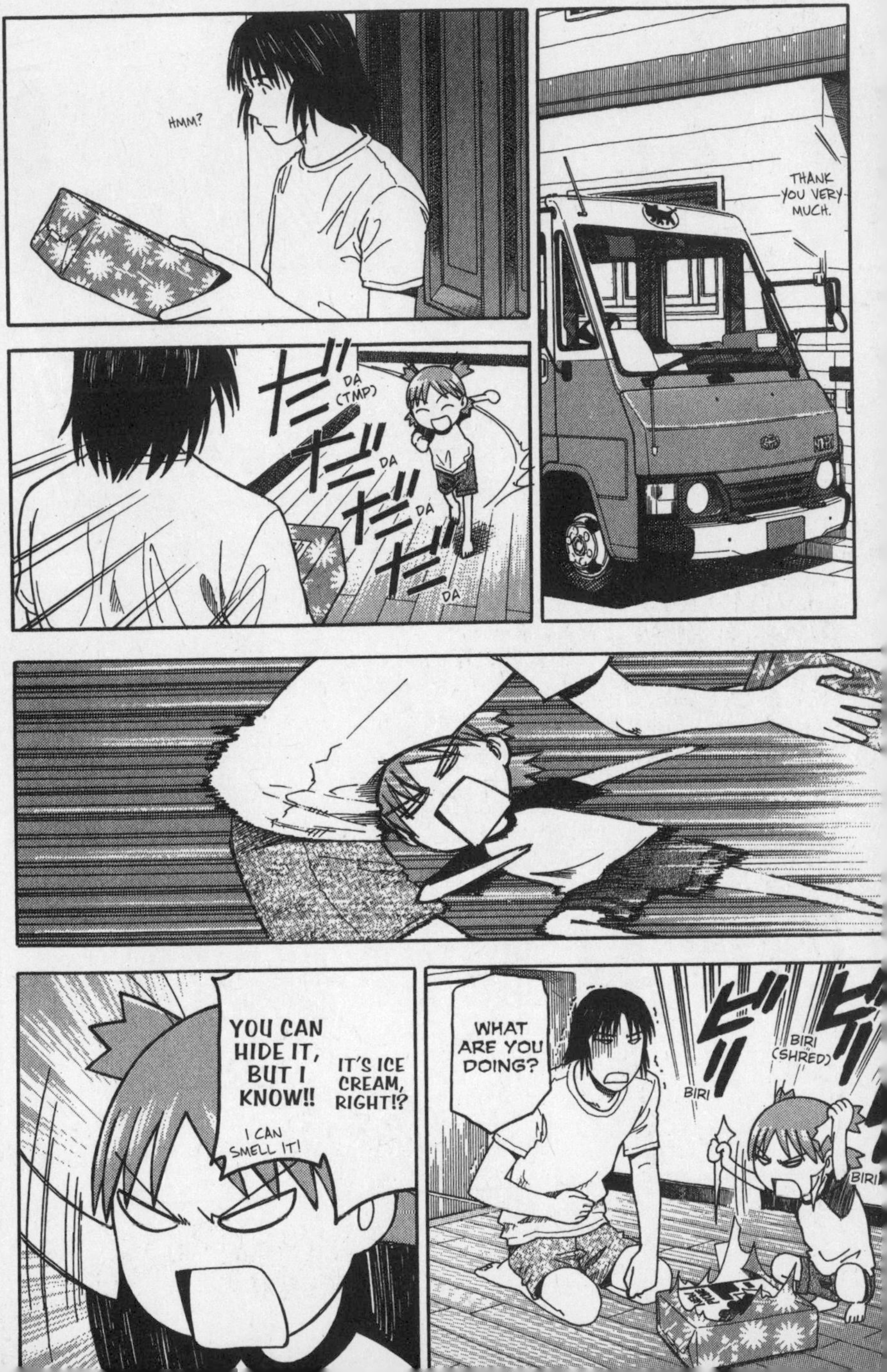
THANK YOU VERY MUCH.
HMM?
DA (TMP)
DA
DA
DA
WHAT ARE YOU DOING?
BIRI (SHRED)
BIRI
BIRI
YOU CAN HIDE IT, BUT I KNOW!!
IT'S ICE CREAM, RIGHT!?
I CAN SMELL IT!

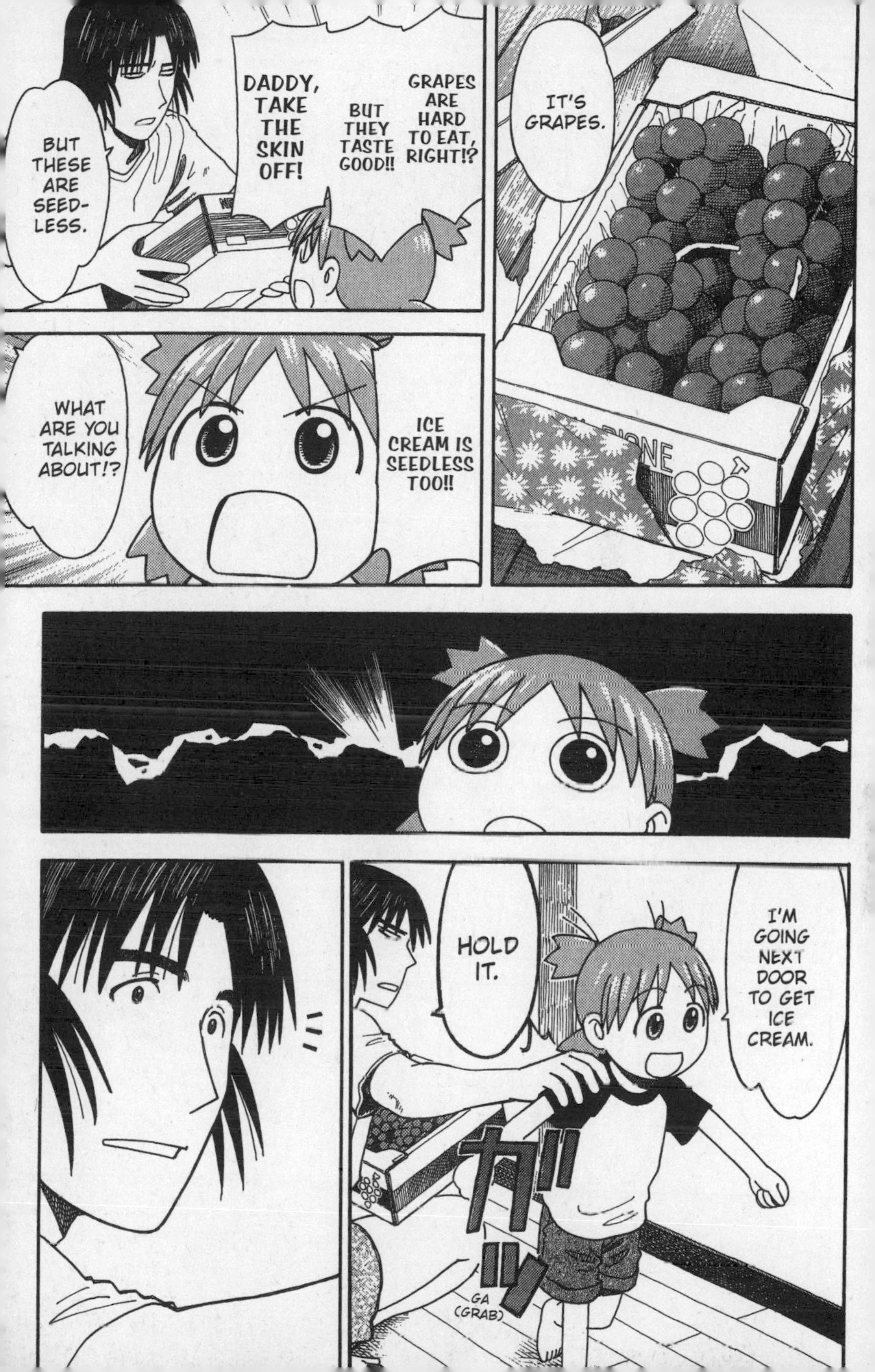
IT'S GRAPES.
GRAPES ARE HARD TO EAT, RIGHT!?
BUT THEY TASTE GOOD!!
DADDY, TAKE THE SKIN OFF!
BUT THESE ARE SEED-LESS.
ICE CREAM IS SEEDLESS TOO!!
WHAT ARE YOU TALKING ABOUT!?
I'M GOING NEXT DOOR TO GET ICE CREAM.
HOLD IT.
GA (GRAB)

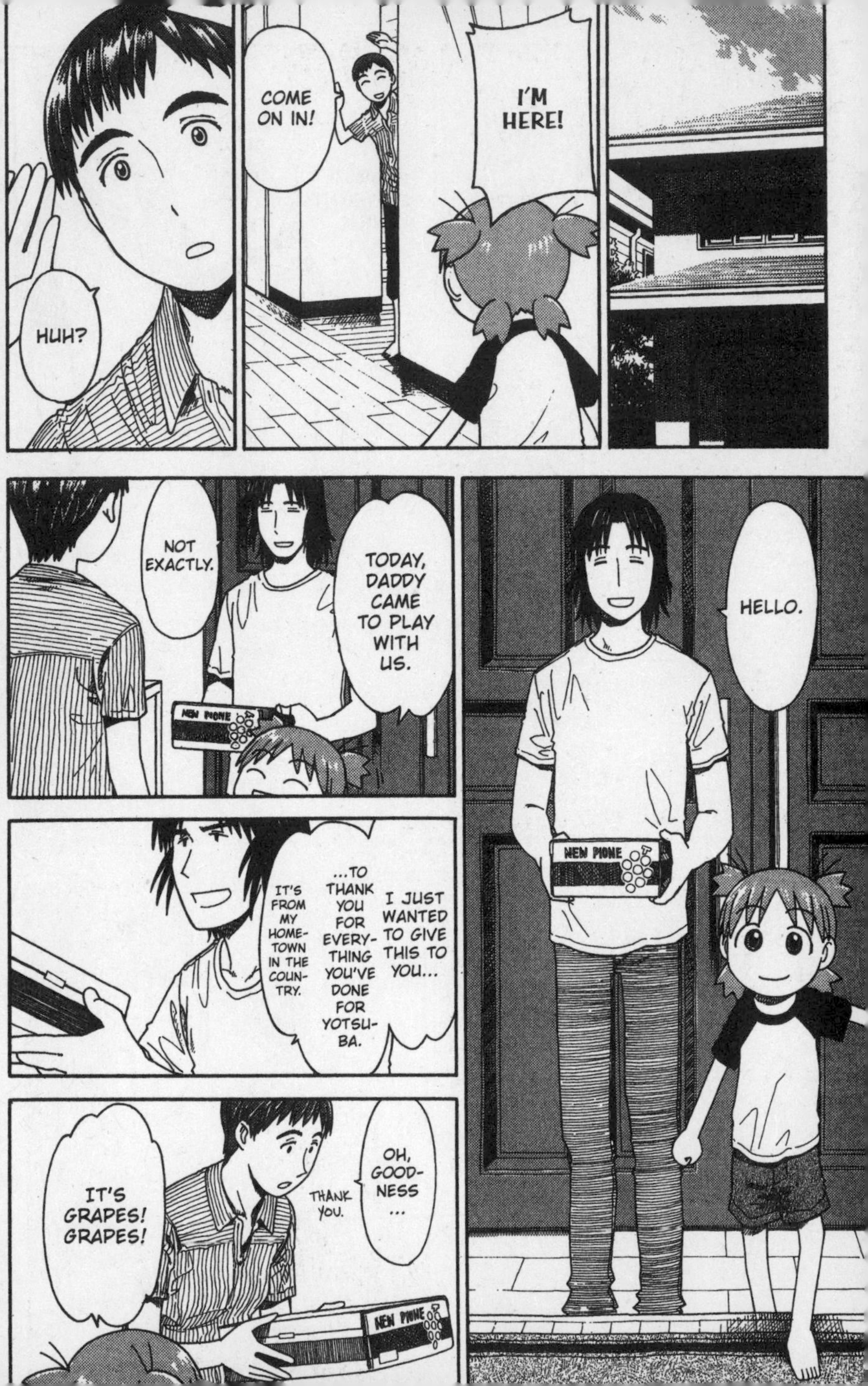
I'M HERE!
COME ON IN!
HUH?
HELLO.
NEW PIONE
TODAY, DADDY CAME TO PLAY WITH US.
NOT EXACTLY.
NEW PIONE
I JUST WANTED TO GIVE THIS TO YOU...
...TO THANK YOU FOR EVERYTHING YOU'VE DONE FOR YOTSUBA.
IT'S FROM MY HOMETOWN IN THE COUNTRY.
OH, GOODNESS...
THANK YOU.
IT'S GRAPES! GRAPES!
NEW PIONE

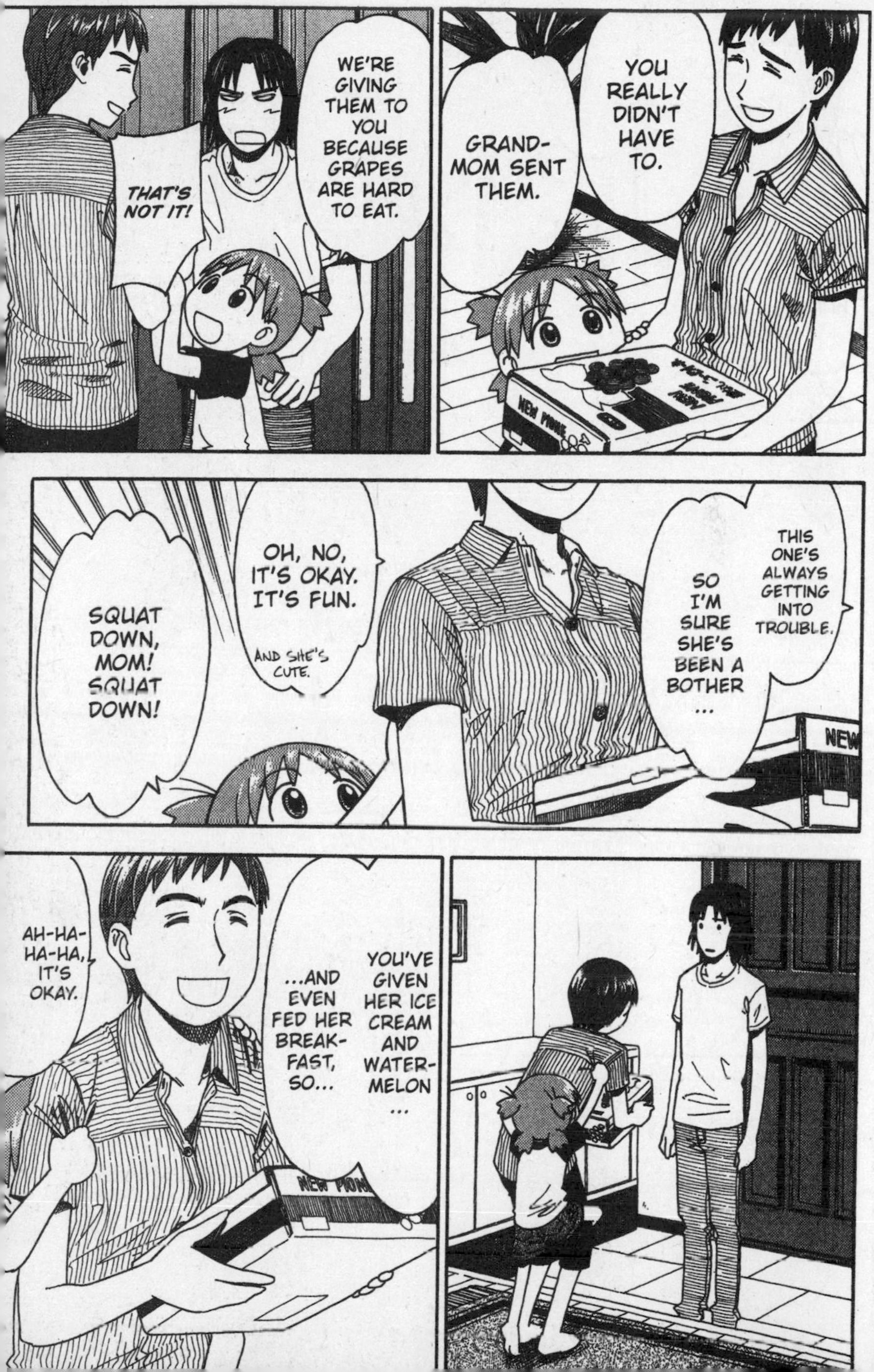
YOU REALLY DIDN'T HAVE TO.
GRAND-MOM SENT THEM.
WE'RE GIVING THEM TO YOU BECAUSE GRAPES ARE HARD TO EAT.
THAT'S NOT IT!
THIS ONE'S ALWAYS GETTING INTO TROUBLE.
SO I'M SURE SHE'S BEEN A BOTHER...
OH, NO, IT'S OKAY. IT'S FUN.
AND SHE'S CUTE.
SQUAT DOWN, MOM! SQUAT DOWN!
YOU'VE GIVEN HER ICE CREAM AND WATER-MELON...
...AND EVEN FED HER BREAK-FAST, SO...
AH-HA-HA-HA, IT'S OKAY.

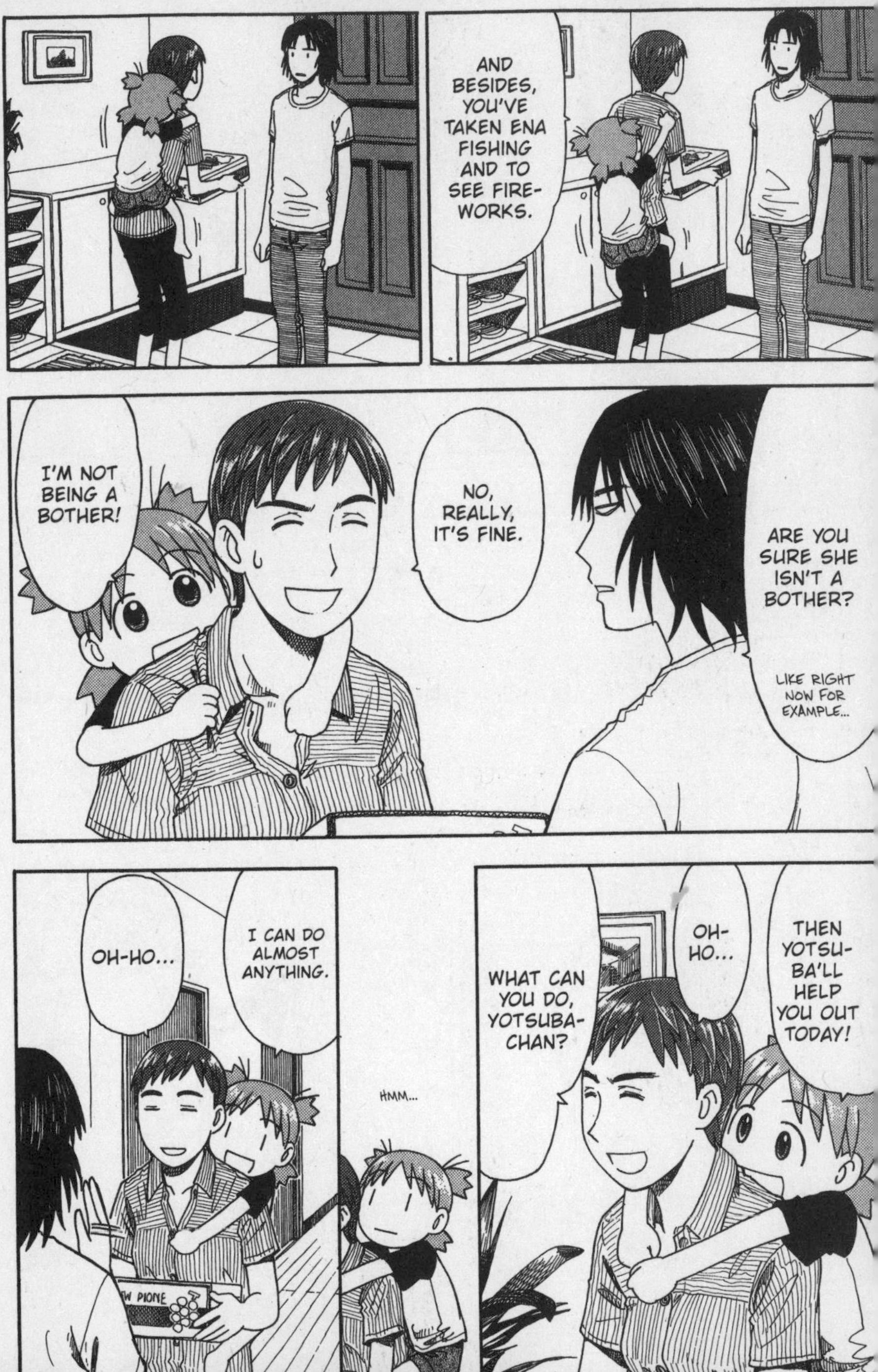
AND BESIDES, YOU'VE TAKEN ENA FISHING AND TO SEE FIRE-WORKS.
ARE YOU SURE SHE ISN'T A BOTHER?
LIKE RIGHT NOW FOR EXAMPLE...
NO, REALLY, IT'S FINE.
I'M NOT BEING A BOTHER!
THEN YOTSUBA'LL HELP YOU OUT TODAY!
OH-HO...
WHAT CAN YOU DO, YOTSUBA-CHAN?
HMM...
I CAN DO ALMOST ANYTHING.
OH-HO...

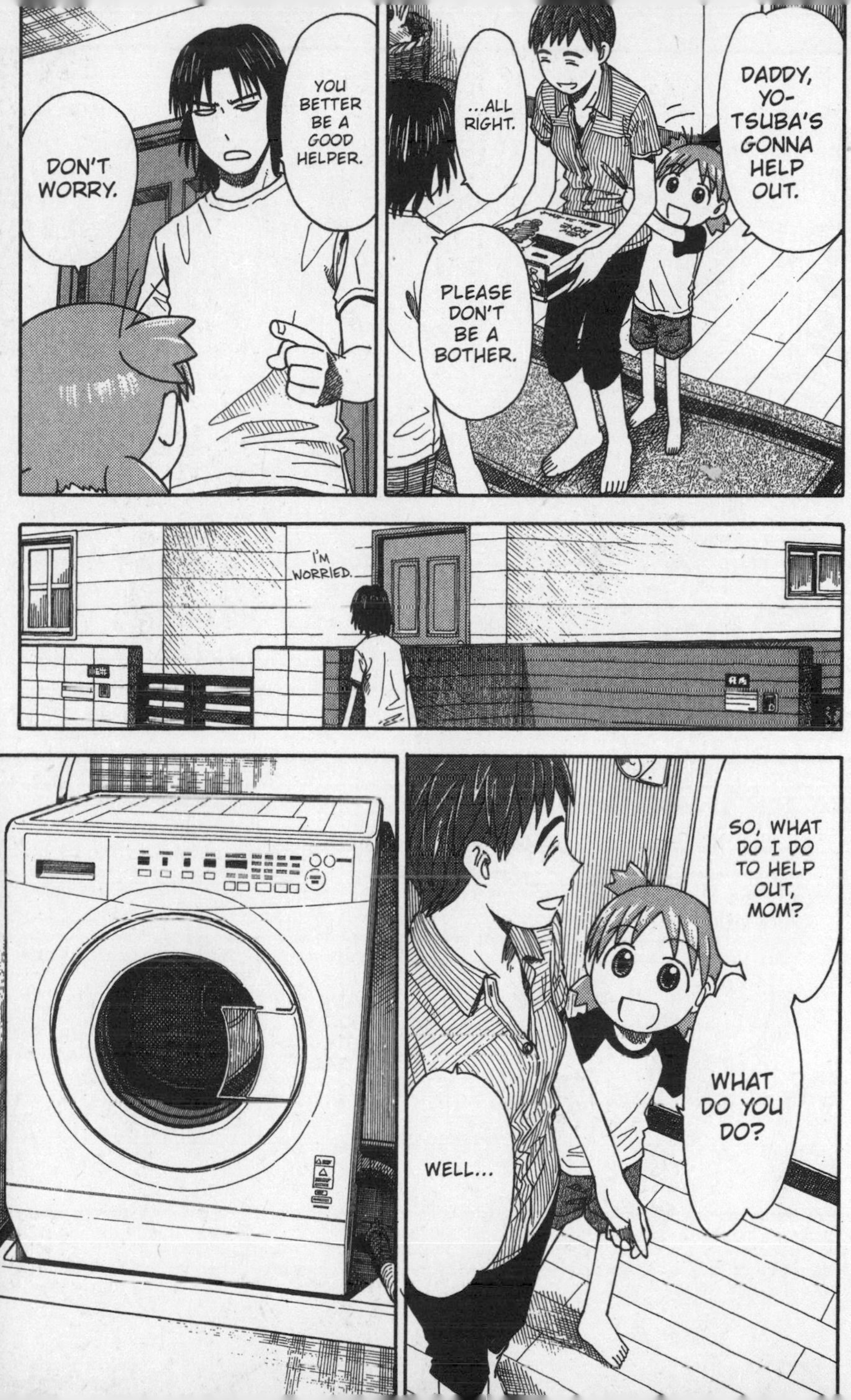
DADDY, YO-TSUBA'S GONNA HELP OUT.
...ALL RIGHT.
PLEASE DON'T BE A BOTHER.
YOU BETTER BE A GOOD HELPER.
DON'T WORRY.
I'M WORRIED.
SO, WHAT DO I DO TO HELP OUT, MOM?
WHAT DO YOU DO?
WELL...

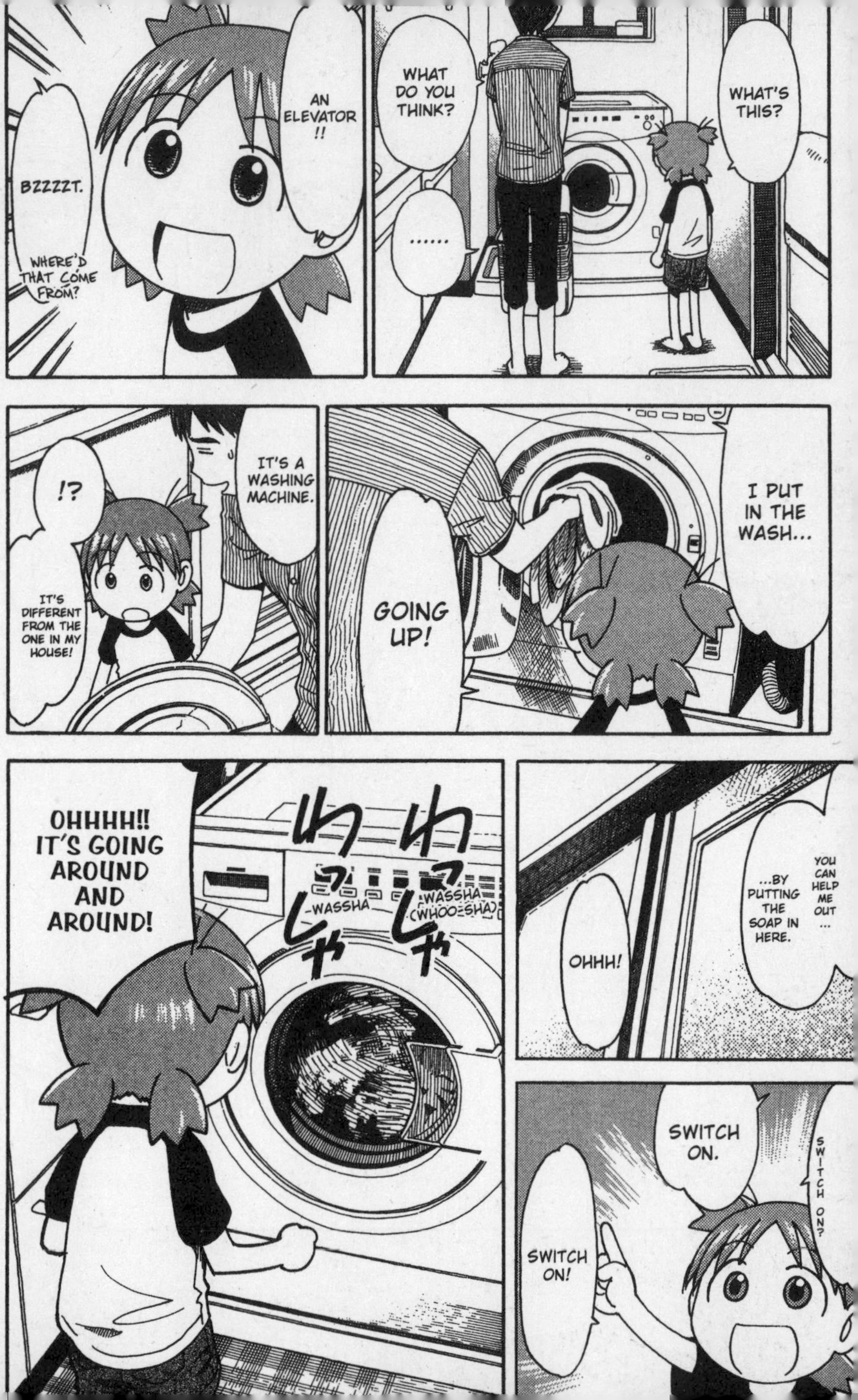
WHAT'S THIS?
WHAT DO YOU THINK?
......
AN ELEVATOR !!
BZZZZT.
WHERE'D THAT COME FROM?
I PUT IN THE WASH...
GOING UP!
IT'S A WASHING MACHINE.
!?
IT'S DIFFERENT FROM THE ONE IN MY HOUSE!
YOU CAN HELP ME OUT ...
...BY PUTTING THE SOAP IN HERE.
OHHH!
SWITCH ON?
SWITCH ON.
SWITCH ON!
わっしゃ
わっしゃ
WASSHA
WASSHA (WHOO-SHA)
OHHHH!! IT'S GOING AROUND AND AROUND!

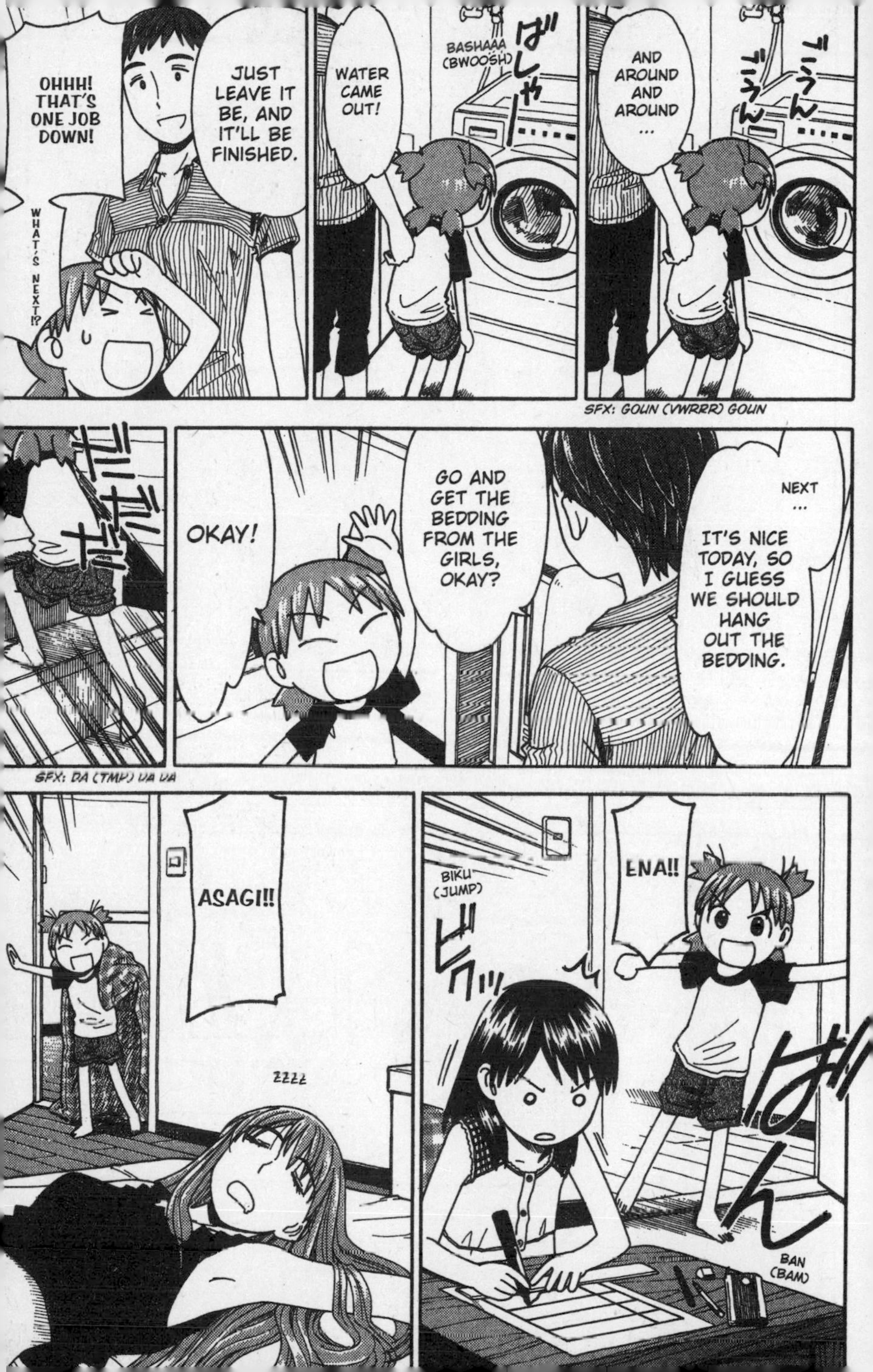

ごうんごうん
AND AROUND AND AROUND ...
ばしゃー
BASHAAA (BWOOSH)
WATER CAME OUT!
JUST LEAVE IT BE, AND IT'LL BE FINISHED.
OHHH! THAT'S ONE JOB DOWN!
WHAT'S NEXT!?
SFX: GOUN (VWRRR) GOUN
NEXT ...
IT'S NICE TODAY, SO I GUESS WE SHOULD HANG OUT THE BEDDING.
GO AND GET THE BEDDING FROM THE GIRLS, OKAY?
OKAY!
SFX: DA (TMP) DA DA
ENA!!
ばん!!
BAN (BAM)
BIKU (JUMP)
ASAGI!!
ZZZZ

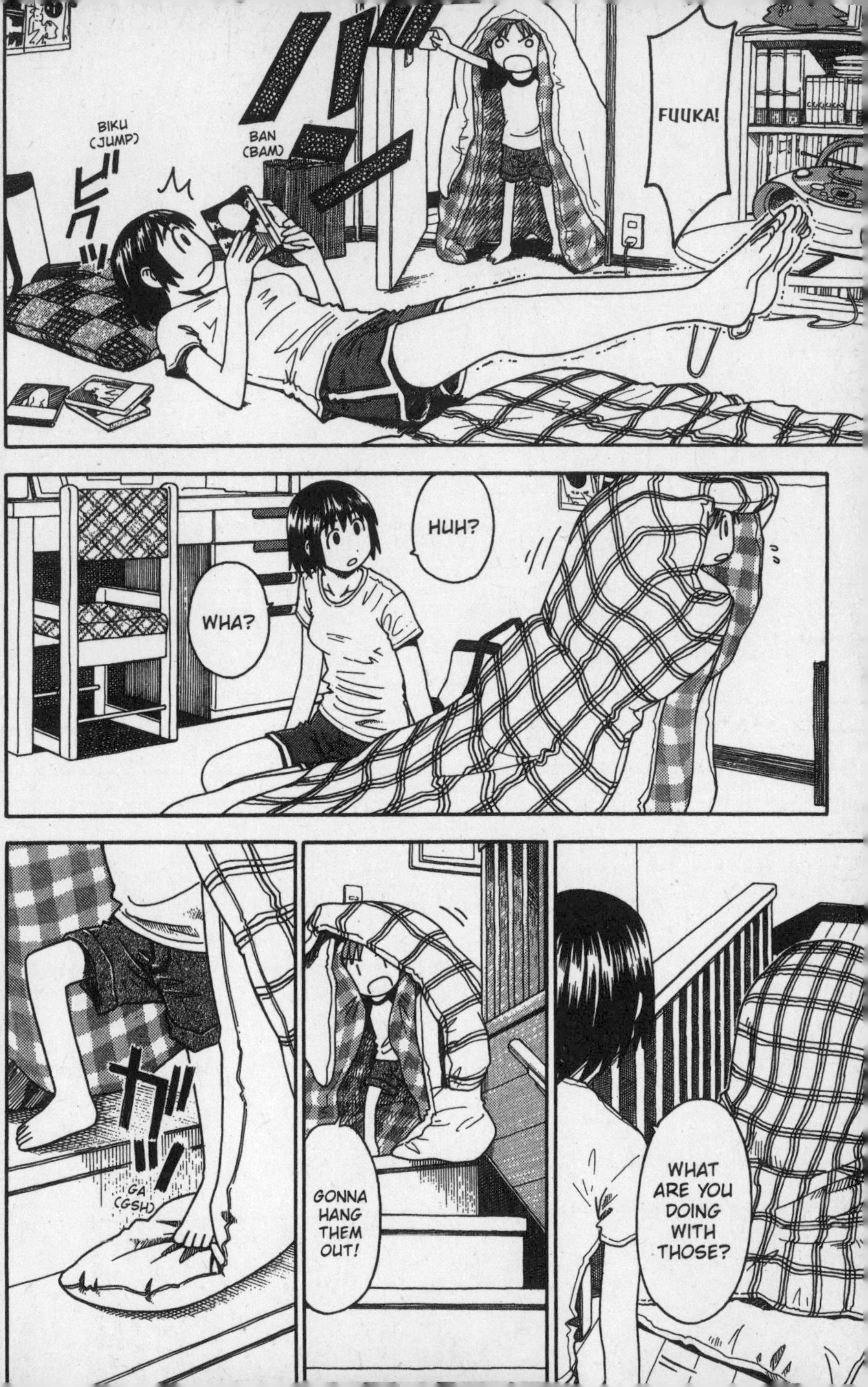
FUUKA!
BAN (BAM)
BIKU (JUMP)
HUH?
WHA?
WHAT ARE YOU DOING WITH THOSE?
GONNA HANG THEM OUT!
GA (GSH)

GYAAAAH!

GORON

GORON (ROLL)

SFX: DA (TMP) DA DA DA

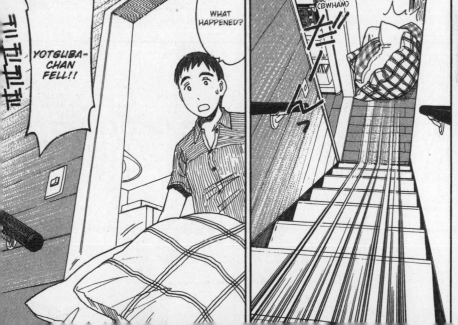

WHAT HAPPENED?

YOTSUBA-CHAN FELL!!

DAAN (BWHAM)

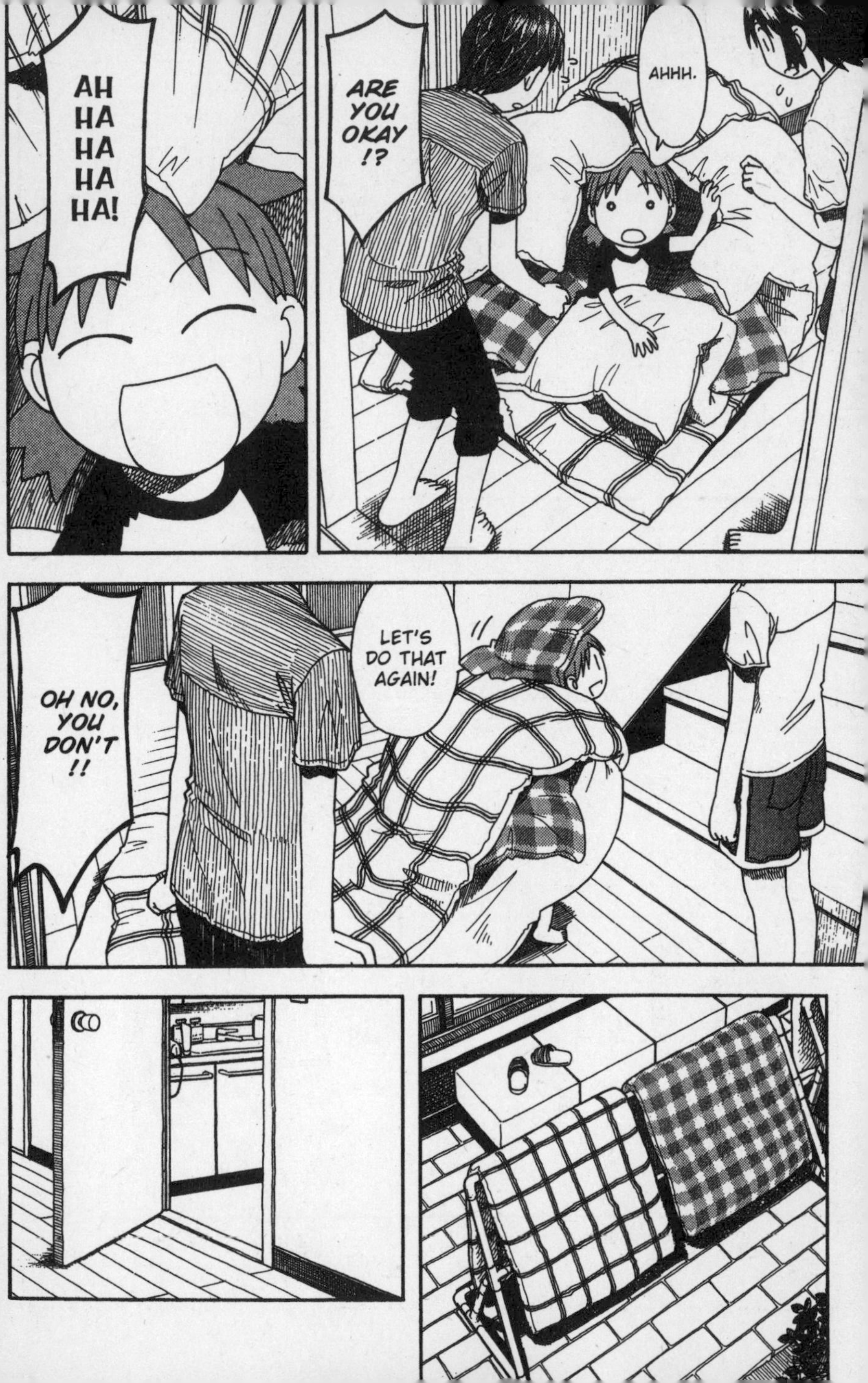
AHHH.
ARE YOU OKAY!?
AH HA HA HA HA!
LET'S DO THAT AGAIN!
OH NO, YOU DON'T!!

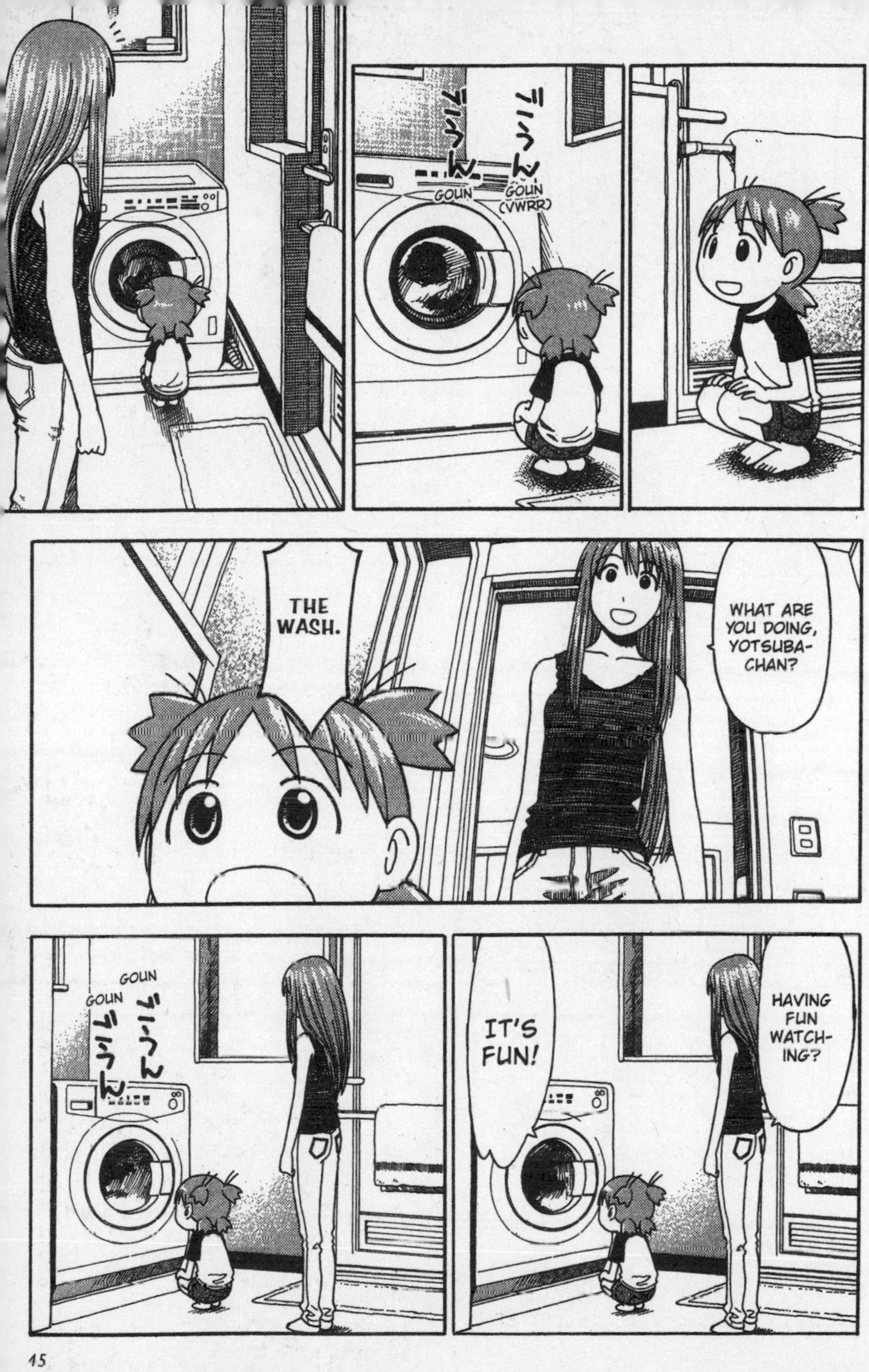
GOUN (VWRR)
GOUN
WHAT ARE YOU DOING, YOTSUBA-CHAN?
THE WASH.
HAVING FUN WATCHING?
IT'S FUN!
GOUN
GOUN

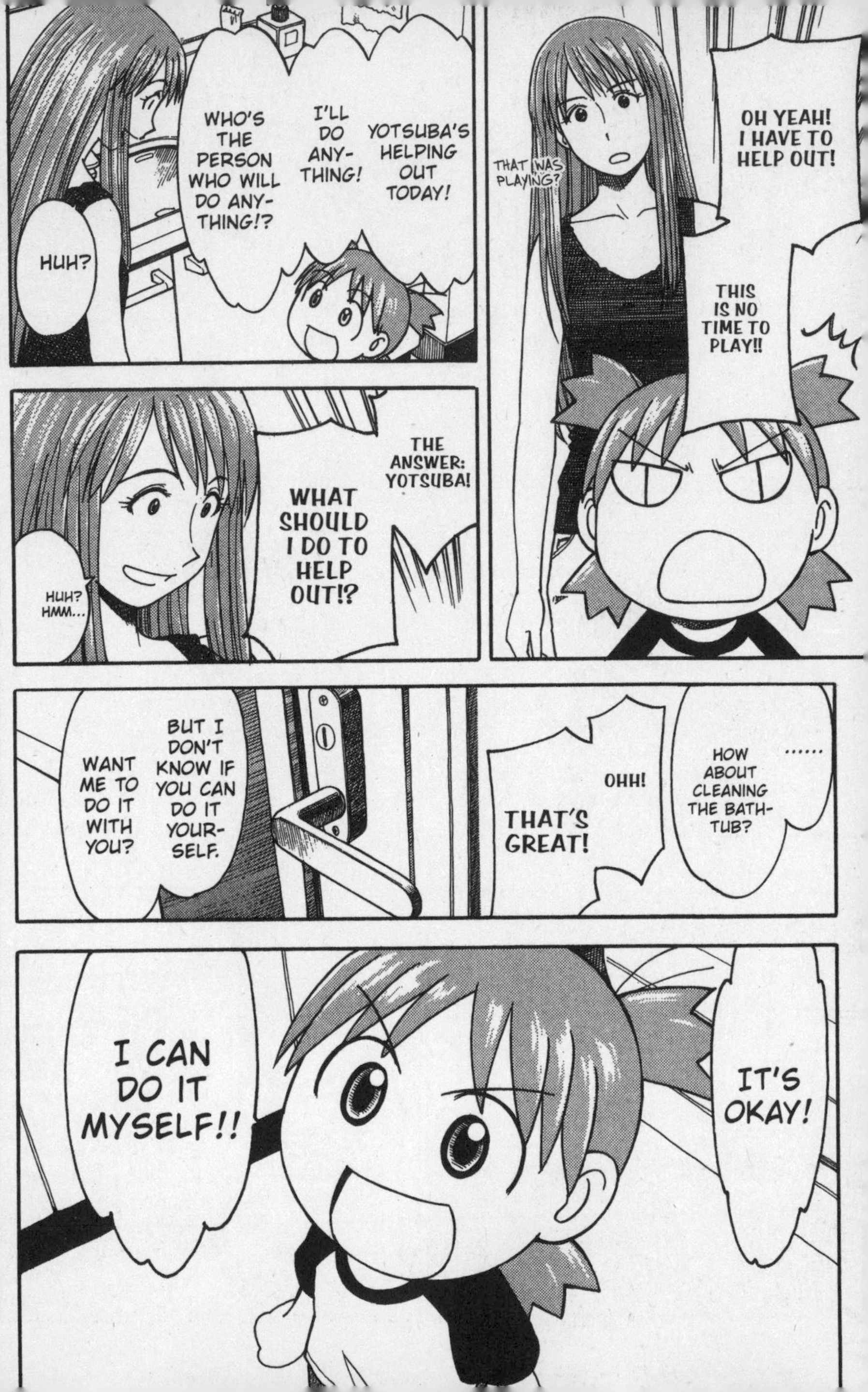
OH YEAH! I HAVE TO HELP OUT!
THIS IS NO TIME TO PLAY!!
THAT WAS PLAYING?
YOTSUBA'S HELPING OUT TODAY!
I'LL DO ANY-THING!
WHO'S THE PERSON WHO WILL DO ANY-THING!?
HUH?
THE ANSWER: YOTSUBA!
WHAT SHOULD I DO TO HELP OUT!?
HUH? HMM...
......
HOW ABOUT CLEANING THE BATH-TUB?
OHH!
THAT'S GREAT!
BUT I DON'T KNOW IF YOU CAN DO IT YOUR-SELF.
WANT ME TO DO IT WITH YOU?
IT'S OKAY!
I CAN DO IT MYSELF!!

GOSHI

HMMM HMM ♪

GOSHI
(SCRUB)

WITH SCRUBBING, BUBBLES,
BATH MAGICLEAN!

HMM ♪

BUSHU

BUSHU
(BSSHT)

HAAA!

BUSHU

BUSHU

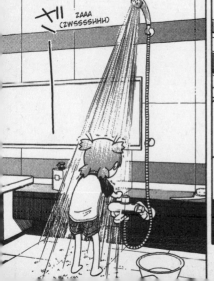

ZAAA
(ZWSSSSSHHH)

KYU
(SQUEAK)

HMM ♪

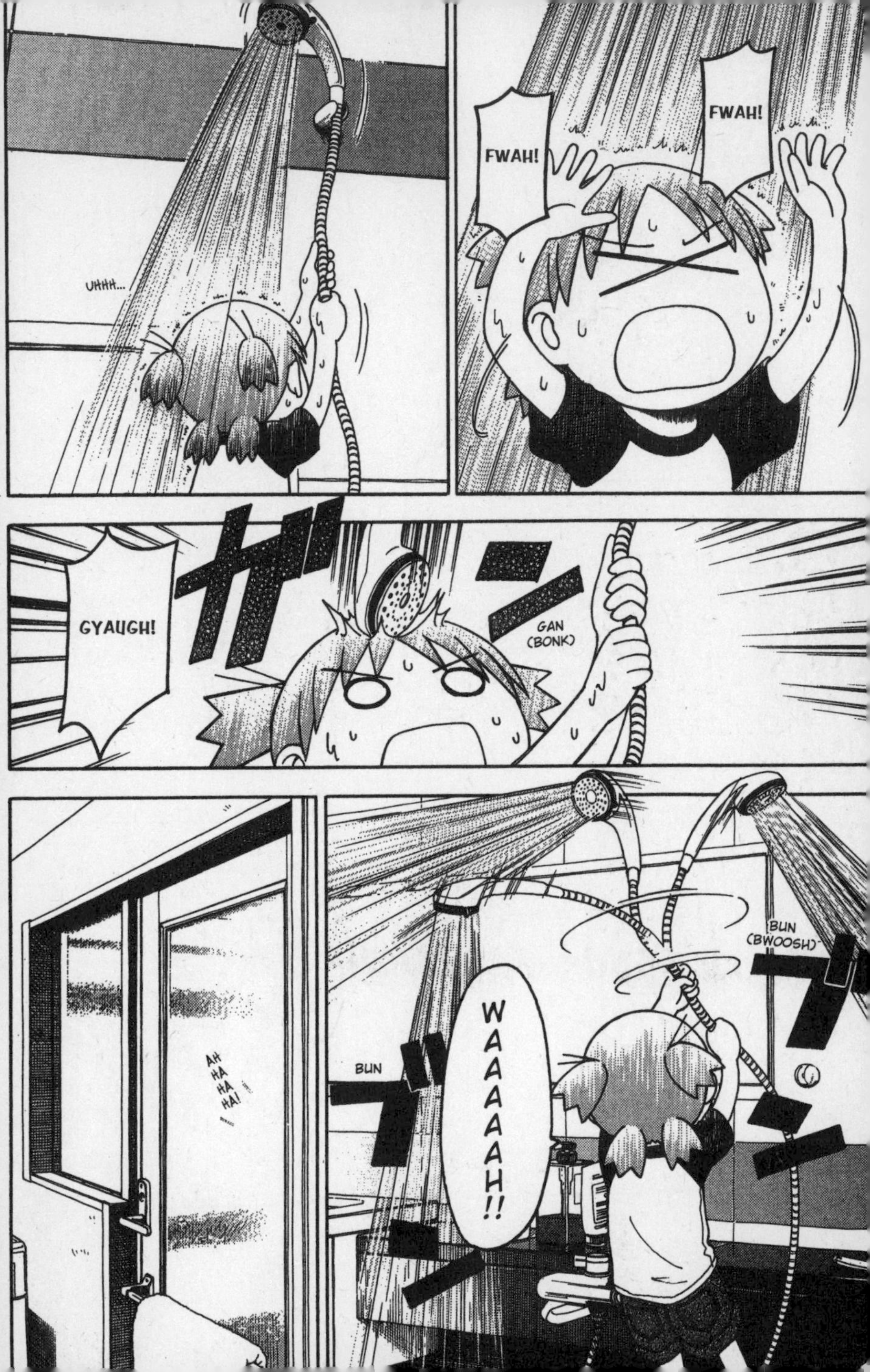
FWAH!
FWAH!
UHHH...
GAN (BONK)
GYAUGH!
BUN (BWOOSH)
WAAAAAAH!!
BUN
AH HA HA HA!

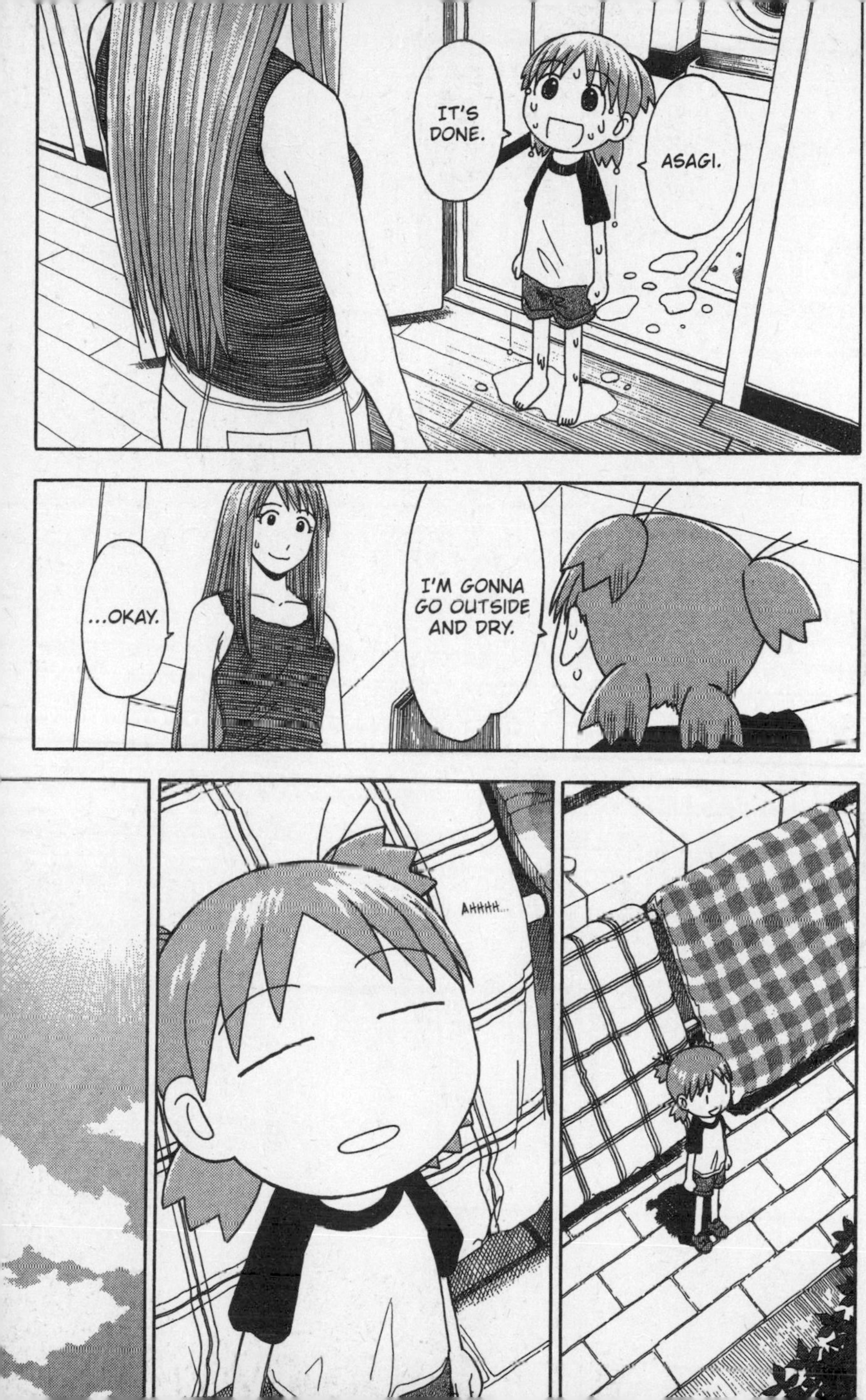
ASAGI.
IT'S DONE.
I'M GONNA GO OUTSIDE AND DRY.
...OKAY.
AHHHH...

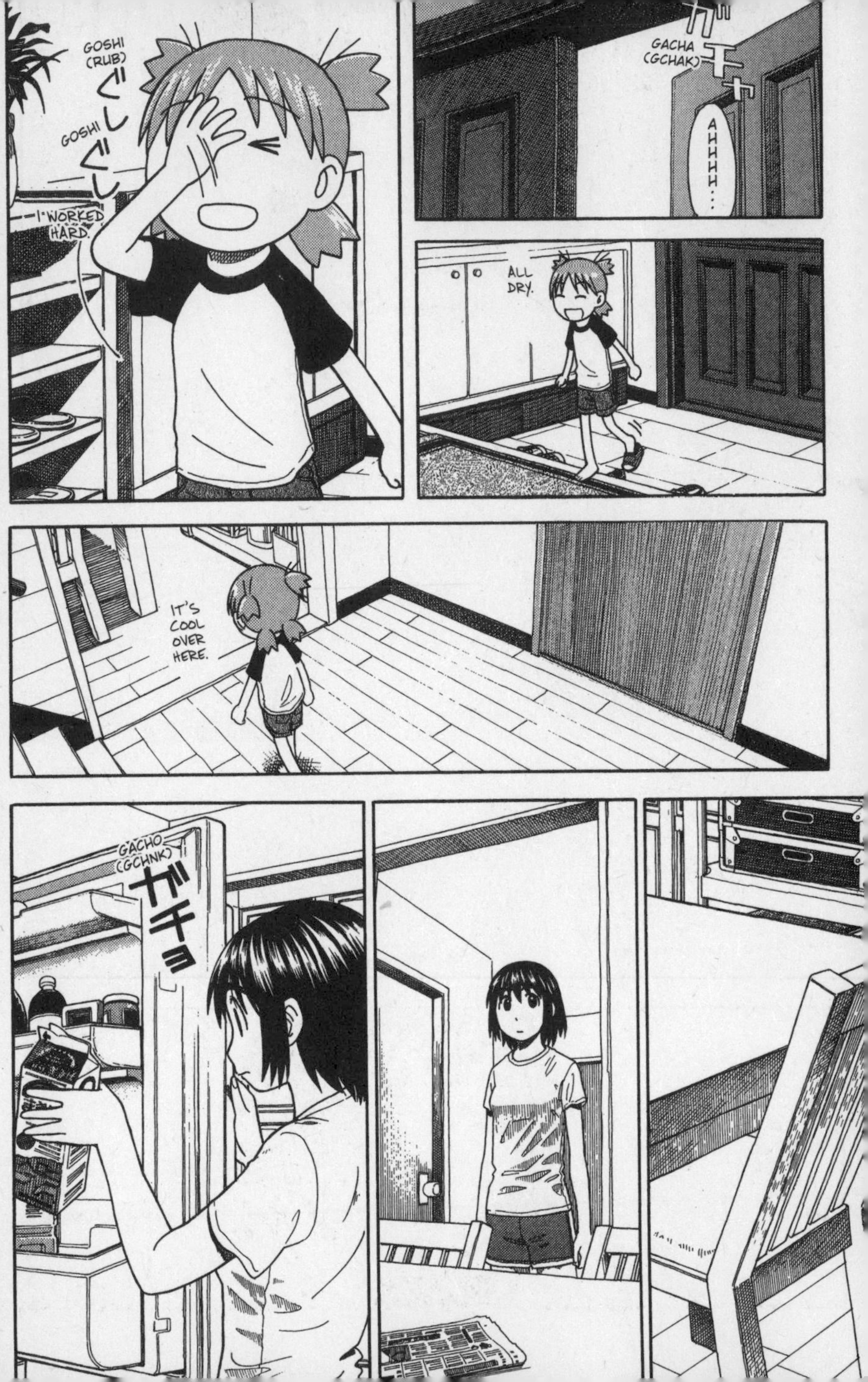
GACHA (GCHAK)
ガチャ
AHHHH...
ALL DRY.
GOSHI (RUB)
ぐし
GOSHI
ぐし
I WORKED HARD.
IT'S COOL OVER HERE.
GACHO (GCHNK)
ガチョ

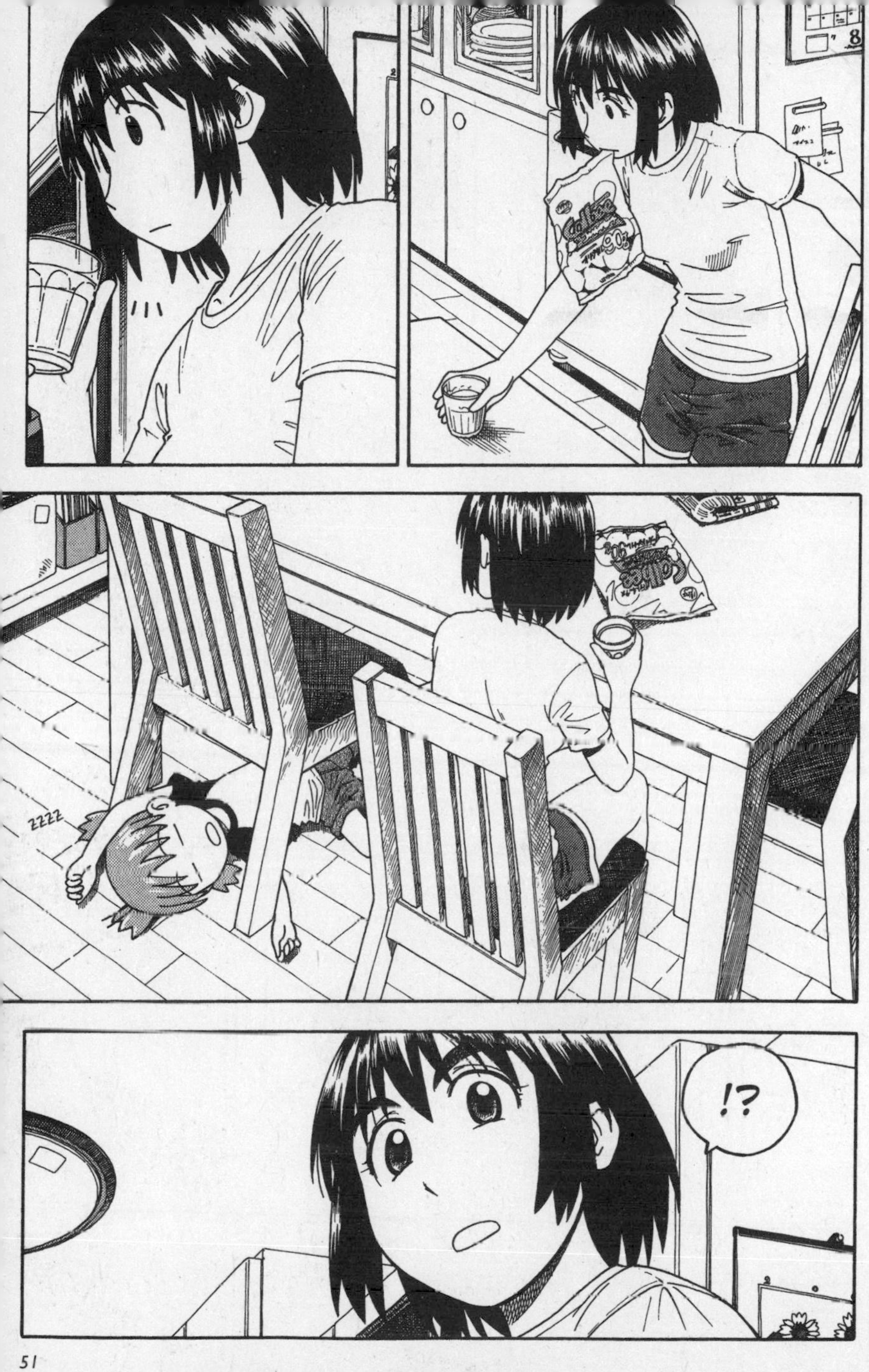
ZZZZ
!?

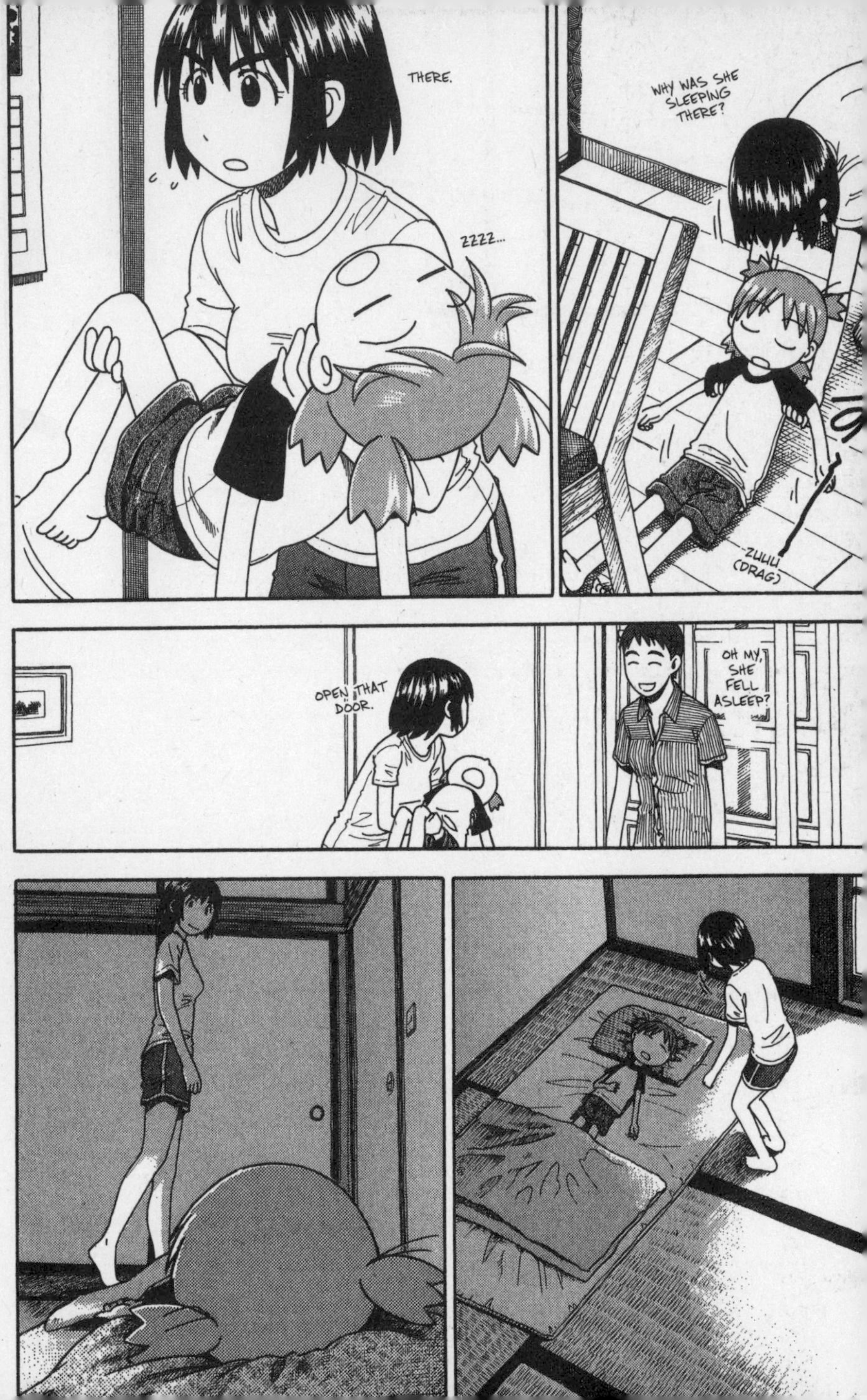
WHY WAS SHE SLEEPING THERE?
-ZUUU (DRAG)
THERE.
ZZZZ...
OH MY, SHE FELL ASLEEP?
OPEN THAT DOOR.

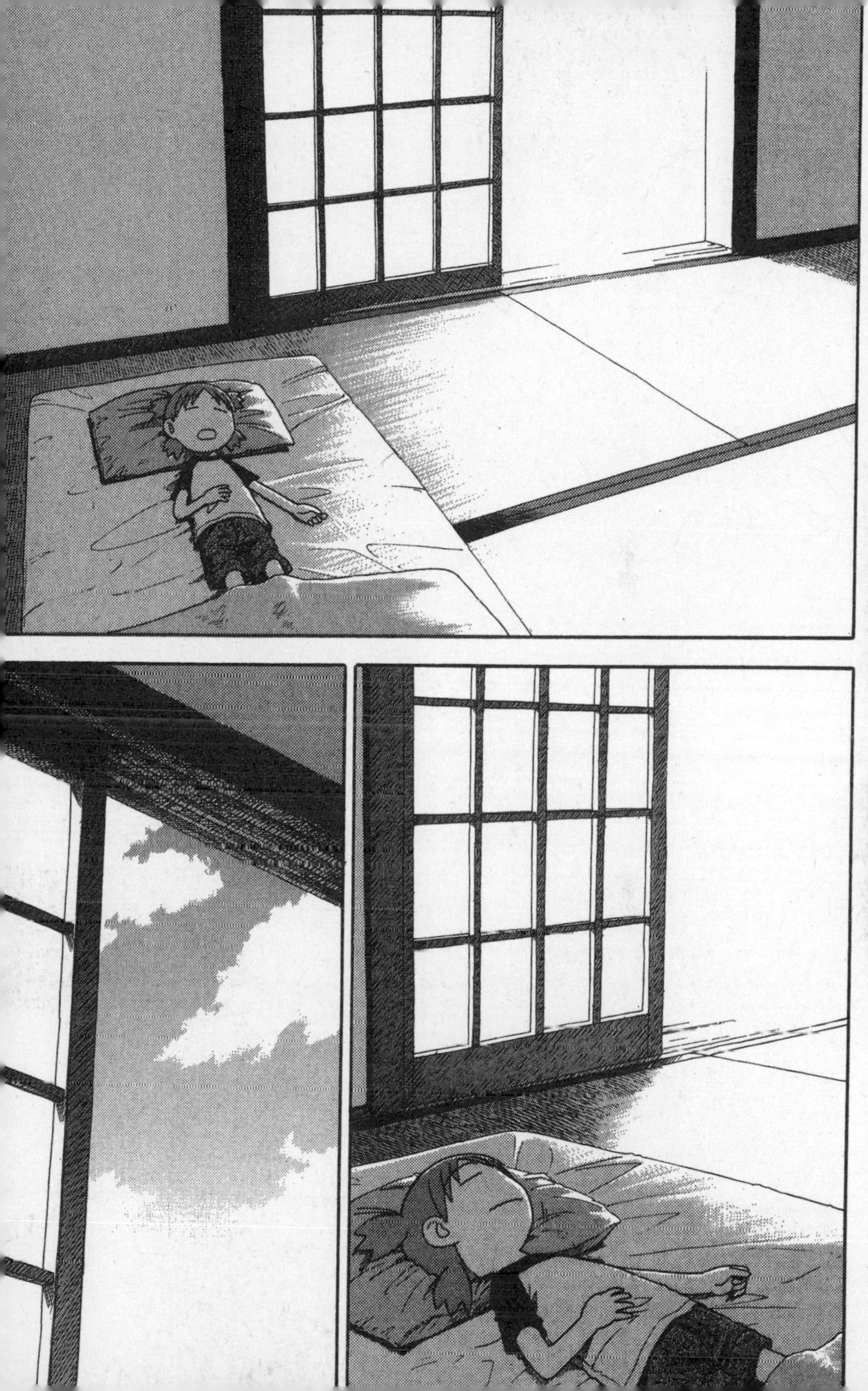

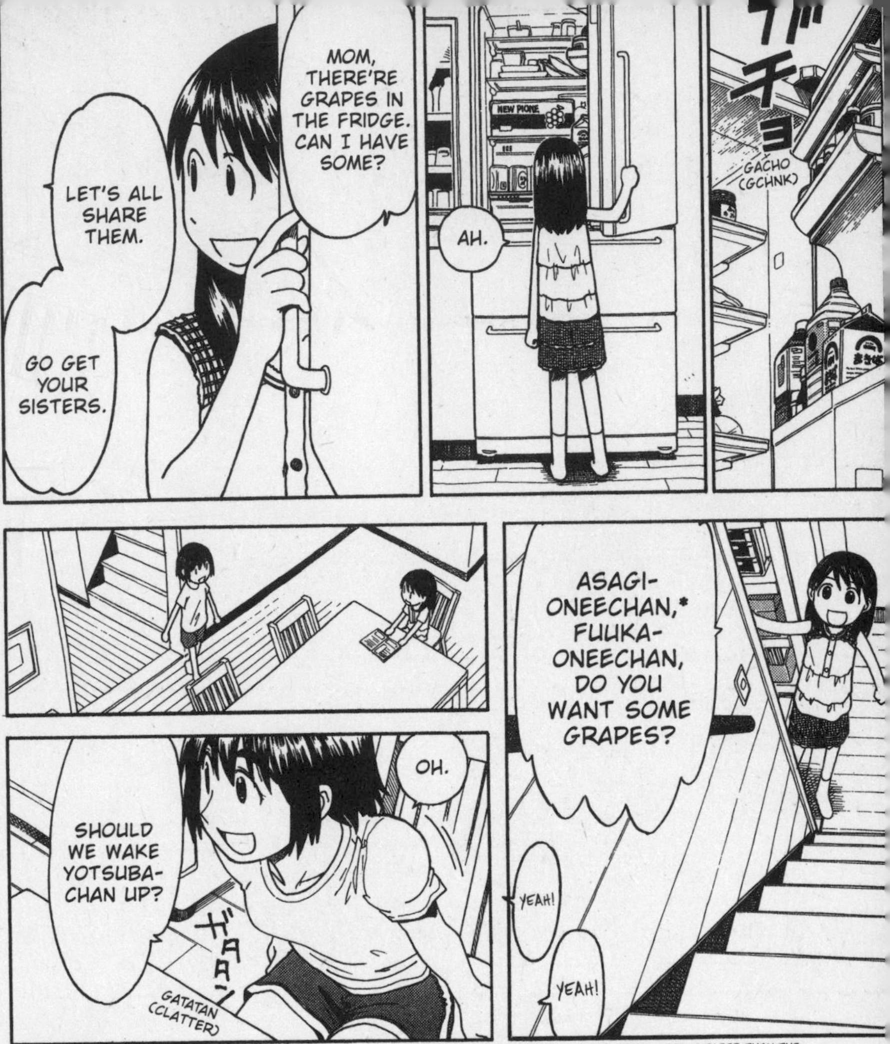
ガチョ
GACHO (GCHNK)
AH.
MOM, THERE'RE GRAPES IN THE FRIDGE. CAN I HAVE SOME?
LET'S ALL SHARE THEM.
GO GET YOUR SISTERS.
ASAGI-ONEECHAN,* FUUKA-ONEECHAN, DO YOU WANT SOME GRAPES?
YEAH!
YEAH!
OH.
SHOULD WE WAKE YOTSUBA-CHAN UP?
ガタ
GATATAN (CLATTER)

*-ONEECHAN: AN HONORIFIC SUFFIX USED TO REFER TO AN OLDER SISTER OR AN UNRELATED YOUNG WOMAN WHO IS OLDER THAN THE SPEAKER.

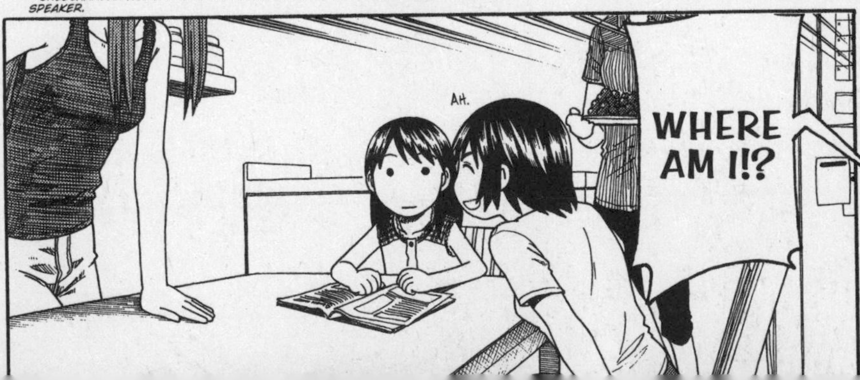
WHERE AM I!?
AH.

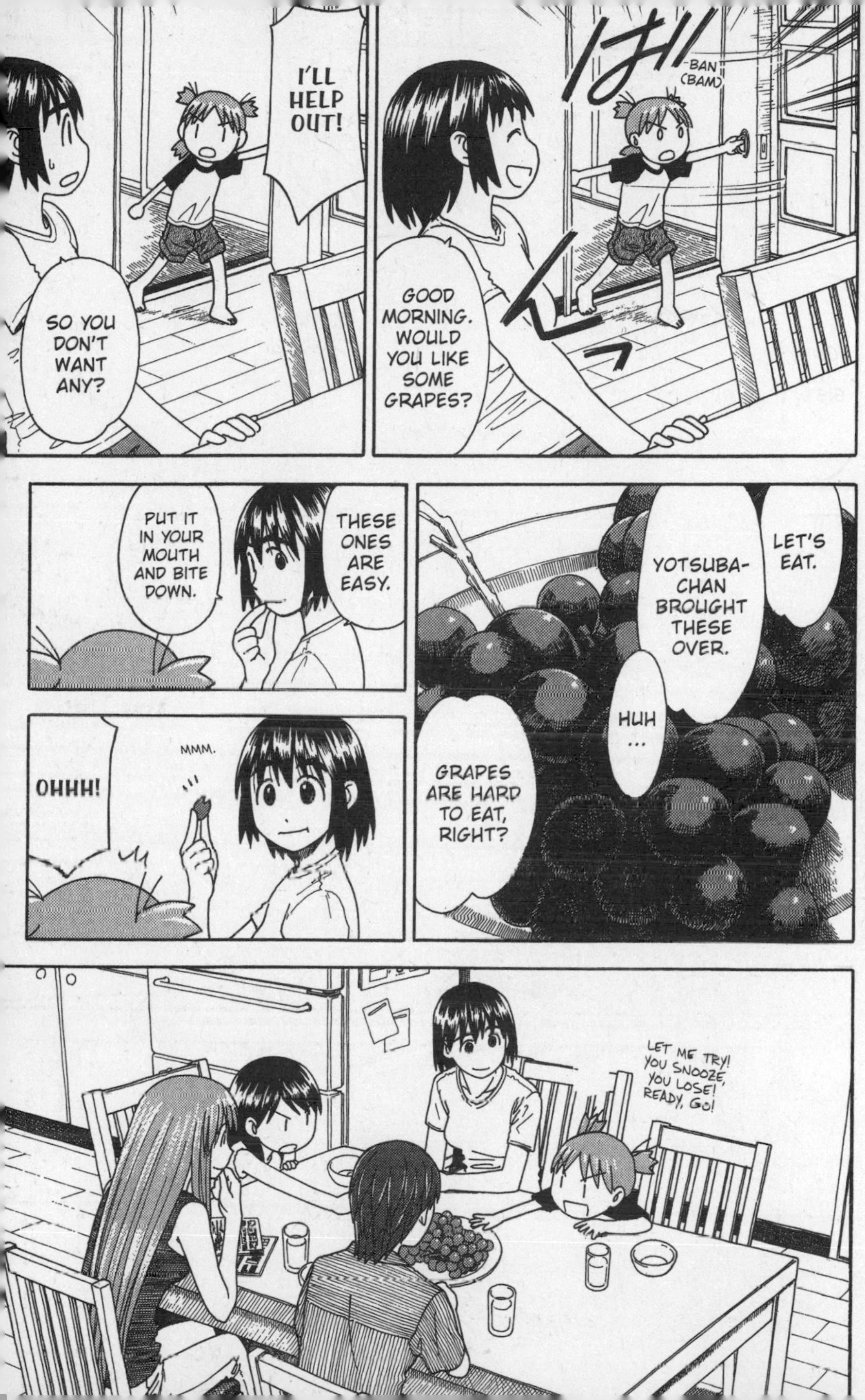
-BAN (BAM)
GOOD MORNING. WOULD YOU LIKE SOME GRAPES?
I'LL HELP OUT!
SO YOU DON'T WANT ANY?
LET'S EAT.
YOTSUBA-CHAN BROUGHT THESE OVER.
HUH ...
GRAPES ARE HARD TO EAT, RIGHT?
THESE ONES ARE EASY.
PUT IT IN YOUR MOUTH AND BITE DOWN.
MMM.
OHHH!
LET ME TRY! YOU SNOOZE, YOU LOSE! READY, GO!

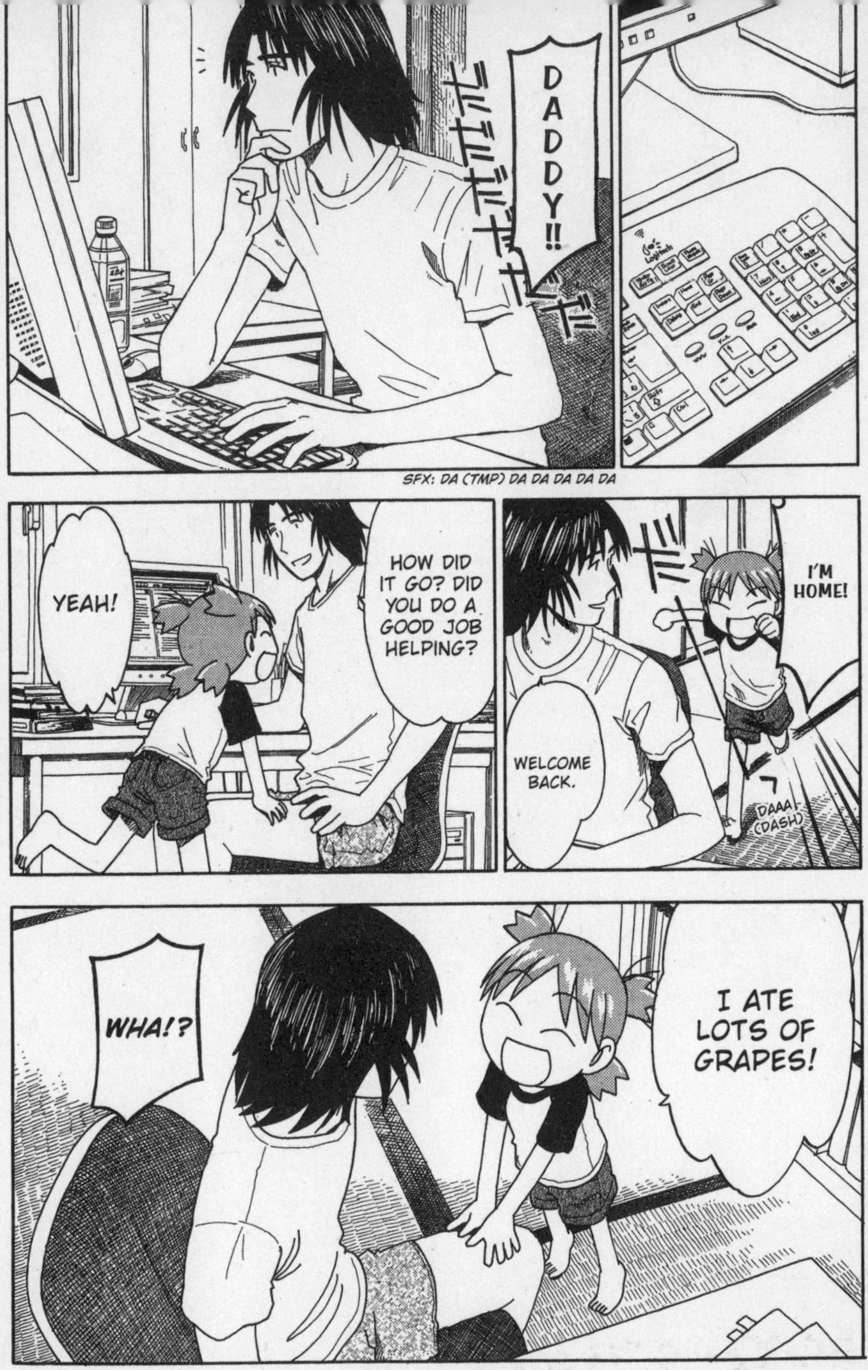
DADDY!!
SFX: DA (TMP) DA DA DA DA DA
I'M HOME!
DAAA (DASH)
WELCOME BACK.
HOW DID IT GO? DID YOU DO A GOOD JOB HELPING?
YEAH!
I ATE LOTS OF GRAPES!
WHA!?

YOTSUBA&!

YOTSUBA& YANDA!

#30

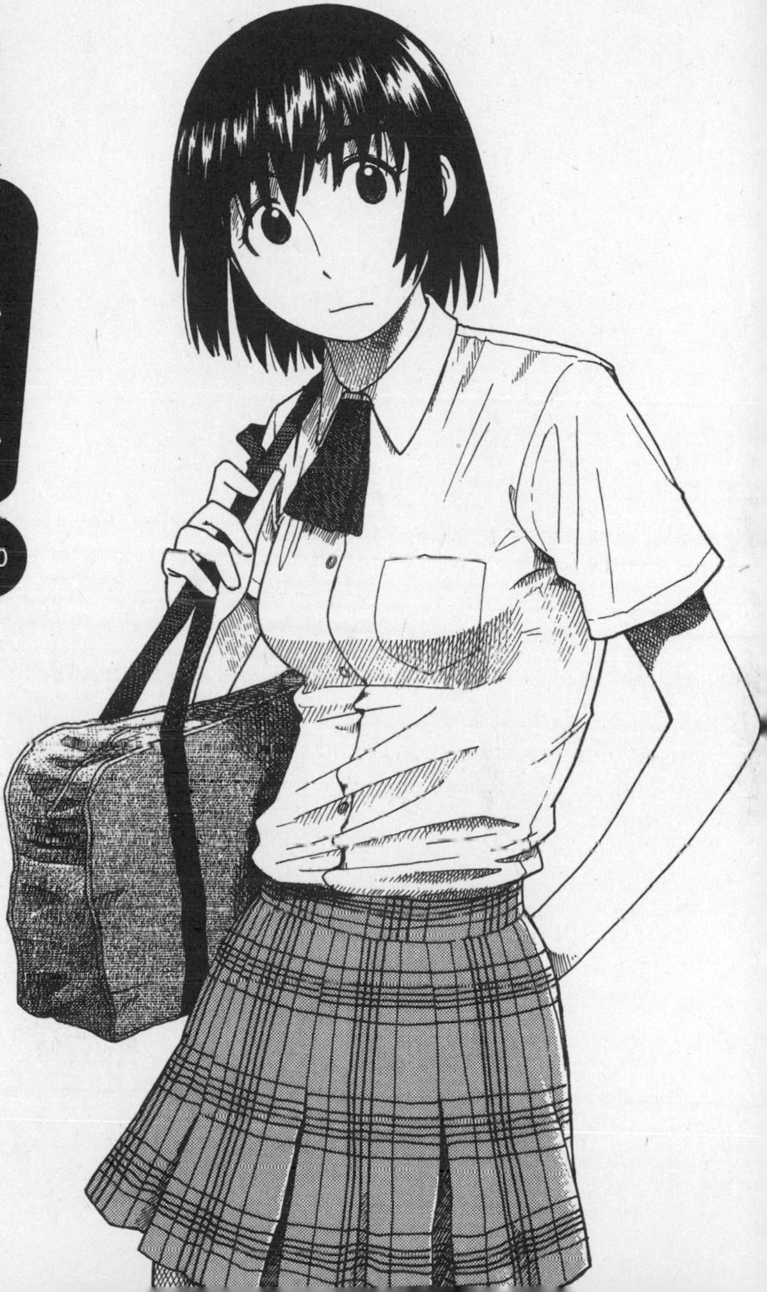

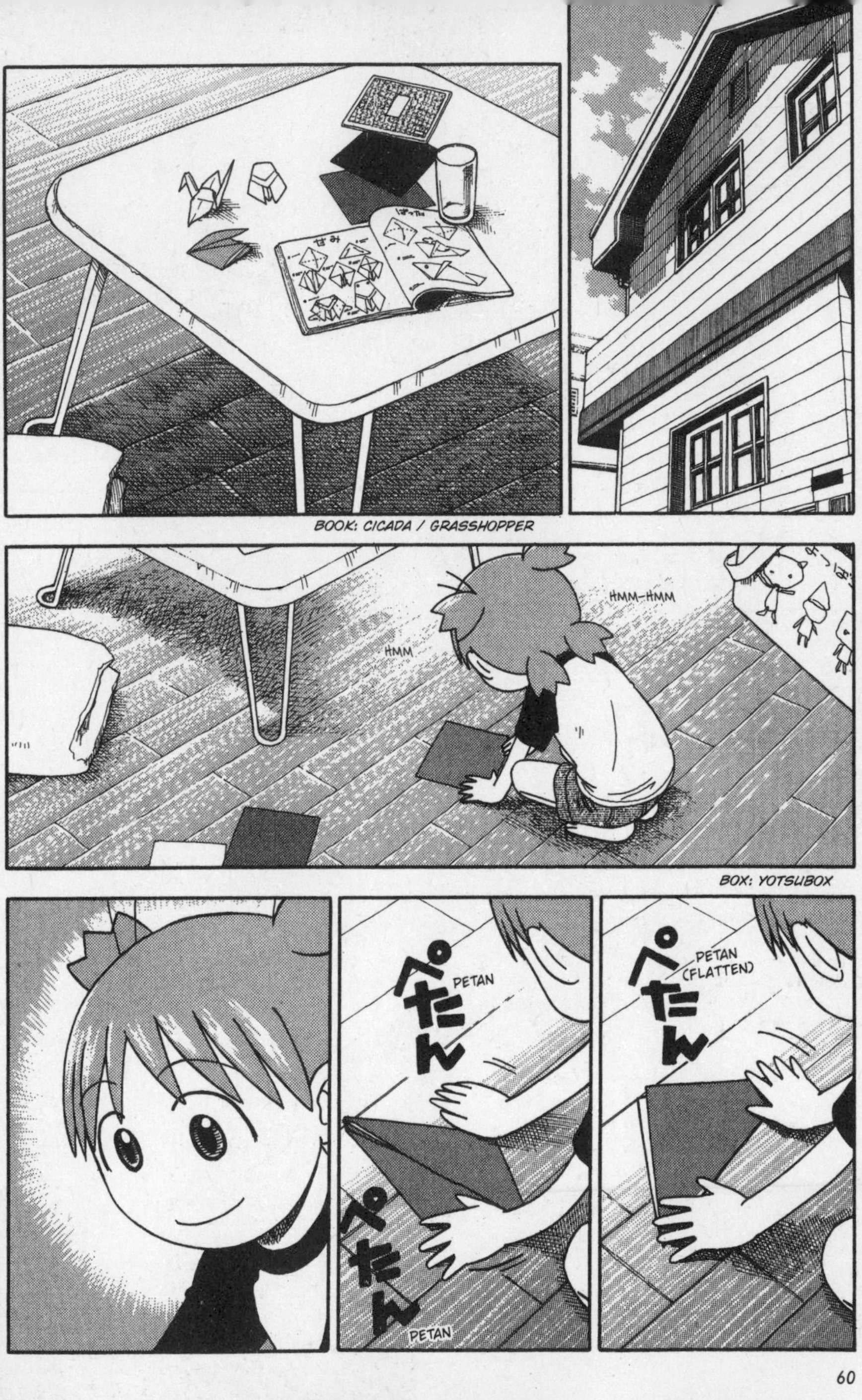
せみ
BOOK: CICADA / GRASSHOPPER
HMM-HMM
HMM
BOX: YOTSUBOX
ぺたん
PETAN (FLATTEN)
ぺたん
PETAN
ぺたん
PETAN

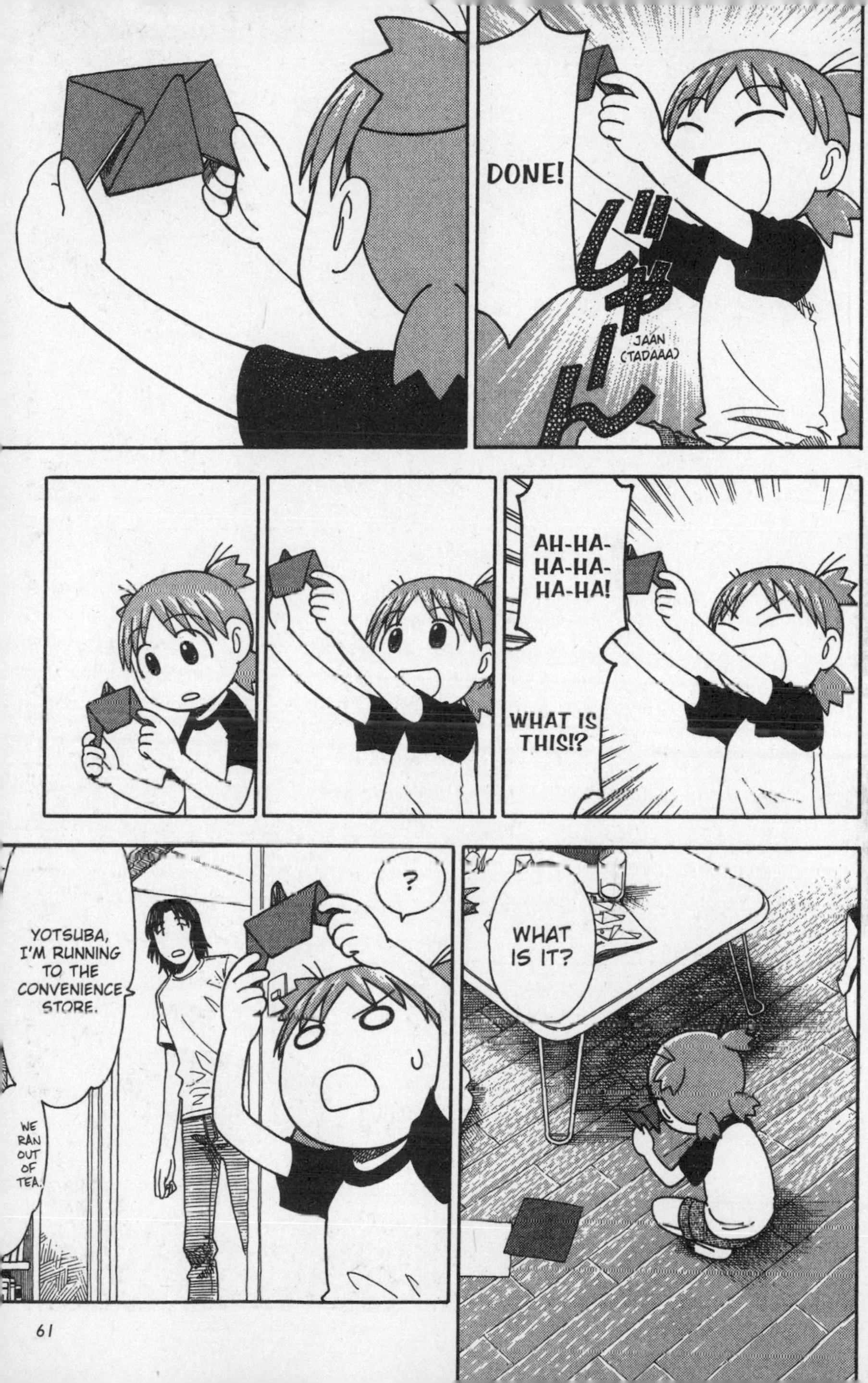
DONE!
じゃーん
JAAN (TADAAA)
AH-HA-HA-HA-HA-HA!
WHAT IS THIS!?
WHAT IS IT?
?
YOTSUBA, I'M RUNNING TO THE CONVENIENCE STORE.
WE RAN OUT OF TEA.

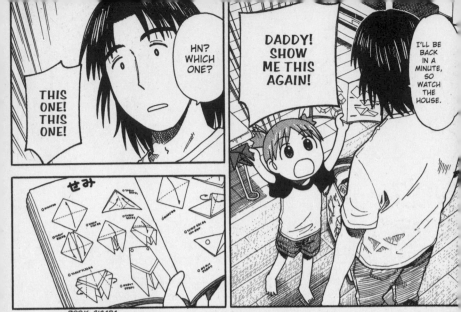

I'LL BE BACK IN A MINUTE, SO WATCH THE HOUSE.
DADDY! SHOW ME THIS AGAIN!
HN? WHICH ONE?
THIS ONE! THIS ONE!
せみ
BOOK: CICADA
HMMM.
TRIANGLE.
TRIANGLE, TRIANGLE.
AND SQUARE.
RIGHT.

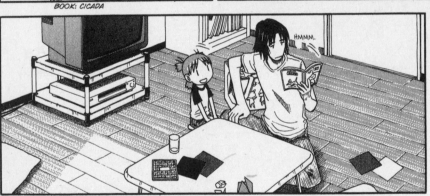

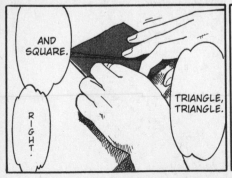

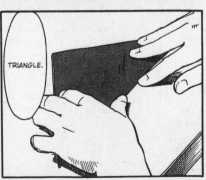

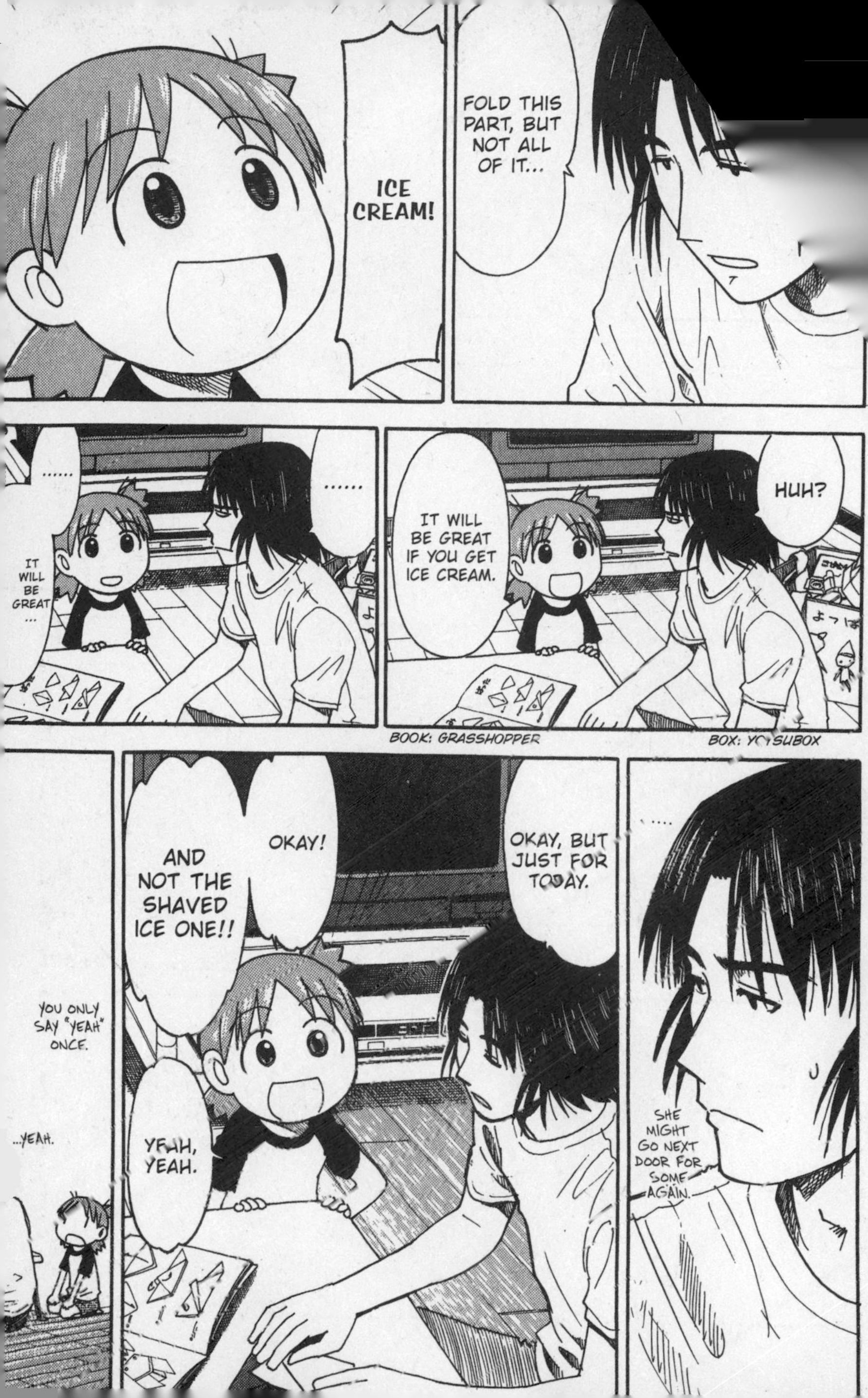
FOLD THIS PART, BUT NOT ALL OF IT...
ICE CREAM!
HUH?
IT WILL BE GREAT IF YOU GET ICE CREAM.
......
......
IT WILL BE GREAT...
BOX: YOTSUBOX
BOOK: GRASSHOPPER
....
SHE MIGHT GO NEXT DOOR FOR SOME AGAIN.
OKAY, BUT JUST FOR TODAY.
OKAY!
AND NOT THE SHAVED ICE ONE!!
YEAH, YEAH.
YOU ONLY SAY "YEAH" ONCE.
...YEAH.

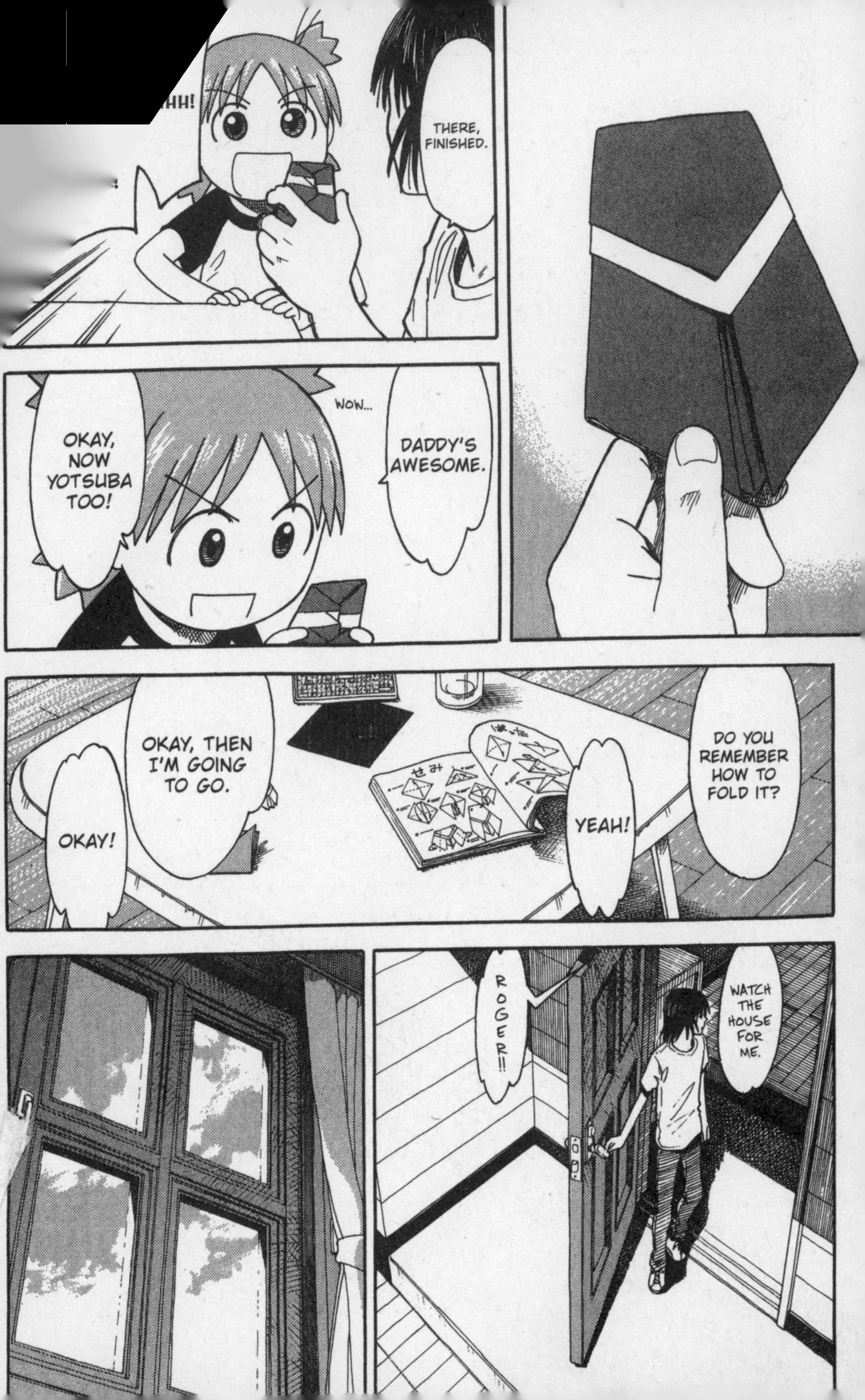
THERE, FINISHED.
[redacted]
WOW...
DADDY'S AWESOME.
OKAY, NOW YOTSUBA TOO!
DO YOU REMEMBER HOW TO FOLD IT?
YEAH!
せみ
OKAY, THEN I'M GOING TO GO.
OKAY!
WATCH THE HOUSE FOR ME.
ROGER!!

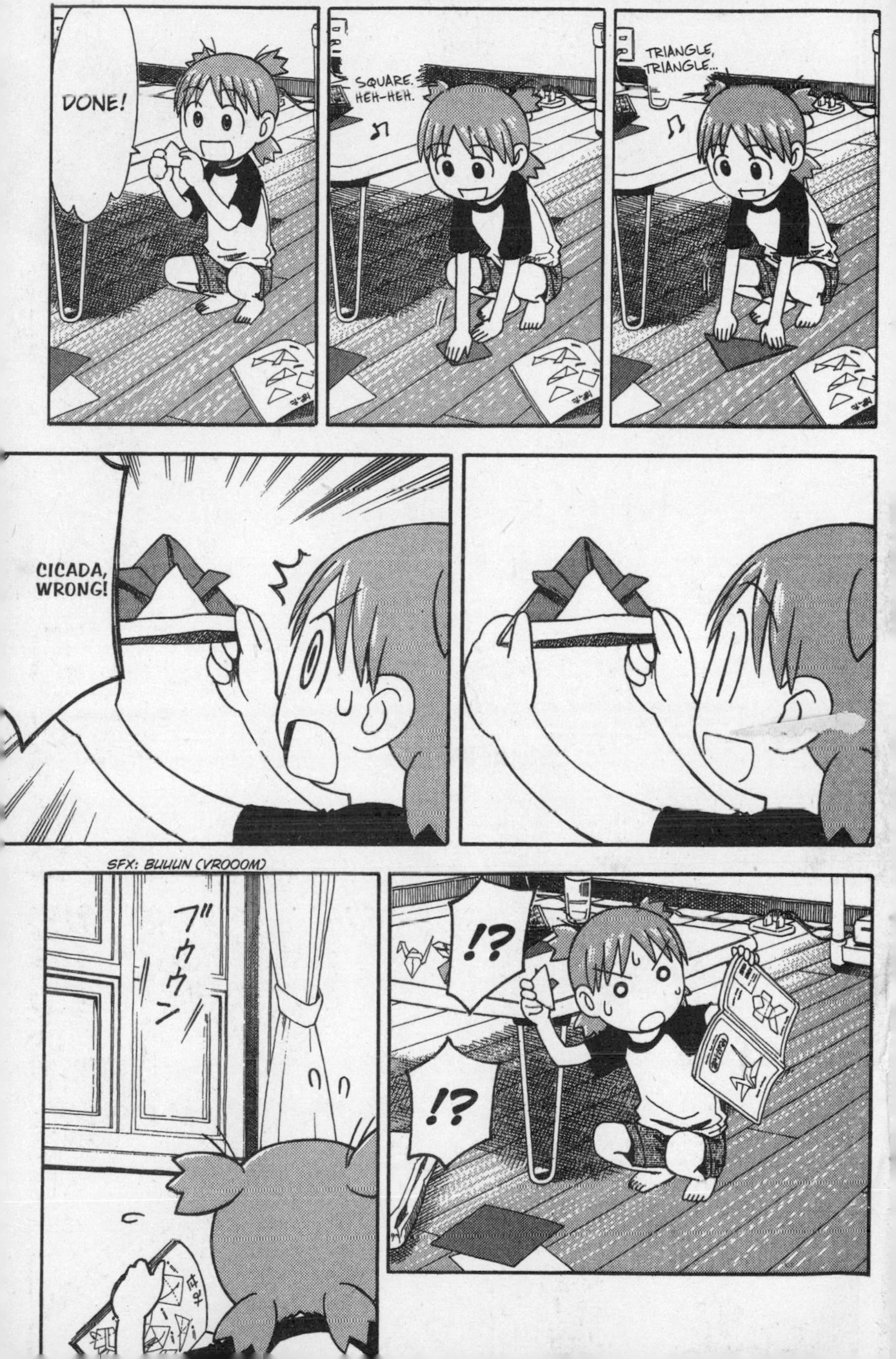
TRIANGLE, TRIANGLE...
SQUARE. HEH-HEH.
DONE!
CICADA, WRONG!
!?
!?
SFX: BUUUN (VROOOM)
ブウウン

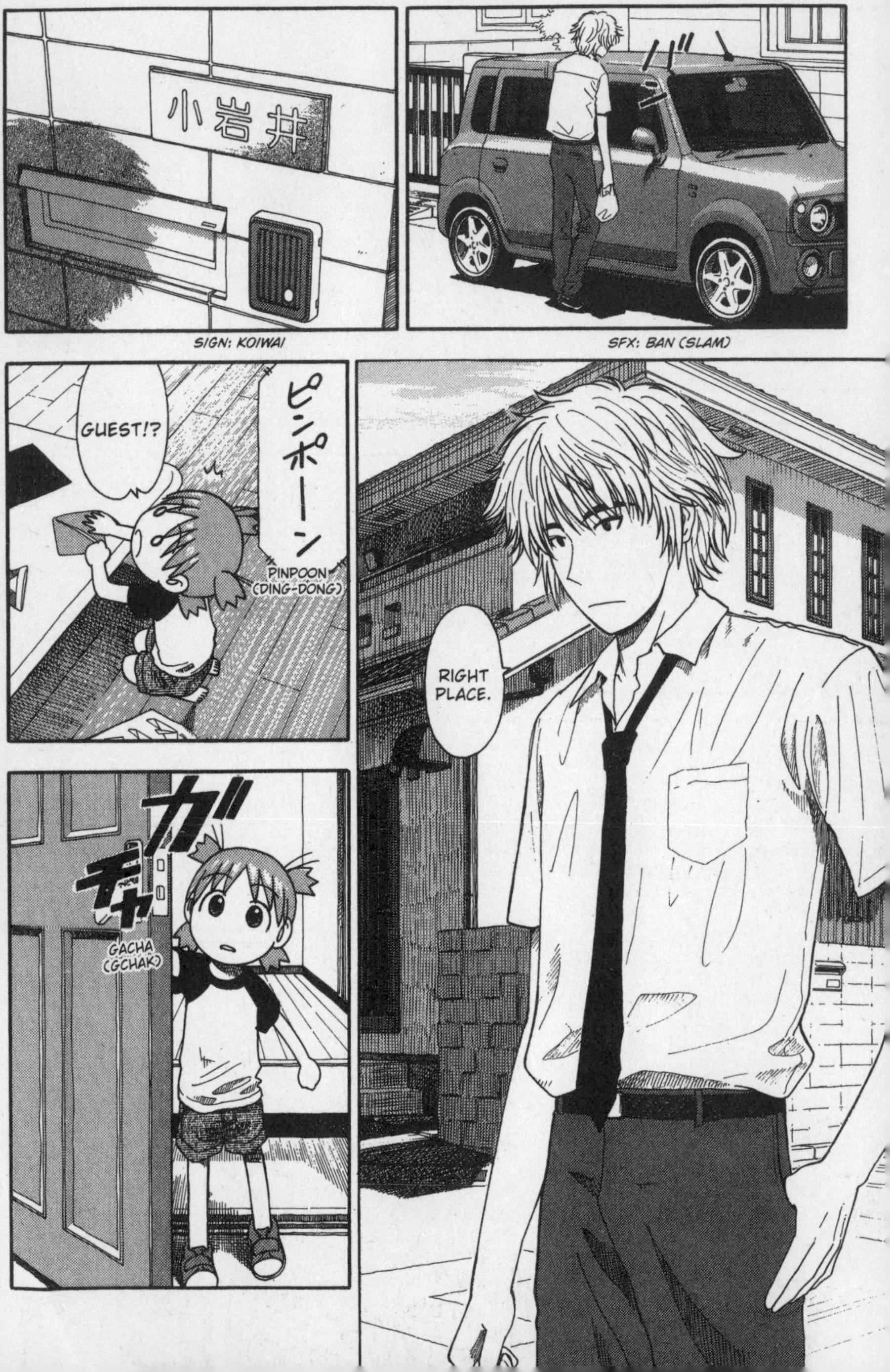
バン
SFX: BAN (SLAM)
小岩井
SIGN: KOIWAI
RIGHT PLACE.
GUEST!?
ピンポーン
PINPOON (DING-DONG)
ガチャ
GACHA (GCHAK)

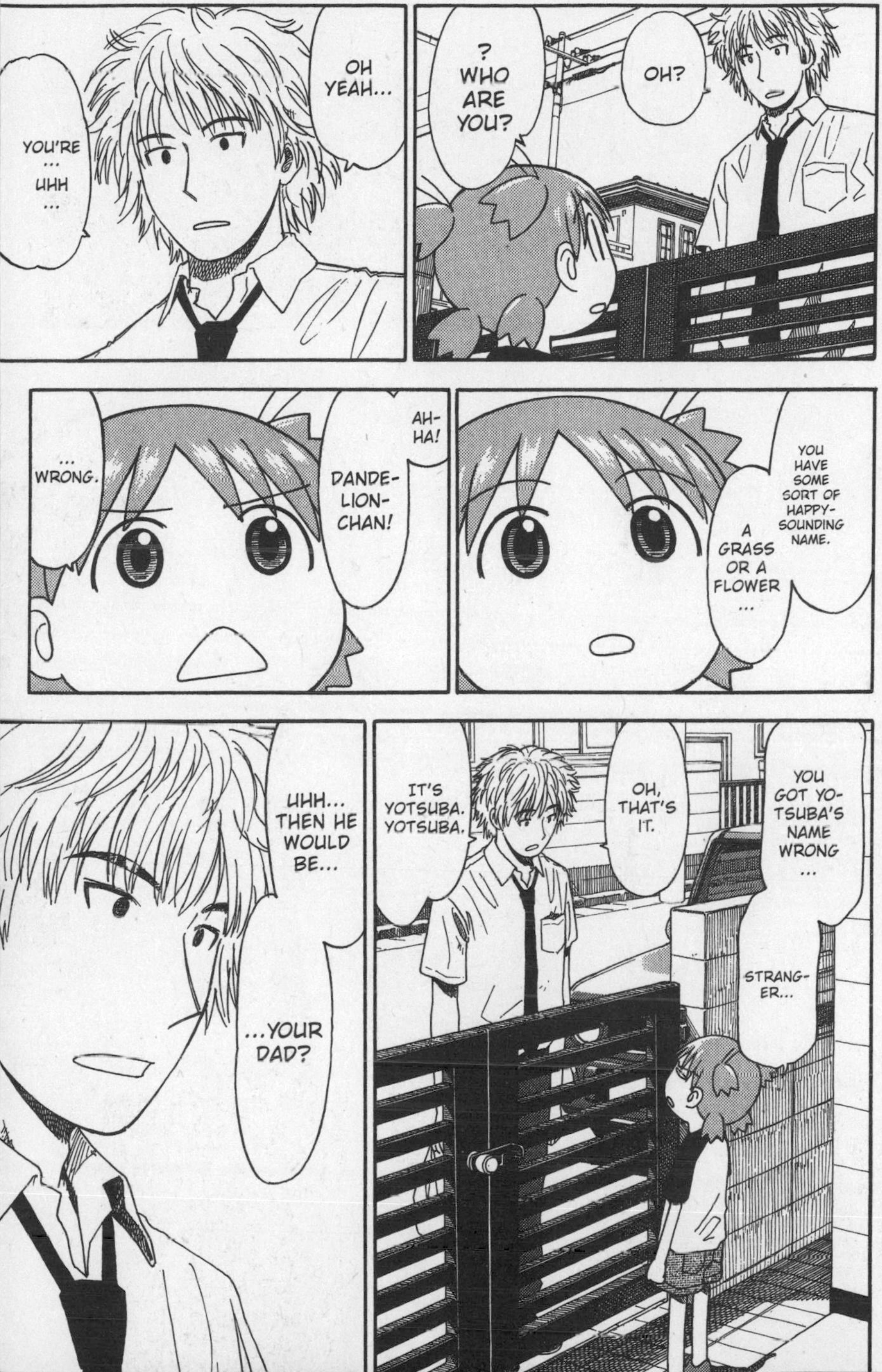
OH?
? WHO ARE YOU?
OH YEAH...
YOU'RE ... UHH ...
YOU HAVE SOME SORT OF HAPPY-SOUNDING NAME.
A GRASS OR A FLOWER ...
AH-HA!
DANDE-LION-CHAN!
... WRONG.
YOU GOT YO-TSUBA'S NAME WRONG ...
STRANG-ER...
OH, THAT'S IT.
IT'S YOTSUBA. YOTSUBA.
UHH... THEN HE WOULD BE...
...YOUR DAD?

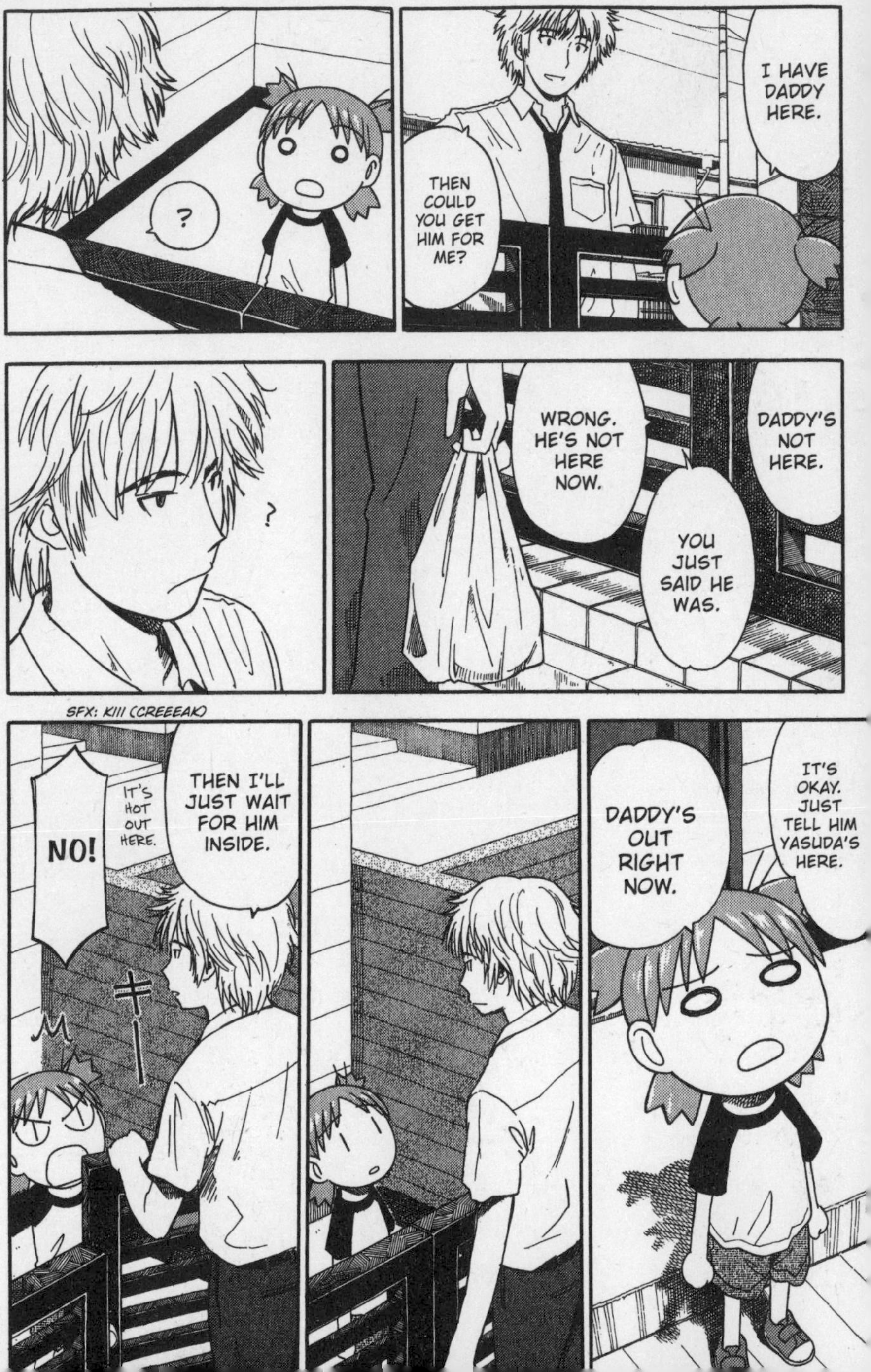
I HAVE DADDY HERE.
THEN COULD YOU GET HIM FOR ME?
?
DADDY'S NOT HERE.
WRONG. HE'S NOT HERE NOW.
YOU JUST SAID HE WAS.
?
SFX: KIII (CREEEAK)
IT'S OKAY. JUST TELL HIM YASUDA'S HERE.
DADDY'S OUT RIGHT NOW.
THEN I'LL JUST WAIT FOR HIM INSIDE.
IT'S HOT OUT HERE.
NO!

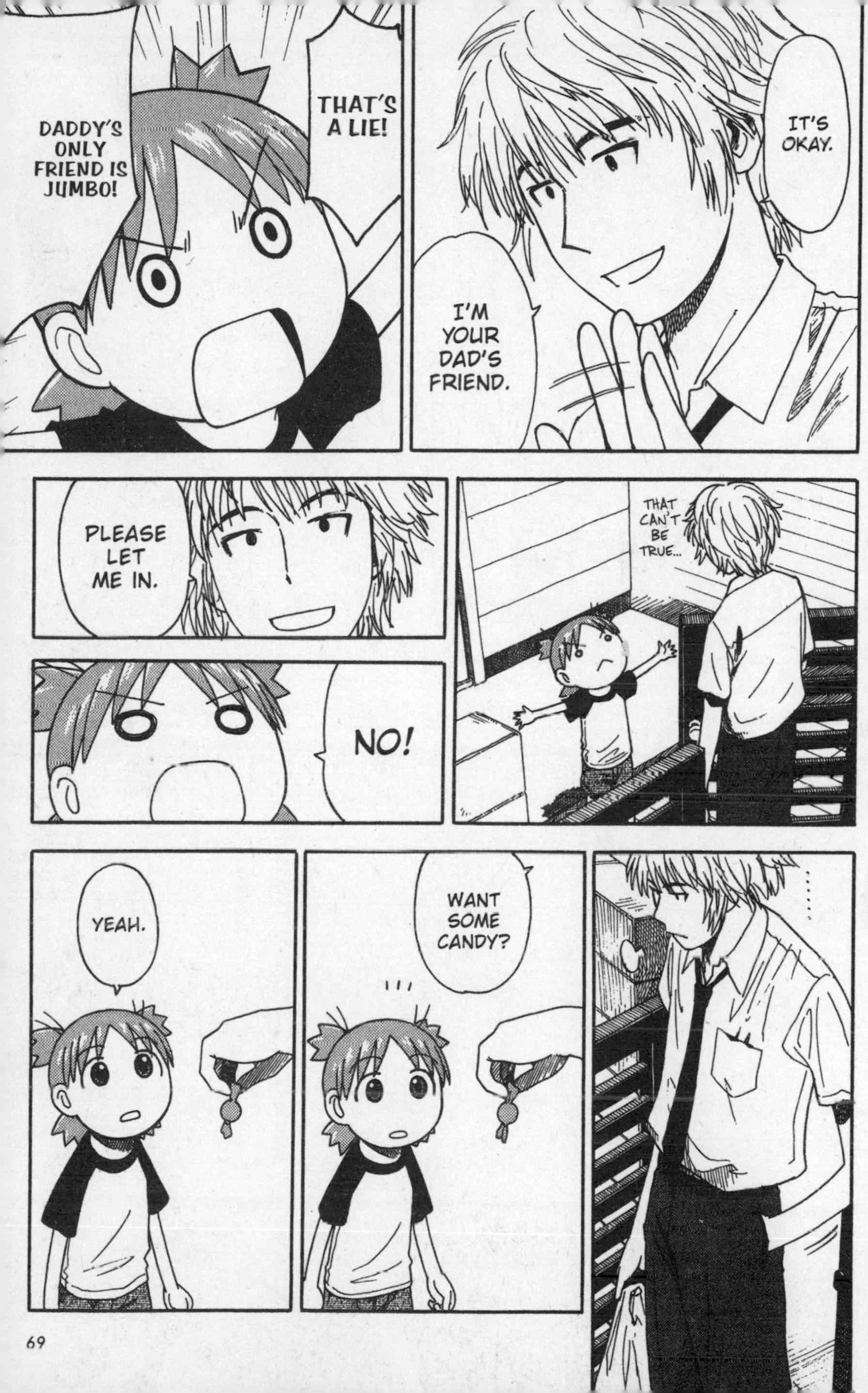
IT'S OKAY.
I'M YOUR DAD'S FRIEND.
THAT'S A LIE!
DADDY'S ONLY FRIEND IS JUMBO!
THAT CAN'T BE TRUE...
PLEASE LET ME IN.
NO!
......
WANT SOME CANDY?
YEAH.

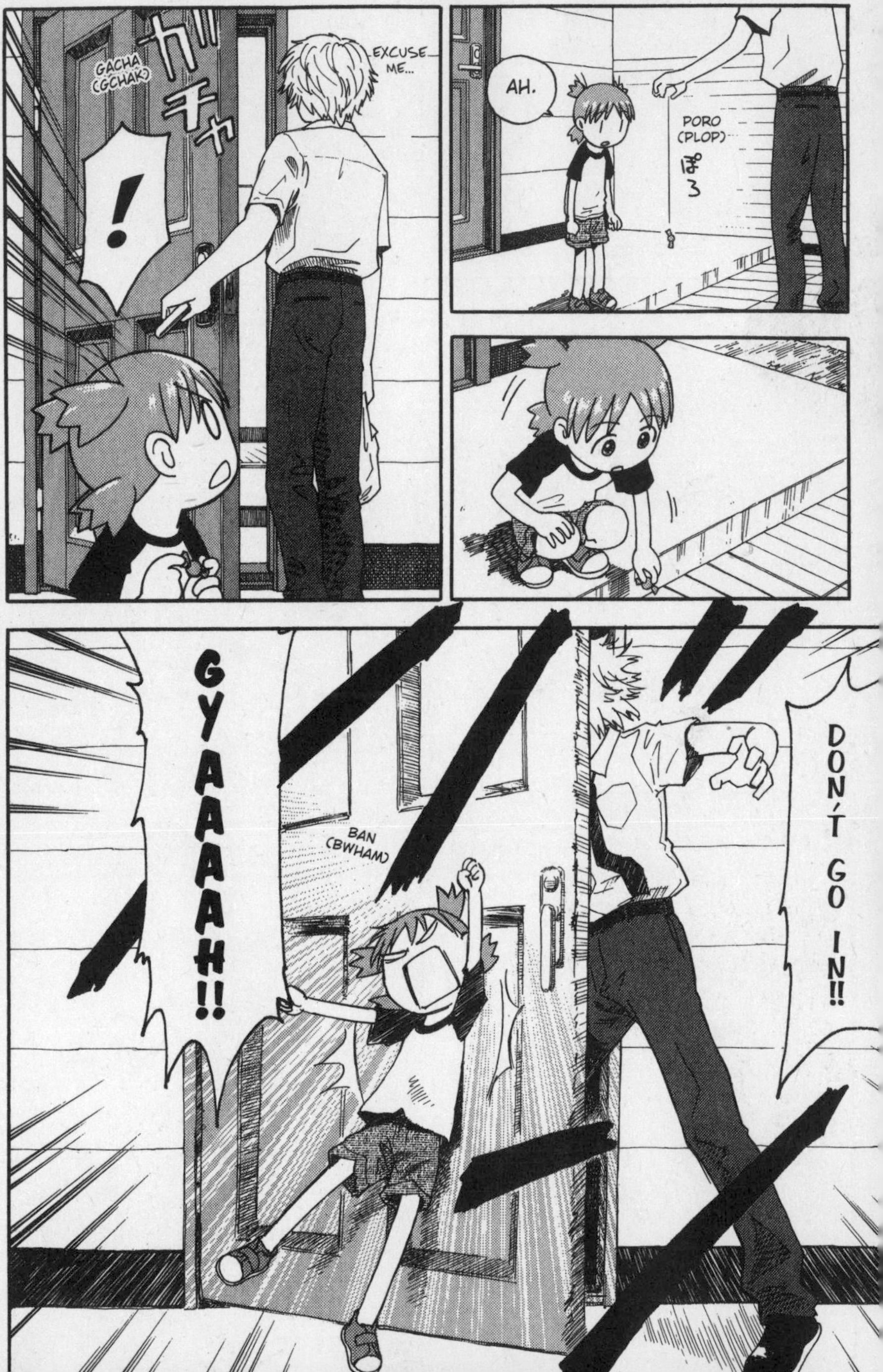
AH.
PORO (PLOP)
ぽろ
EXCUSE ME...
カチャ
GACHA (GCHAK)
!
DON'T GO IN!!
BAN (BWHAM)
GYAAAAAH!!

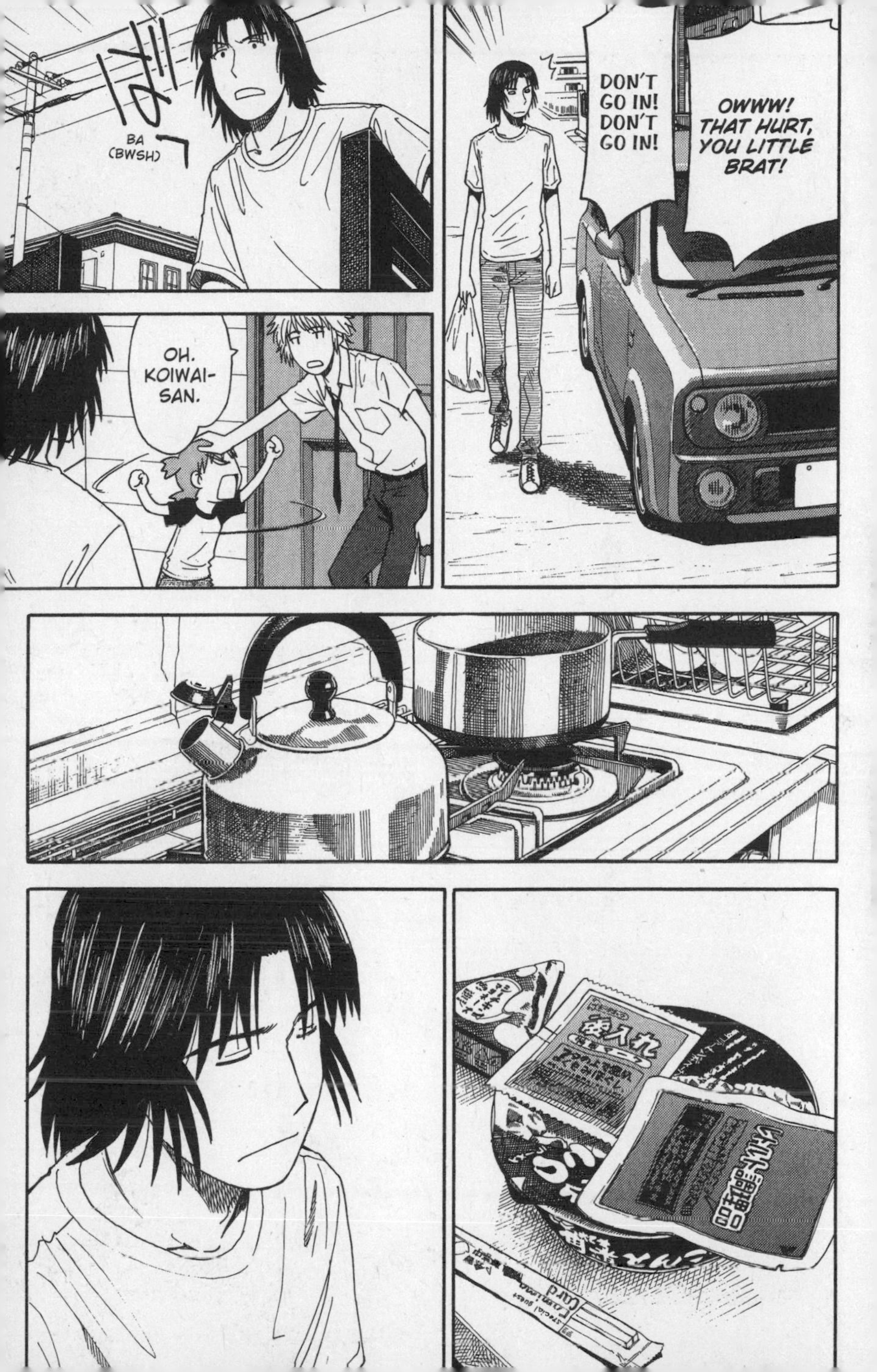
OWWW! THAT HURT, YOU LITTLE BRAT!
DON'T GO IN! DON'T GO IN!
BA (BWSH)
OH. KOIWAI-SAN.

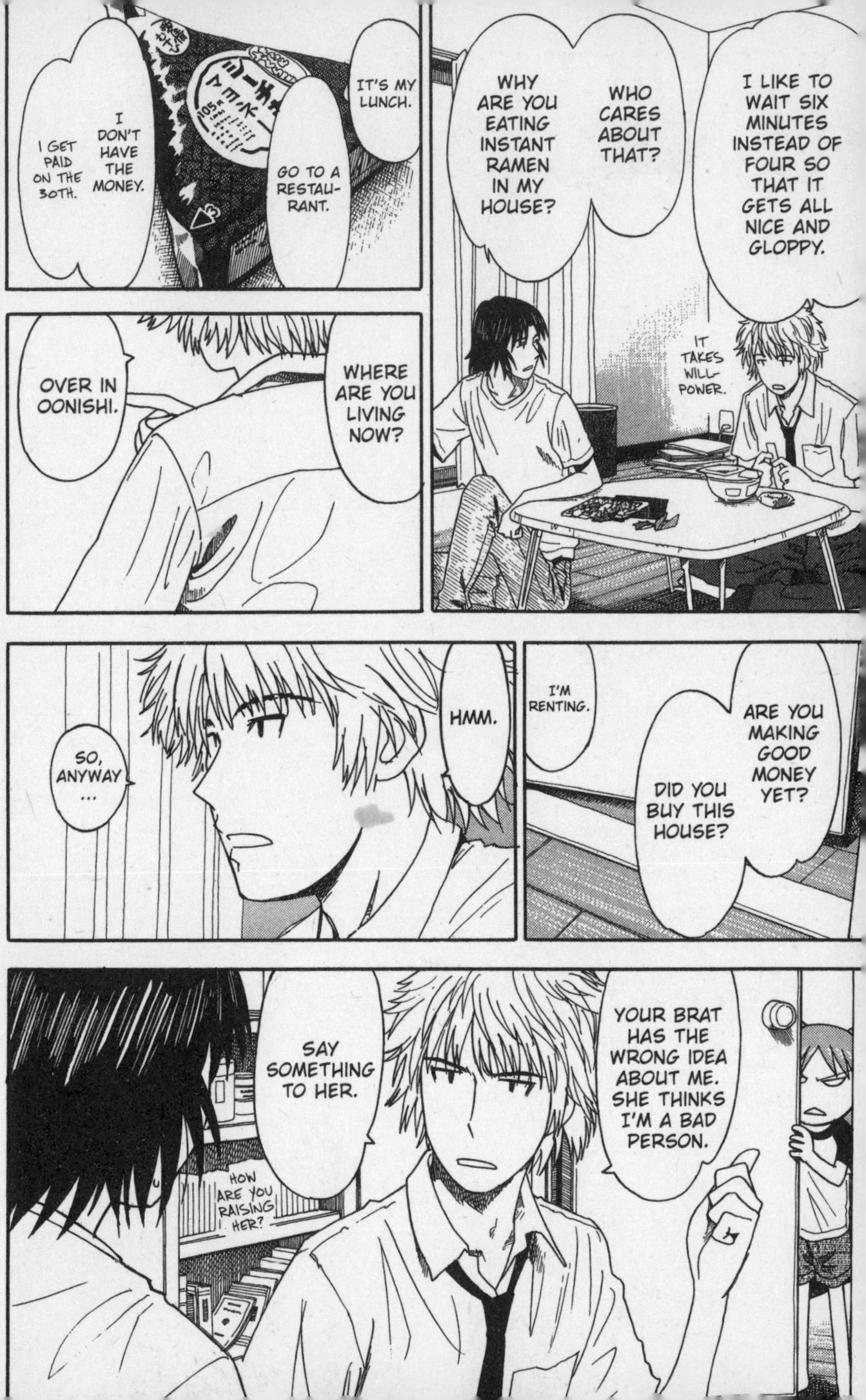
I LIKE TO WAIT SIX MINUTES INSTEAD OF FOUR SO THAT IT GETS ALL NICE AND GLOPPY.
WHO CARES ABOUT THAT?
WHY ARE YOU EATING INSTANT RAMEN IN MY HOUSE?
IT TAKES WILL-POWER.
IT'S MY LUNCH.
GO TO A RESTAU-RANT.
I DON'T HAVE THE MONEY.
I GET PAID ON THE 30TH.
WHERE ARE YOU LIVING NOW?
OVER IN OONISHI.
ARE YOU MAKING GOOD MONEY YET?
DID YOU BUY THIS HOUSE?
I'M RENTING.
HMM.
SO, ANYWAY ...
YOUR BRAT HAS THE WRONG IDEA ABOUT ME. SHE THINKS I'M A BAD PERSON.
SAY SOMETHING TO HER.
HOW ARE YOU RAISING HER?

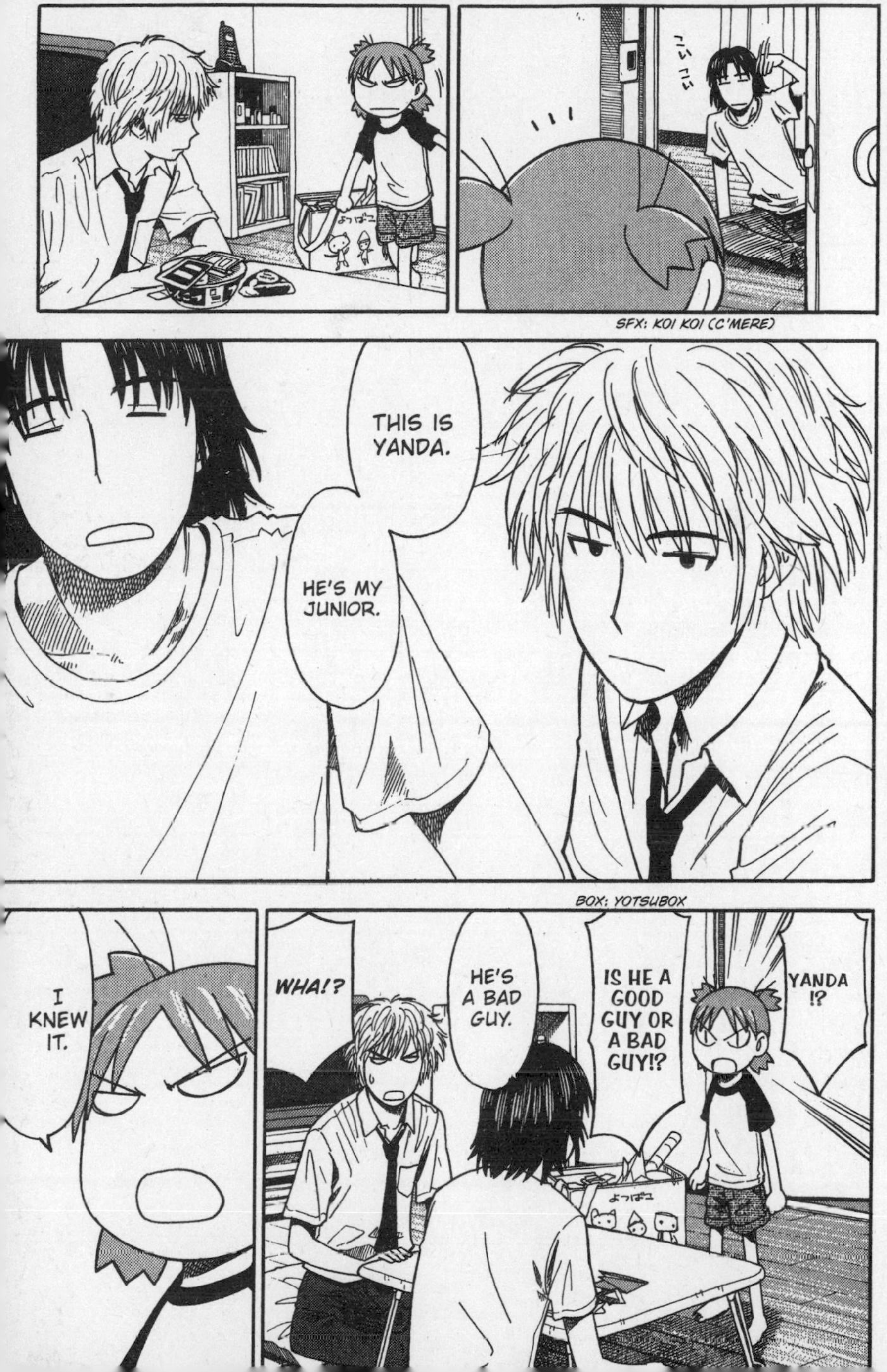
SFX: KOI KOI (C'MERE)
THIS IS YANDA.
HE'S MY JUNIOR.
BOX: YOTSUBOX
YANDA !?
IS HE A GOOD GUY OR A BAD GUY!?
HE'S A BAD GUY.
WHA!?
I KNEW IT.

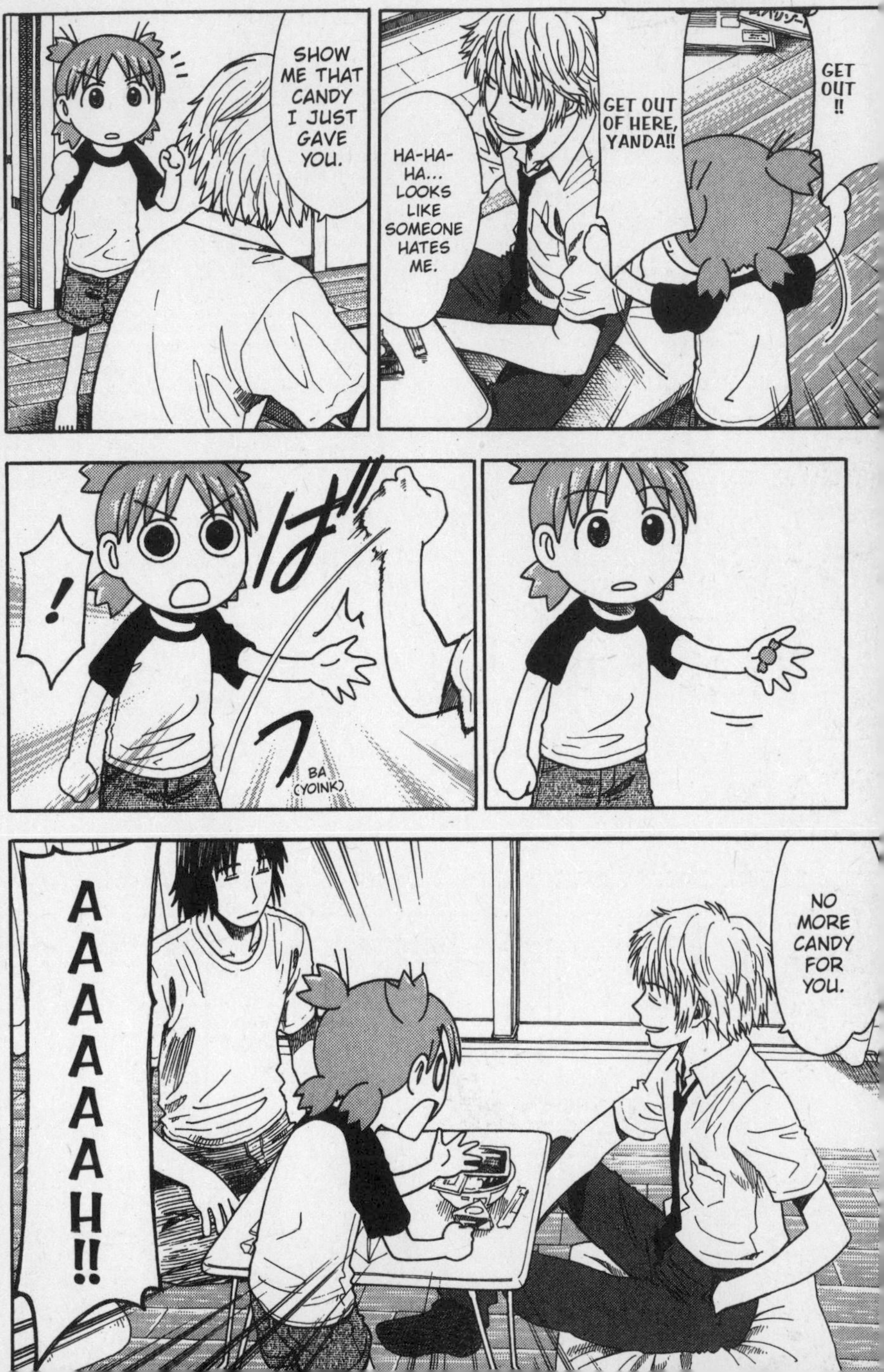
GET OUT!!
GET OUT OF HERE, YANDA!!
HA-HA-HA... LOOKS LIKE SOMEONE HATES ME.
SHOW ME THAT CANDY I JUST GAVE YOU.
!
BA (YOINK)
NO MORE CANDY FOR YOU.
AAAAAAAH!!

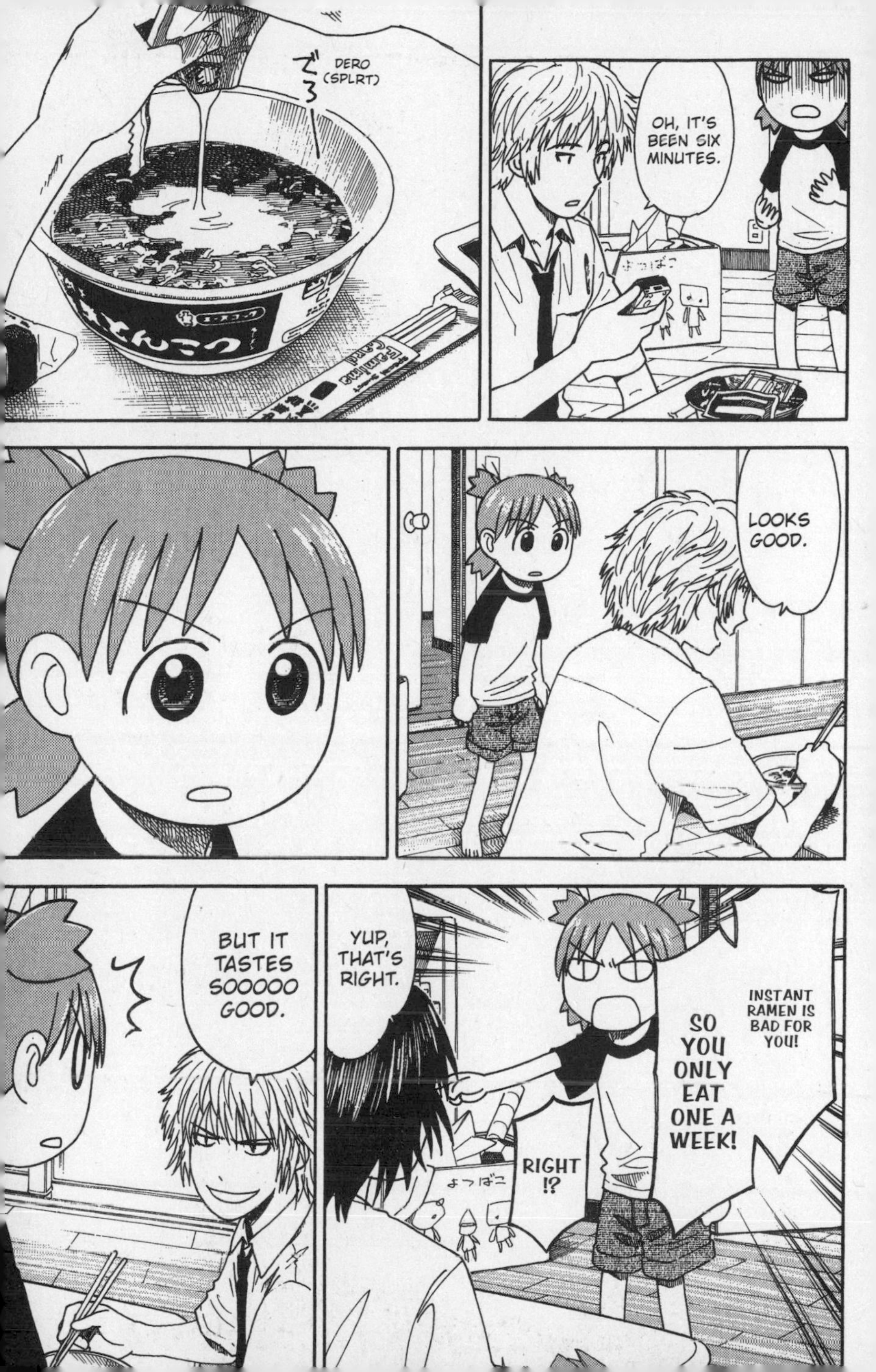
OH, IT'S BEEN SIX MINUTES.
でろ
DERO (SPLRT)
LOOKS GOOD.
INSTANT RAMEN IS BAD FOR YOU!
SO YOU ONLY EAT ONE A WEEK!
RIGHT !?
よつばこ
YUP, THAT'S RIGHT.
BUT IT TASTES SOOOOO GOOD.

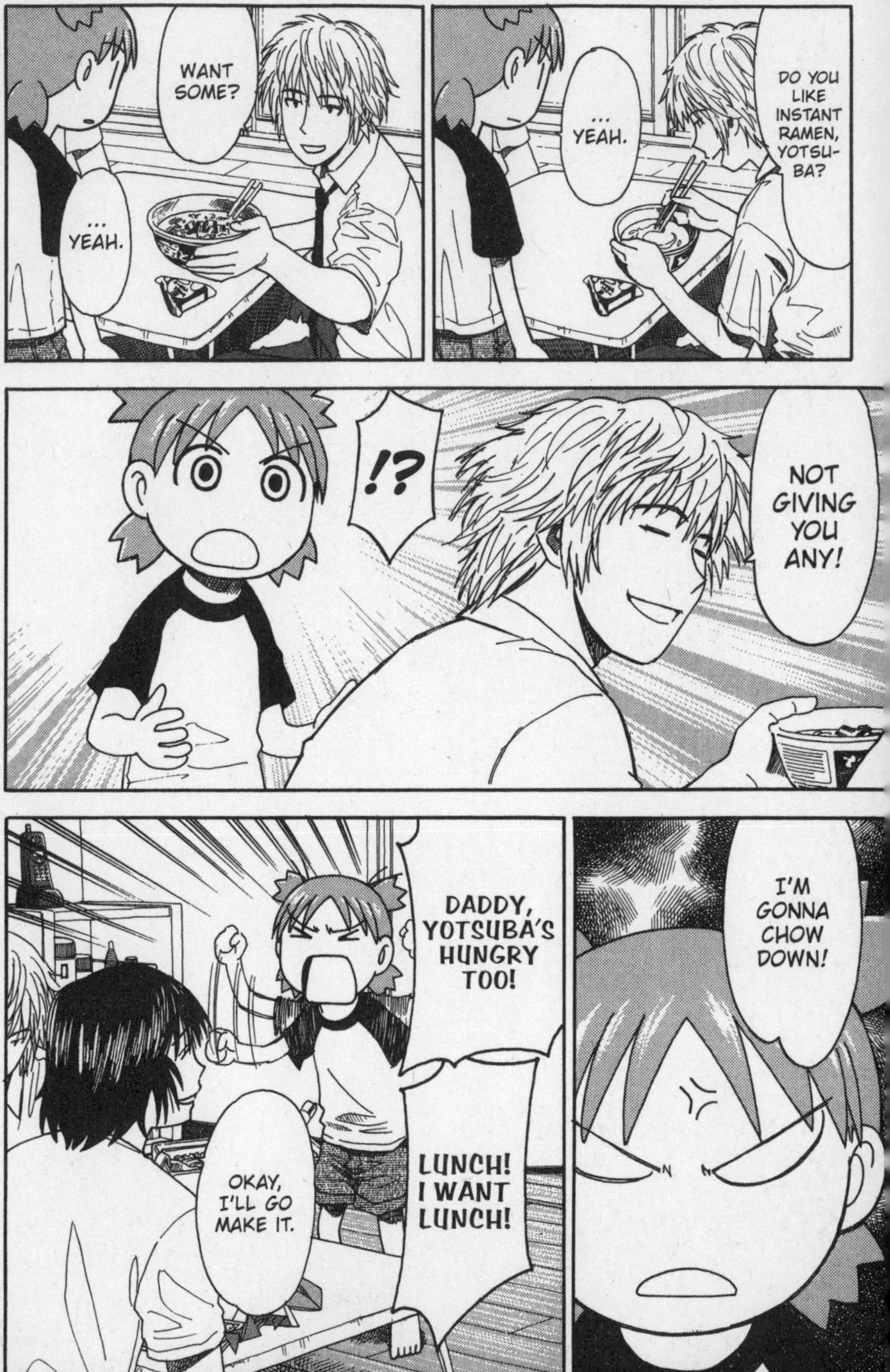
DO YOU LIKE INSTANT RAMEN, YOTSU-BA?
... YEAH.
WANT SOME?
... YEAH.
NOT GIVING YOU ANY!
!?
I'M GONNA CHOW DOWN!
DADDY, YOTSUBA'S HUNGRY TOO!
LUNCH! I WANT LUNCH!
OKAY, I'LL GO MAKE IT.

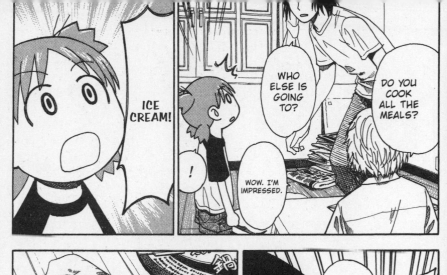

DO YOU COOK ALL THE MEALS?
WHO ELSE IS GOING TO?
!
WOW. I'M IMPRESSED.
ICE CREAM!
I WANT TO HAVE ICE CREAM!!
RIGHT NOW? HAVE IT AFTER LUNCH.
NOW! I'M GONNA EAT IT RIGHT NOW!
PACKAGE: CHOCOLATE AND VANILLA

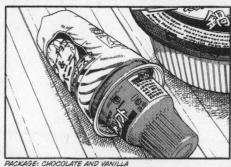

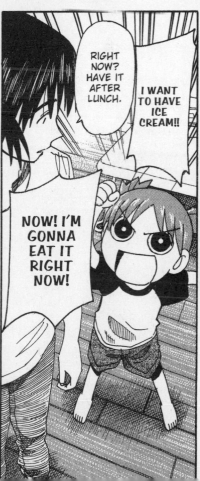

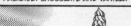

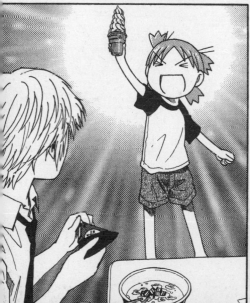

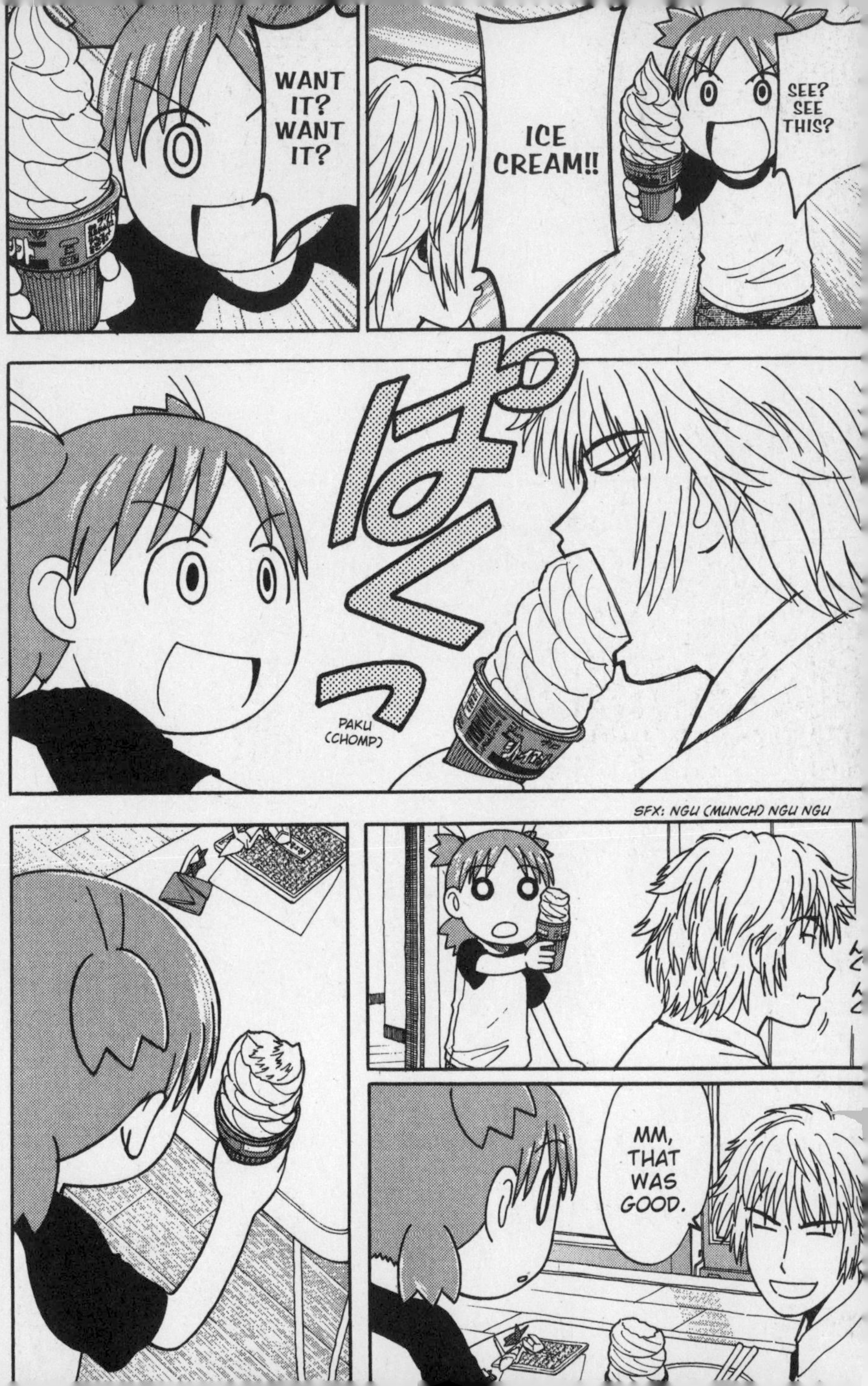
SEE? SEE THIS?
ICE CREAM!!
WANT IT? WANT IT?
ぱくっ
PAKU (CHOMP)
SFX: NGU (MUNCH) NGU NGU
MM, THAT WAS GOOD.

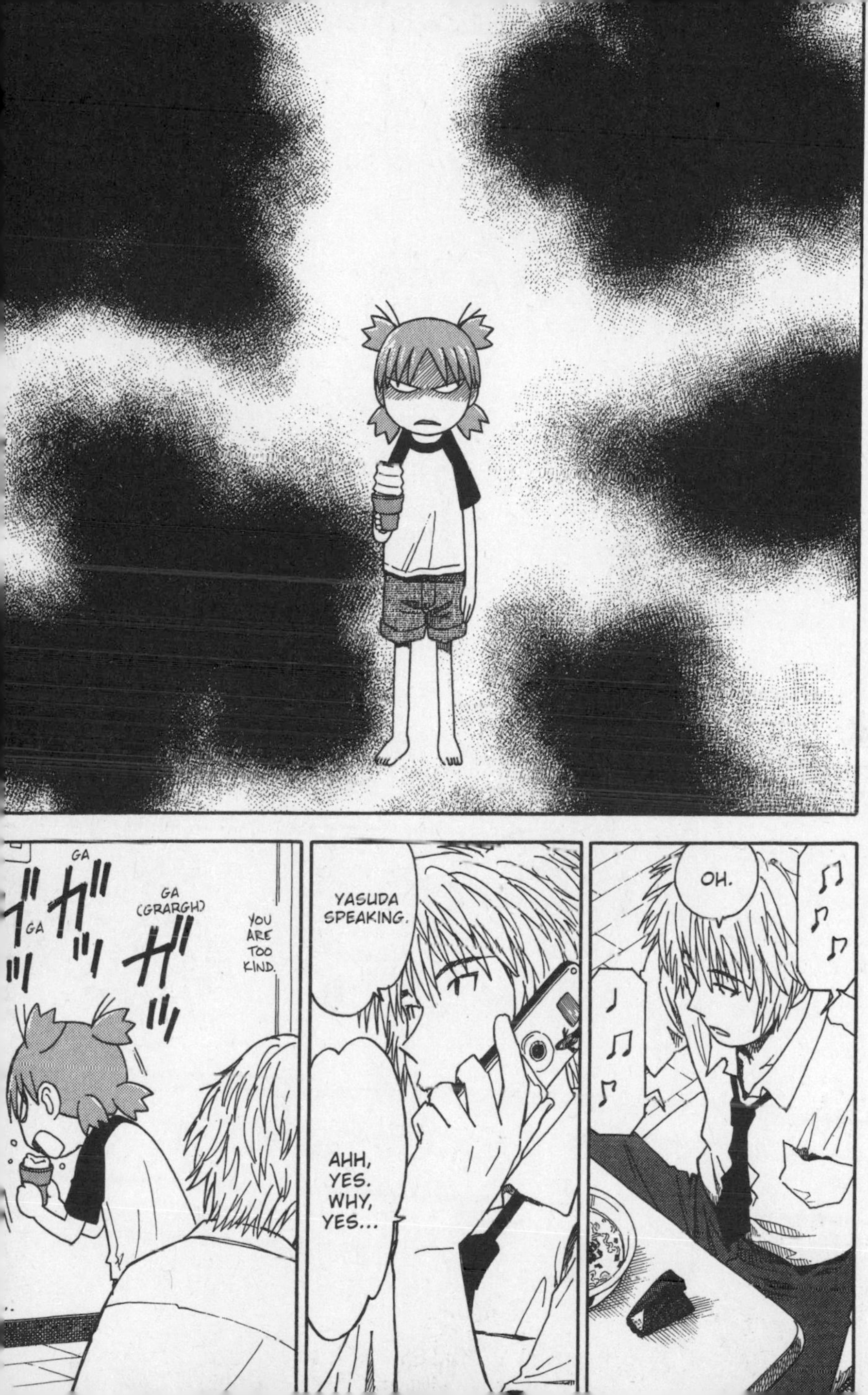
OH.
YASUDA SPEAKING.
AHH, YES. WHY, YES...
YOU ARE TOO KIND.
GA (GRARGH)
GA
GA

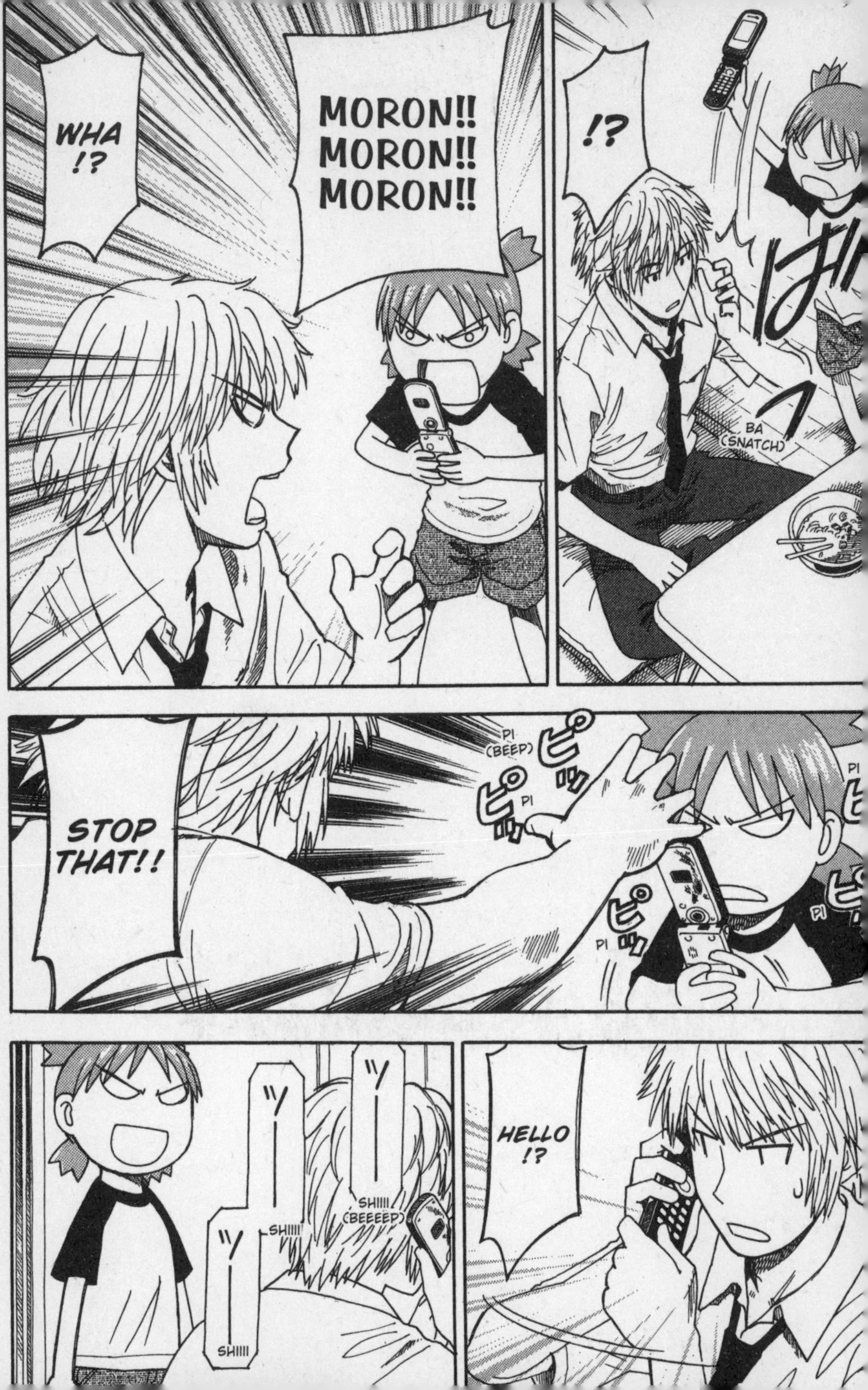
!?
BA
(SNATCH)
MORON!!
MORON!!
MORON!!
WHA
!?
PI
PI
PI
(BEEP)
PI
PI
STOP
THAT!!
HELLO
!?
SHI!!!!
(BEEEEP)
SHI!!!!
SHI!!!!

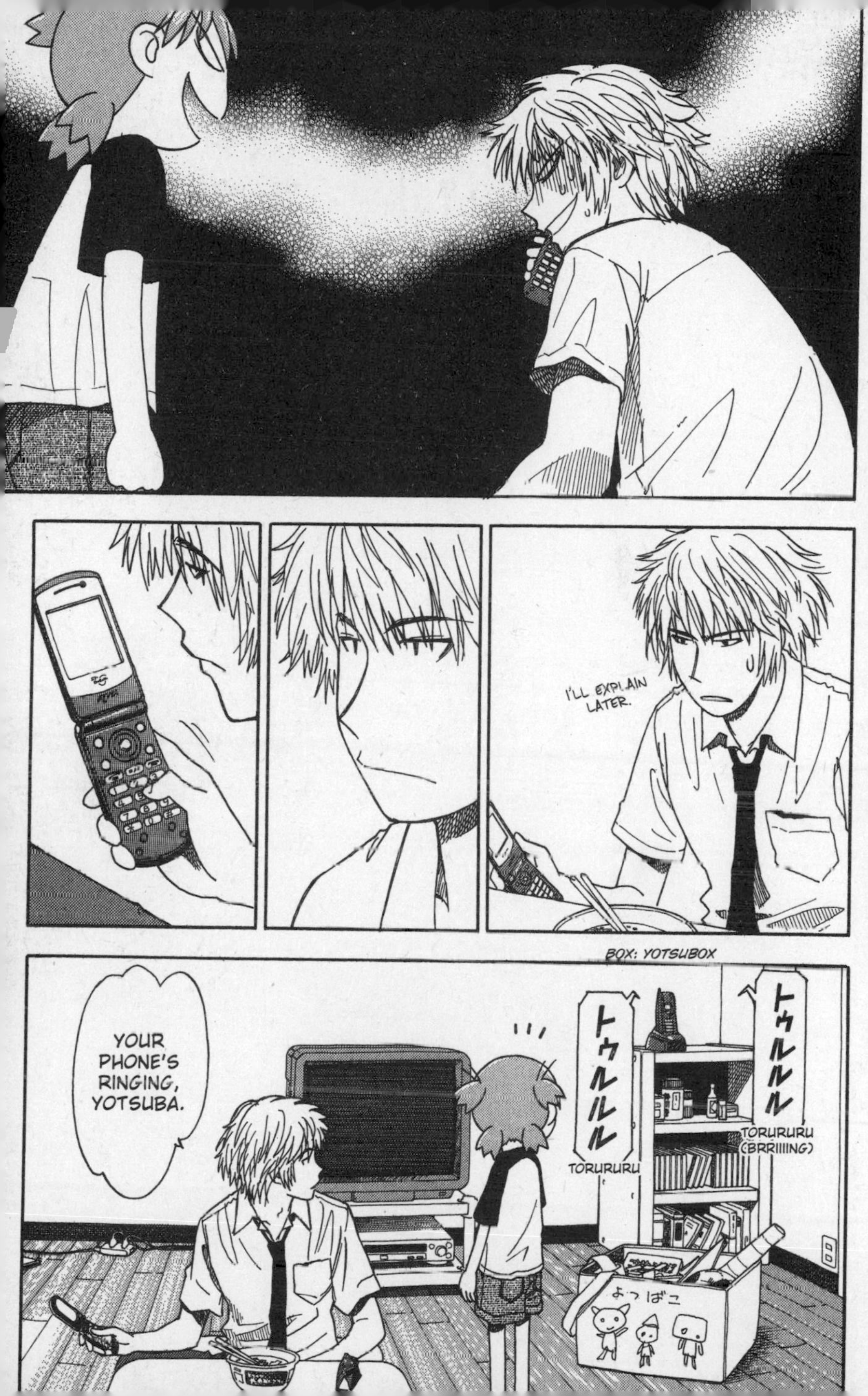
I'LL EXPLAIN LATER.
BOX: YOTSUBOX
トゥルルル
TORURURU (BRRIIIING)
トゥルルル
TORURURU
よつばこ
YOUR PHONE'S RINGING, YOTSUBA.

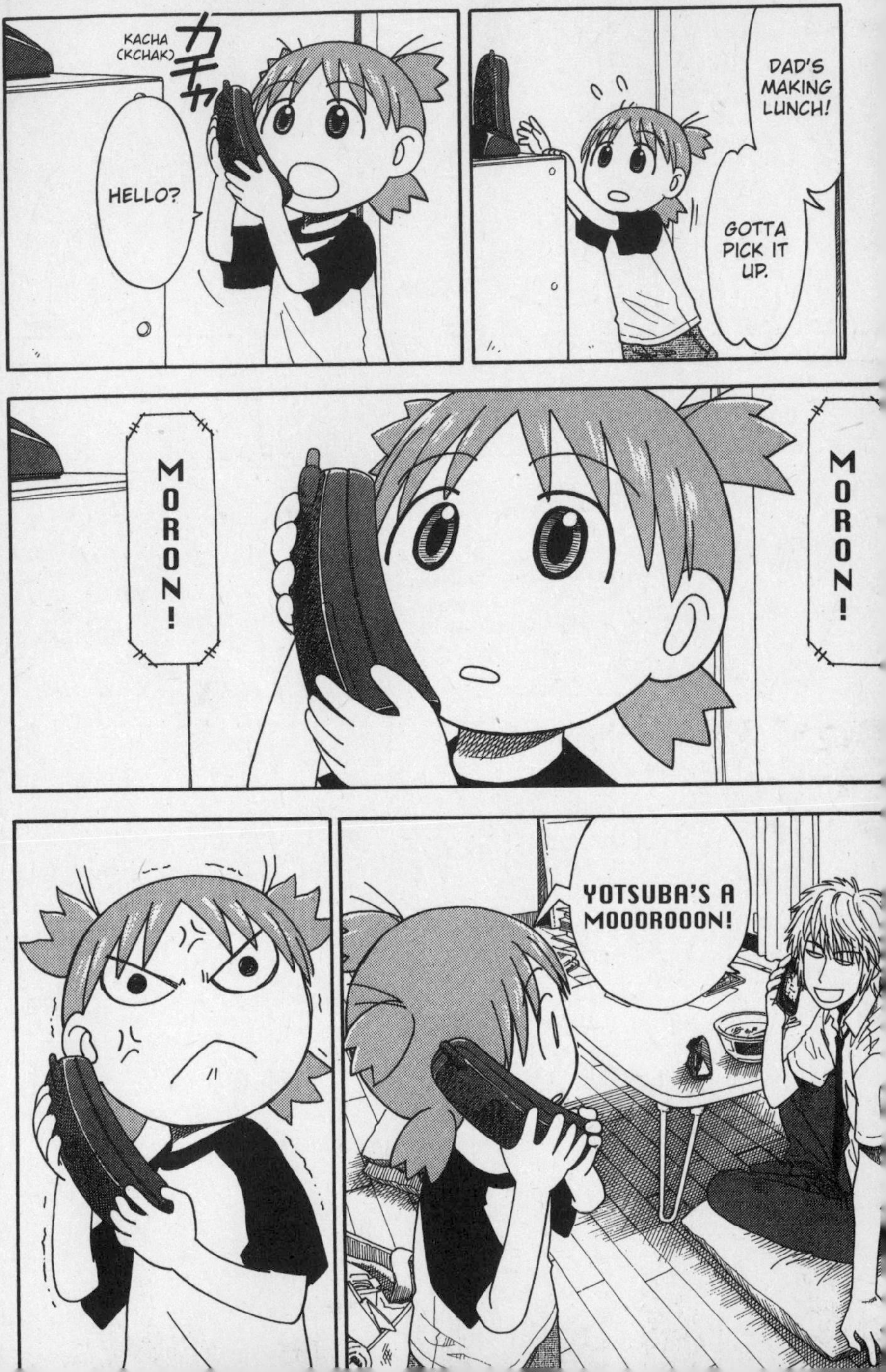
DAD'S MAKING LUNCH!
GOTTA PICK IT UP.
カチャ
KACHA (KCHAK)
HELLO?
MORON!
MORON!
YOTSUBA'S A MOOOROOON!

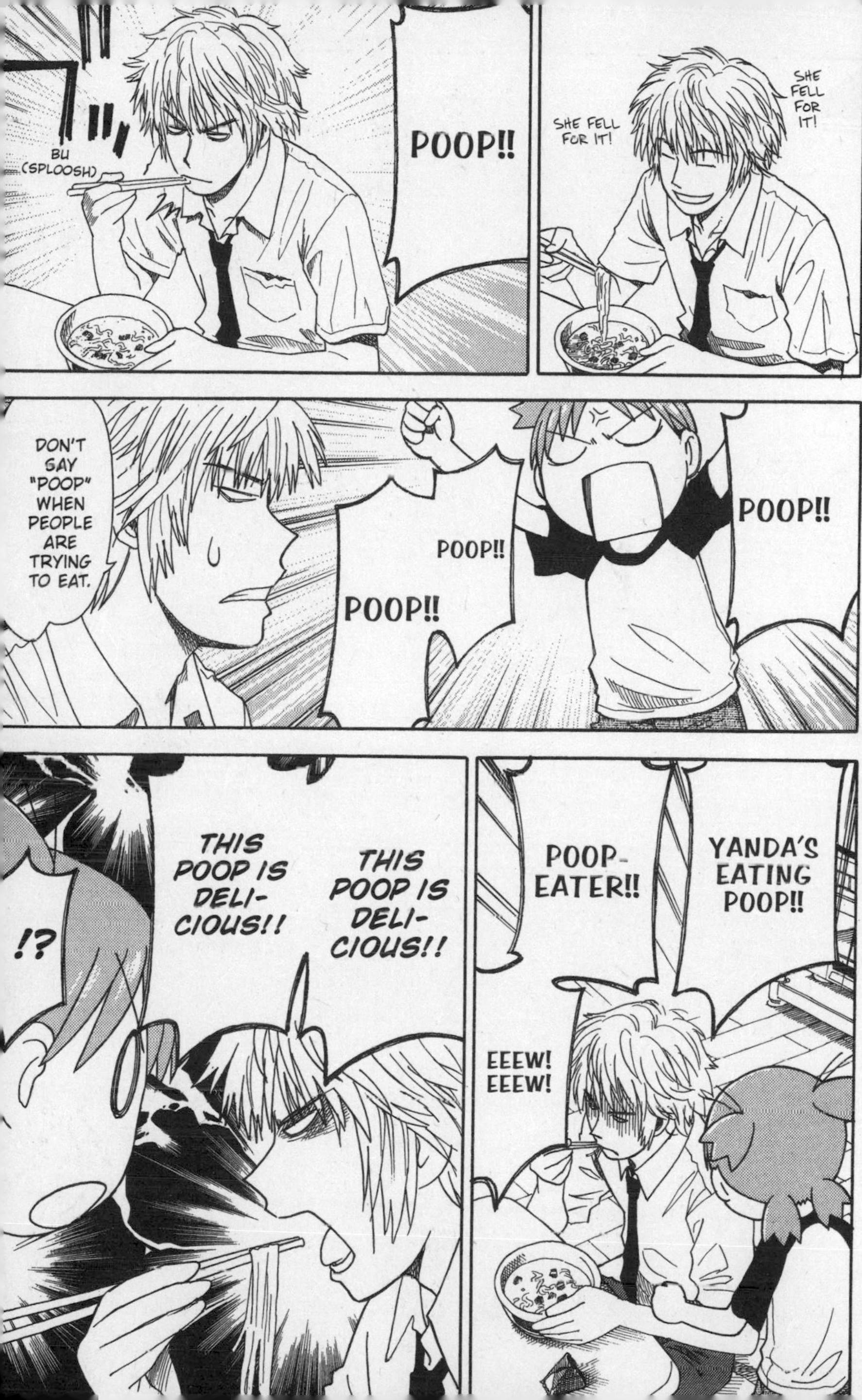
SHE FELL FOR IT!
SHE FELL FOR IT!
POOP!!
BU (SPLOOSH)
POOP!!
POOP!!
POOP!!
DON'T SAY "POOP" WHEN PEOPLE ARE TRYING TO EAT.
YANDA'S EATING POOP!!
POOP-EATER!!
EEEW! EEEW!
THIS POOP IS DELI-CIOUS!!
THIS POOP IS DELI-CIOUS!!
!?

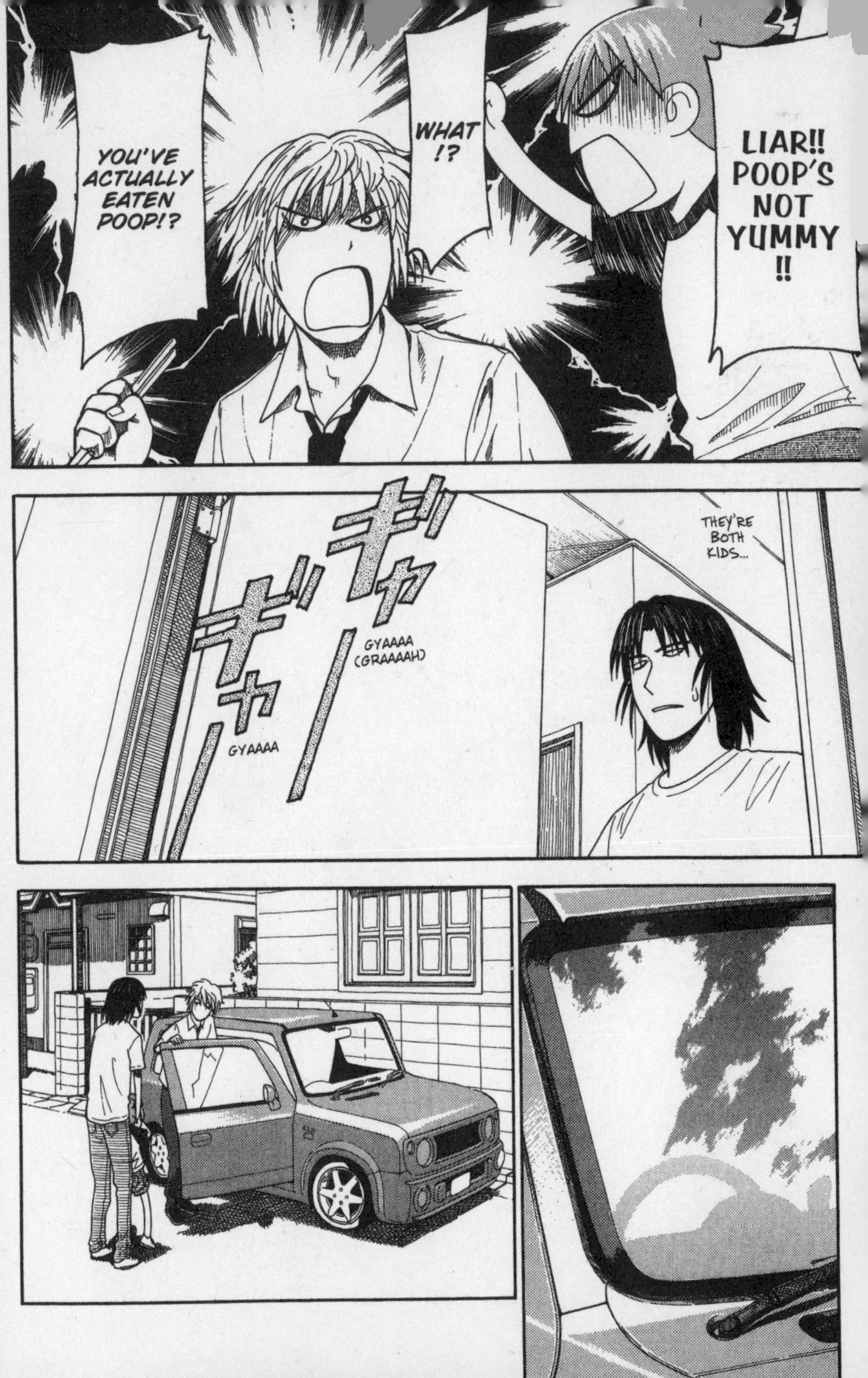
LIAR!! POOP'S NOT YUMMY!!
WHAT!?
YOU'VE ACTUALLY EATEN POOP!?
THEY'RE BOTH KIDS...
ギャー
GYAAAA (GRAAAAH)
ギャー
GYAAAA

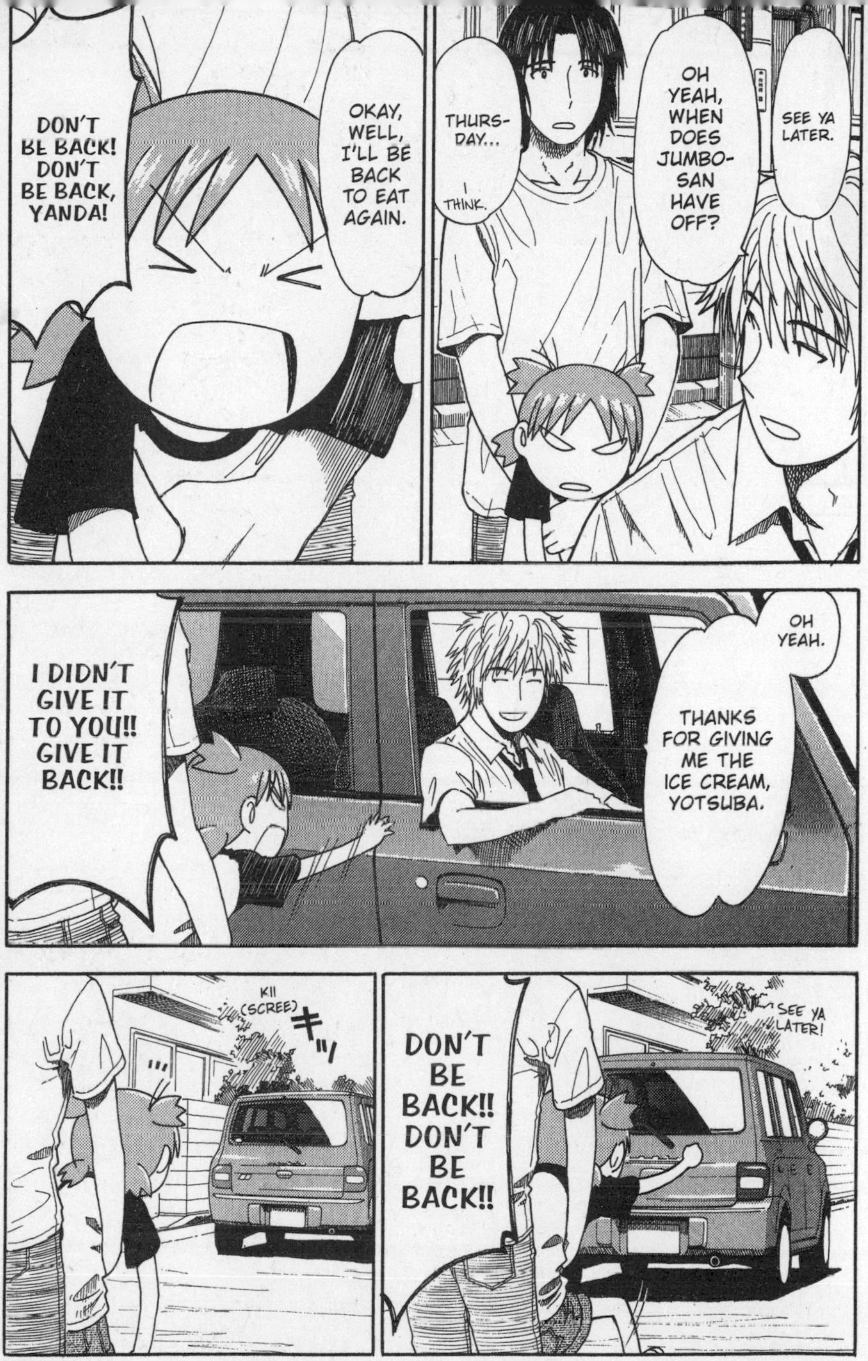

SEE YA LATER.
OH YEAH, WHEN DOES JUMBO-SAN HAVE OFF?
THURS-DAY...
I THINK.
OKAY, WELL, I'LL BE BACK TO EAT AGAIN.
DON'T BE BACK! DON'T BE BACK, YANDA!
OH YEAH.
THANKS FOR GIVING ME THE ICE CREAM, YOTSUBA.
I DIDN'T GIVE IT TO YOU!! GIVE IT BACK!!
SEE YA LATER!
DON'T BE BACK!! DON'T BE BACK!!
KII (SCREE)
キッ
...

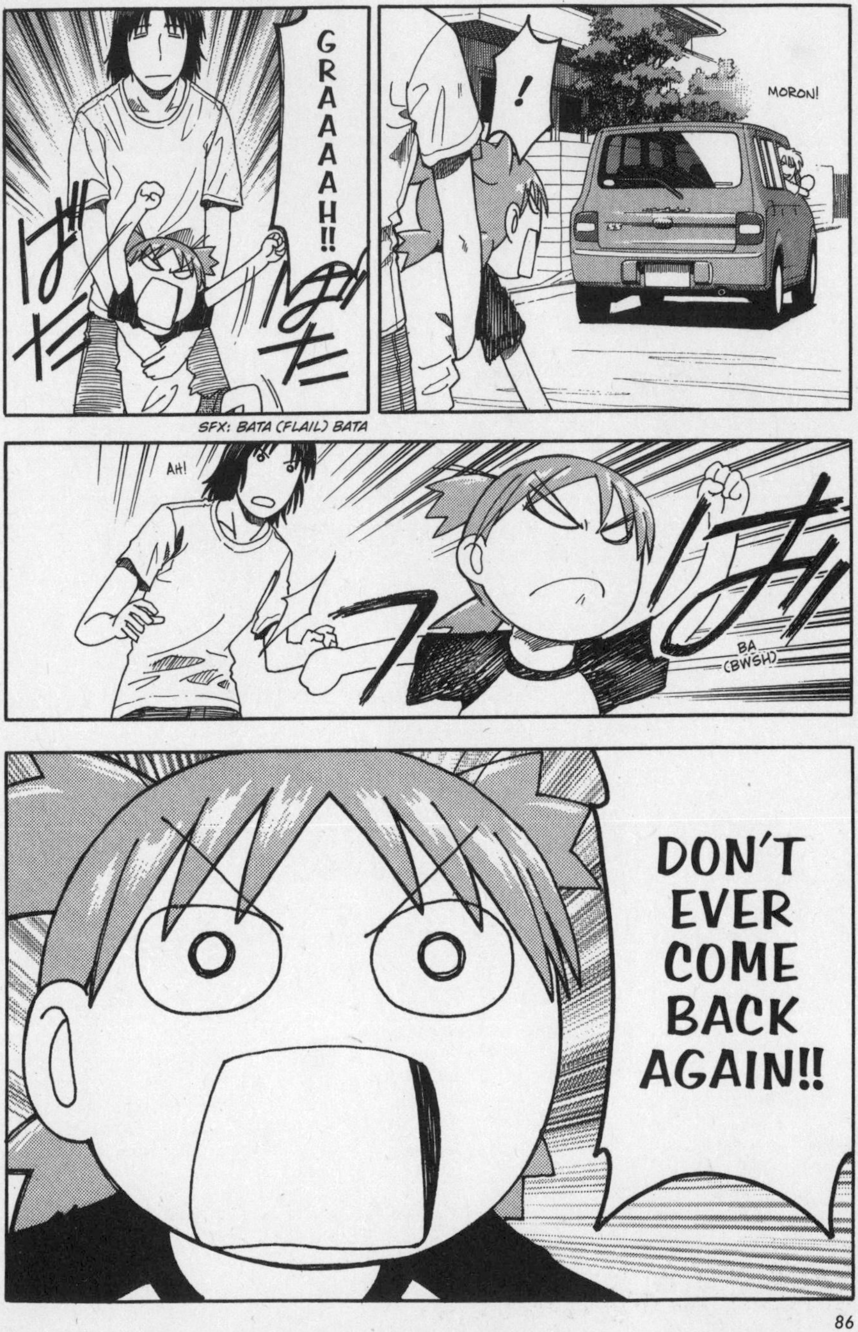
!
MORON!
GRAAAAAH!!
SFX: BATA (FLAIL) BATA
AH!
BA
(BWSH)
DON'T EVER COME BACK AGAIN!!

YOTSUBA&!

YOTSUBA&!
STARS
#31

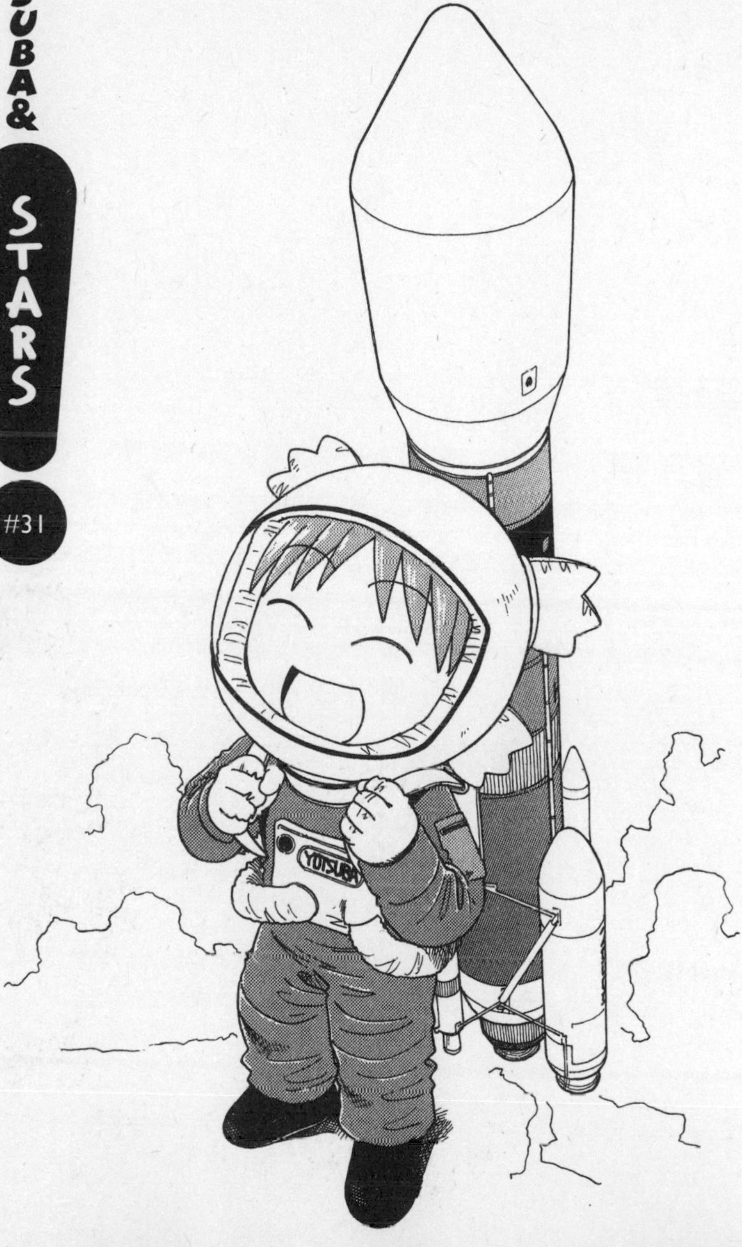
YOTSUBA

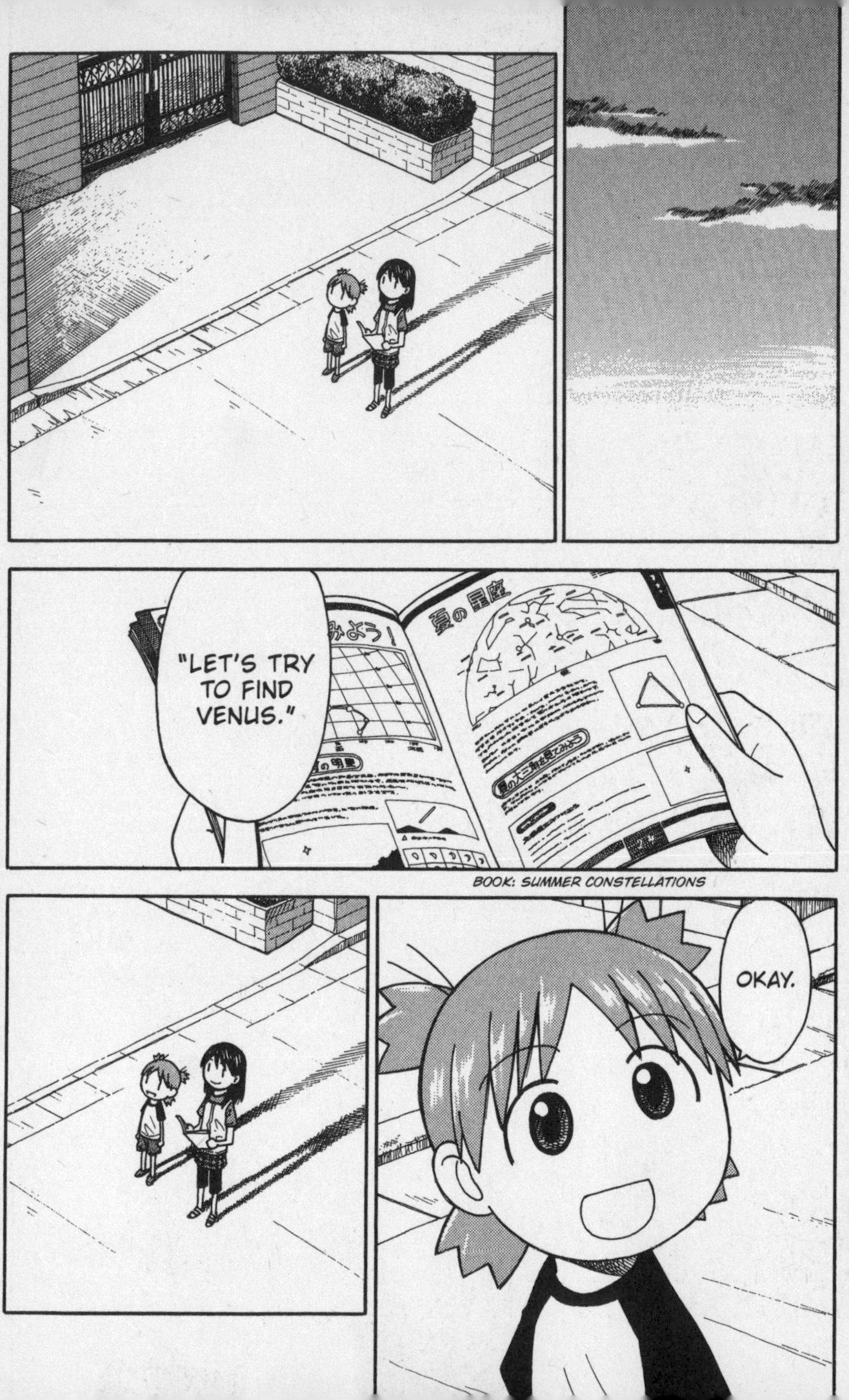
夏の星座
"LET'S TRY TO FIND VENUS."
BOOK: SUMMER CONSTELLATIONS
OKAY.

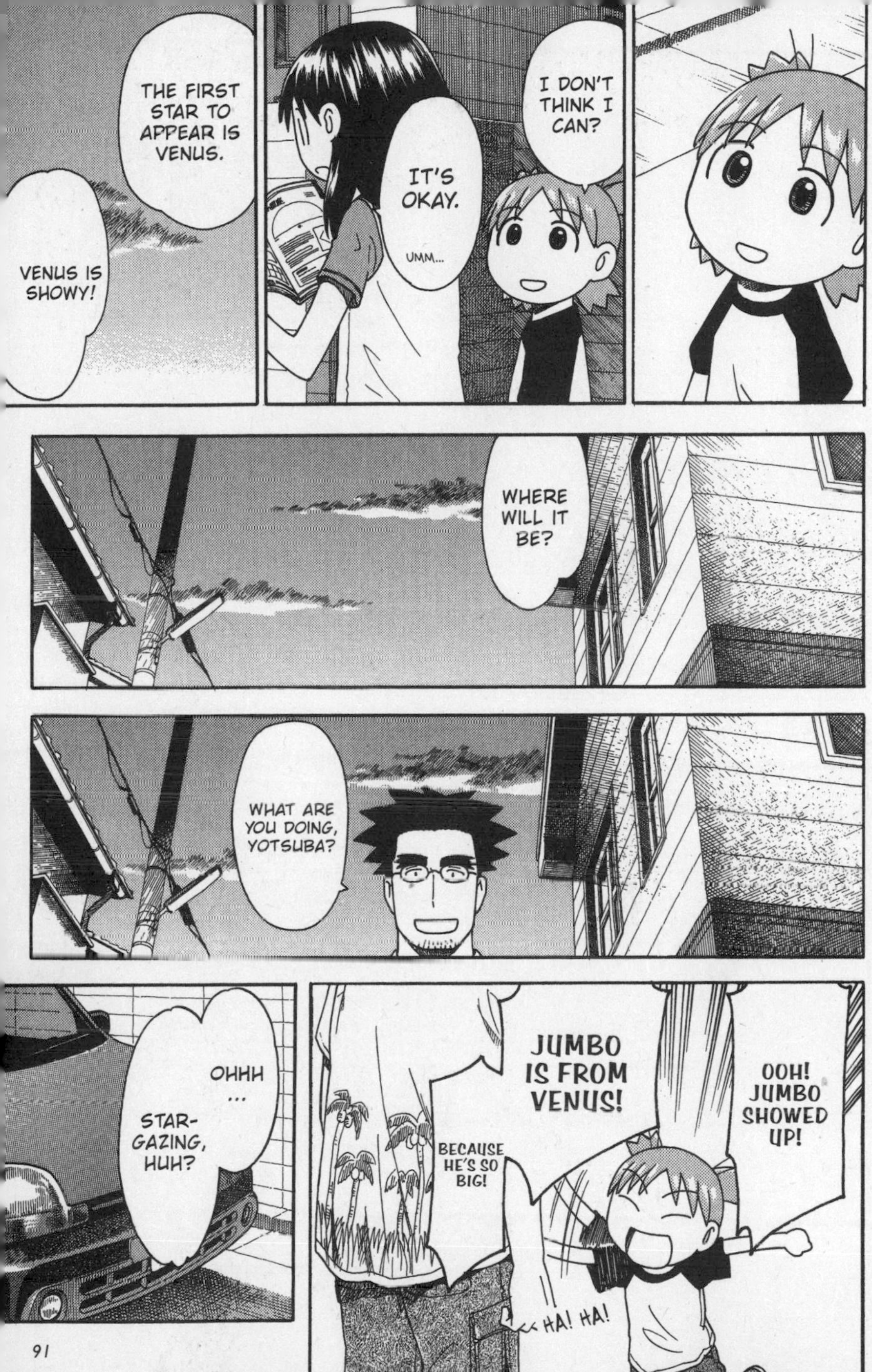
I DON'T THINK I CAN?
IT'S OKAY.
UMM...
THE FIRST STAR TO APPEAR IS VENUS.
VENUS IS SHOWY!
WHERE WILL IT BE?
WHAT ARE YOU DOING, YOTSUBA?
OOH! JUMBO SHOWED UP!
JUMBO IS FROM VENUS!
BECAUSE HE'S SO BIG!
HA! HA!
OHHH ...
STAR-GAZING, HUH?

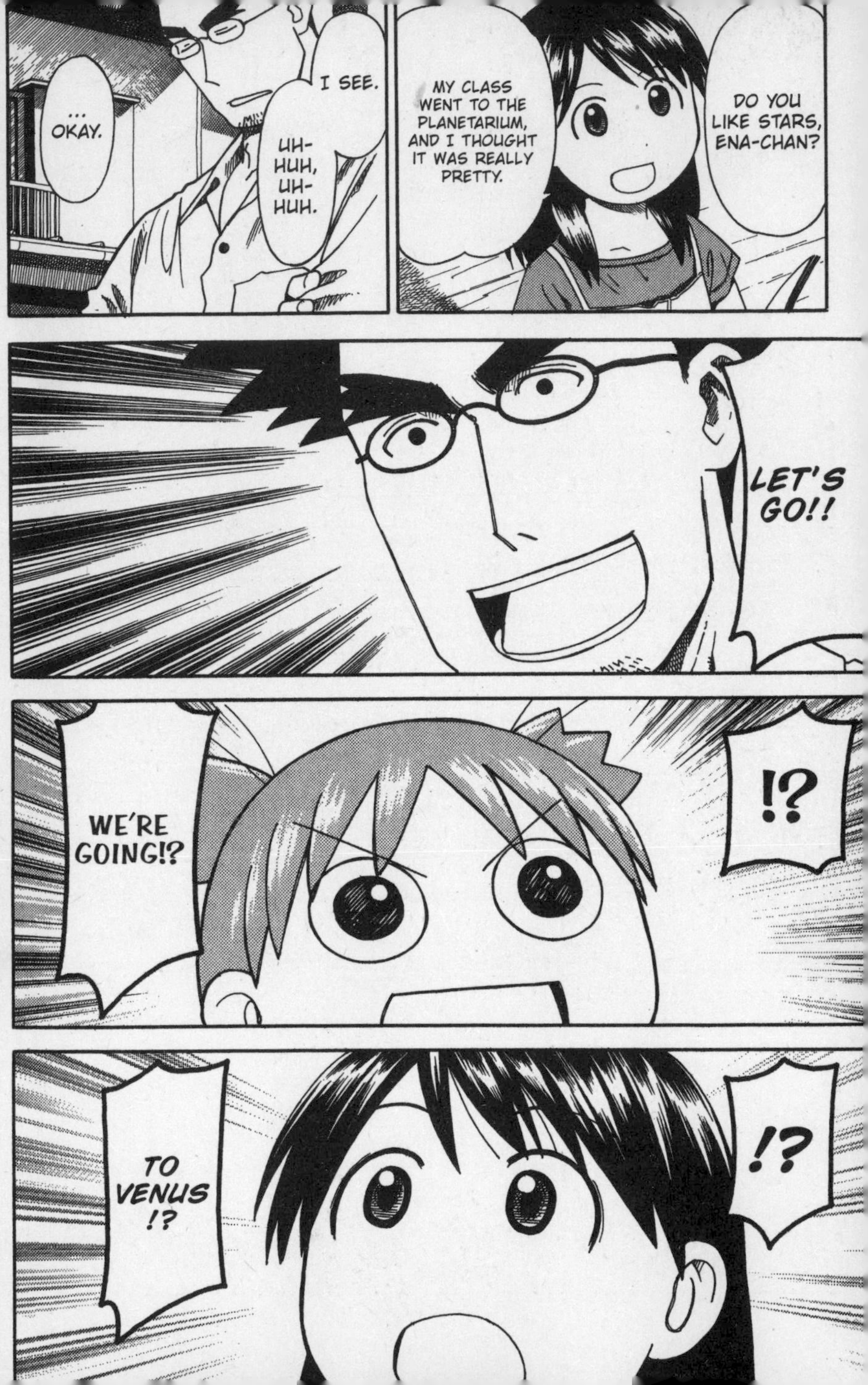
DO YOU LIKE STARS, ENA-CHAN?
MY CLASS WENT TO THE PLANETARIUM, AND I THOUGHT IT WAS REALLY PRETTY.
I SEE.
UH-HUH, UH-HUH.
... OKAY.
LET'S GO!!
!?
WE'RE GOING!?
!?
TO VENUS !?

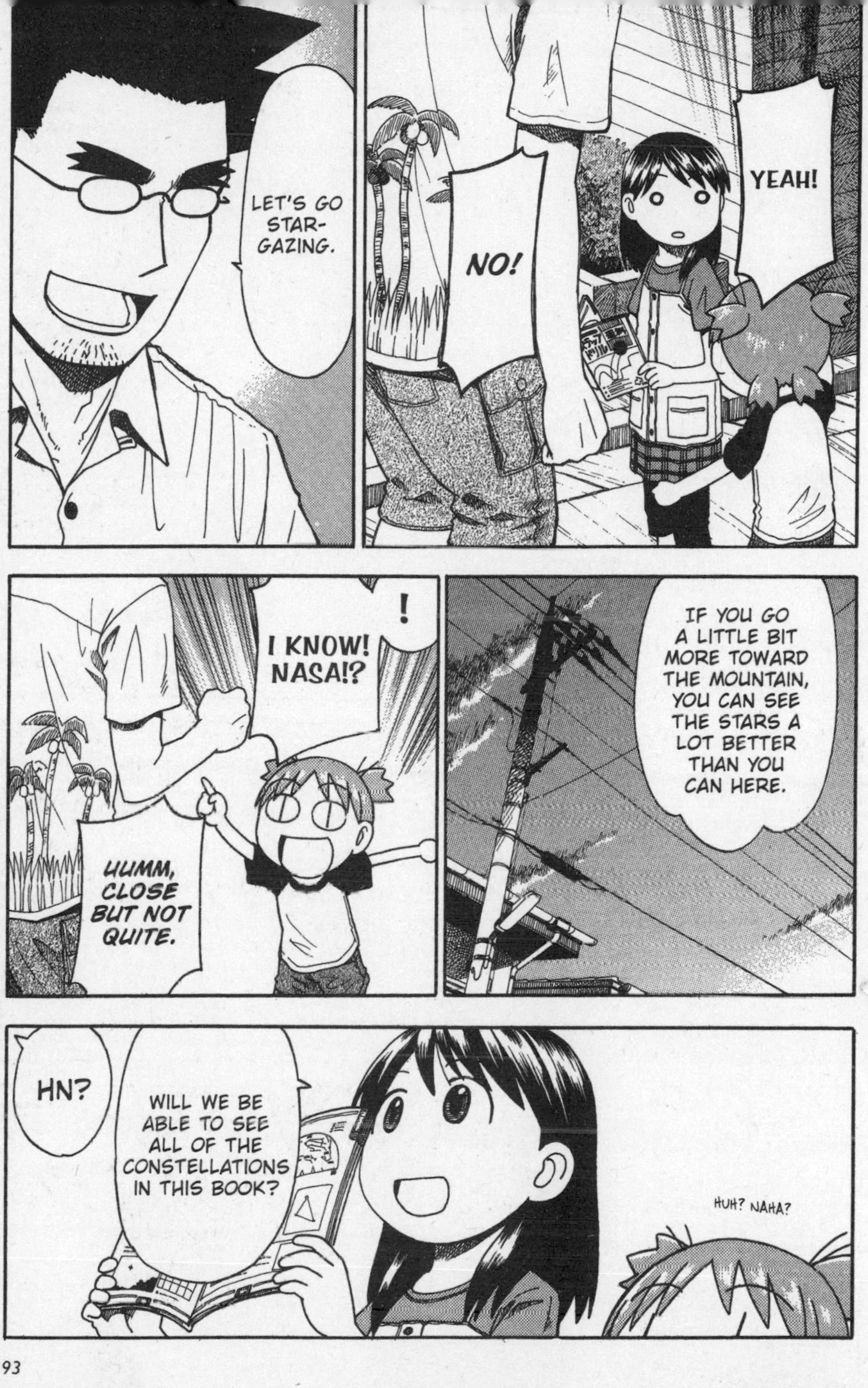
YEAH!
NO!
LET'S GO STAR-GAZING.
IF YOU GO A LITTLE BIT MORE TOWARD THE MOUNTAIN, YOU CAN SEE THE STARS A LOT BETTER THAN YOU CAN HERE.
!
I KNOW! NASA!?
UUMM, CLOSE BUT NOT QUITE.
HUH? NAHA?
WILL WE BE ABLE TO SEE ALL OF THE CONSTELLATIONS IN THIS BOOK?
HN?

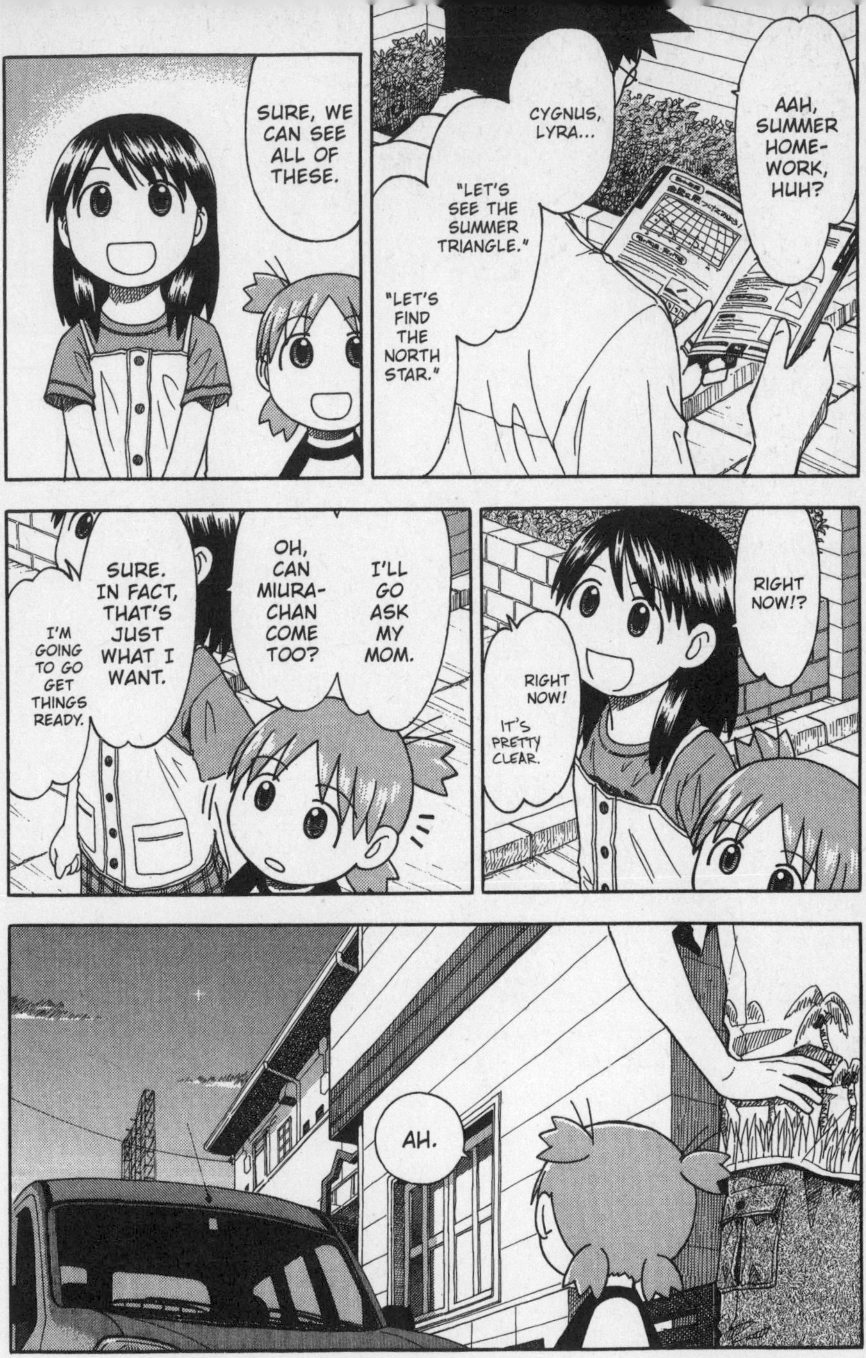
AAH, SUMMER HOMEWORK, HUH?
CYGNUS, LYRA...
"LET'S SEE THE SUMMER TRIANGLE."
"LET'S FIND THE NORTH STAR."
SURE, WE CAN SEE ALL OF THESE.
RIGHT NOW!?
RIGHT NOW!
IT'S PRETTY CLEAR.
I'LL GO ASK MY MOM.
OH, CAN MIURA-CHAN COME TOO?
SURE. IN FACT, THAT'S JUST WHAT I WANT.
I'M GOING TO GO GET THINGS READY.
AH.

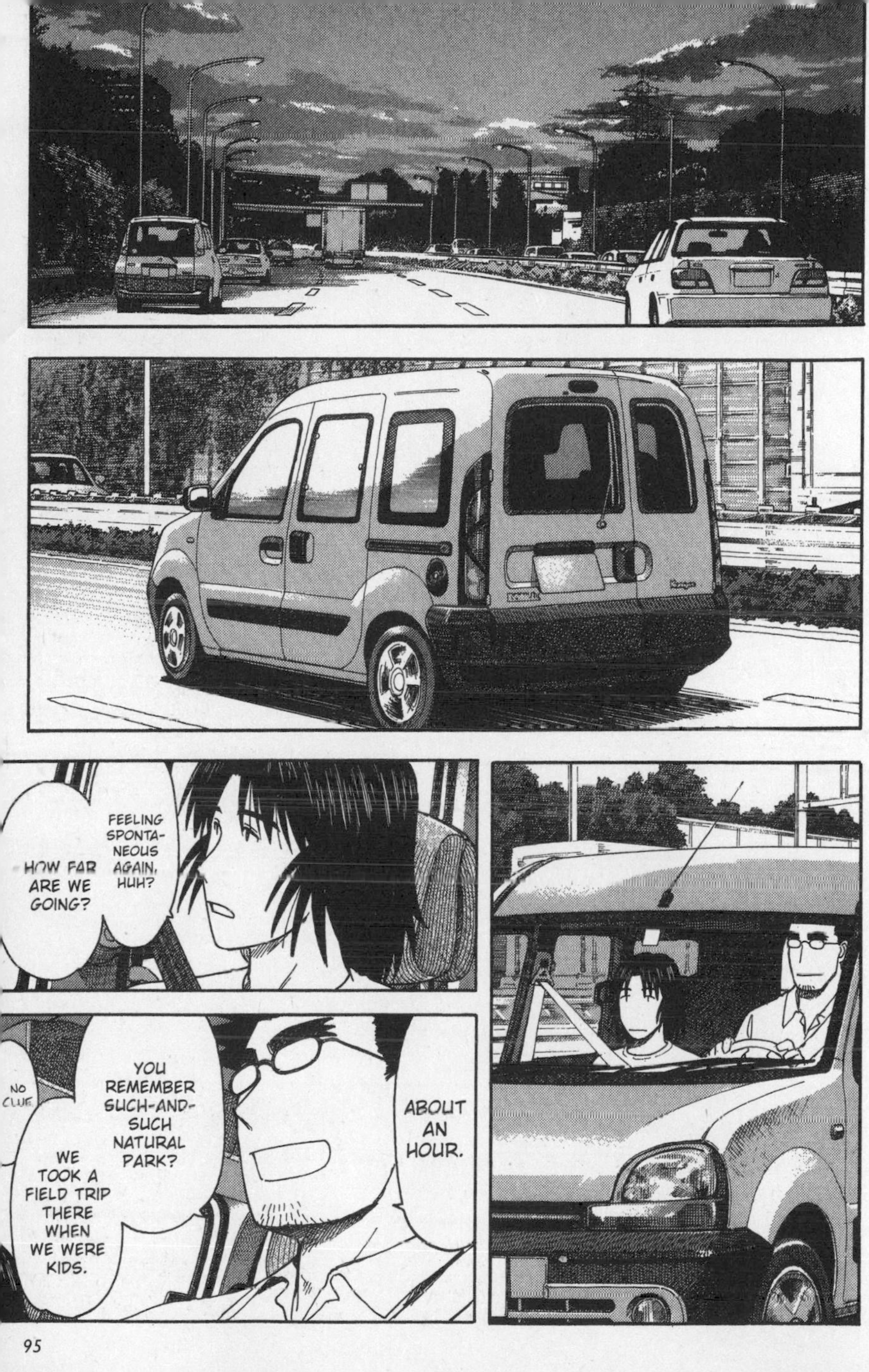
FEELING SPONTANEOUS AGAIN, HUH?
HOW FAR ARE WE GOING?
ABOUT AN HOUR.
YOU REMEMBER SUCH-AND-SUCH NATURAL PARK?
WE TOOK A FIELD TRIP THERE WHEN WE WERE KIDS.
NO CLUE.

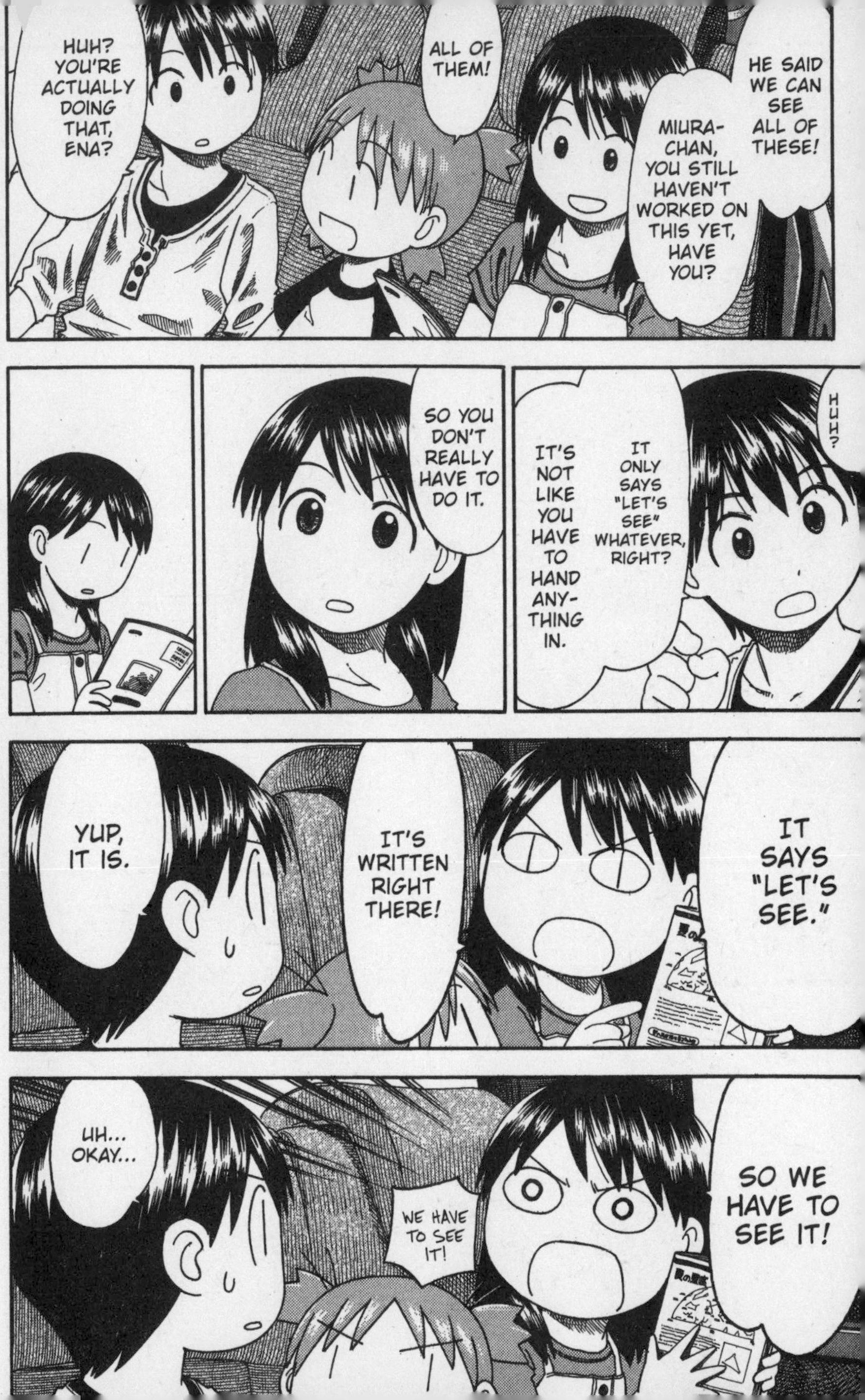
HE SAID WE CAN SEE ALL OF THESE!
MIURA-CHAN, YOU STILL HAVEN'T WORKED ON THIS YET, HAVE YOU?
ALL OF THEM!
HUH? YOU'RE ACTUALLY DOING THAT, ENA?
HUH?
IT ONLY SAYS "LET'S SEE" WHATEVER, RIGHT?
IT'S NOT LIKE YOU HAVE TO HAND ANY-THING IN.
SO YOU DON'T REALLY HAVE TO DO IT.
IT SAYS "LET'S SEE."
IT'S WRITTEN RIGHT THERE!
YUP, IT IS.
SO WE HAVE TO SEE IT!
WE HAVE TO SEE IT!
UH... OKAY...

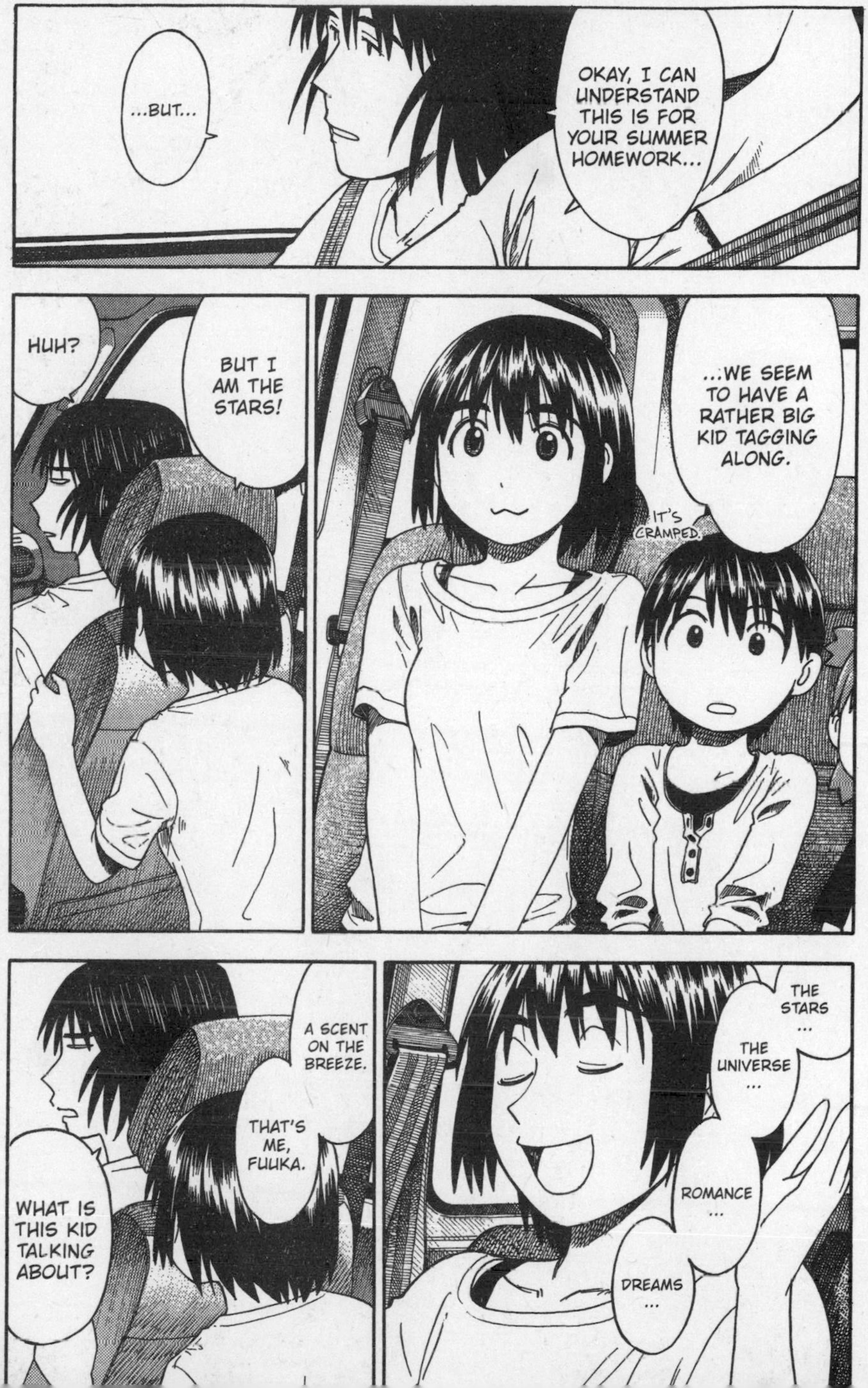
OKAY, I CAN UNDERSTAND THIS IS FOR YOUR SUMMER HOMEWORK...
...BUT...
...WE SEEM TO HAVE A RATHER BIG KID TAGGING ALONG.
IT'S CRAMPED.
BUT I AM THE STARS!
HUH?
THE STARS...
THE UNIVERSE...
ROMANCE...
DREAMS...
A SCENT ON THE BREEZE.
THAT'S ME, FUUKA.
WHAT IS THIS KID TALKING ABOUT?

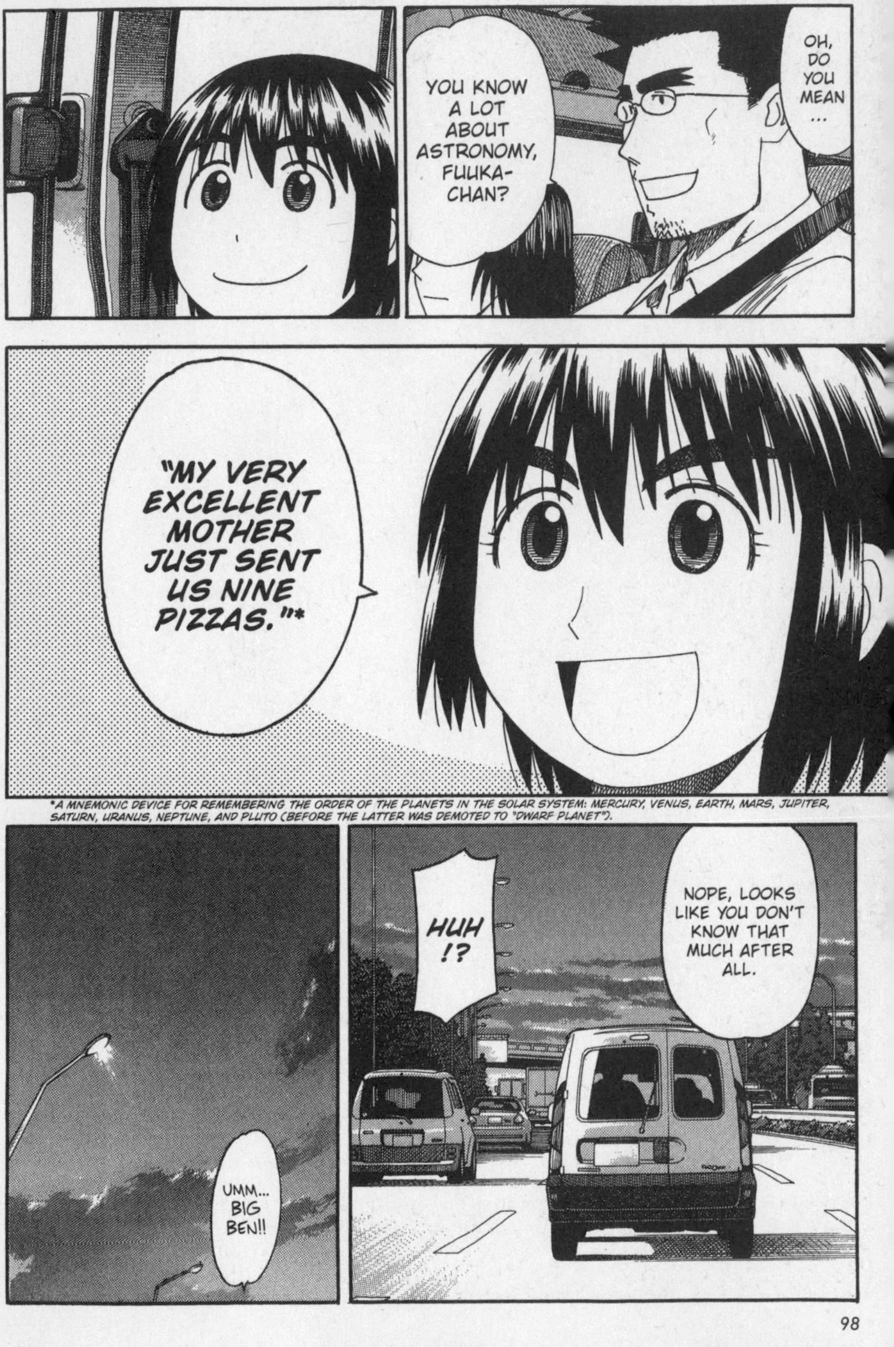
OH, DO YOU MEAN ...
YOU KNOW A LOT ABOUT ASTRONOMY, FUUKA-CHAN?
"MY VERY EXCELLENT MOTHER JUST SENT US NINE PIZZAS."*
NOPE, LOOKS LIKE YOU DON'T KNOW THAT MUCH AFTER ALL.
HUH!?
UMM... BIG BEN!!

*A MNEMONIC DEVICE FOR REMEMBERING THE ORDER OF THE PLANETS IN THE SOLAR SYSTEM: MERCURY, VENUS, EARTH, MARS, JUPITER, SATURN, URANUS, NEPTUNE, AND PLUTO (BEFORE THE LATTER WAS DEMOTED TO "DWARF PLANET").

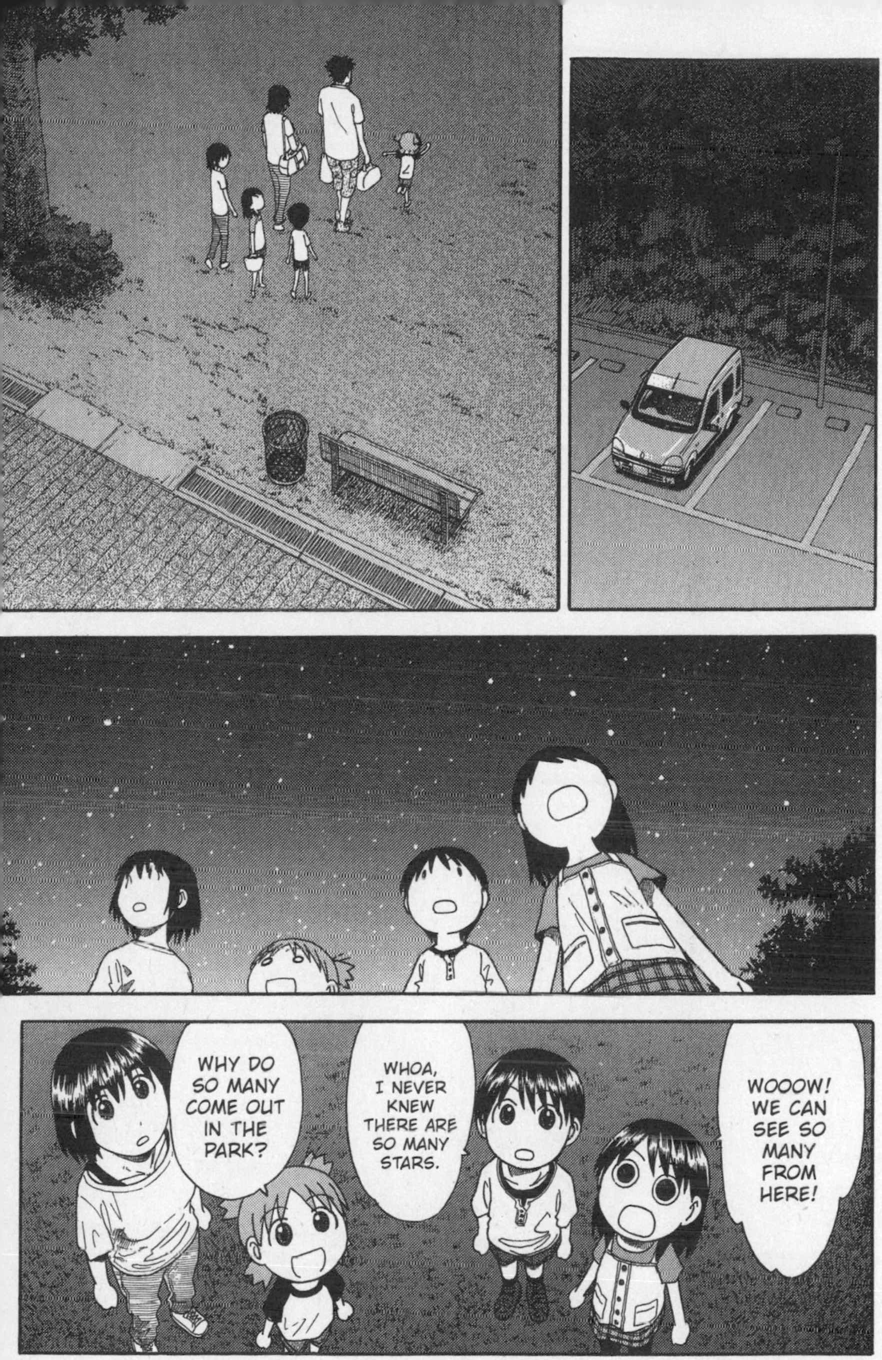
WOOOW! WE CAN SEE SO MANY FROM HERE!
WHOA, I NEVER KNEW THERE ARE SO MANY STARS.
WHY DO SO MANY COME OUT IN THE PARK?

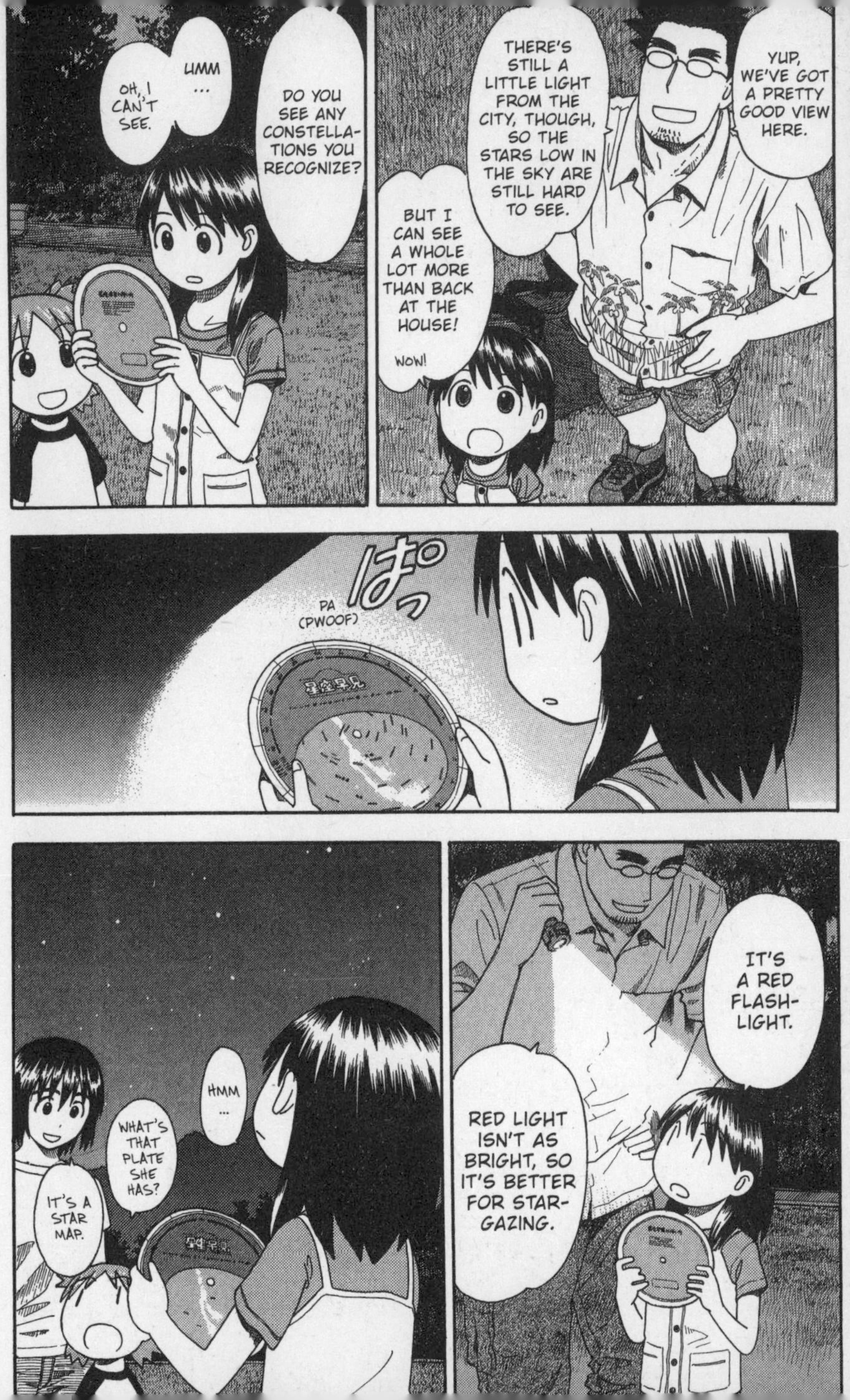
YUP, WE'VE GOT A PRETTY GOOD VIEW HERE.
THERE'S STILL A LITTLE LIGHT FROM THE CITY, THOUGH, SO THE STARS LOW IN THE SKY ARE STILL HARD TO SEE.
BUT I CAN SEE A WHOLE LOT MORE THAN BACK AT THE HOUSE!
WOW!
DO YOU SEE ANY CONSTELLATIONS YOU RECOGNIZE?
UMM ...
OH, I CAN'T SEE.
ぱっ
PA (PWOOF)
IT'S A RED FLASHLIGHT.
RED LIGHT ISN'T AS BRIGHT, SO IT'S BETTER FOR STARGAZING.
HMM ...
WHAT'S THAT PLATE SHE HAS?
IT'S A STAR MAP.

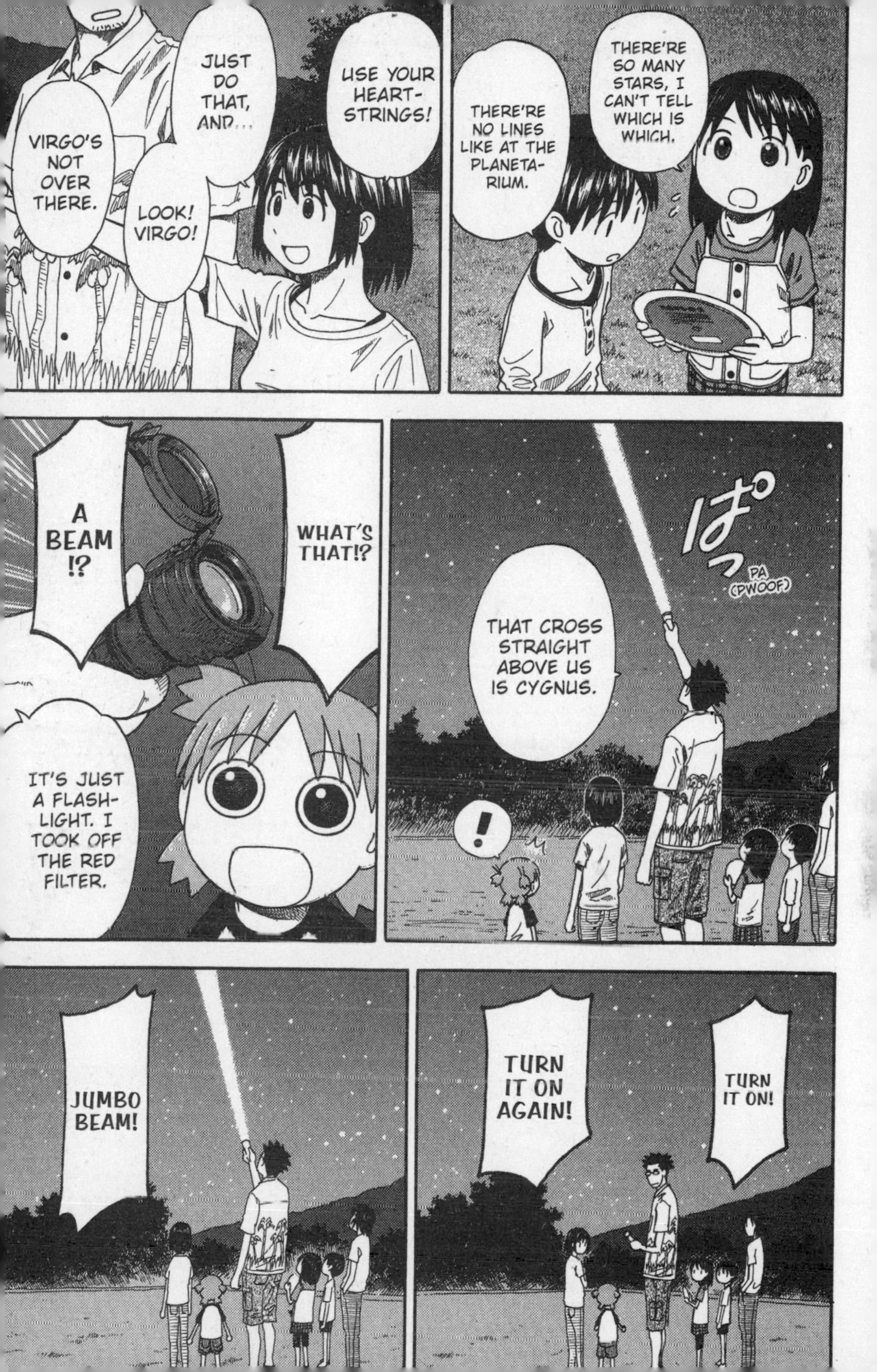
THERE'RE SO MANY STARS, I CAN'T TELL WHICH IS WHICH.
THERE'RE NO LINES LIKE AT THE PLANETARIUM.
USE YOUR HEART-STRINGS!
JUST DO THAT, AND...
LOOK! VIRGO!
VIRGO'S NOT OVER THERE.
ぱっ
PA (PWOOF)
THAT CROSS STRAIGHT ABOVE US IS CYGNUS.
!
WHAT'S THAT!?
A BEAM!?
IT'S JUST A FLASH-LIGHT. I TOOK OFF THE RED FILTER.
TURN IT ON!
TURN IT ON AGAIN!
JUMBO BEAM!

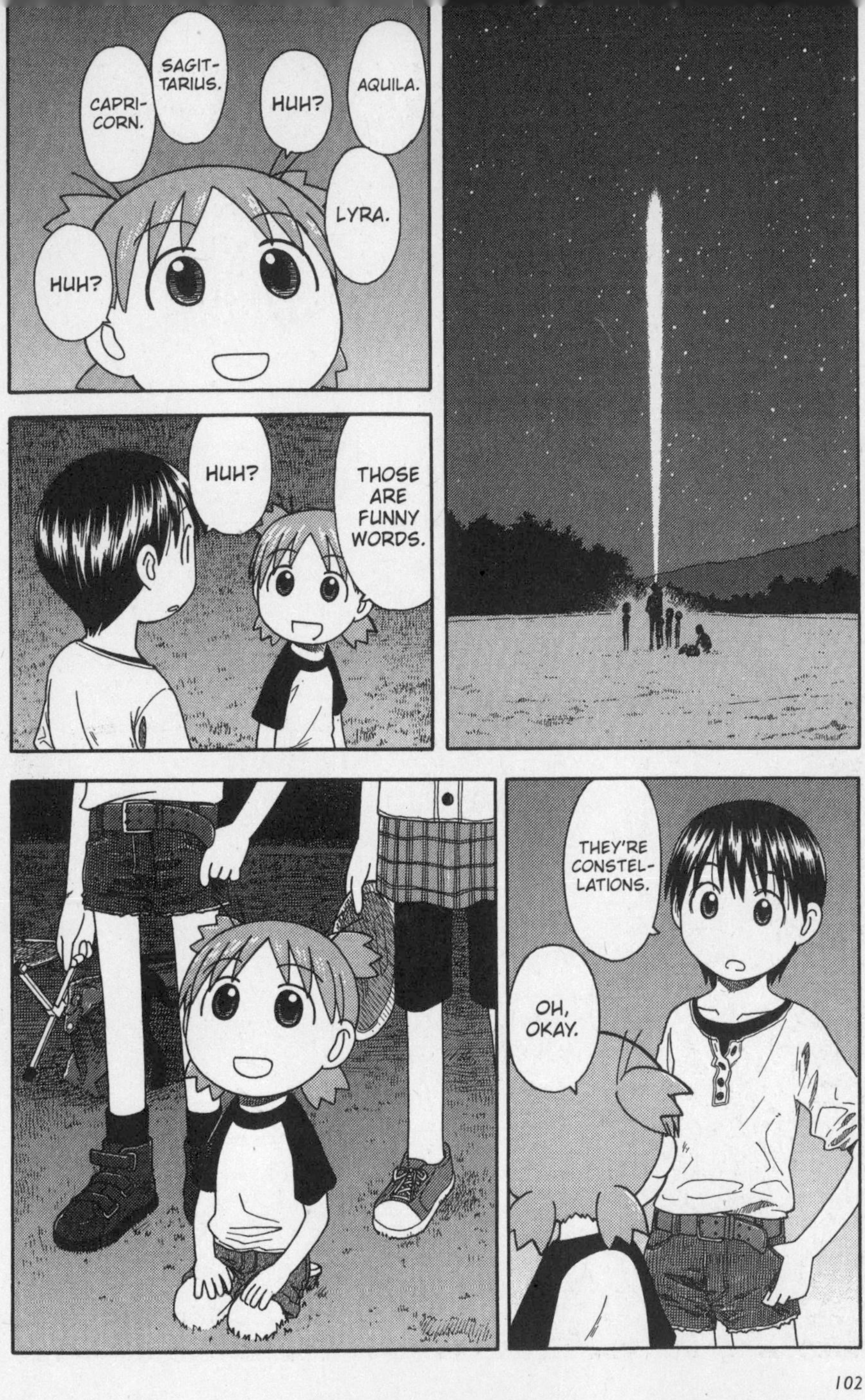
AQUILA.
HUH?
SAGIT-
TARIUS.
CAPRI-
CORN.
LYRA.
HUH?
THOSE ARE FUNNY WORDS.
HUH?
THEY'RE CONSTEL-
LATIONS.
OH, OKAY.

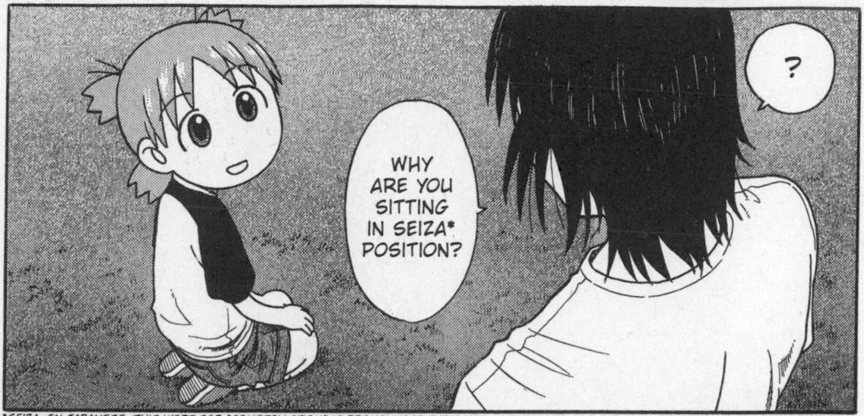
?
WHY ARE YOU SITTING IN SEIZA* POSITION?

*SEIZA: IN JAPANESE, THIS WORD FOR "CONSTELLATION" IS PRONOUNCED THE SAME AS THE NAME FOR THE TRADITIONAL JAPANESE WAY OF SITTING. YOTSUBA MISTAKES ONE FOR THE OTHER!

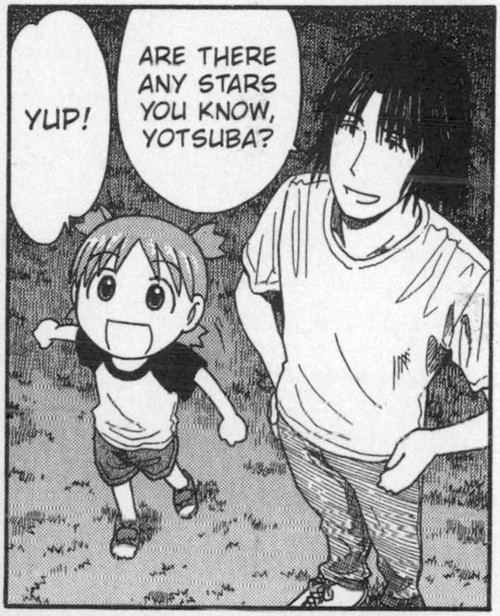
ARE THERE ANY STARS YOU KNOW, YOTSUBA?
YUP!

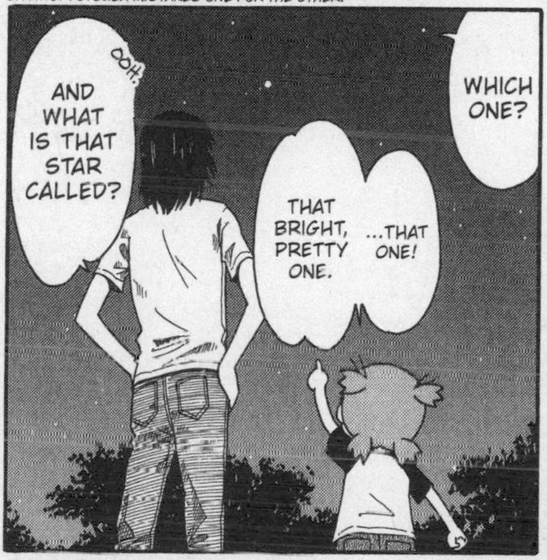
WHICH ONE?
...THAT ONE!
THAT BRIGHT, PRETTY ONE.
OOH.
AND WHAT IS THAT STAR CALLED?

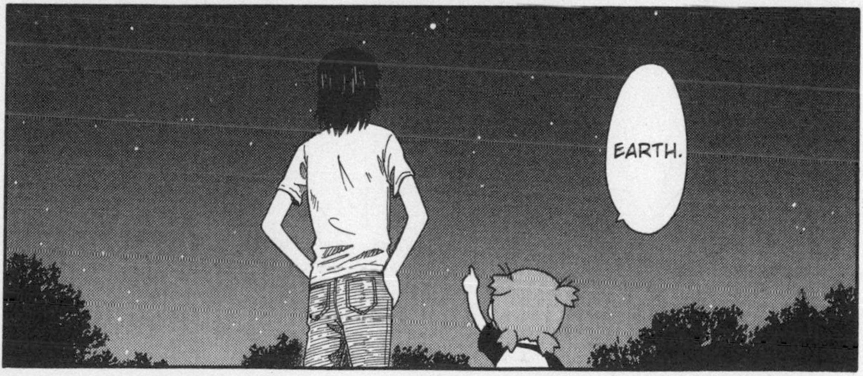
EARTH.

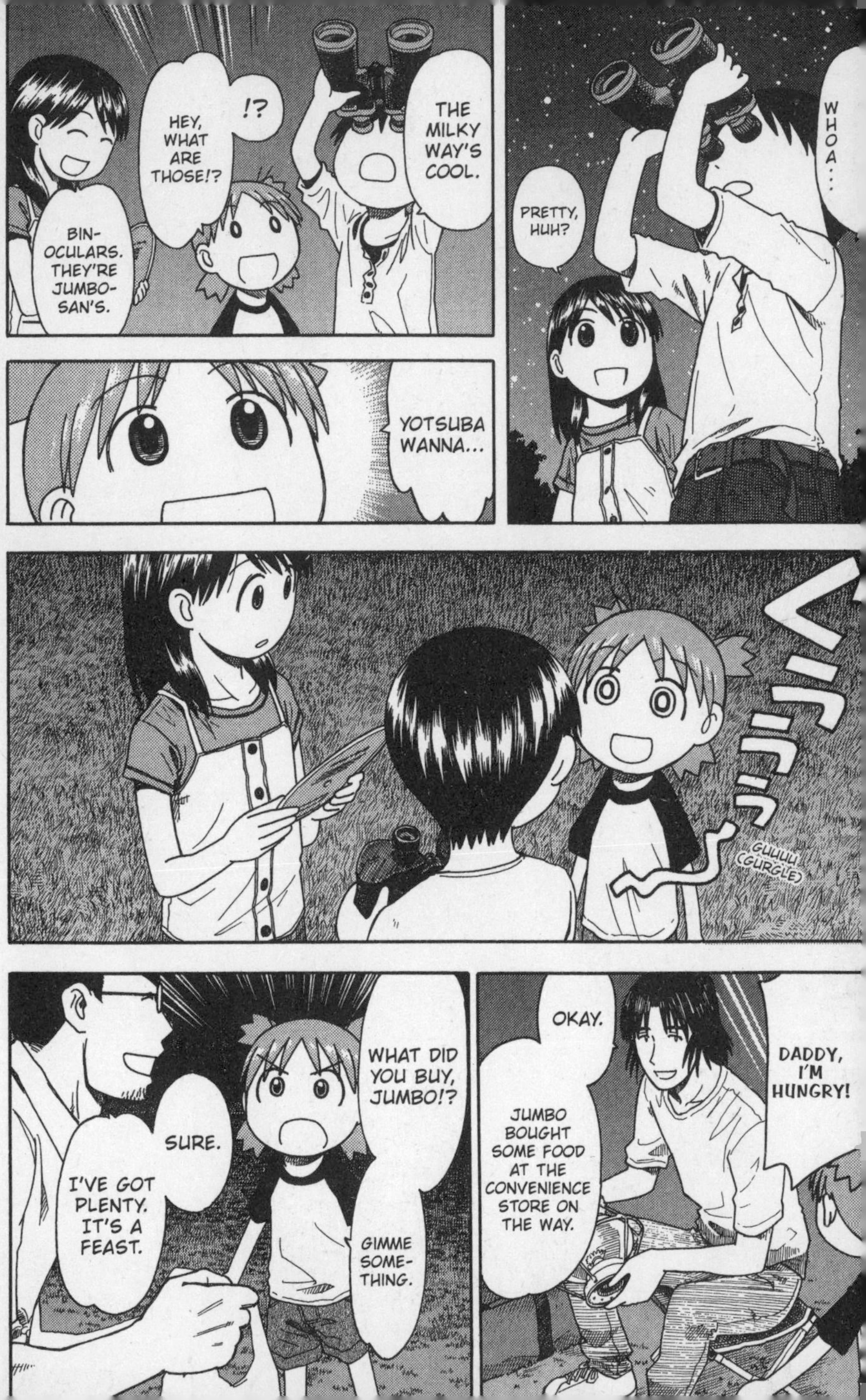
WHOA...
PRETTY, HUH?
THE MILKY WAY'S COOL.
!?
HEY, WHAT ARE THOSE!?
BIN-OCULARS. THEY'RE JUMBO-SAN'S.
YOTSUBA WANNA...
GUUUU (GURGLE)
DADDY, I'M HUNGRY!
OKAY.
JUMBO BOUGHT SOME FOOD AT THE CONVENIENCE STORE ON THE WAY.
WHAT DID YOU BUY, JUMBO!?
SURE.
I'VE GOT PLENTY. IT'S A FEAST.
GIMME SOMETHING.

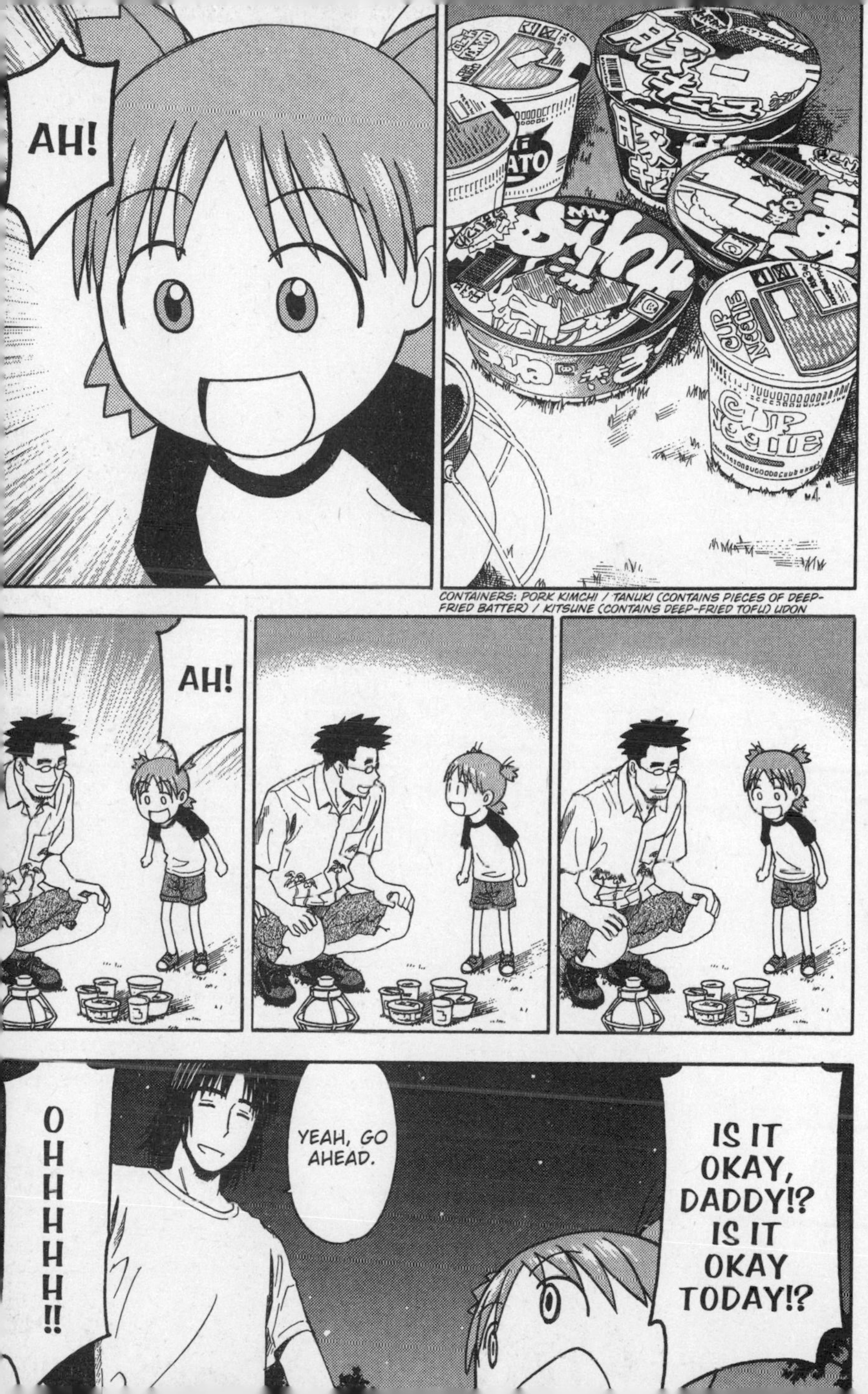
AH!
CONTAINERS: PORK KIMCHI / TANUKI (CONTAINS PIECES OF DEEP-FRIED BATTER) / KITSUNE (CONTAINS DEEP-FRIED TOFU) UDON
AH!
IS IT OKAY, DADDY!? IS IT OKAY TODAY!?
YEAH, GO AHEAD.
OHHHHHH!!

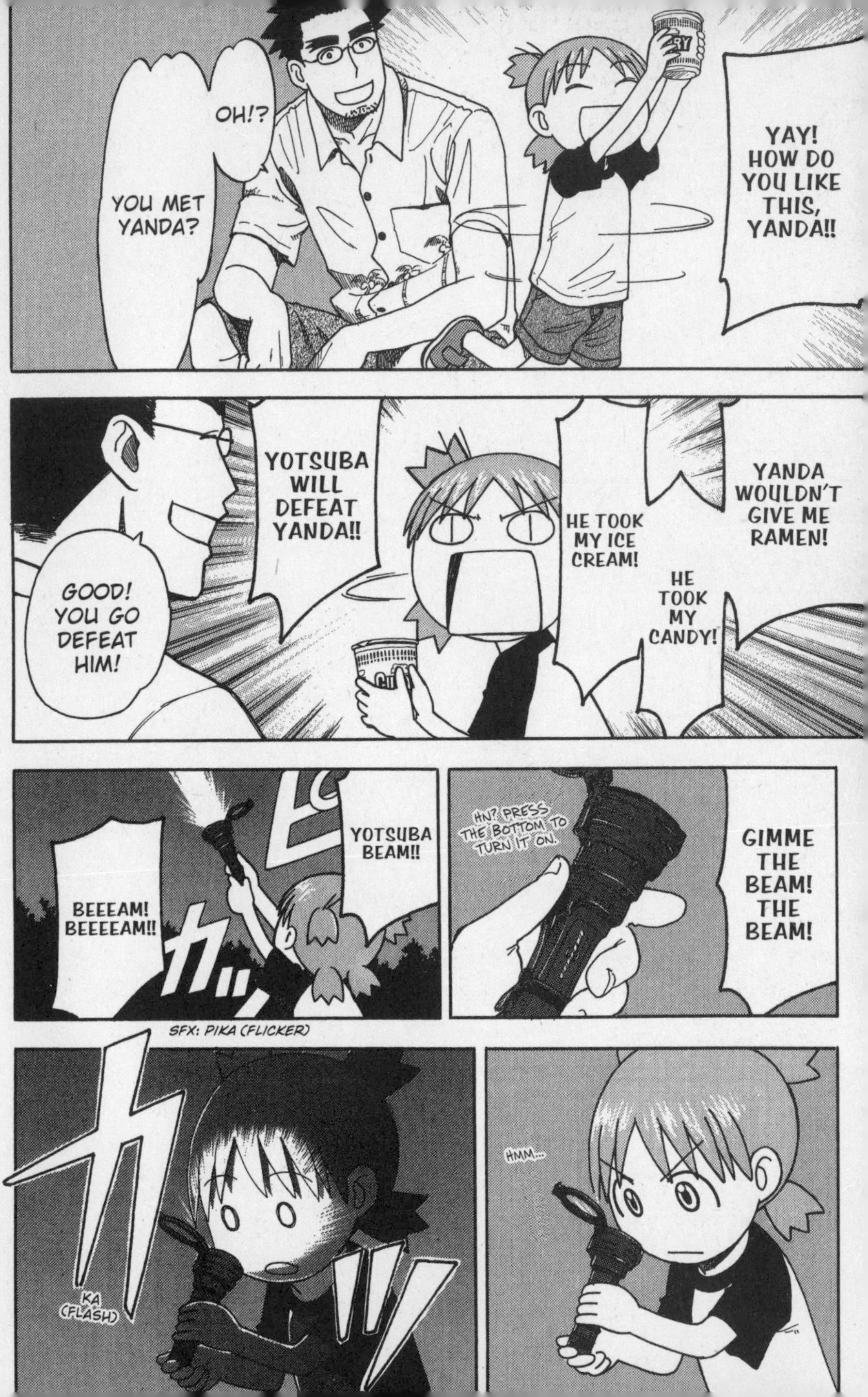
YAY! HOW DO YOU LIKE THIS, YANDA!!
OH!?
YOU MET YANDA?
YANDA WOULDN'T GIVE ME RAMEN!
HE TOOK MY CANDY!
HE TOOK MY ICE CREAM!
YOTSUBA WILL DEFEAT YANDA!!
GOOD! YOU GO DEFEAT HIM!
GIMME THE BEAM! THE BEAM!
HN? PRESS THE BOTTOM TO TURN IT ON.
YOTSUBA BEAM!!
BEEEAM! BEEEEAM!!
SFX: PIKA (FLICKER)
HMM...
KA (FLASH)

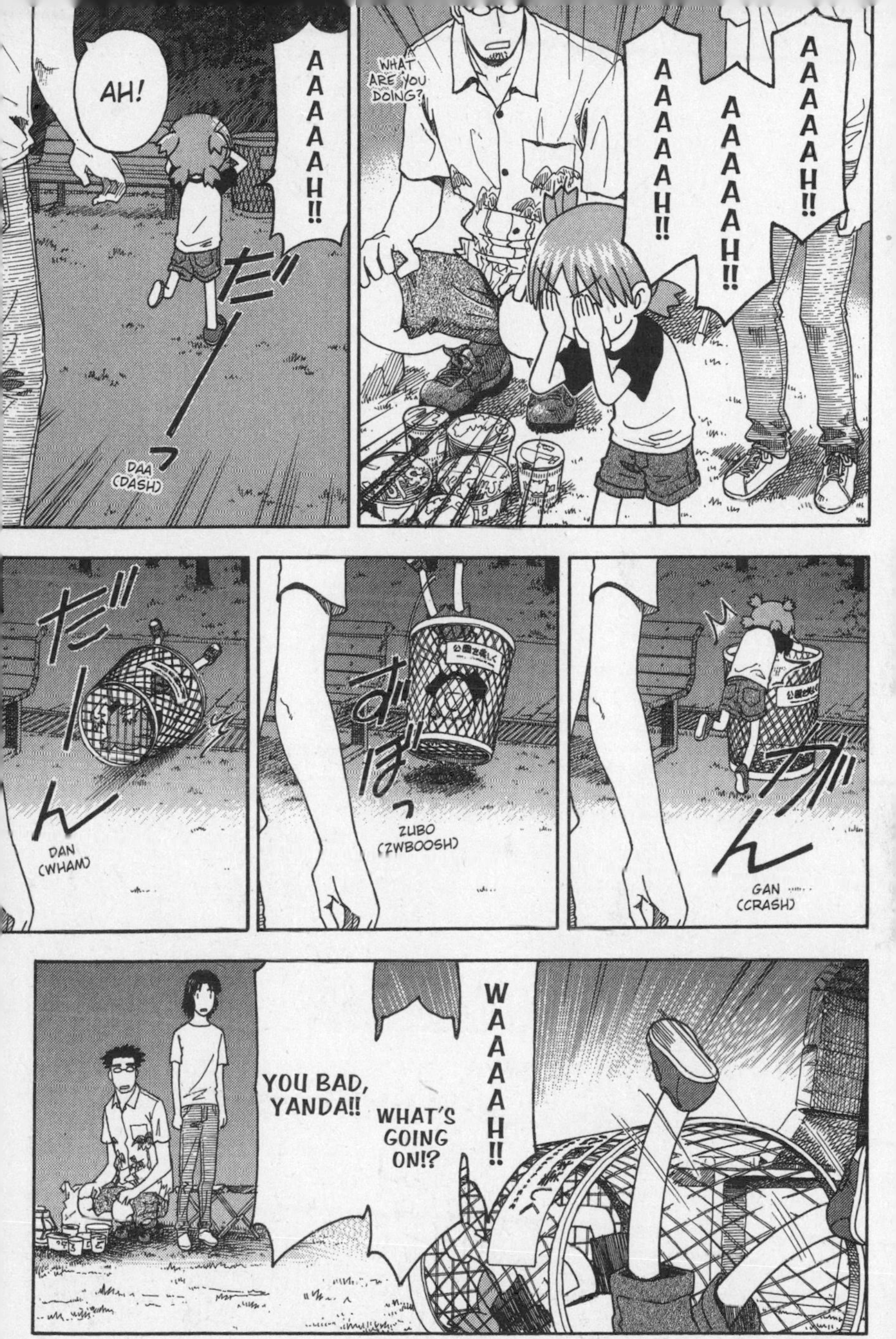
AAAAAH!!
AAAAAH!!
AAAAAH!!
WHAT ARE YOU DOING?
AH!
AAAAAH!!
だーっ
DAA (DASH)
がん
GAN (CRASH)
ずぼっ
ZUBO (ZWBOOSH)
だーん
DAN (WHAM)
WAAAAAH!!
WHAT'S GOING ON!?
YOU BAD, YANDA!!

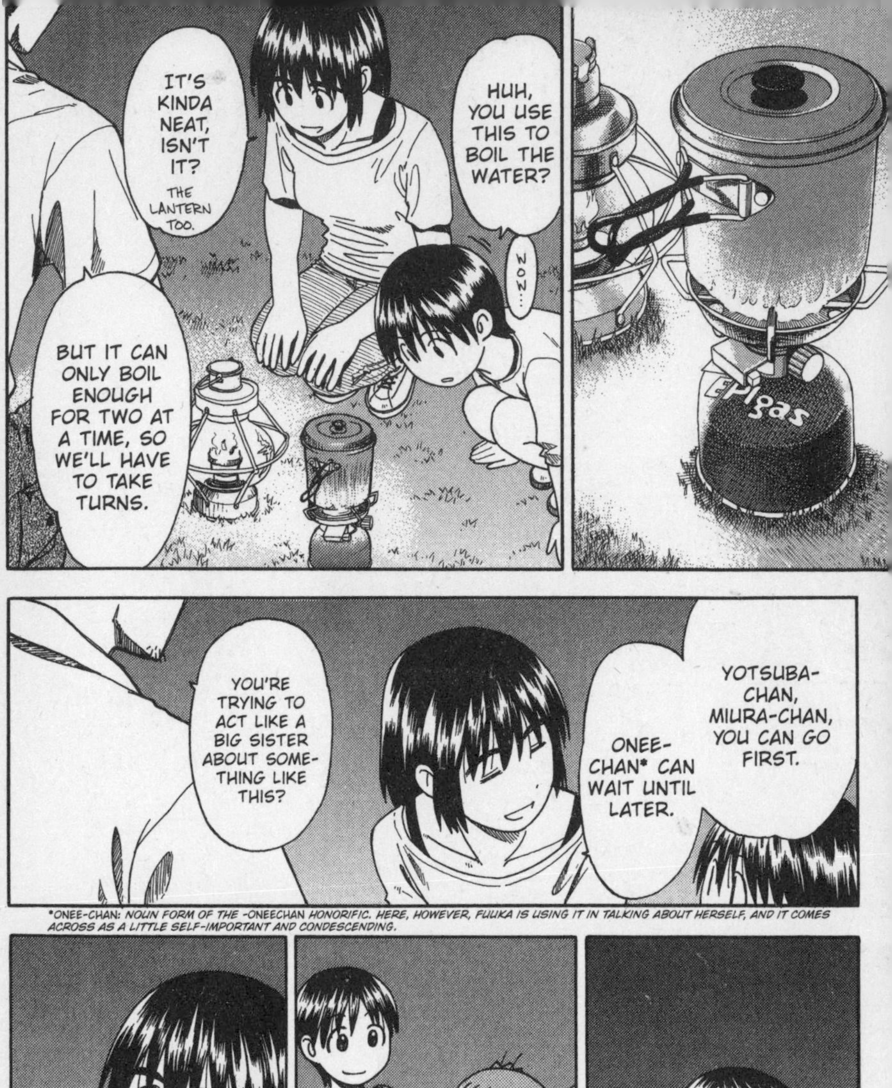
HUH, YOU USE THIS TO BOIL THE WATER?
IT'S KINDA NEAT, ISN'T IT? THE LANTERN TOO.
WOW...
BUT IT CAN ONLY BOIL ENOUGH FOR TWO AT A TIME, SO WE'LL HAVE TO TAKE TURNS.
YOTSUBA-CHAN, MIURA-CHAN, YOU CAN GO FIRST.
ONEE-CHAN* CAN WAIT UNTIL LATER.
YOU'RE TRYING TO ACT LIKE A BIG SISTER ABOUT SOMETHING LIKE THIS?

*ONEE-CHAN: *NOUN FORM OF THE -ONEECHAN HONORIFIC. HERE, HOWEVER, FUUKA IS USING IT IN TALKING ABOUT HERSELF, AND IT COMES ACROSS AS A LITTLE SELF-IMPORTANT AND CONDESCENDING.*

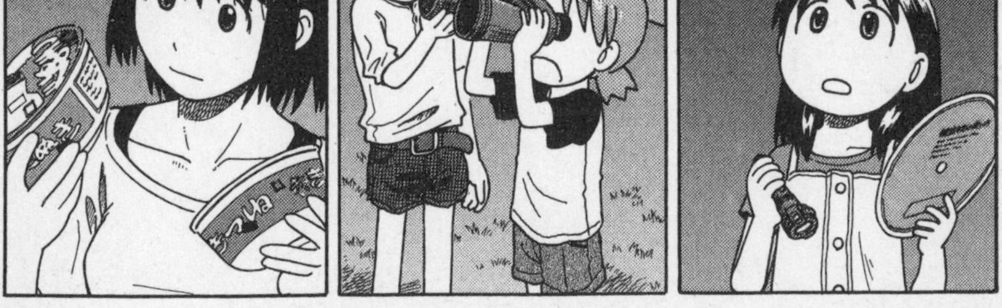

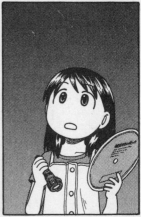

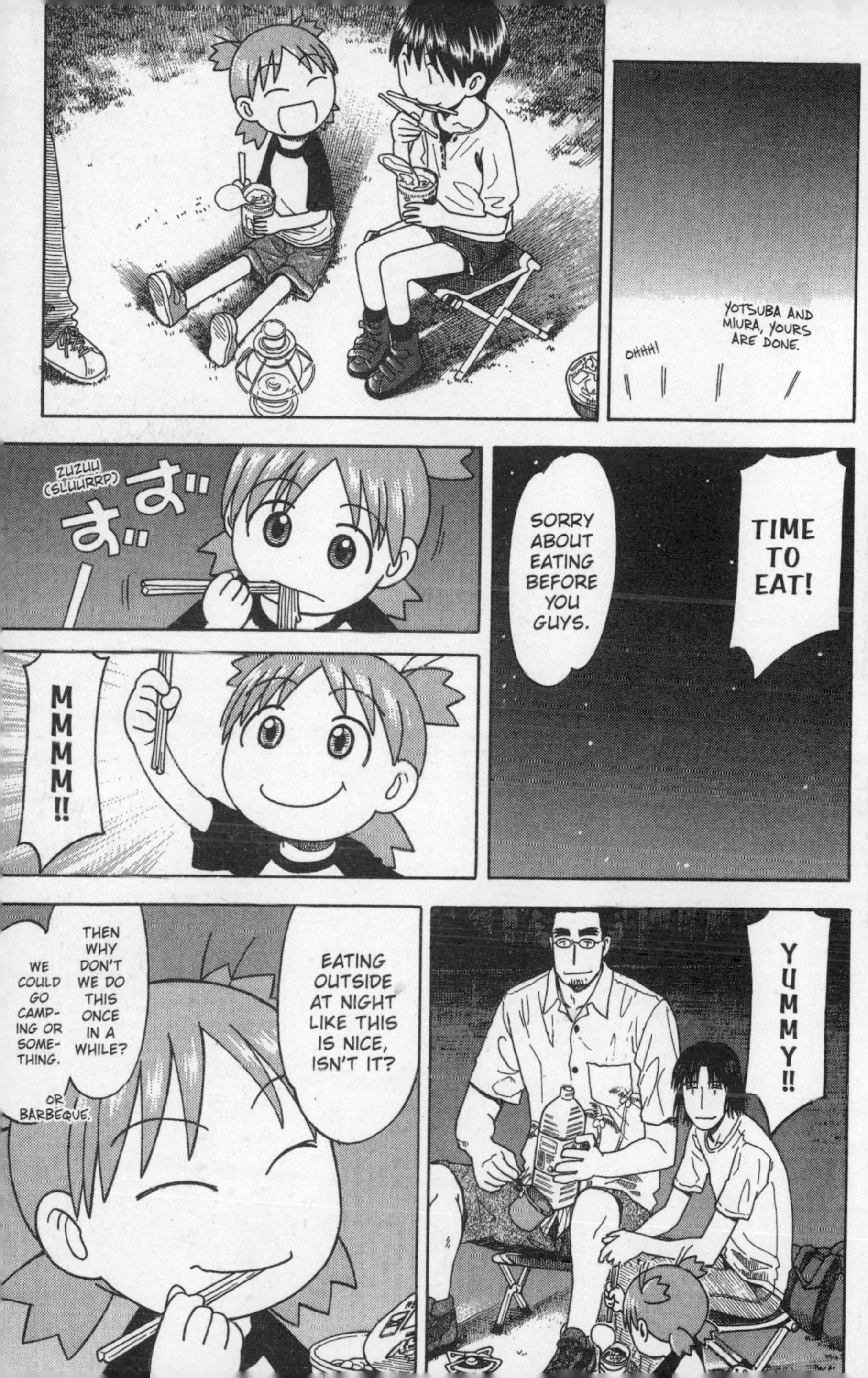
YOTSUBA AND MIURA, YOURS ARE DONE.
OHHH!
TIME TO EAT!
SORRY ABOUT EATING BEFORE YOU GUYS.
ZUZUU (SLUUURP)
MMMM!!
YUMMY!!
EATING OUTSIDE AT NIGHT LIKE THIS IS NICE, ISN'T IT?
THEN WHY DON'T WE DO THIS ONCE IN A WHILE?
WE COULD GO CAMPING OR SOMETHING.
OR BARBEQUE.

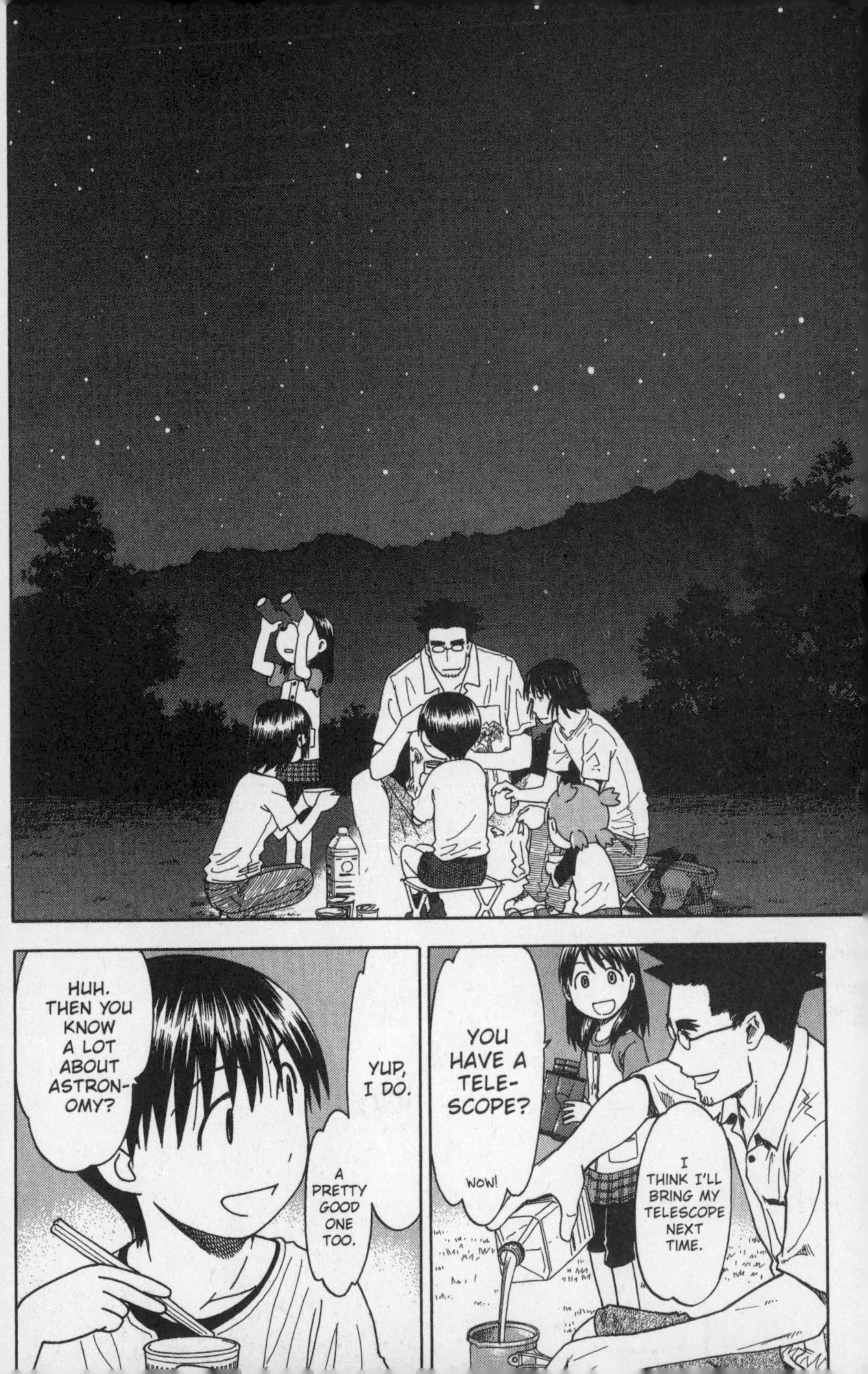
I THINK I'LL BRING MY TELESCOPE NEXT TIME.
YOU HAVE A TELE-SCOPE?
WOW!
YUP, I DO.
A PRETTY GOOD ONE TOO.
HUH. THEN YOU KNOW A LOT ABOUT ASTRON-OMY?

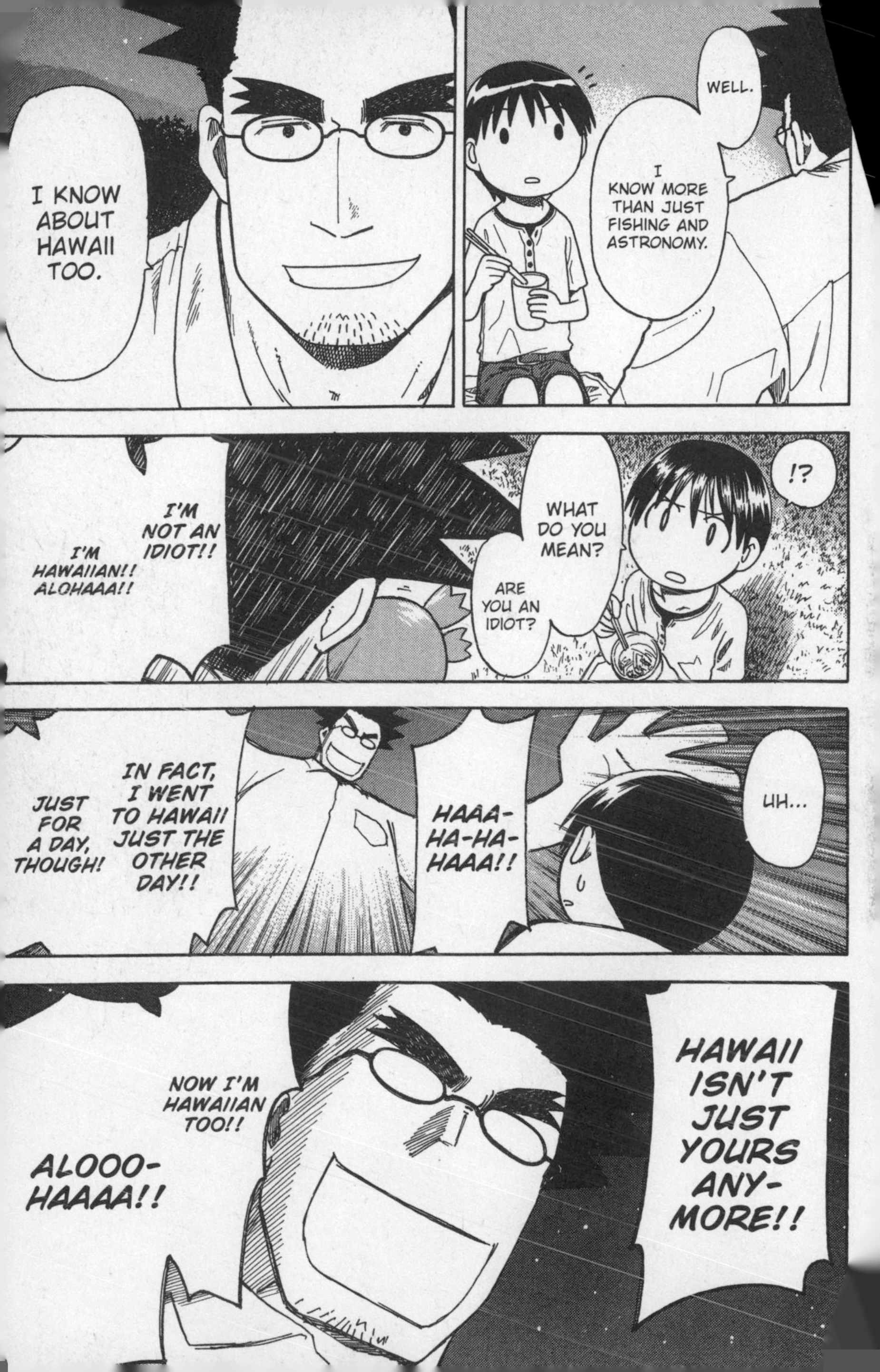
WELL.
I KNOW MORE THAN JUST FISHING AND ASTRONOMY.
I KNOW ABOUT HAWAII TOO.
!?
WHAT DO YOU MEAN?
ARE YOU AN IDIOT?
I'M NOT AN IDIOT!!
I'M HAWAIIAN!! ALOHAAA!!
UH...
HAAA-HA-HA-HAAA!!
IN FACT, I WENT TO HAWAII JUST THE OTHER DAY!!
JUST FOR A DAY, THOUGH!
HAWAII ISN'T JUST YOURS ANY-MORE!!
NOW I'M HAWAIIAN TOO!!
ALOOO-HAAAA!!

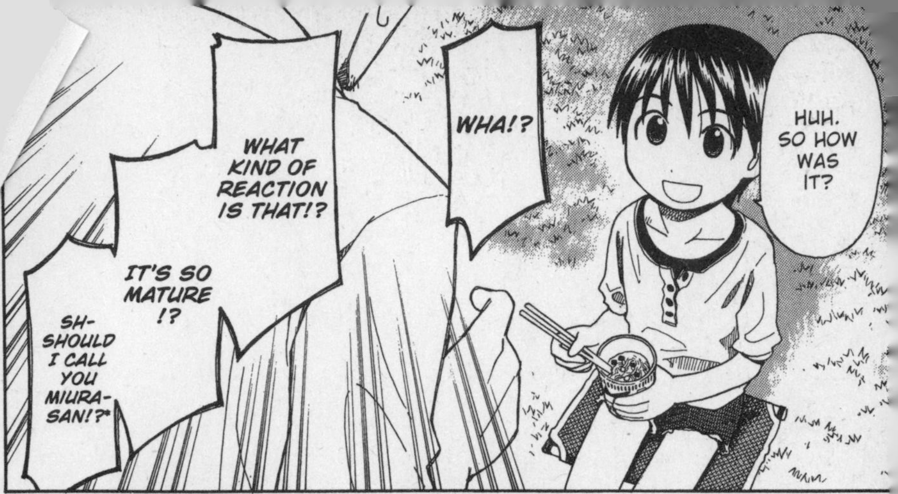
HUH. SO HOW WAS IT?
WHA!?
WHAT KIND OF REACTION IS THAT!?
IT'S SO MATURE!?
SH-SHOULD I CALL YOU MIURA-SAN!?*

*-SAN: A POLITE HONORIFIC SUFFIX THAT IS THE EQUIVALENT OF "MR.," "MRS.," OR "MISS."

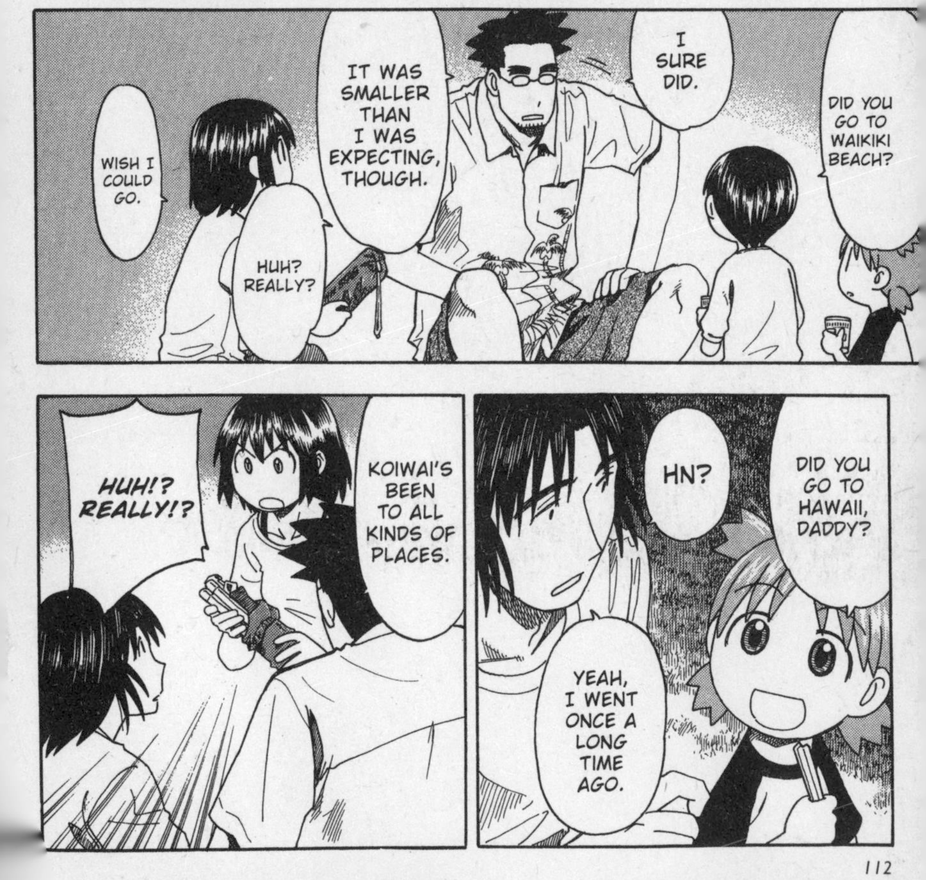
DID YOU GO TO WAIKIKI BEACH?
I SURE DID.
IT WAS SMALLER THAN I WAS EXPECTING, THOUGH.
WISH I COULD GO.
HUH? REALLY?
DID YOU GO TO HAWAII, DADDY?
HN?
YEAH, I WENT ONCE A LONG TIME AGO.
KOIWAI'S BEEN TO ALL KINDS OF PLACES.
HUH!? REALLY!?

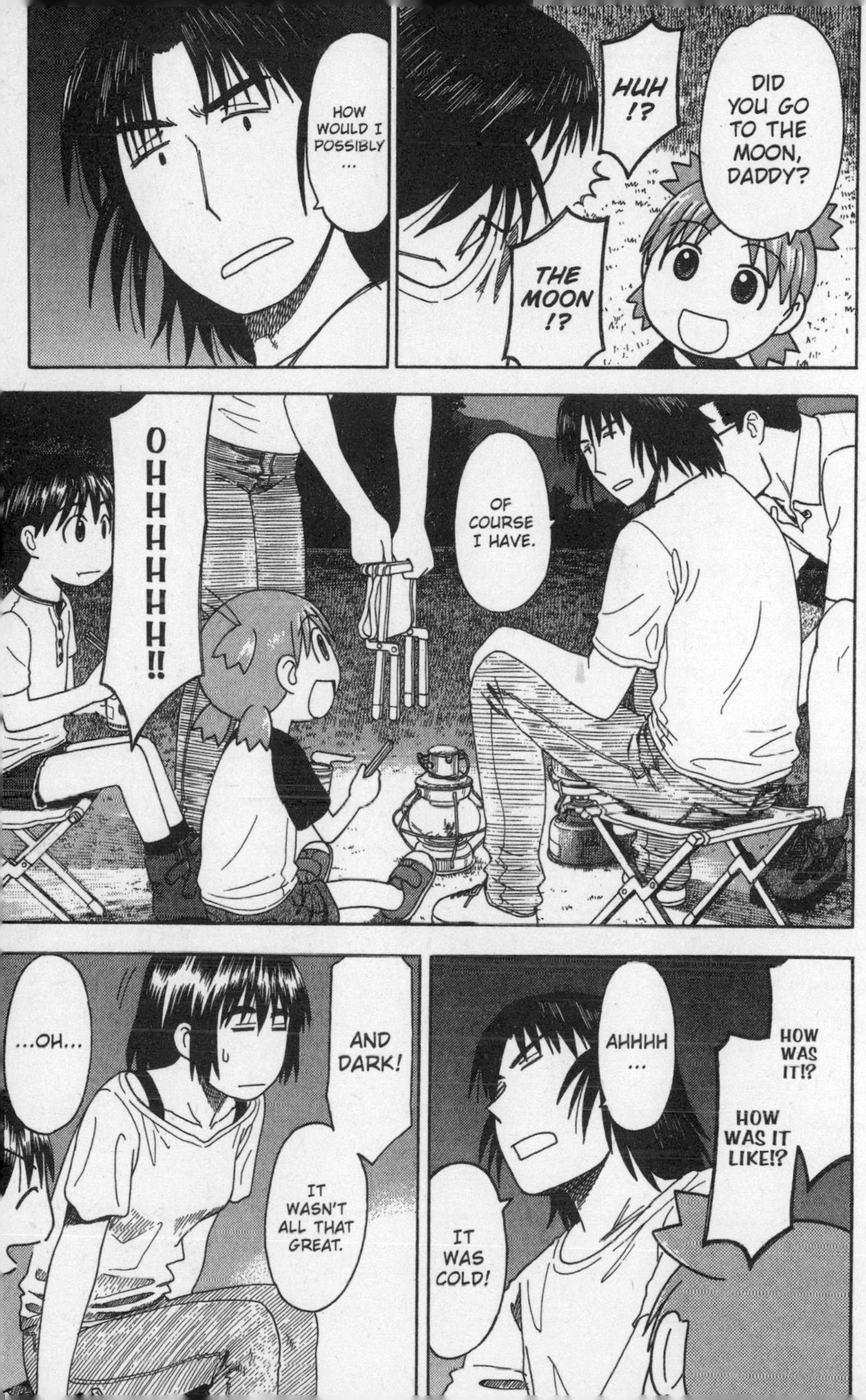
DID YOU GO TO THE MOON, DADDY?
HUH!?
THE MOON!?
HOW WOULD I POSSIBLY ...
OF COURSE I HAVE.
OHHHHHHH!!
HOW WAS IT!?
HOW WAS IT LIKE!?
AHHHH ...
IT WAS COLD!
AND DARK!
...OH...
IT WASN'T ALL THAT GREAT.

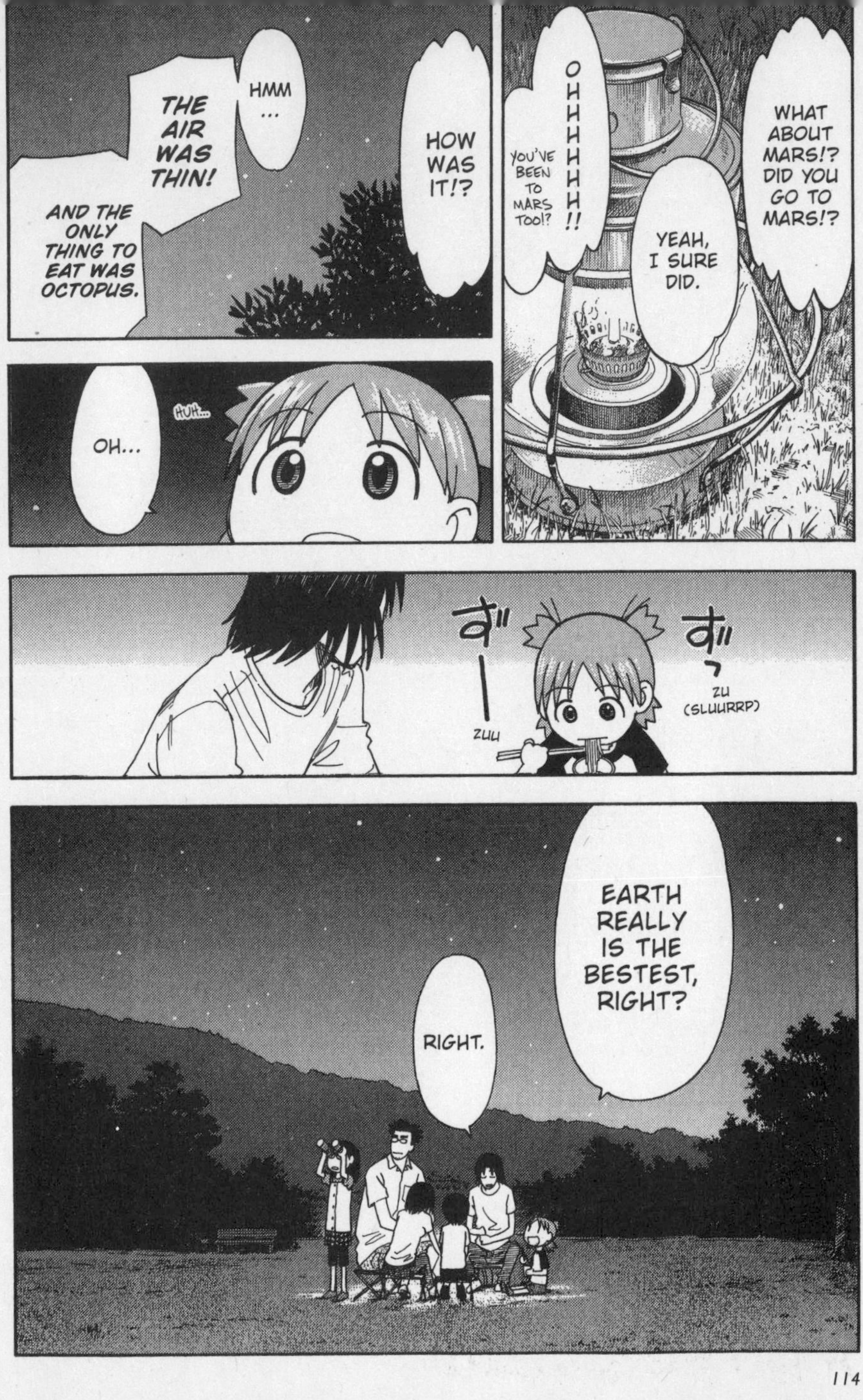
WHAT ABOUT MARS!? DID YOU GO TO MARS!?
YEAH, I SURE DID.
OHHHHHHH!!
YOU'VE BEEN TO MARS TOO!?
HOW WAS IT!?
HMM ...
THE AIR WAS THIN!
AND THE ONLY THING TO EAT WAS OCTOPUS.
HUH...
OH...
ずっ
ZU (SLUURRP)
ずー
ZUU
EARTH REALLY IS THE BESTEST, RIGHT?
RIGHT.

YOTSUBA&!

YOTSUBA&

RAIN

#32

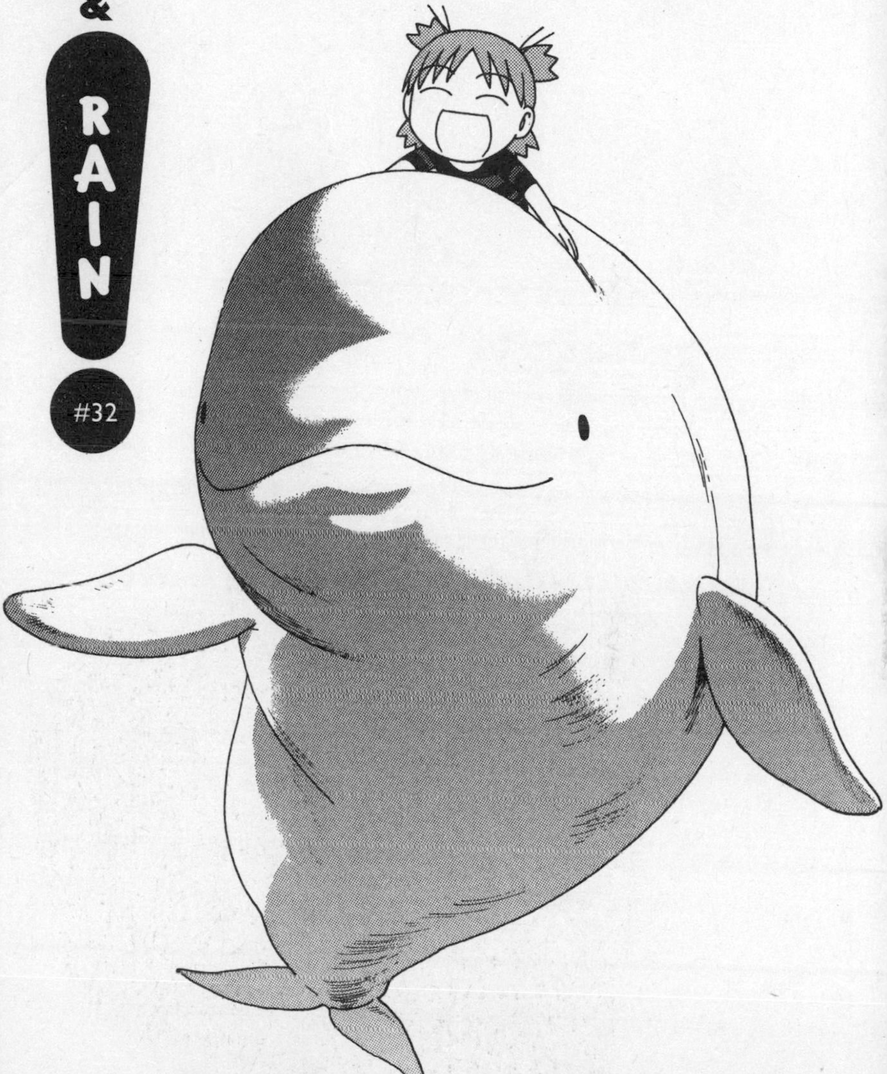

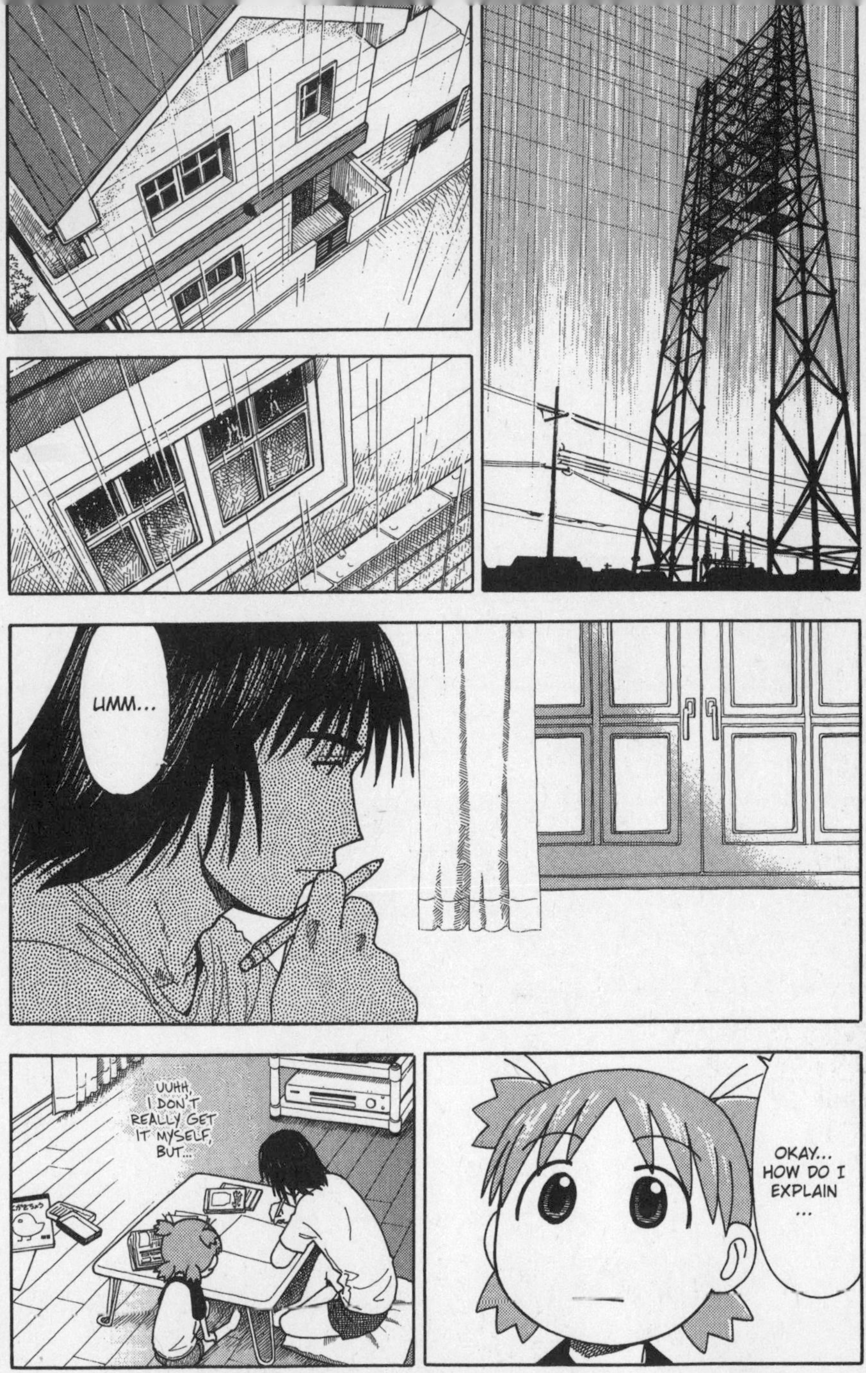
UMM...
OKAY... HOW DO I EXPLAIN ...
UUHH, I DON'T REALLY GET IT MYSELF, BUT...

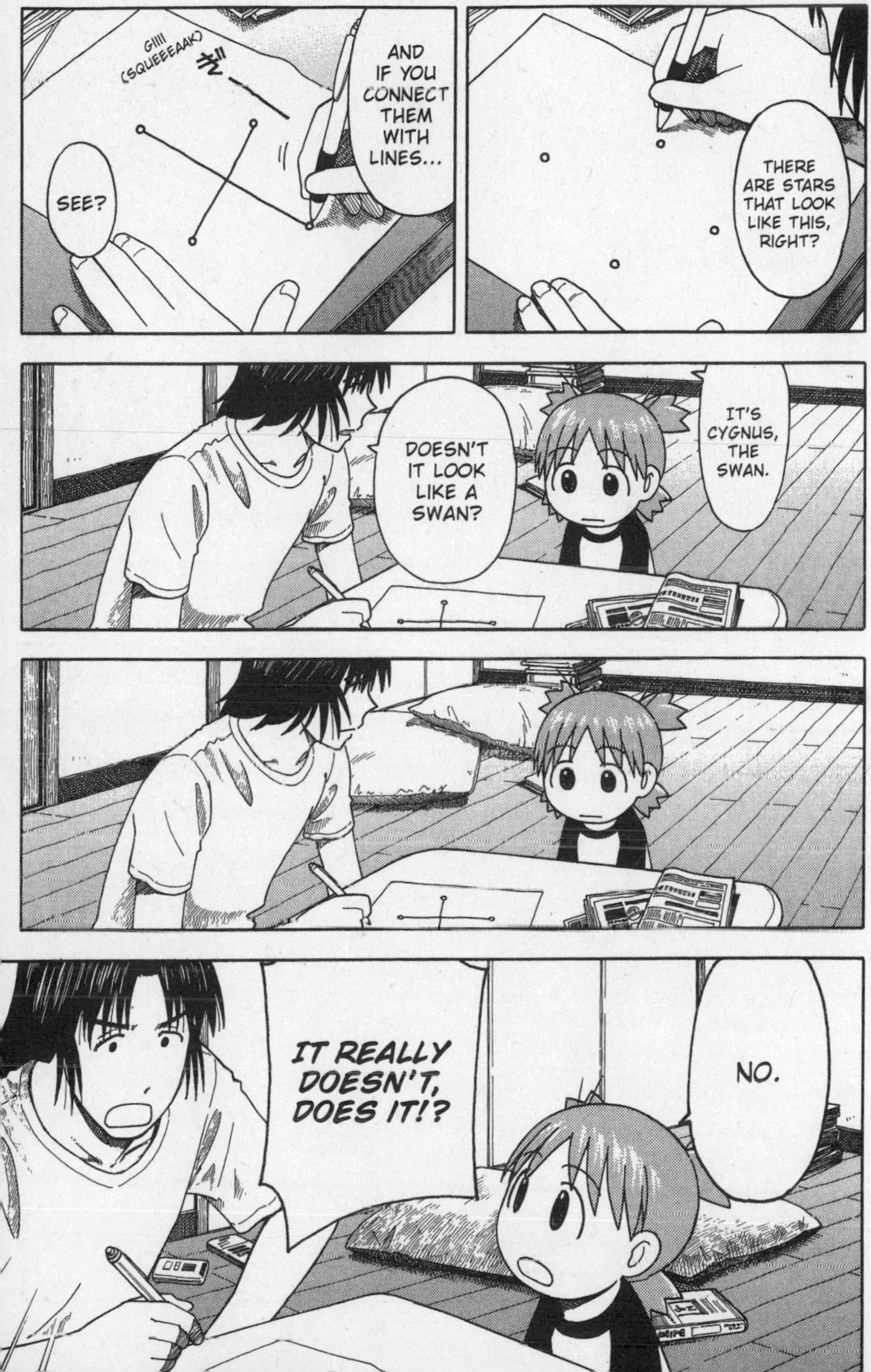
THERE ARE STARS THAT LOOK LIKE THIS, RIGHT?
AND IF YOU CONNECT THEM WITH LINES...
GIIII (SQUEEEAAK)
SEE?
IT'S CYGNUS, THE SWAN.
DOESN'T IT LOOK LIKE A SWAN?
NO.
IT REALLY DOESN'T, DOES IT!?

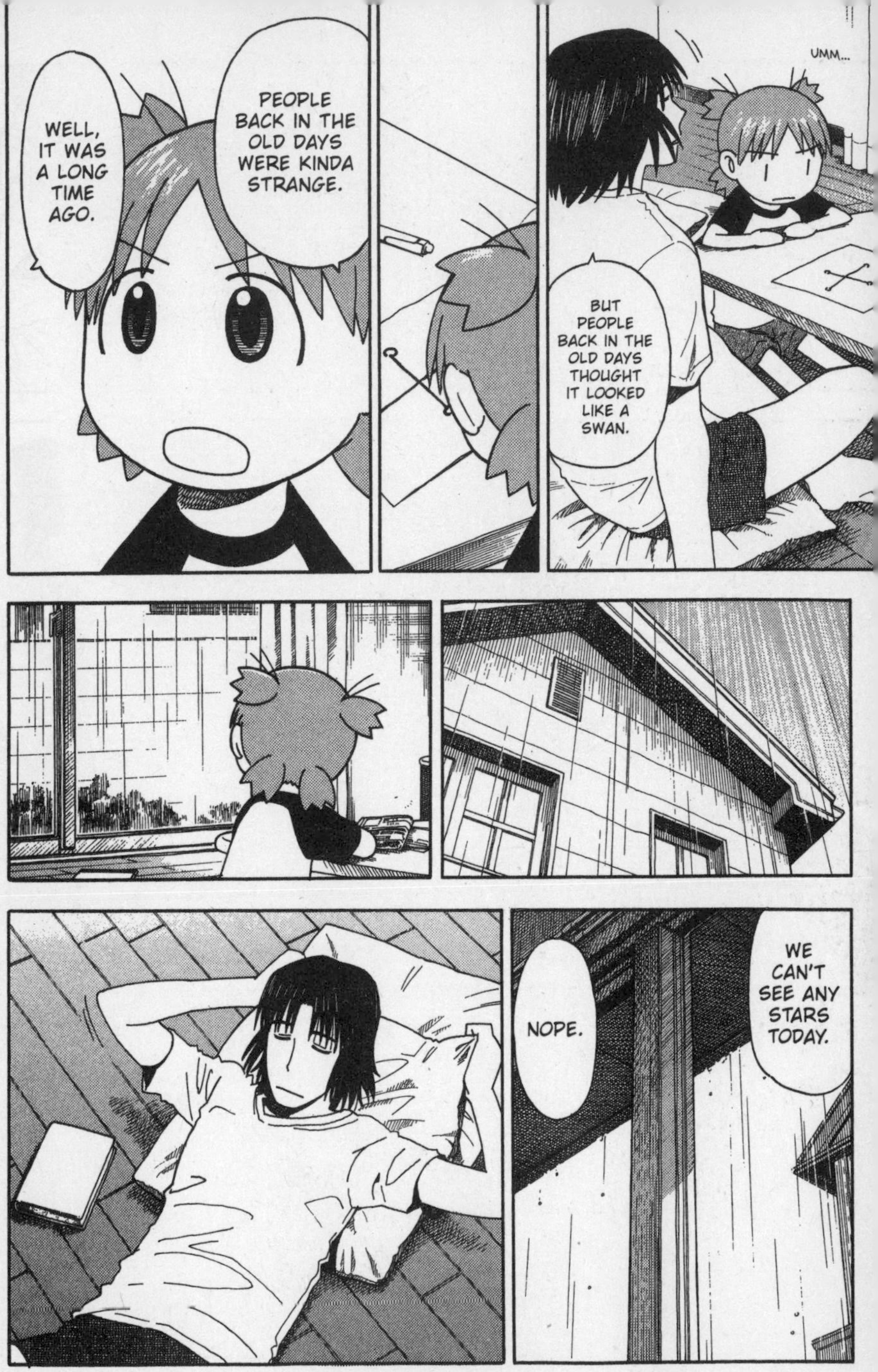
UMM...
BUT PEOPLE BACK IN THE OLD DAYS THOUGHT IT LOOKED LIKE A SWAN.
PEOPLE BACK IN THE OLD DAYS WERE KINDA STRANGE.
WELL, IT WAS A LONG TIME AGO.
WE CAN'T SEE ANY STARS TODAY.
NOPE.

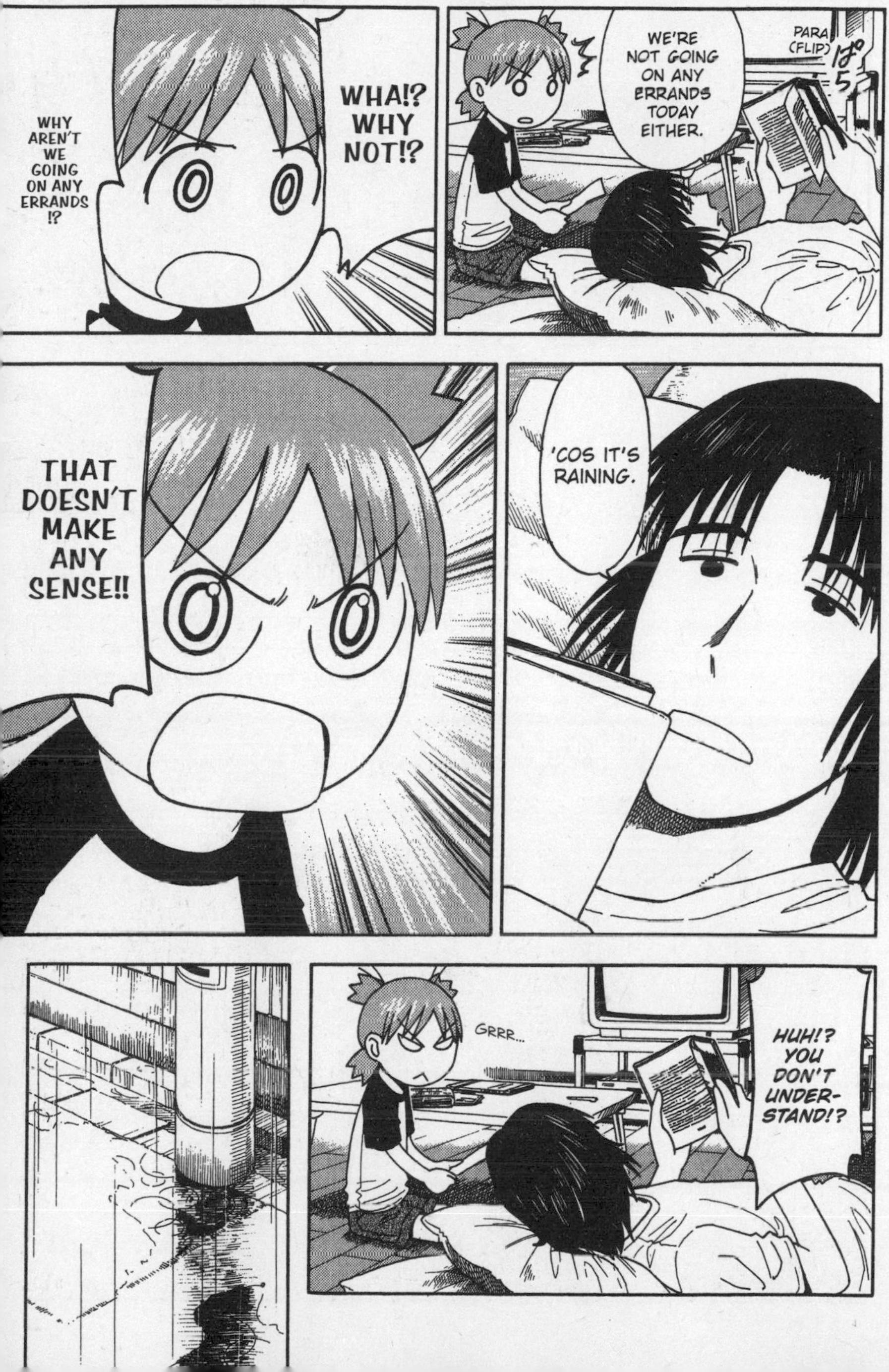
PARA (FLIP)
WE'RE NOT GOING ON ANY ERRANDS TODAY EITHER.
WHA!? WHY NOT!?
WHY AREN'T WE GOING ON ANY ERRANDS !?
'COS IT'S RAINING.
THAT DOESN'T MAKE ANY SENSE!!
HUH!? YOU DON'T UNDER-STAND!?
GRRR...

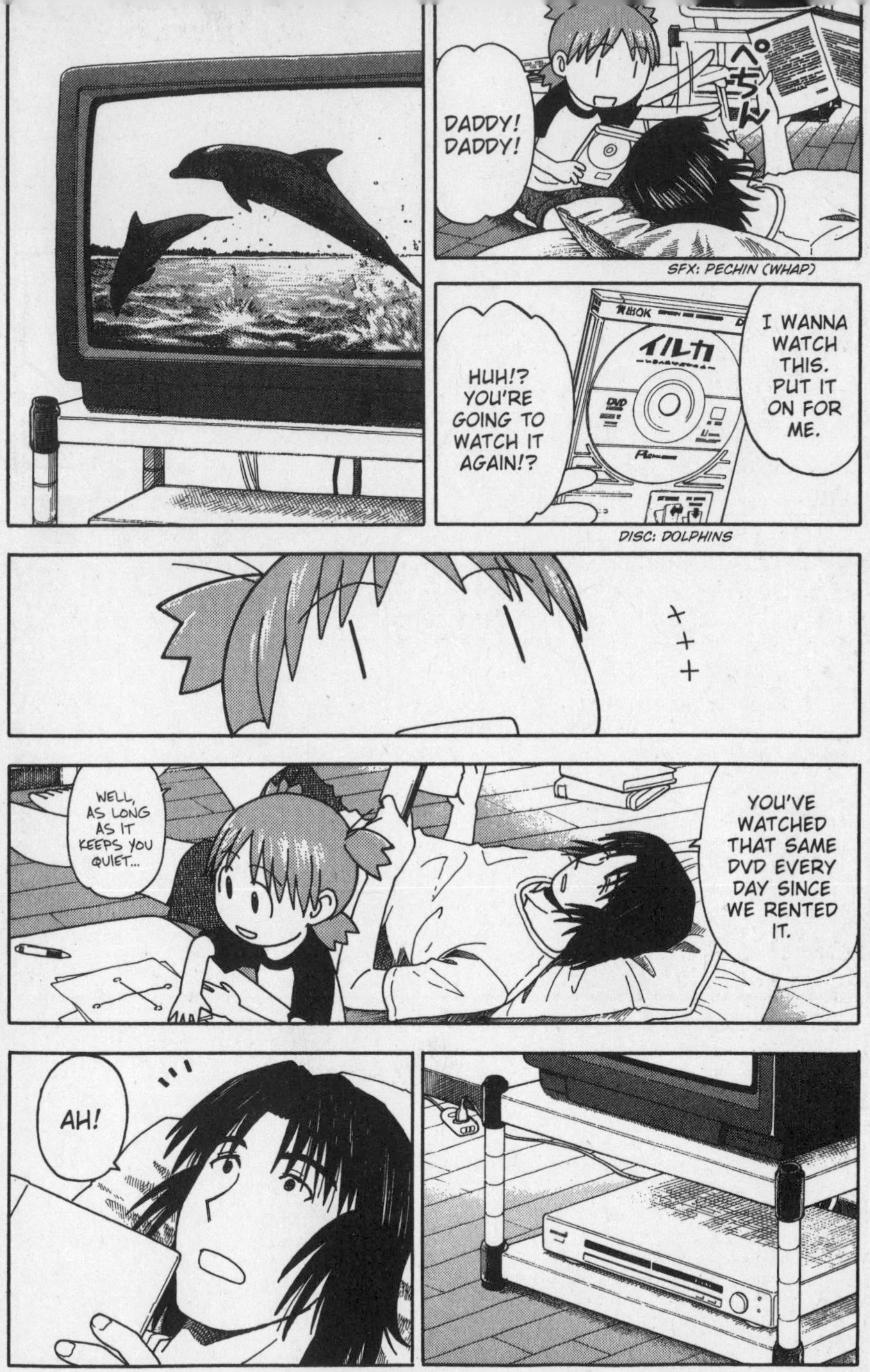
DADDY! DADDY!
ぺちん
SFX: PECHIN (WHAP)
I WANNA WATCH THIS. PUT IT ON FOR ME.
HUH!? YOU'RE GOING TO WATCH IT AGAIN!?
イルカ
DISC: DOLPHINS
YOU'VE WATCHED THAT SAME DVD EVERY DAY SINCE WE RENTED IT.
WELL, AS LONG AS IT KEEPS YOU QUIET...
AH!

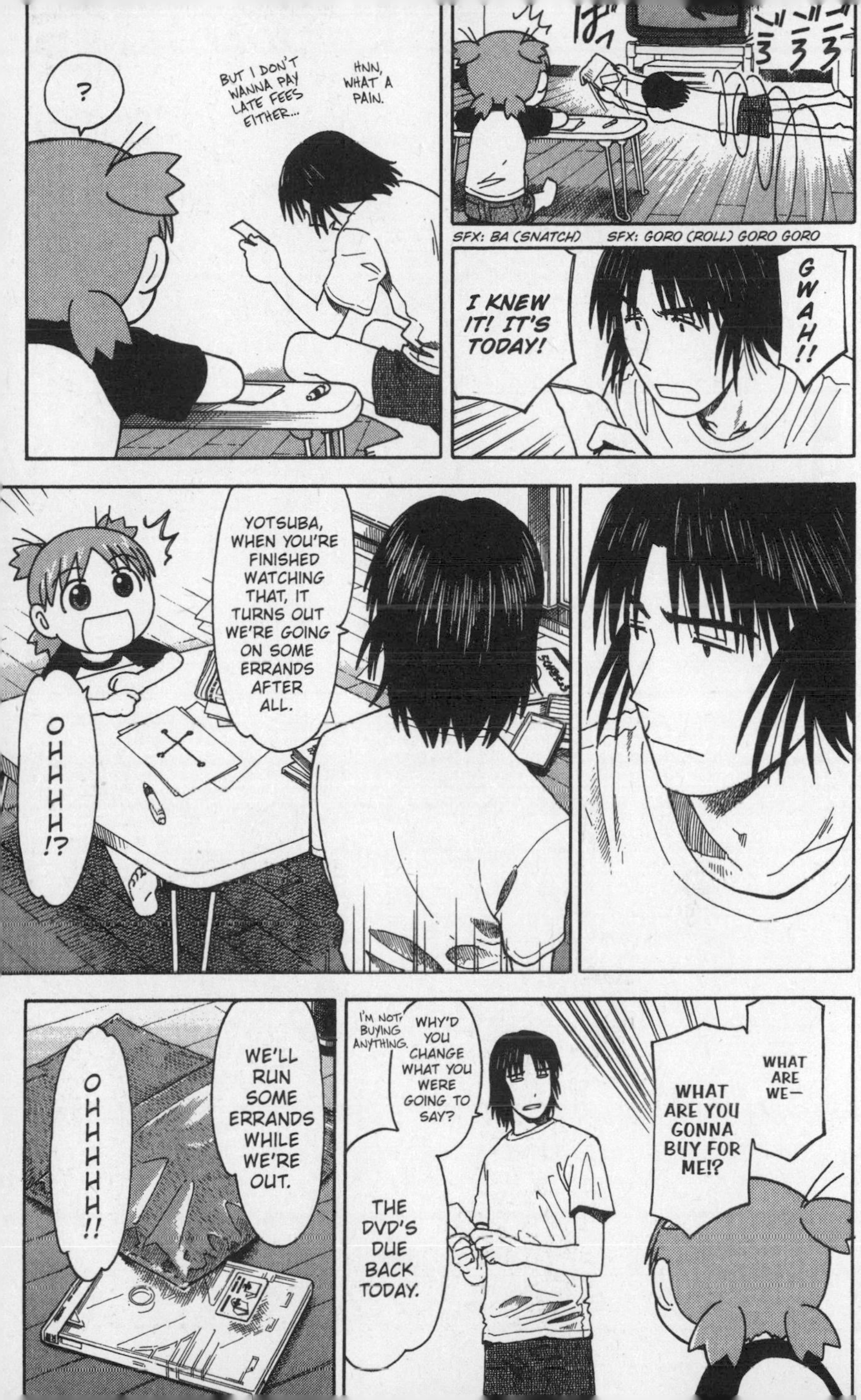

ば
ゴロ ゴロ ゴロ
SFX: BA (SNATCH)
SFX: GORO (ROLL) GORO GORO
GWAH!!
I KNEW IT! IT'S TODAY!
HNN, WHAT A PAIN.
BUT I DON'T WANNA PAY LATE FEES EITHER...
?
YOTSUBA, WHEN YOU'RE FINISHED WATCHING THAT, IT TURNS OUT WE'RE GOING ON SOME ERRANDS AFTER ALL.
OHHHHH!?
WHAT ARE WE—
WHAT ARE YOU GONNA BUY FOR ME!?
WHY'D YOU CHANGE WHAT YOU WERE GOING TO SAY?
I'M NOT BUYING ANYTHING.
THE DVD'S DUE BACK TODAY.
WE'LL RUN SOME ERRANDS WHILE WE'RE OUT.
OHHHHHH!!

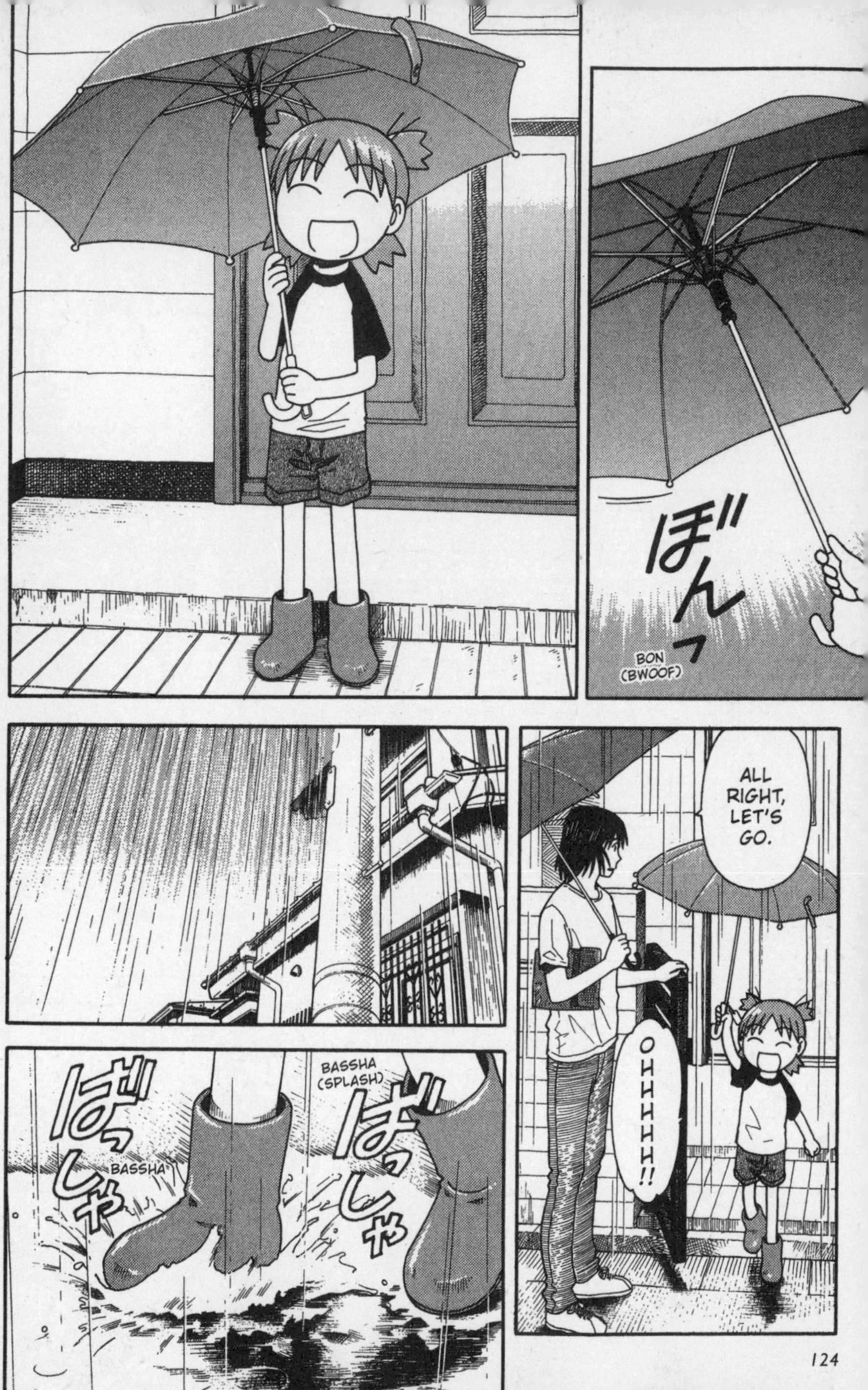
ぼんっ
BON (BWOOF)
ALL RIGHT, LET'S GO.
OHHHHHH!!
ばっしゃ
BASSHA (SPLASH)
ばっしゃ
BASSHA

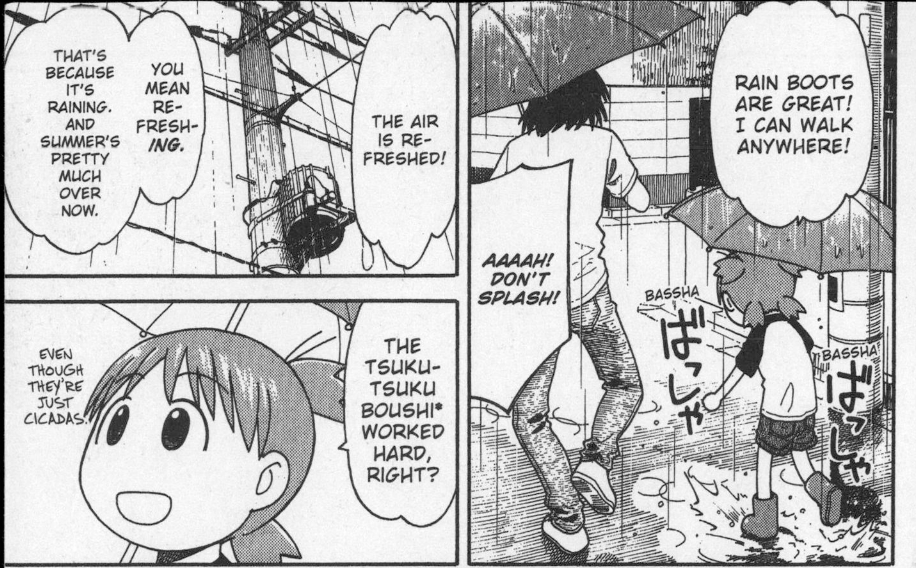
RAIN BOOTS ARE GREAT! I CAN WALK ANYWHERE!
AAAAH! DON'T SPLASH!
BASSHA
ばっしゃ
BASSHA
ばっしゃ
THE AIR IS RE-FRESHED!
YOU MEAN RE-FRESH-*ING*.
THAT'S BECAUSE IT'S RAINING. AND SUMMER'S PRETTY MUCH OVER NOW.
THE TSUKU-TSUKU BOUSHI* WORKED HARD, RIGHT?
EVEN THOUGH THEY'RE JUST CICADAS.

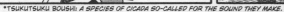

*TSUKUTSUKU BOUSHI: A SPECIES OF CICADA SO-CALLED FOR THE SOUND THEY MAKE.

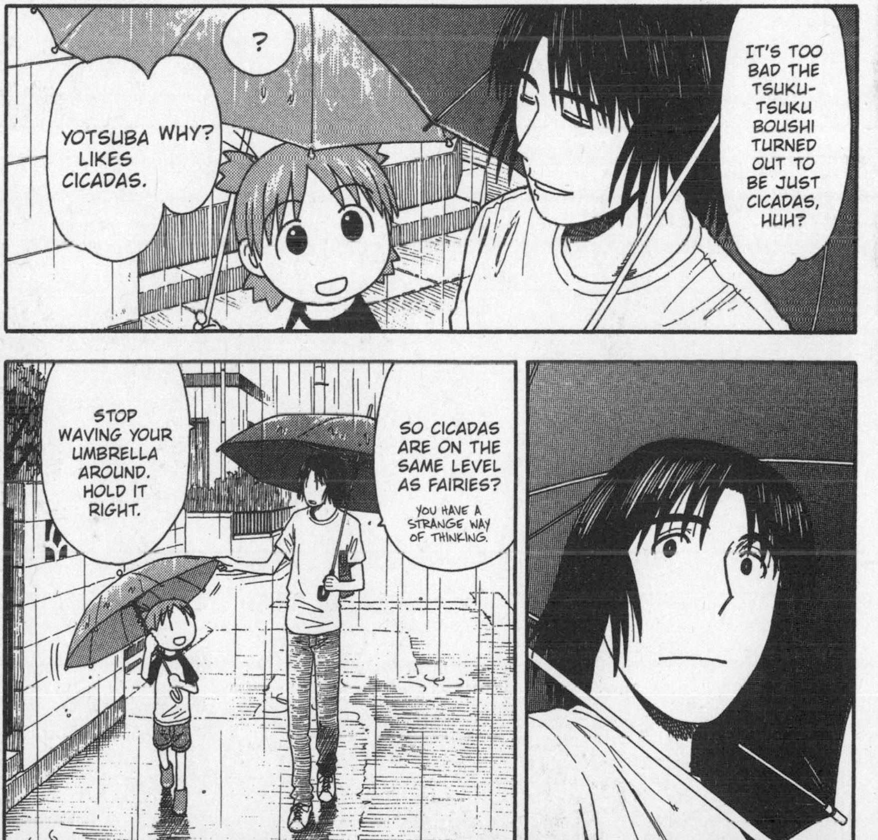
IT'S TOO BAD THE TSUKU-TSUKU BOUSHI TURNED OUT TO BE JUST CICADAS, HUH?
?
WHY?
YOTSUBA LIKES CICADAS.
SO CICADAS ARE ON THE SAME LEVEL AS FAIRIES?
YOU HAVE A STRANGE WAY OF THINKING.
STOP WAVING YOUR UMBRELLA AROUND. HOLD IT RIGHT.

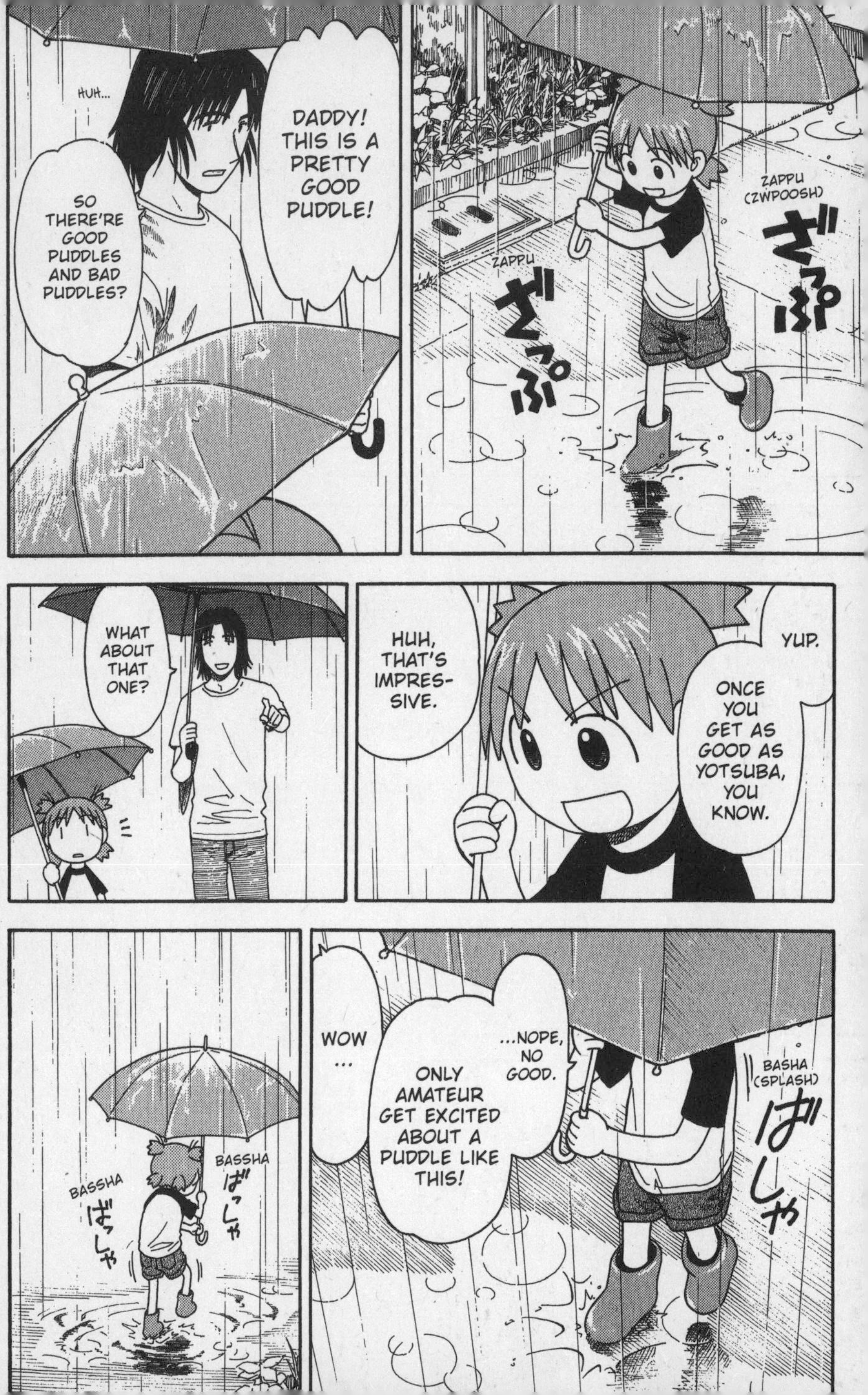
ZAPPU (ZWPOOSH)
ざっぷ
ZAPPU
ざっぷ
DADDY! THIS IS A PRETTY GOOD PUDDLE!
HUH...
SO THERE'RE GOOD PUDDLES AND BAD PUDDLES?
YUP.
ONCE YOU GET AS GOOD AS YOTSUBA, YOU KNOW.
HUH, THAT'S IMPRES-SIVE.
WHAT ABOUT THAT ONE?
BASHA (SPLASH)
ばしゃ
...NOPE, NO GOOD.
ONLY AMATEUR GET EXCITED ABOUT A PUDDLE LIKE THIS!
WOW ...
BASSHA
ばっしゃ
BASSHA
ばっしゃ

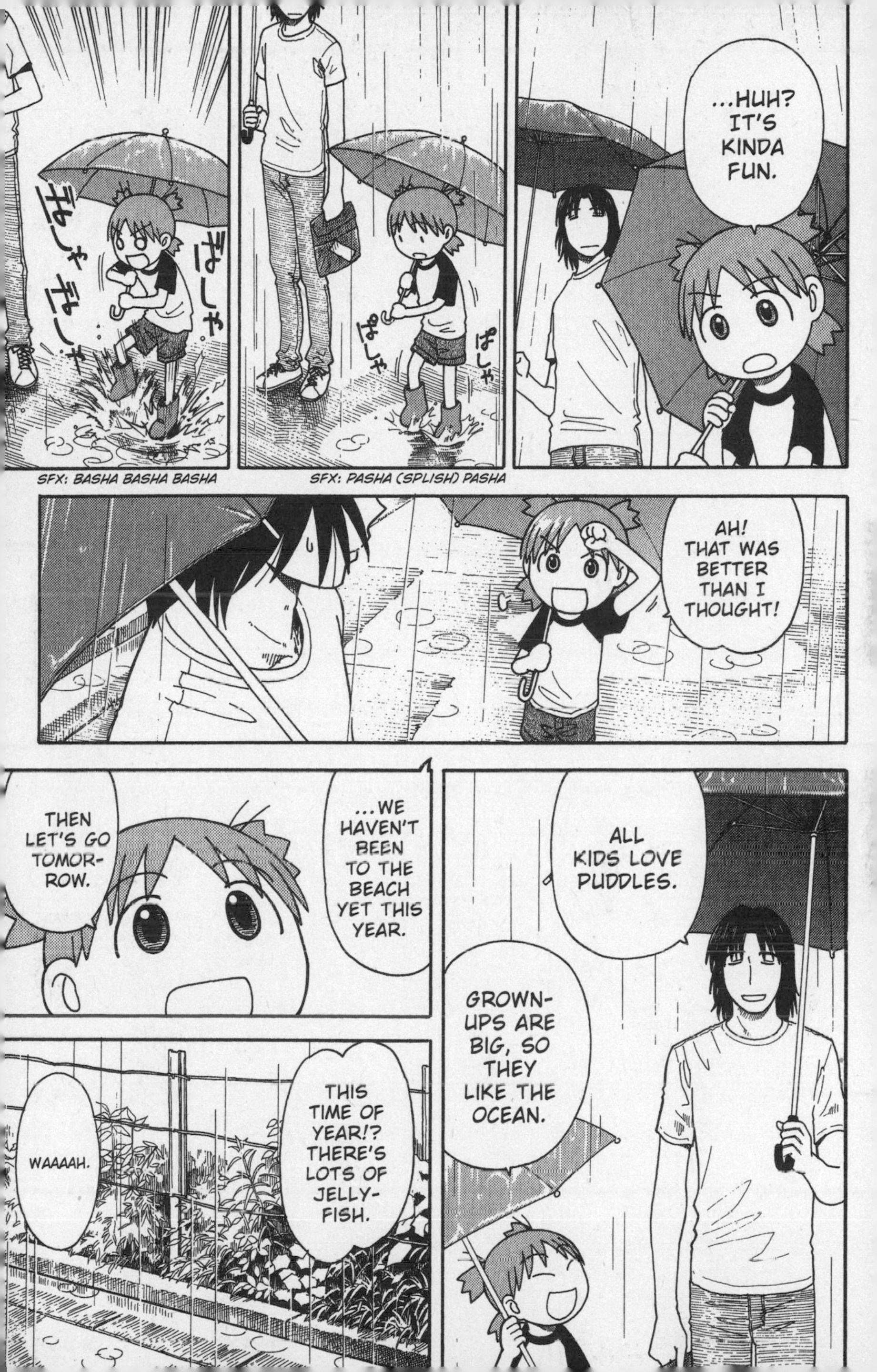
...HUH? IT'S KINDA FUN.
ぱしゃ ぱしゃ
SFX: PASHA (SPLISH) PASHA
ばしゃ ばしゃ ばしゃ
SFX: BASHA BASHA BASHA
AH! THAT WAS BETTER THAN I THOUGHT!
ALL KIDS LOVE PUDDLES.
GROWN-UPS ARE BIG, SO THEY LIKE THE OCEAN.
...WE HAVEN'T BEEN TO THE BEACH YET THIS YEAR.
THEN LET'S GO TOMORROW.
THIS TIME OF YEAR!? THERE'S LOTS OF JELLYFISH.
WAAAAH.

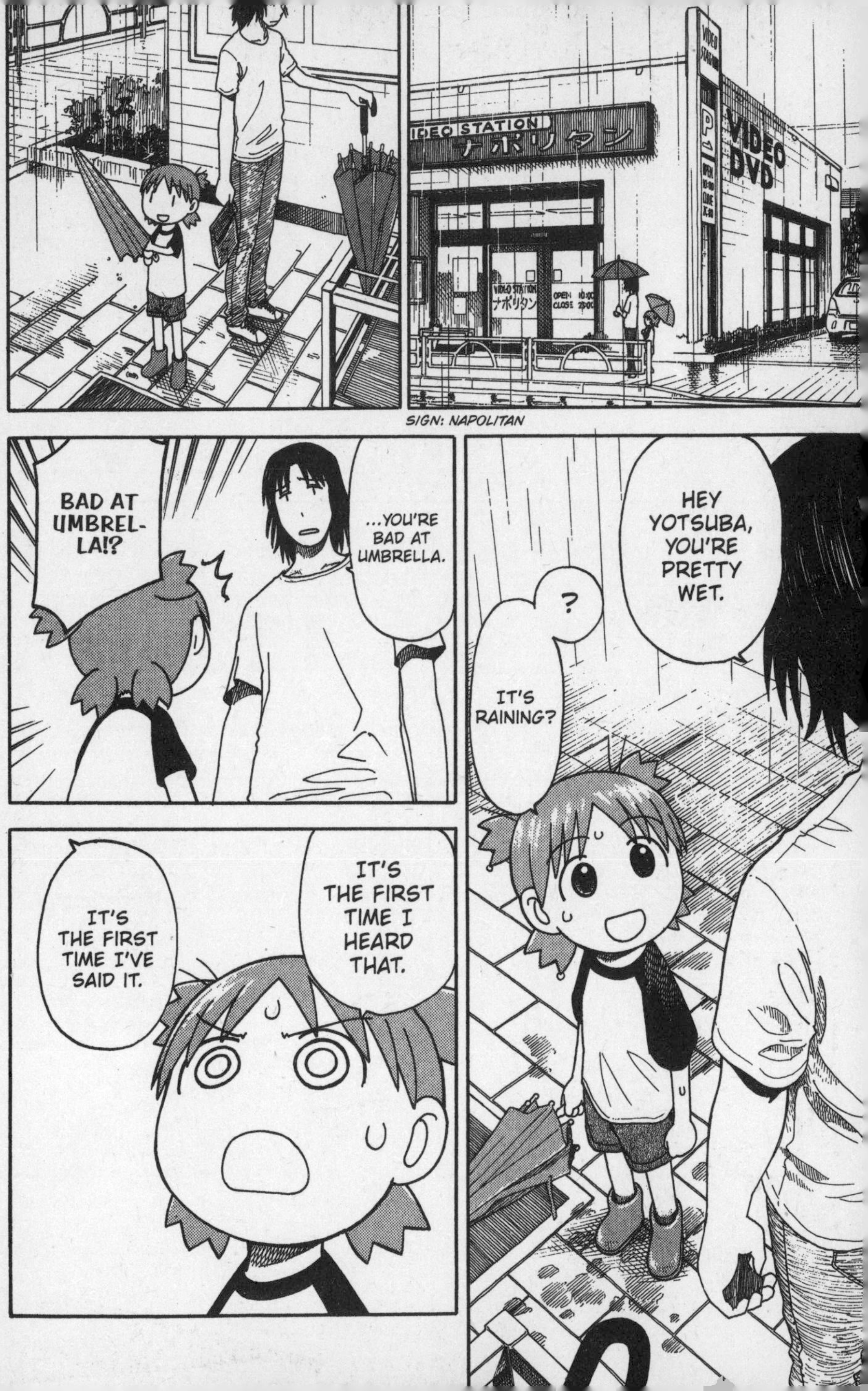
VIDEO STATION
ナポリタン
VIDEO
DVD
VIDEO STATION
ナポリタン
OPEN 10:00
CLOSE 23:00
SIGN: NAPOLITAN
HEY YOTSUBA, YOU'RE PRETTY WET.
?
IT'S RAINING?
...YOU'RE BAD AT UMBRELLA.
BAD AT UMBREL-LA!?
IT'S THE FIRST TIME I HEARD THAT.
IT'S THE FIRST TIME I'VE SAID IT.

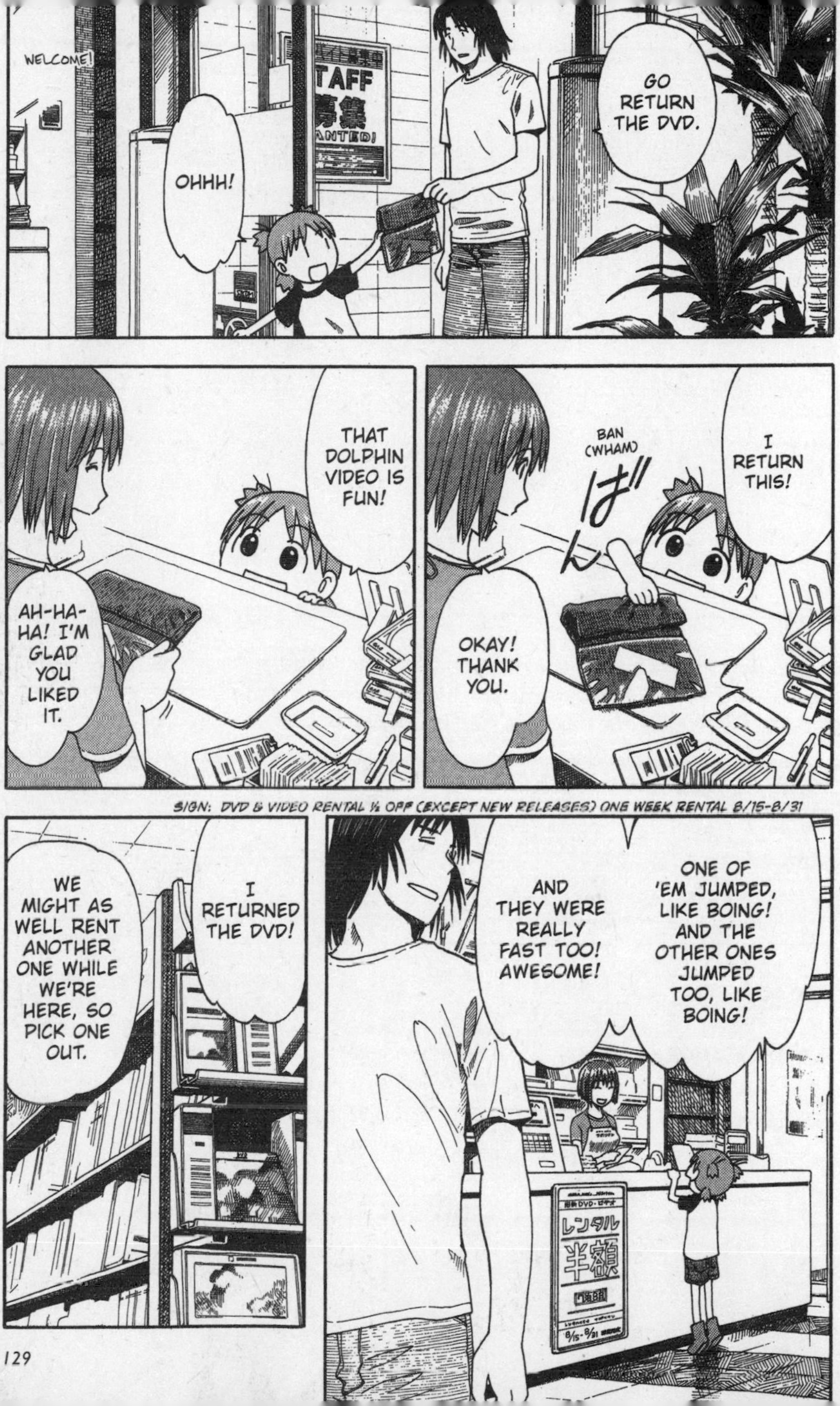
GO RETURN THE DVD.
WELCOME!
OHHH!
I RETURN THIS!
BAN (WHAM)
ばん
OKAY! THANK YOU.
THAT DOLPHIN VIDEO IS FUN!
AH-HA-HA! I'M GLAD YOU LIKED IT.
SIGN: DVD & VIDEO RENTAL ½ OFF (EXCEPT NEW RELEASES) ONE WEEK RENTAL 8/15-8/31
ONE OF 'EM JUMPED, LIKE BOING! AND THE OTHER ONES JUMPED TOO, LIKE BOING!
AND THEY WERE REALLY FAST TOO! AWESOME!
レンタル
半額
I RETURNED THE DVD!
WE MIGHT AS WELL RENT ANOTHER ONE WHILE WE'RE HERE, SO PICK ONE OUT.

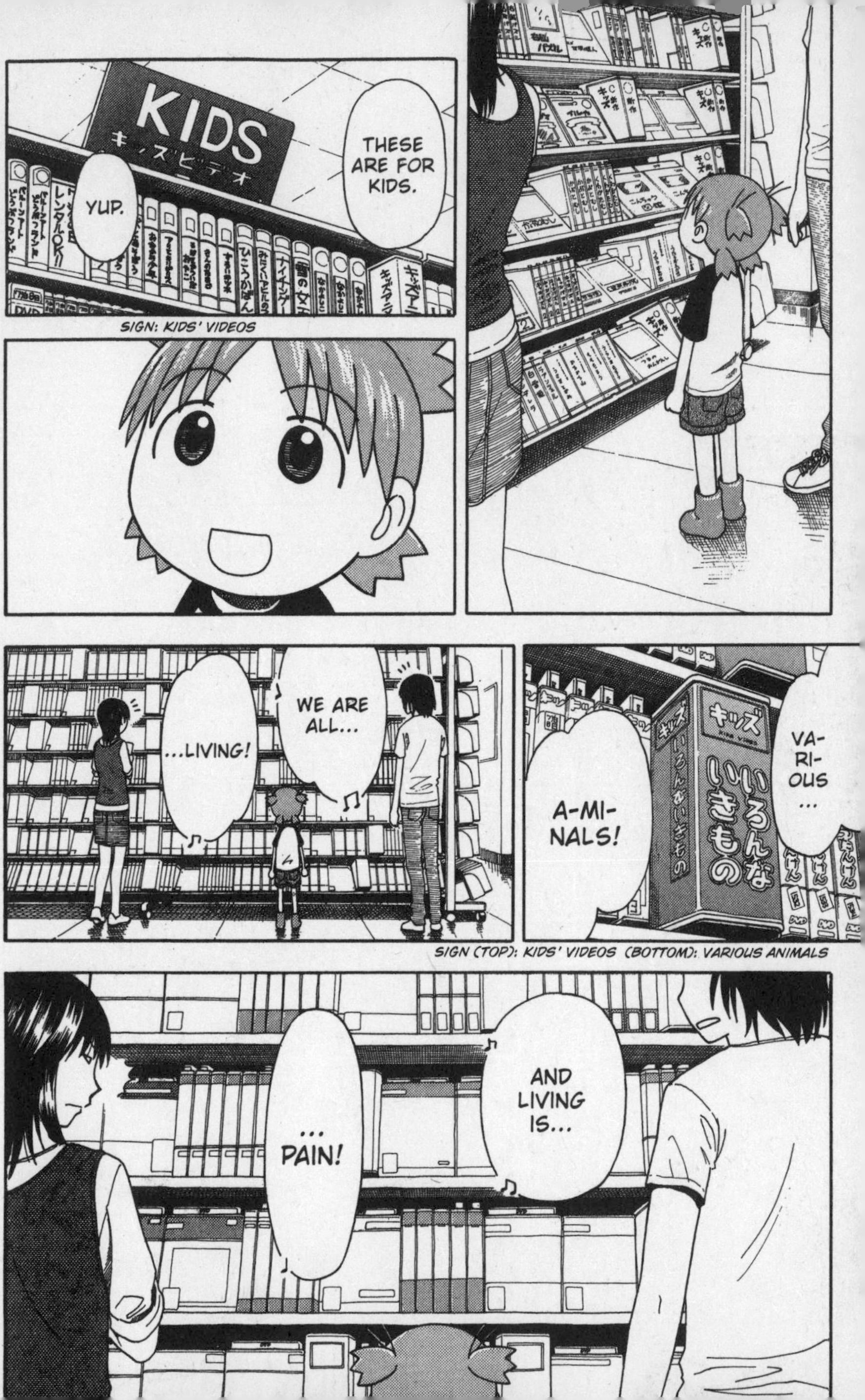
KIDS
キッズビデオ
THESE ARE FOR KIDS.
YUP.
SIGN: KIDS' VIDEOS
VA-RI-OUS ...
A-MI-NALS!
キッズ
いろんないきもの
SIGN (TOP): KIDS' VIDEOS (BOTTOM): VARIOUS ANIMALS
WE ARE ALL...
...LIVING!
AND LIVING IS...
... PAIN!

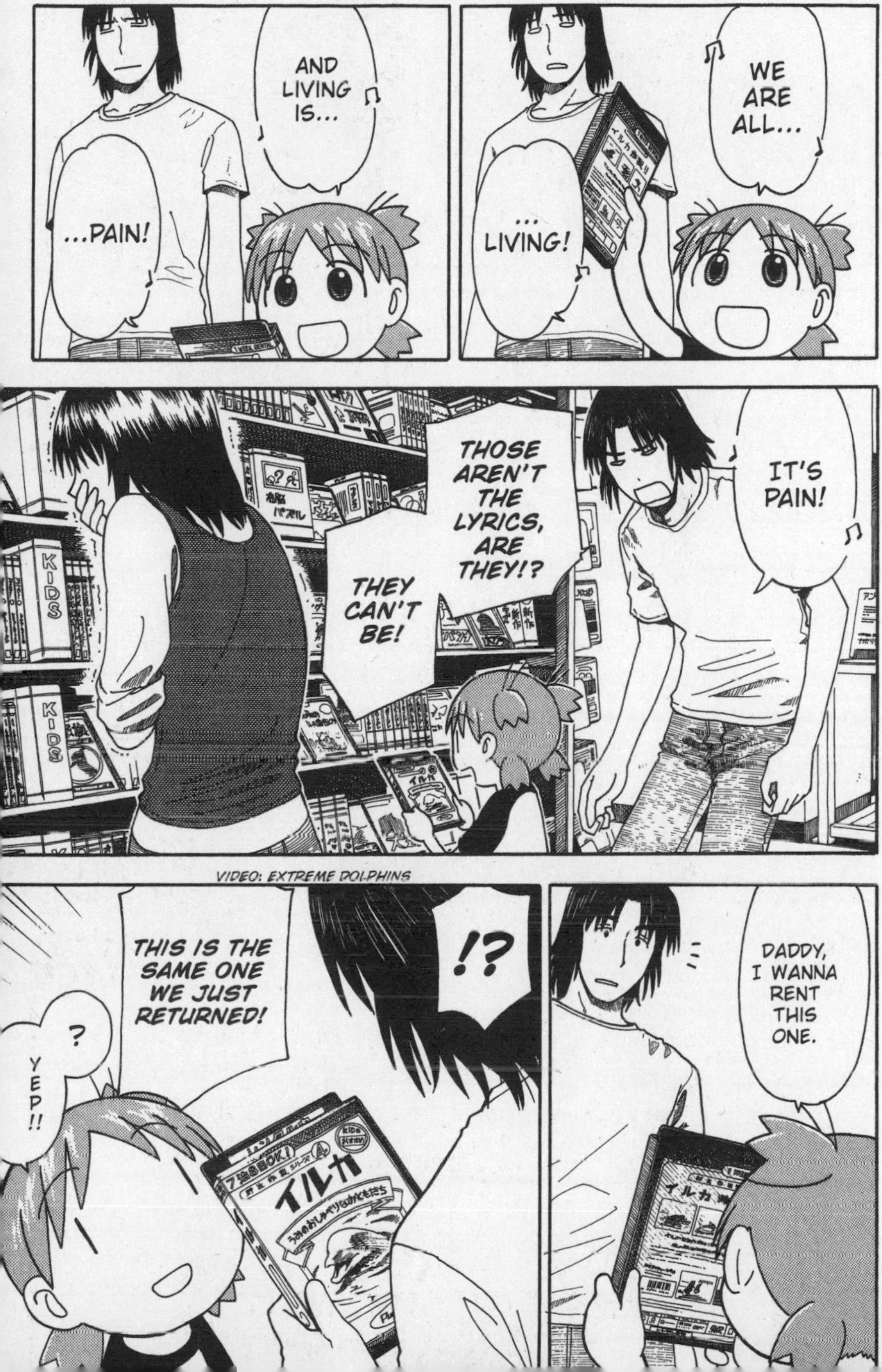
WE ARE ALL...
... LIVING!
AND LIVING IS...
...PAIN!
IT'S PAIN!
THOSE AREN'T THE LYRICS, ARE THEY!?
THEY CAN'T BE!
VIDEO: EXTREME DOLPHINS
DADDY, I WANNA RENT THIS ONE.
!?
THIS IS THE SAME ONE WE JUST RETURNED!
?
YEP!!

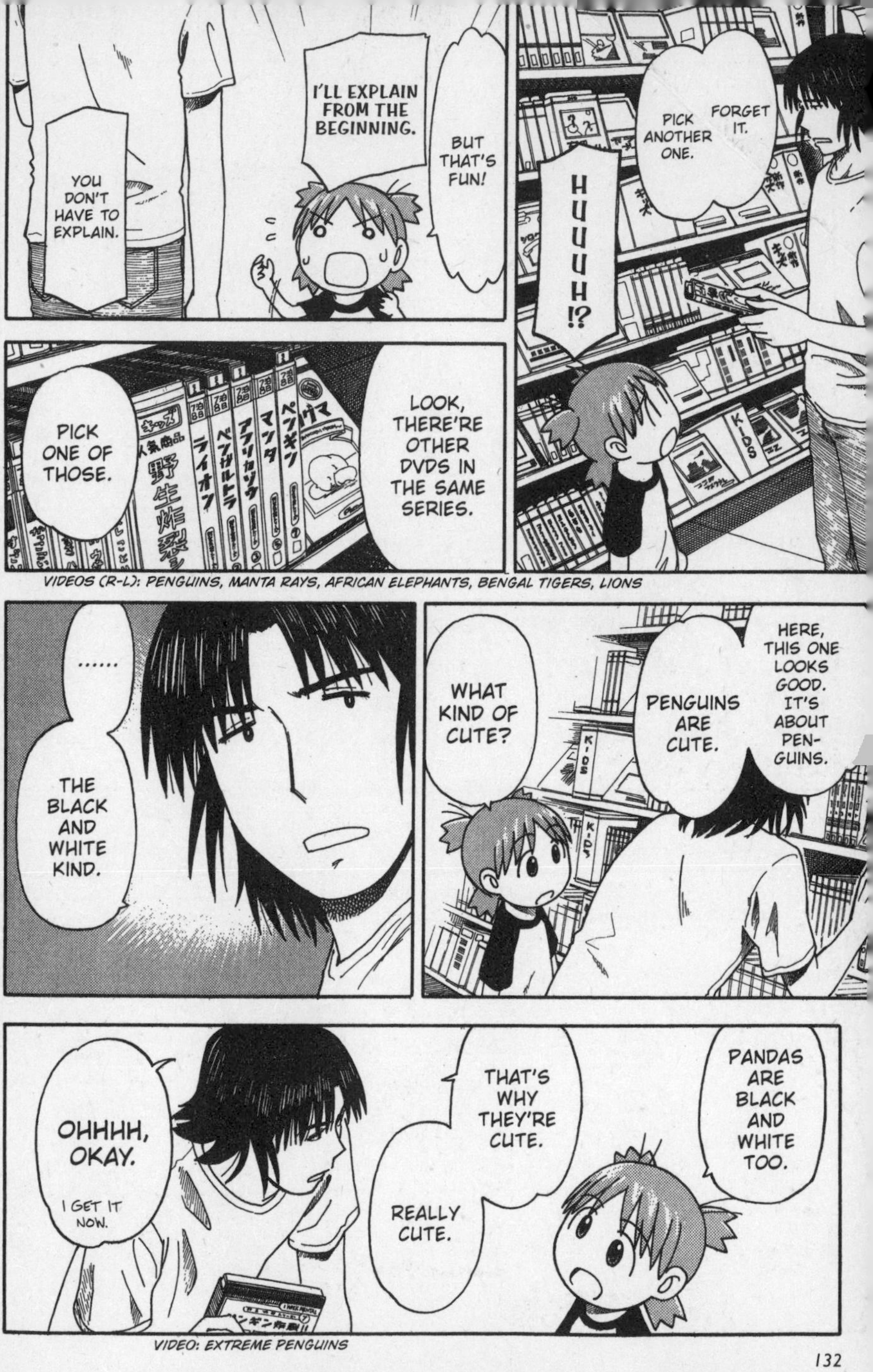
FORGET IT. PICK ANOTHER ONE.
HUUUUH!?
BUT THAT'S FUN!
I'LL EXPLAIN FROM THE BEGINNING.
YOU DON'T HAVE TO EXPLAIN.
LOOK, THERE'RE OTHER DVDS IN THE SAME SERIES.
PICK ONE OF THOSE.
KIDS
HERE, THIS ONE LOOKS GOOD. IT'S ABOUT PEN-GUINS.
PENGUINS ARE CUTE.
WHAT KIND OF CUTE?
......
THE BLACK AND WHITE KIND.
PANDAS ARE BLACK AND WHITE TOO.
THAT'S WHY THEY'RE CUTE.
REALLY CUTE.
OHHHH, OKAY.
I GET IT NOW.

VIDEOS (R-L): PENGUINS, MANTA RAYS, AFRICAN ELEPHANTS, BENGAL TIGERS, LIONS

VIDEO: EXTREME PENGUINS

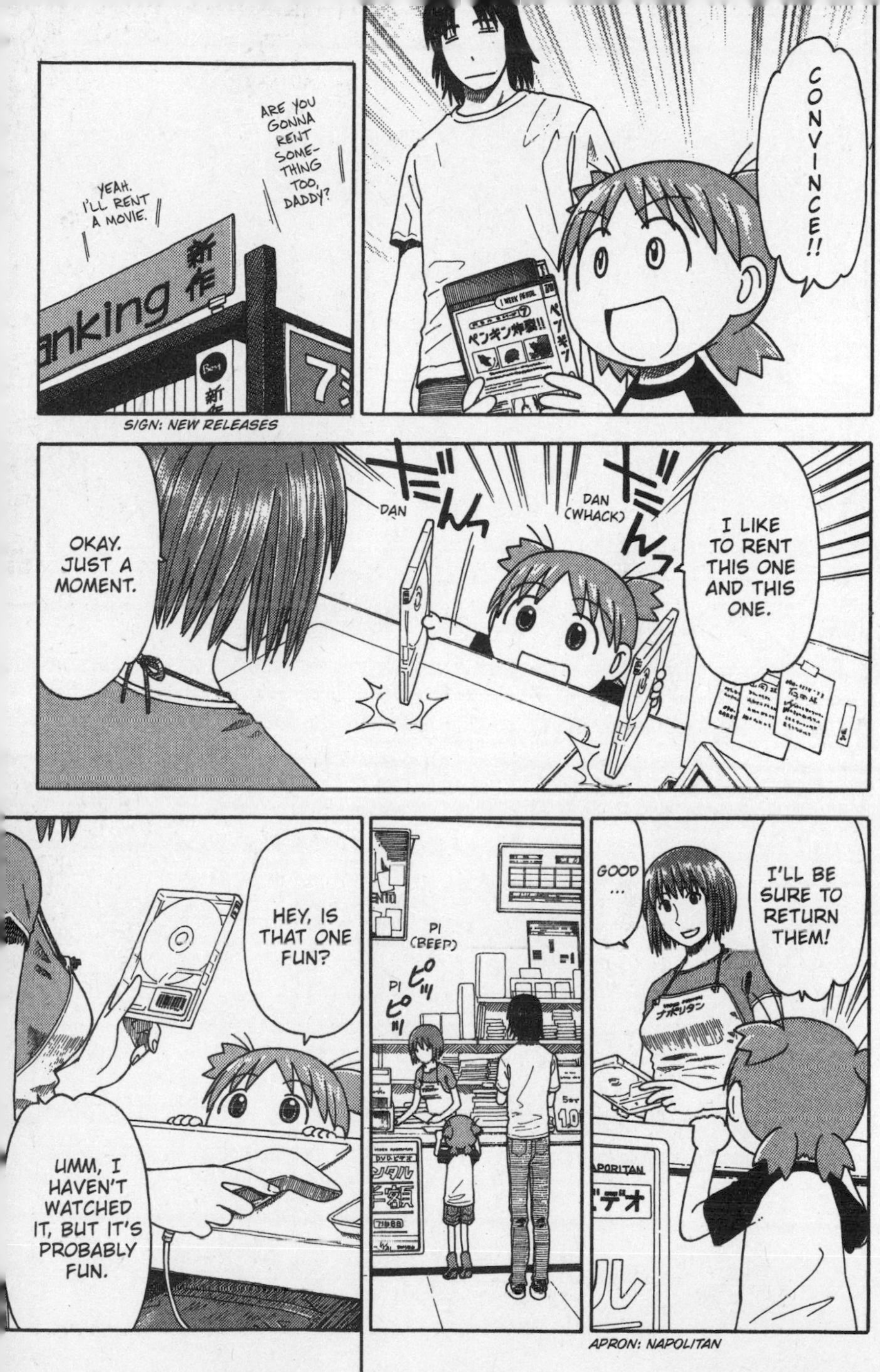
CONVINCE!!
ARE YOU GONNA RENT SOMETHING TOO, DADDY?
YEAH. I'LL RENT A MOVIE.
anking
新作
I LIKE TO RENT THIS ONE AND THIS ONE.
DAN (WHACK)
DAN
OKAY. JUST A MOMENT.
I'LL BE SURE TO RETURN THEM!
GOOD ...
PI (BEEP)
PI
NAPOLITAN
HEY, IS THAT ONE FUN?
UMM, I HAVEN'T WATCHED IT, BUT IT'S PROBABLY FUN.

SIGN: NEW RELEASES

APRON: NAPOLITAN

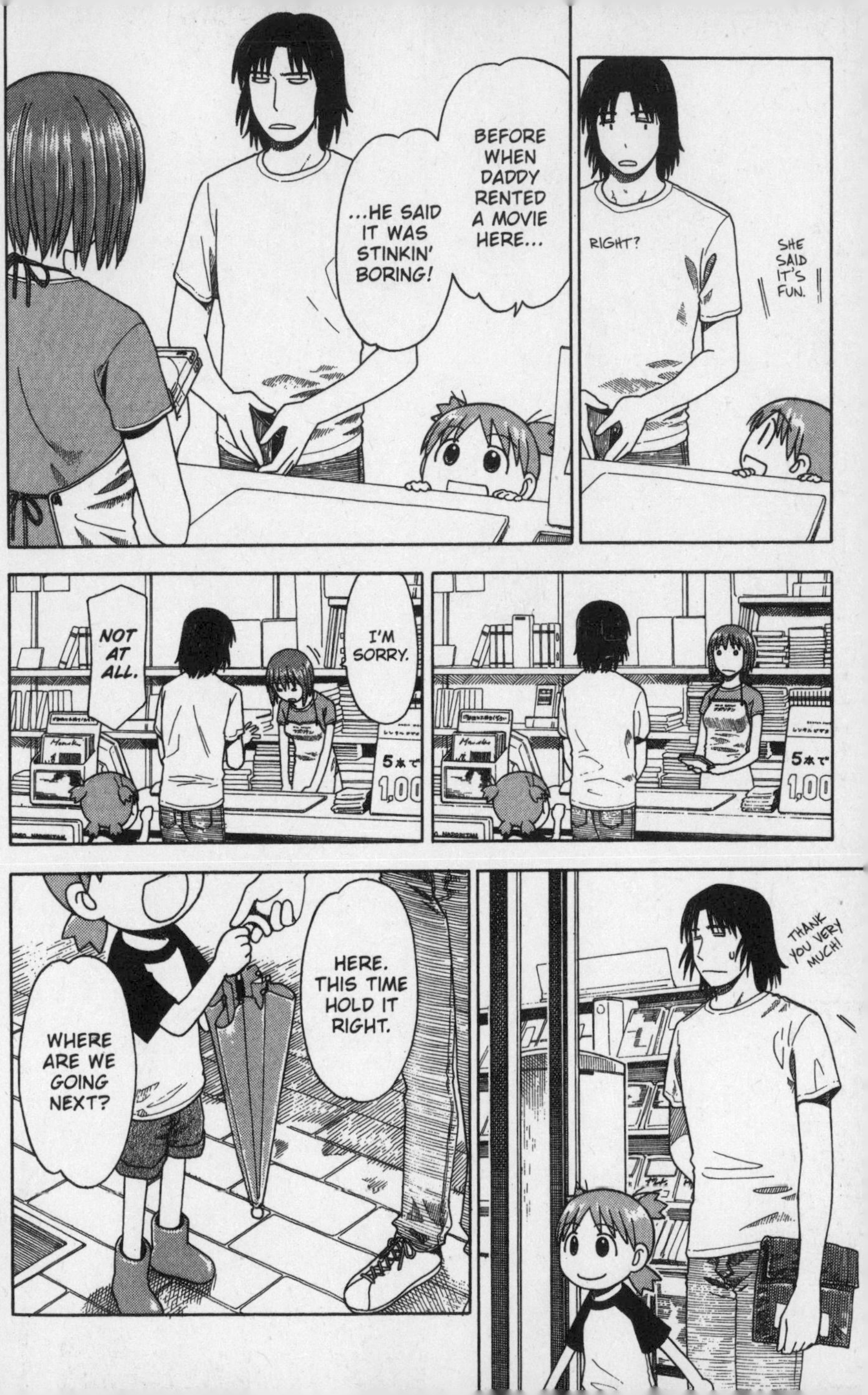
RIGHT?
SHE SAID IT'S FUN.
BEFORE WHEN DADDY RENTED A MOVIE HERE...
...HE SAID IT WAS STINKIN' BORING!
I'M SORRY.
NOT AT ALL.
THANK YOU VERY MUCH!
HERE. THIS TIME HOLD IT RIGHT.
WHERE ARE WE GOING NEXT?

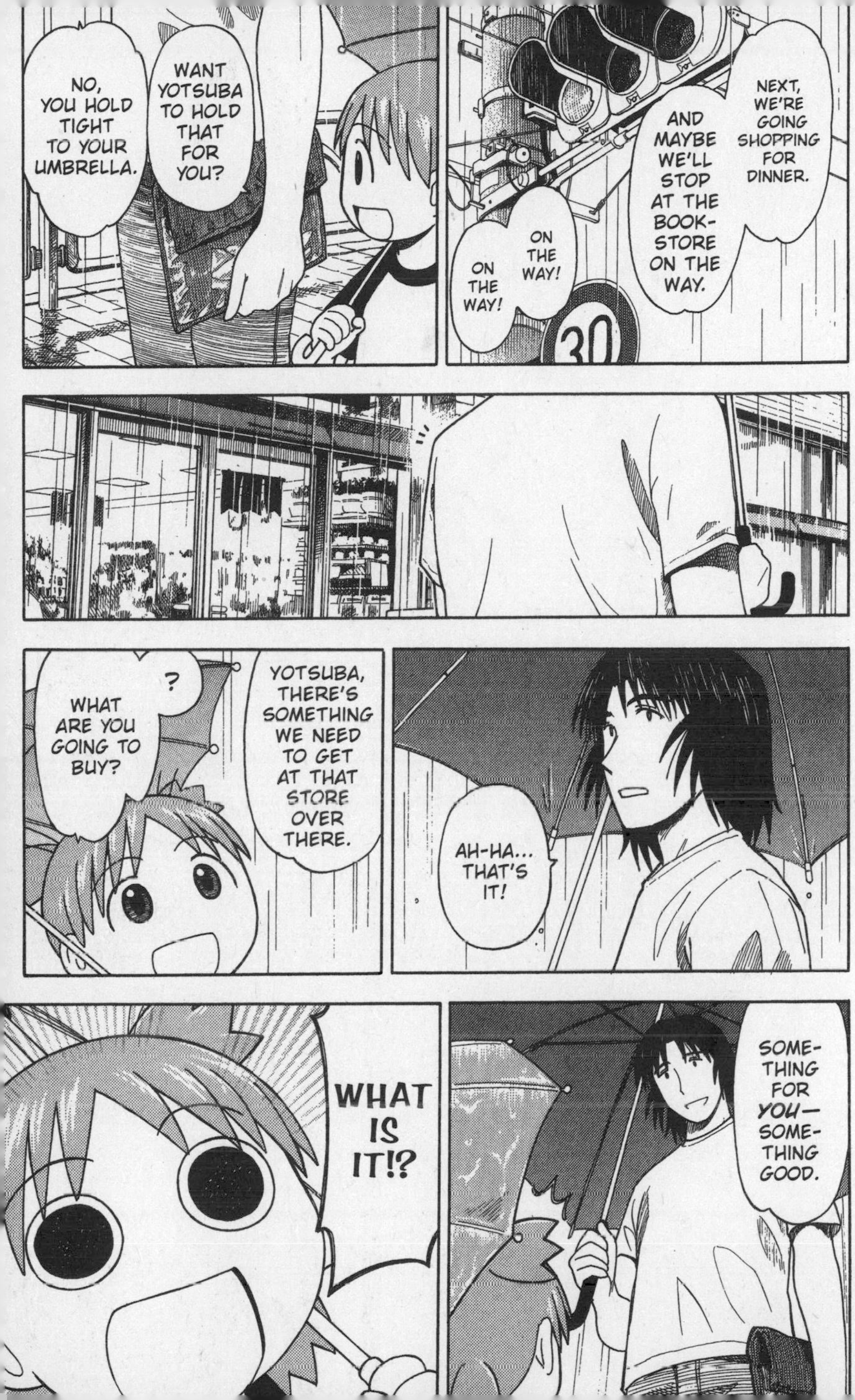
NEXT, WE'RE GOING SHOPPING FOR DINNER.
AND MAYBE WE'LL STOP AT THE BOOKSTORE ON THE WAY.
ON THE WAY!
ON THE WAY!
30
WANT YOTSUBA TO HOLD THAT FOR YOU?
NO, YOU HOLD TIGHT TO YOUR UMBRELLA.
AH-HA... THAT'S IT!
YOTSUBA, THERE'S SOMETHING WE NEED TO GET AT THAT STORE OVER THERE.
?
WHAT ARE YOU GOING TO BUY?
SOMETHING FOR *YOU*—SOMETHING GOOD.
WHAT IS IT!?

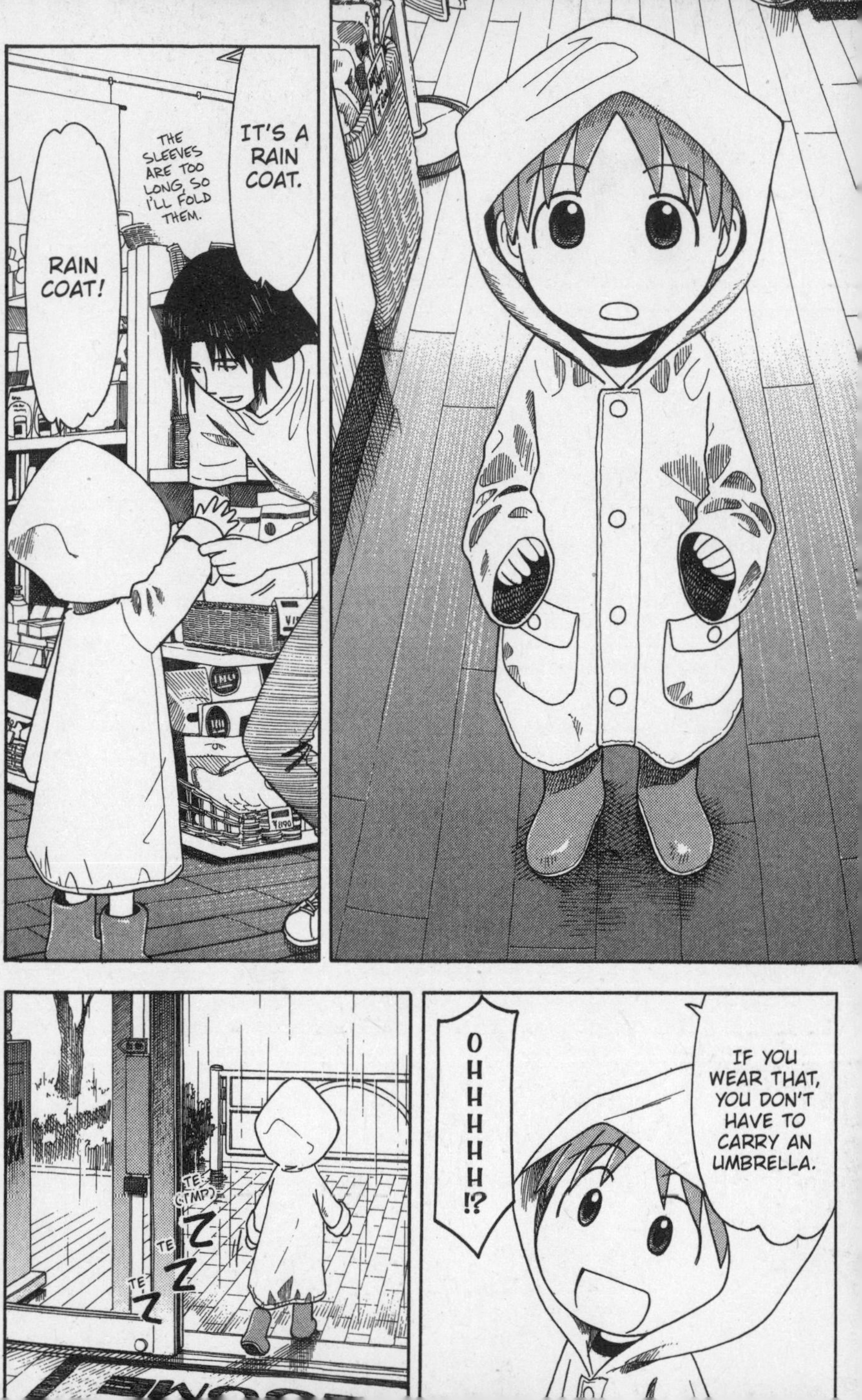
IT'S A RAIN COAT.
THE SLEEVES ARE TOO LONG, SO I'LL FOLD THEM.
RAIN COAT!
IF YOU WEAR THAT, YOU DON'T HAVE TO CARRY AN UMBRELLA.
OHHHHHH!?
TE (TMP)
TE
TE

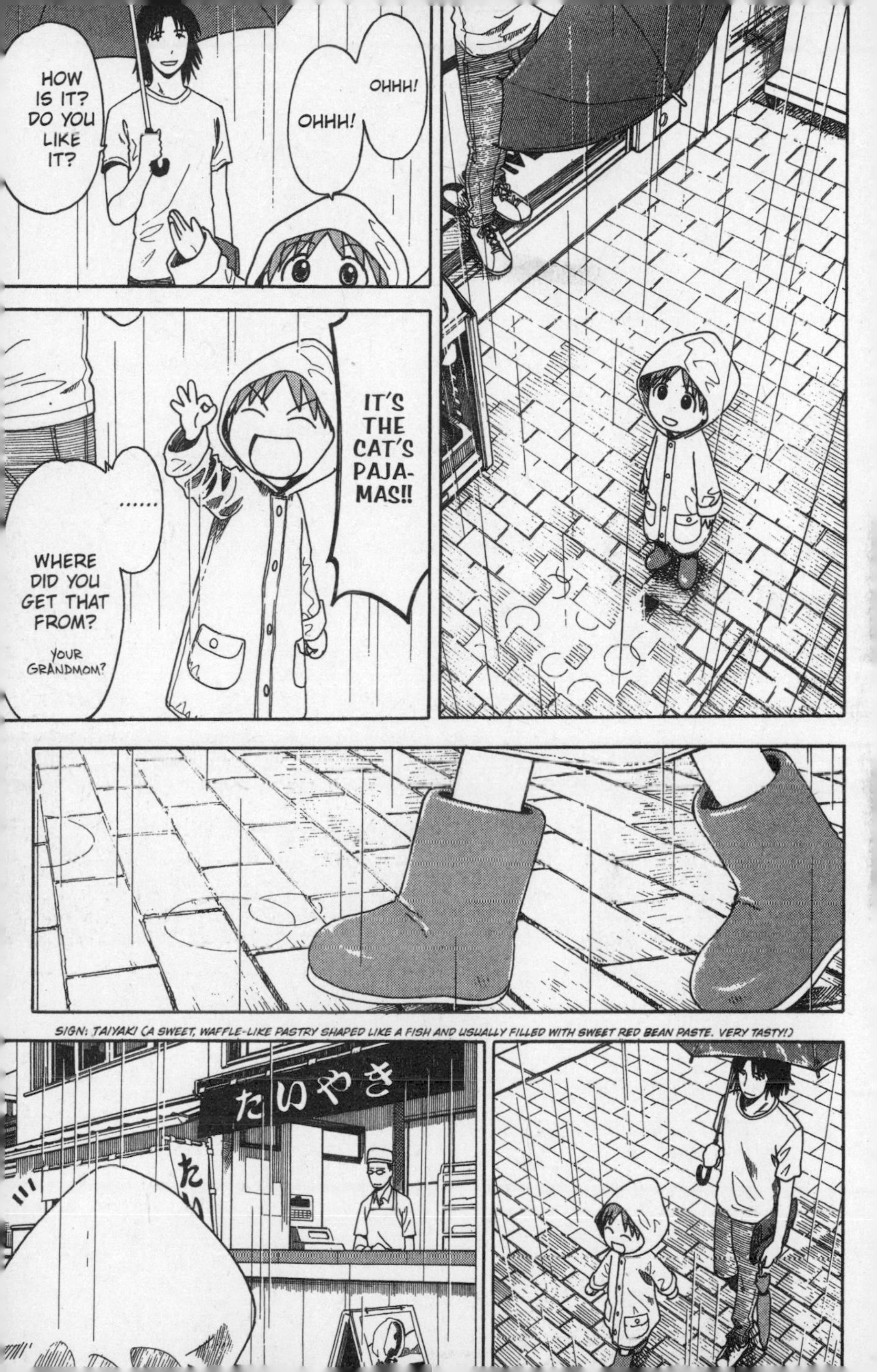
OHHH!
OHHH!
HOW IS IT? DO YOU LIKE IT?
IT'S THE CAT'S PAJAMAS!!
......
WHERE DID YOU GET THAT FROM?
YOUR GRANDMOM?
SIGN: TAIYAKI (A SWEET, WAFFLE-LIKE PASTRY SHAPED LIKE A FISH AND USUALLY FILLED WITH SWEET RED BEAN PASTE. VERY TASTY!)
たいやき
たい

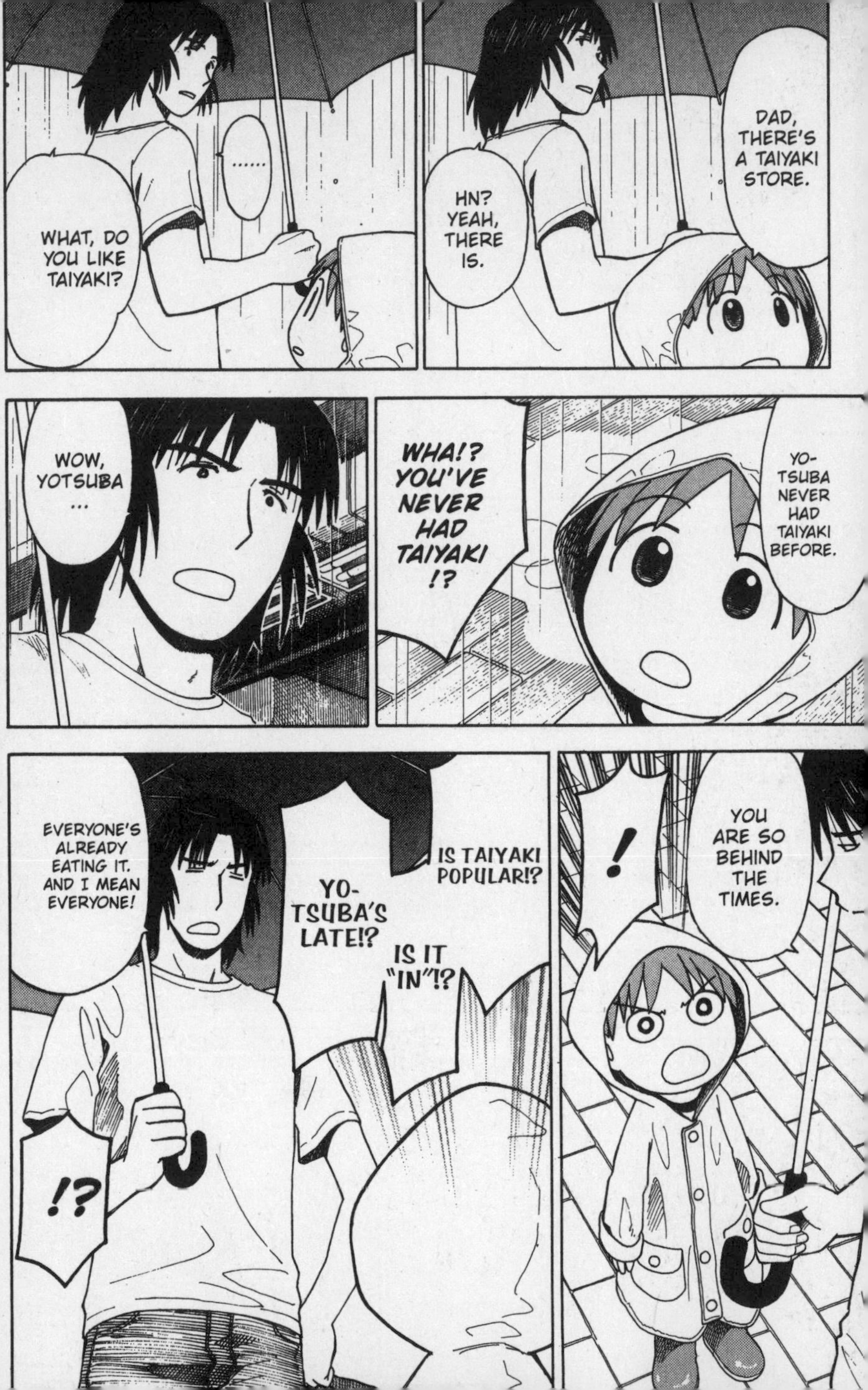
DAD, THERE'S A TAIYAKI STORE.
HN? YEAH, THERE IS.
......
WHAT, DO YOU LIKE TAIYAKI?
YO-TSUBA NEVER HAD TAIYAKI BEFORE.
WHA!? YOU'VE NEVER HAD TAIYAKI !?
WOW, YOTSUBA ...
YOU ARE SO BEHIND THE TIMES.
!
IS TAIYAKI POPULAR!?
YO-TSUBA'S LATE!?
IS IT "IN"!?
EVERYONE'S ALREADY EATING IT. AND I MEAN EVERYONE!
!?

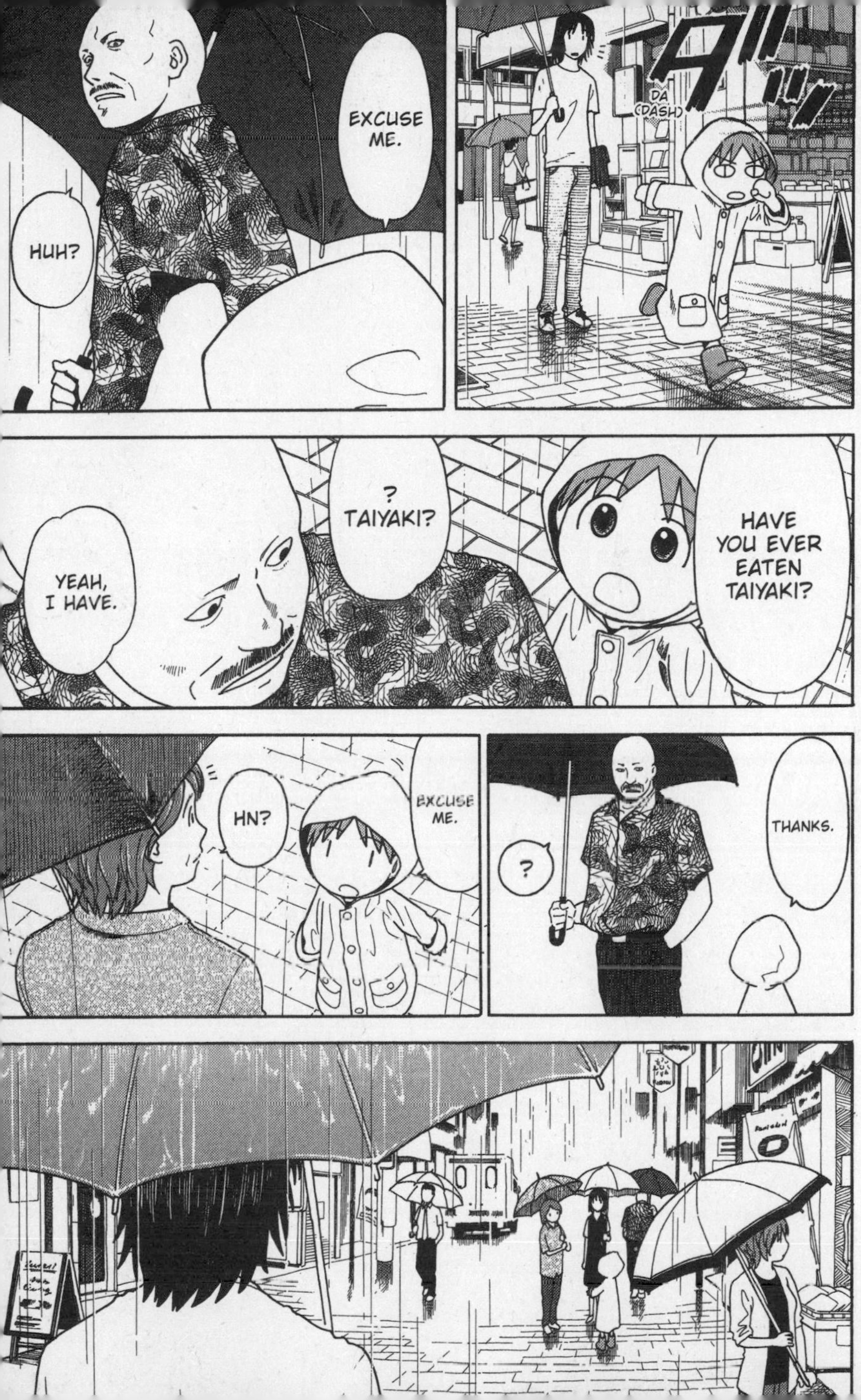

ダッ
DA (DASH)
EXCUSE ME.
HUH?
HAVE YOU EVER EATEN TAIYAKI?
? TAIYAKI?
YEAH, I HAVE.
THANKS.
?
EXCUSE ME.
HN?

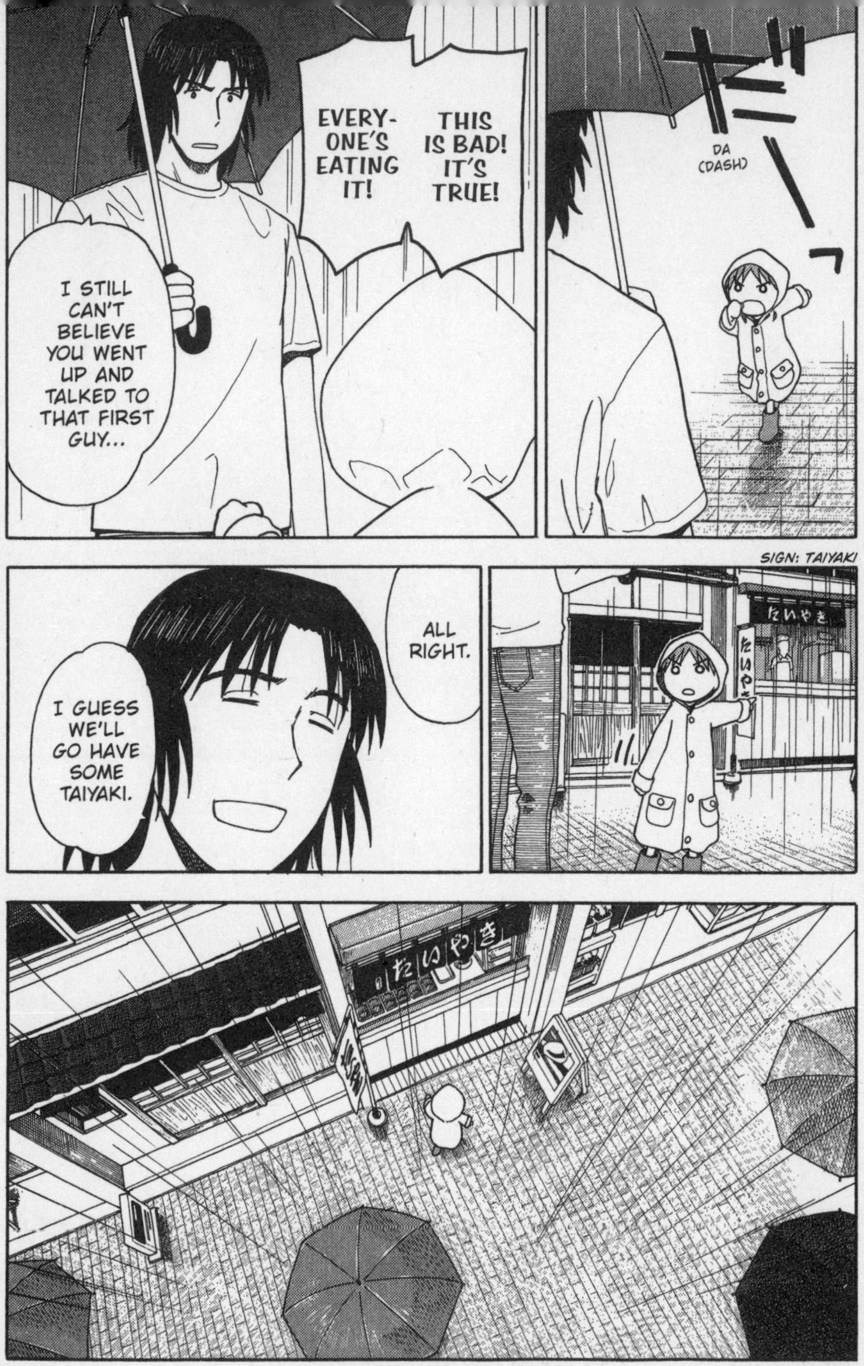
DA
(DASH)
THIS IS BAD! IT'S TRUE!
EVERY-ONE'S EATING IT!
I STILL CAN'T BELIEVE YOU WENT UP AND TALKED TO THAT FIRST GUY...
SIGN: TAIYAKI
たいやき
ALL RIGHT.
I GUESS WE'LL GO HAVE SOME TAIYAKI.
たいやき

YOTSUBA&!

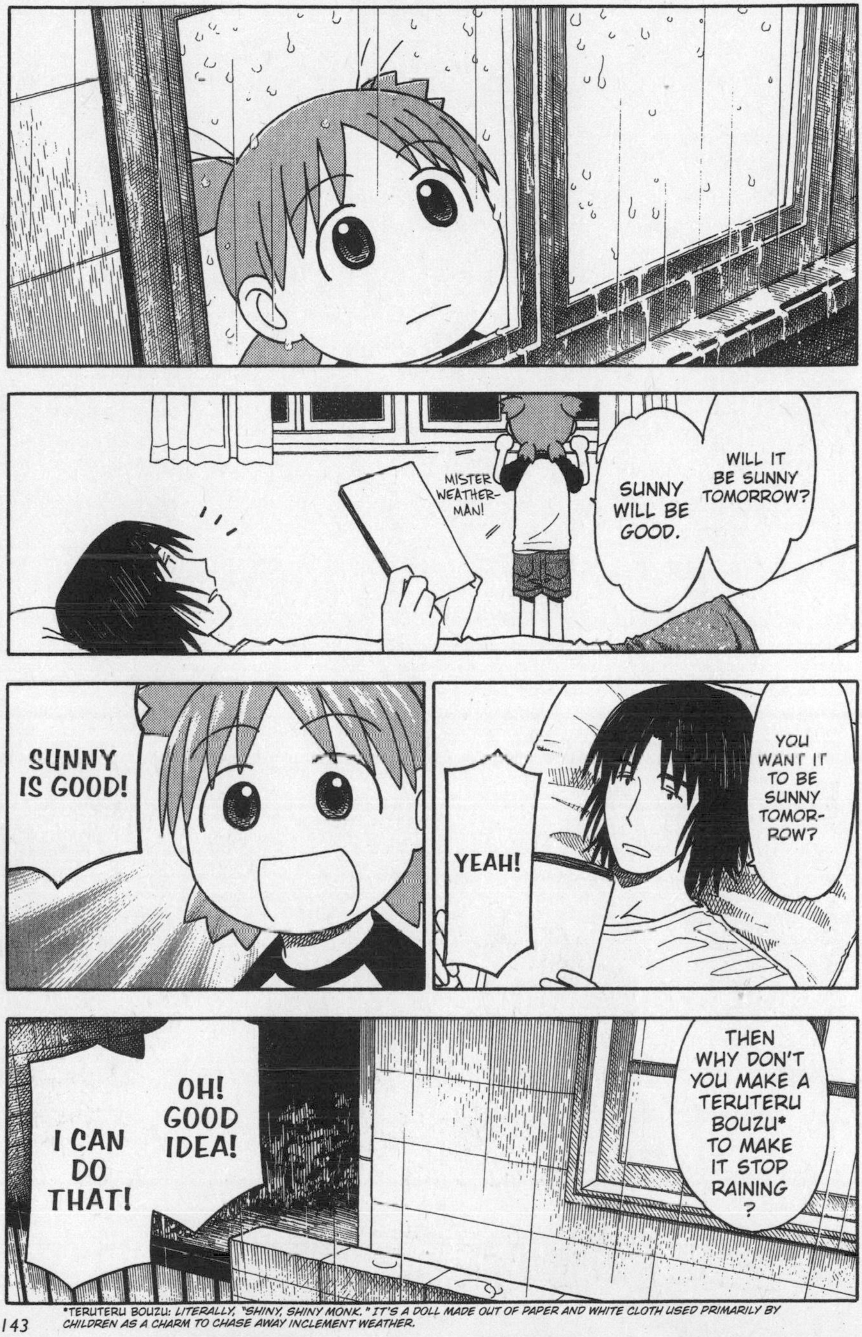
WILL IT BE SUNNY TOMORROW?
SUNNY WILL BE GOOD.
MISTER WEATHER-MAN!
YOU WANT IT TO BE SUNNY TOMOR-ROW?
YEAH!
SUNNY IS GOOD!
THEN WHY DON'T YOU MAKE A TERUTERU BOUZU* TO MAKE IT STOP RAINING?
OH! GOOD IDEA!
I CAN DO THAT!

*TERUTERU BOUZU: *LITERALLY, "SHINY, SHINY MONK."* IT'S A DOLL MADE OUT OF PAPER AND WHITE CLOTH USED PRIMARILY BY CHILDREN AS A CHARM TO CHASE AWAY INCLEMENT WEATHER.

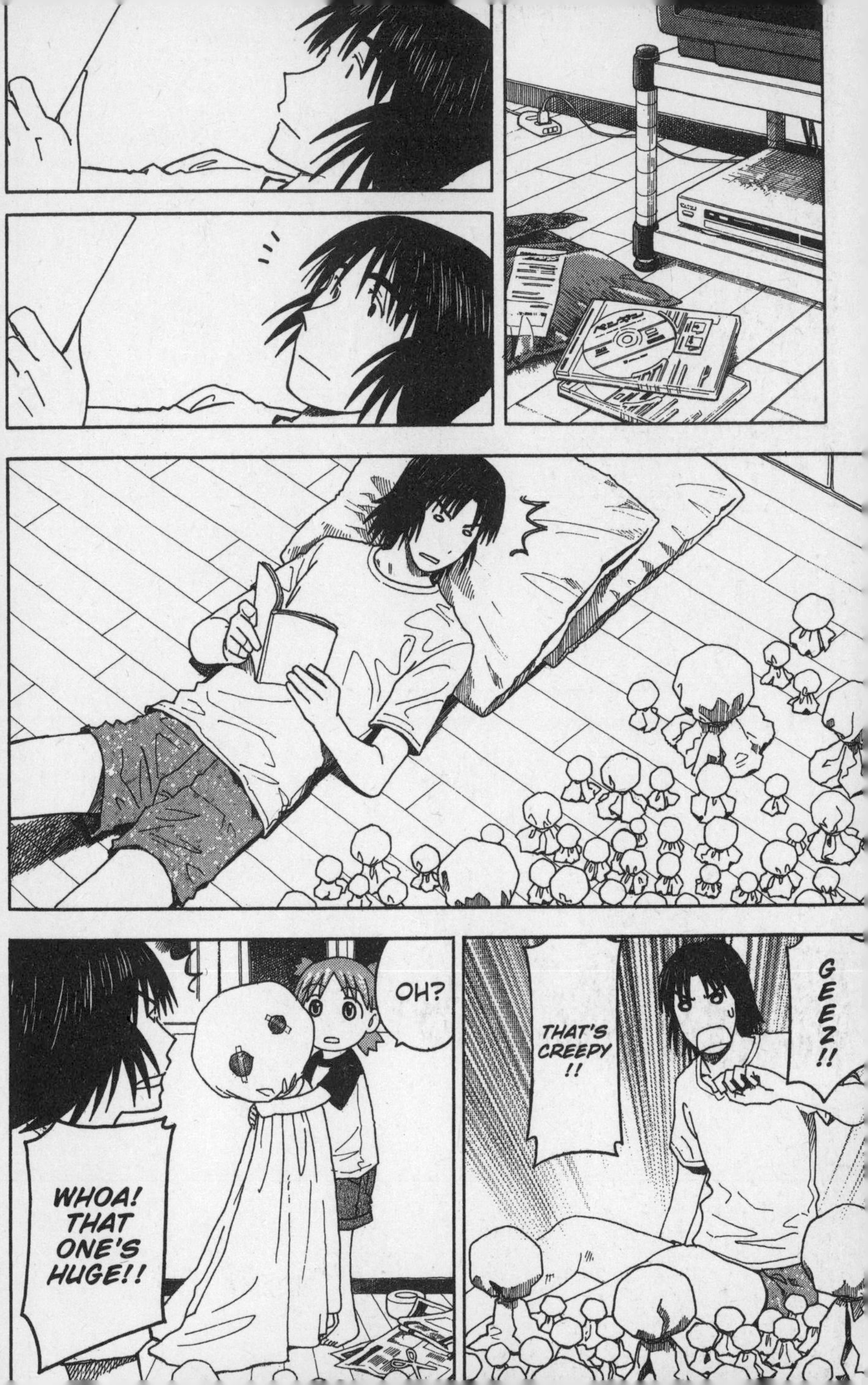
GEEZ!!
THAT'S CREEPY!!
OH?
WHOA! THAT ONE'S HUGE!!

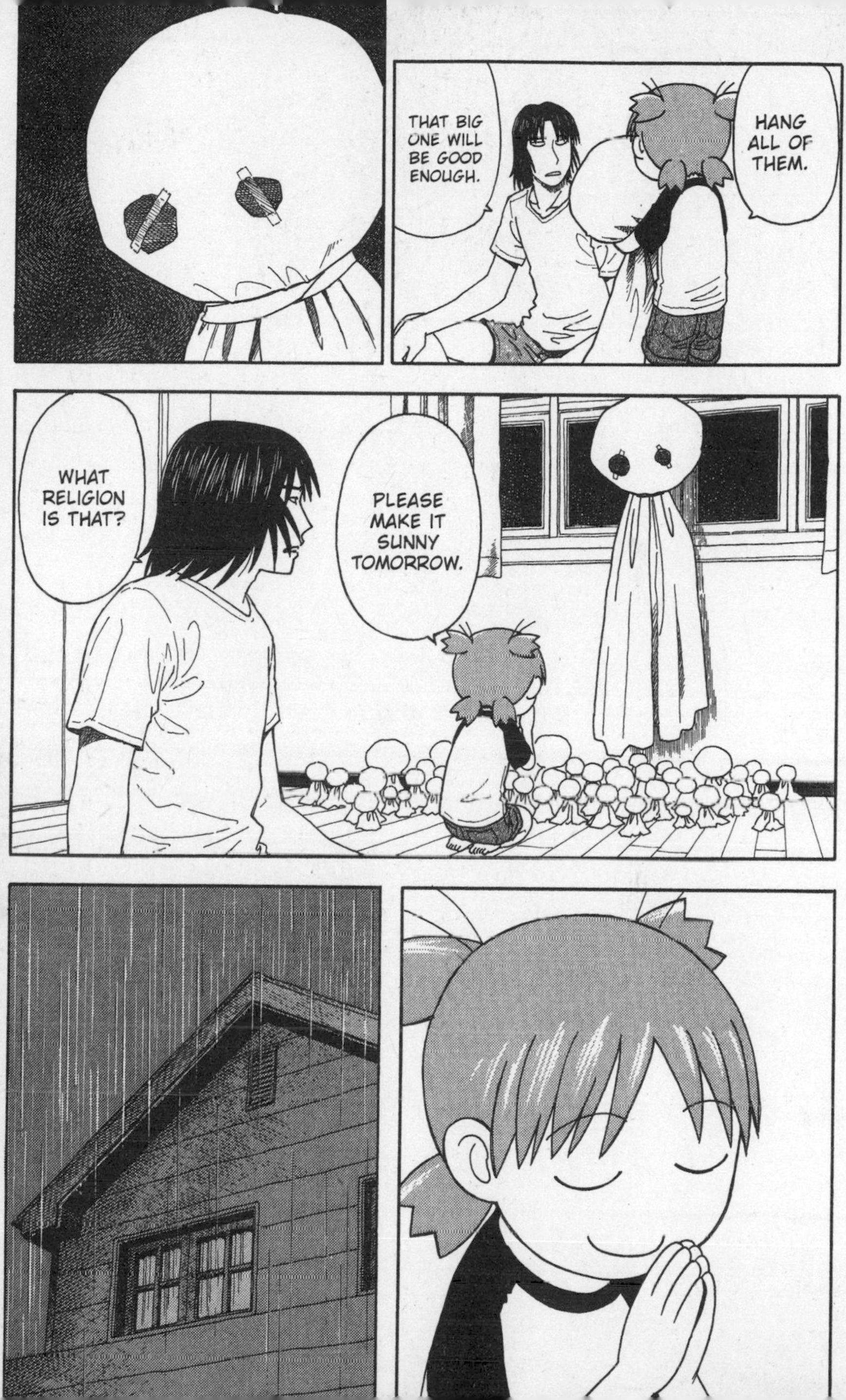
HANG ALL OF THEM.
THAT BIG ONE WILL BE GOOD ENOUGH.
PLEASE MAKE IT SUNNY TOMORROW.
WHAT RELIGION IS THAT?

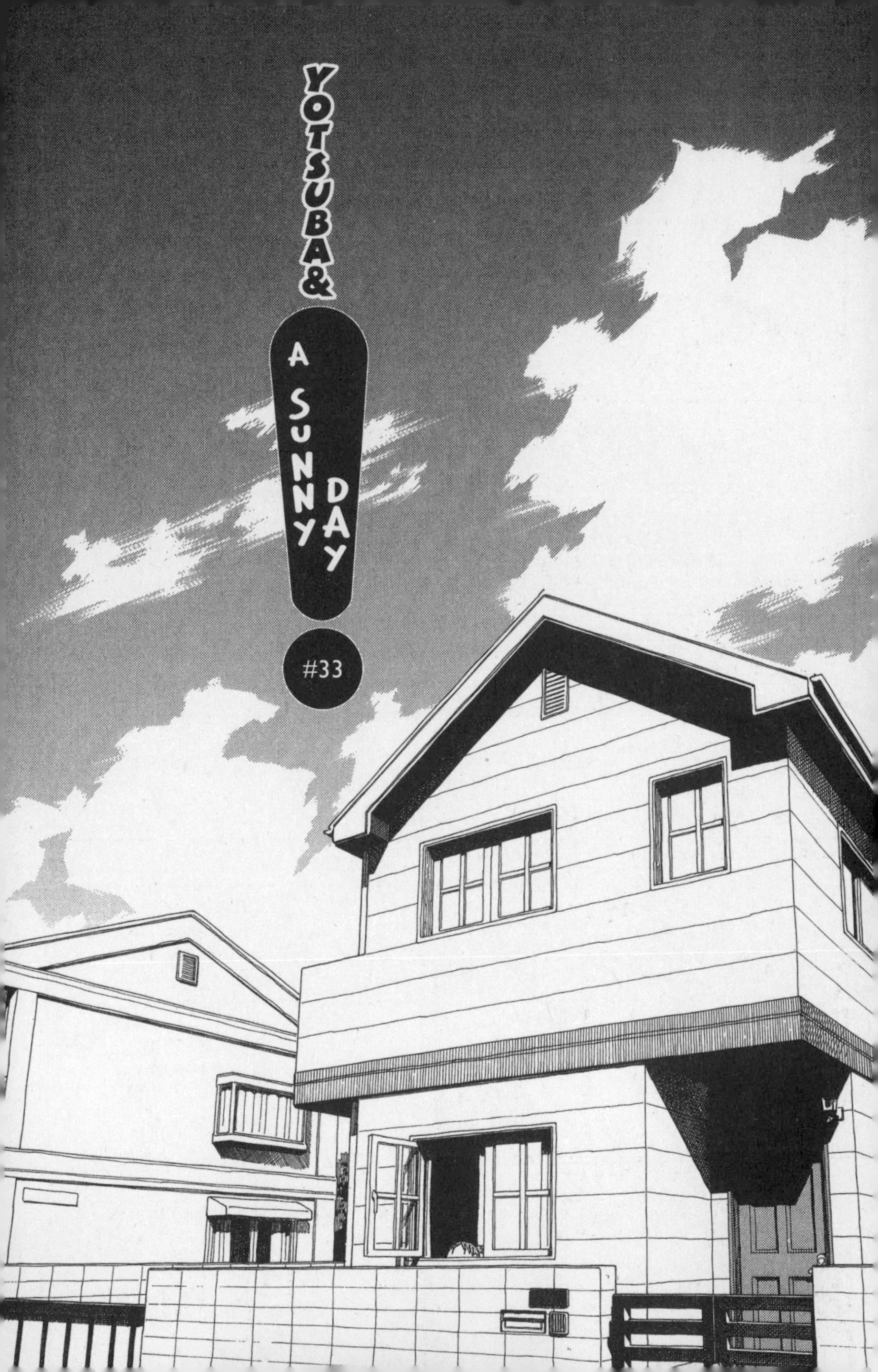
YOTSUBA&!
A SUNNY DAY
#33

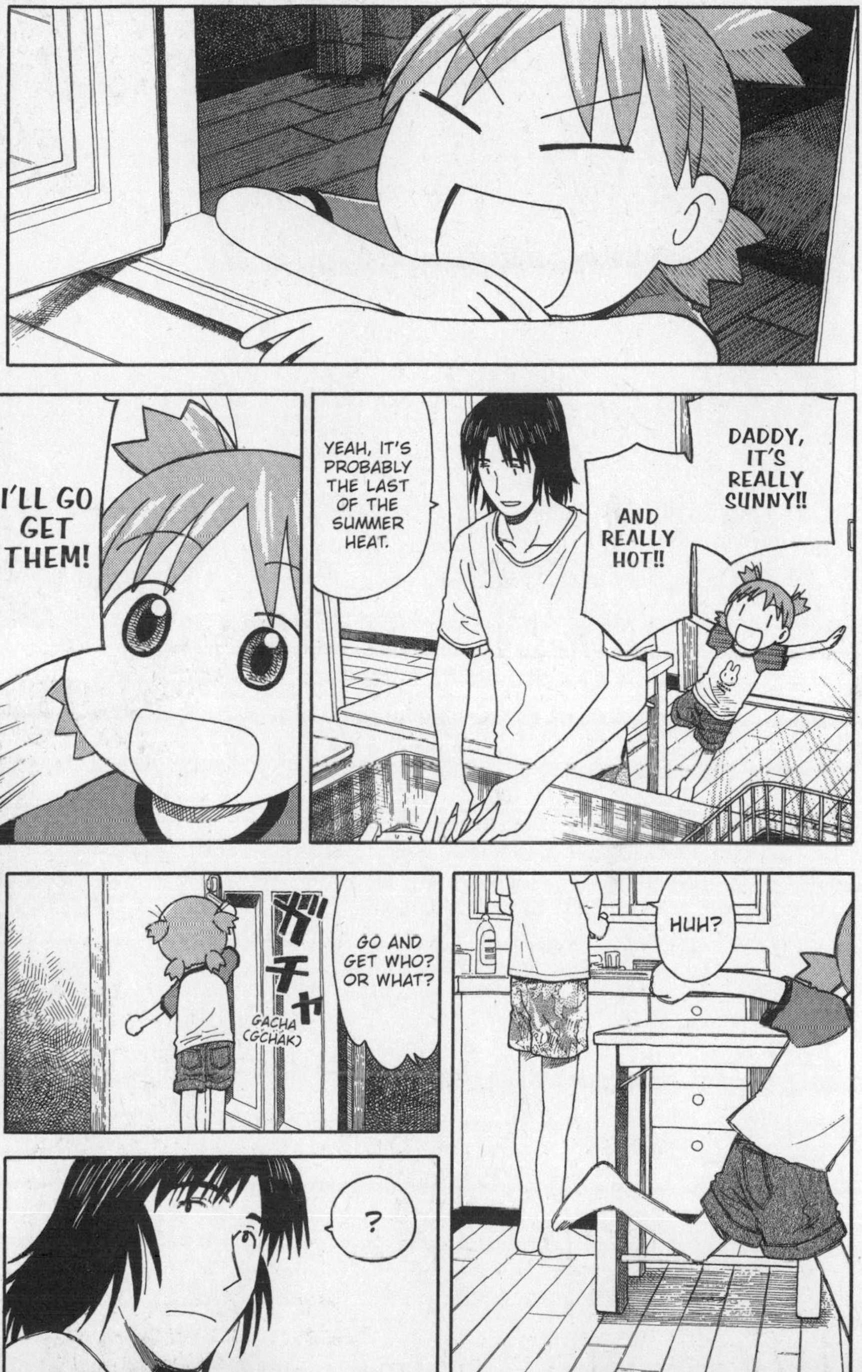
DADDY, IT'S REALLY SUNNY!!
AND REALLY HOT!!
YEAH, IT'S PROBABLY THE LAST OF THE SUMMER HEAT.
I'LL GO GET THEM!
HUH?
GO AND GET WHO? OR WHAT?
ガチャ
GACHA (GCHAK)
?

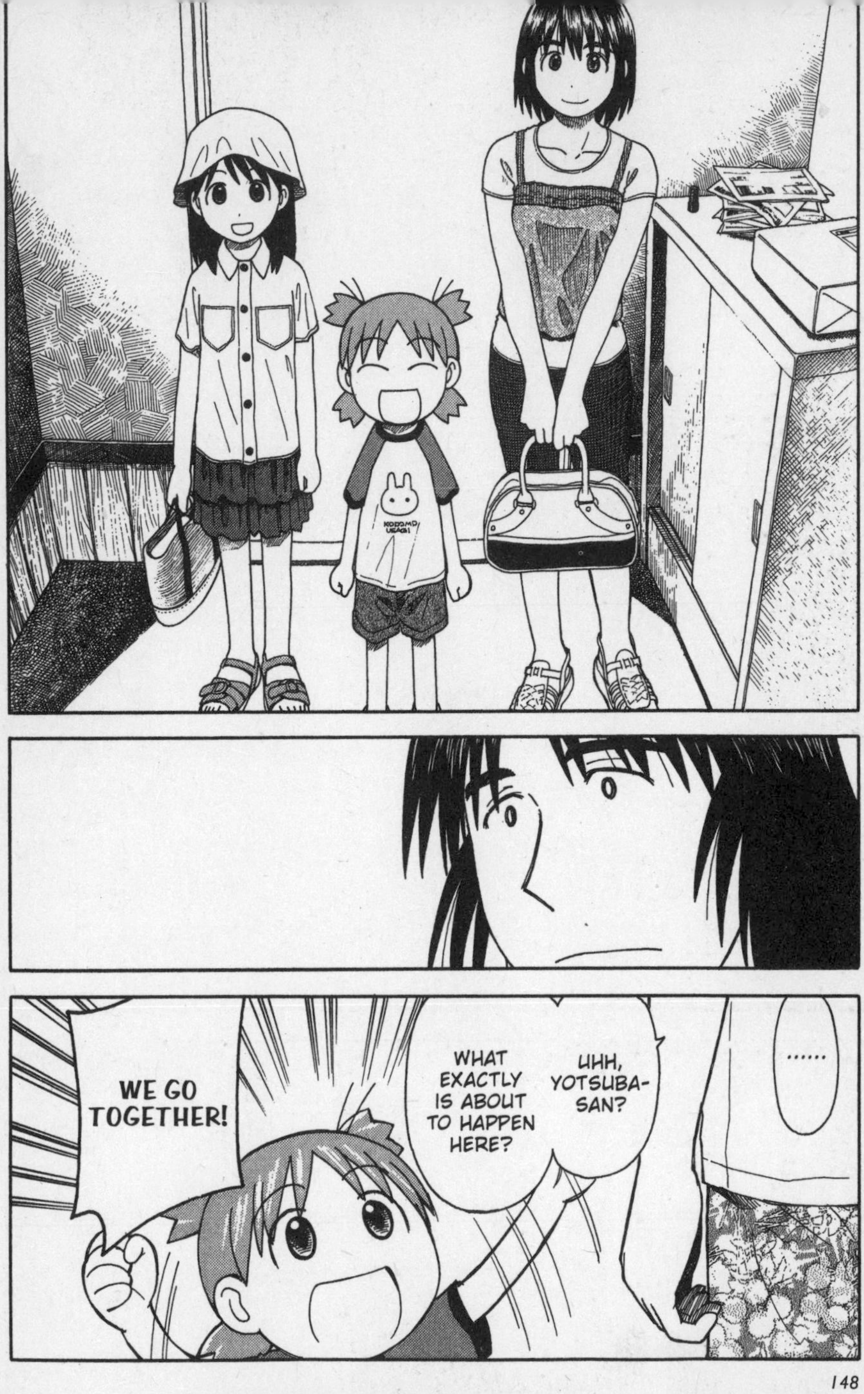
......
UHH, YOTSUBA-SAN?
WHAT EXACTLY IS ABOUT TO HAPPEN HERE?
WE GO TOGETHER!

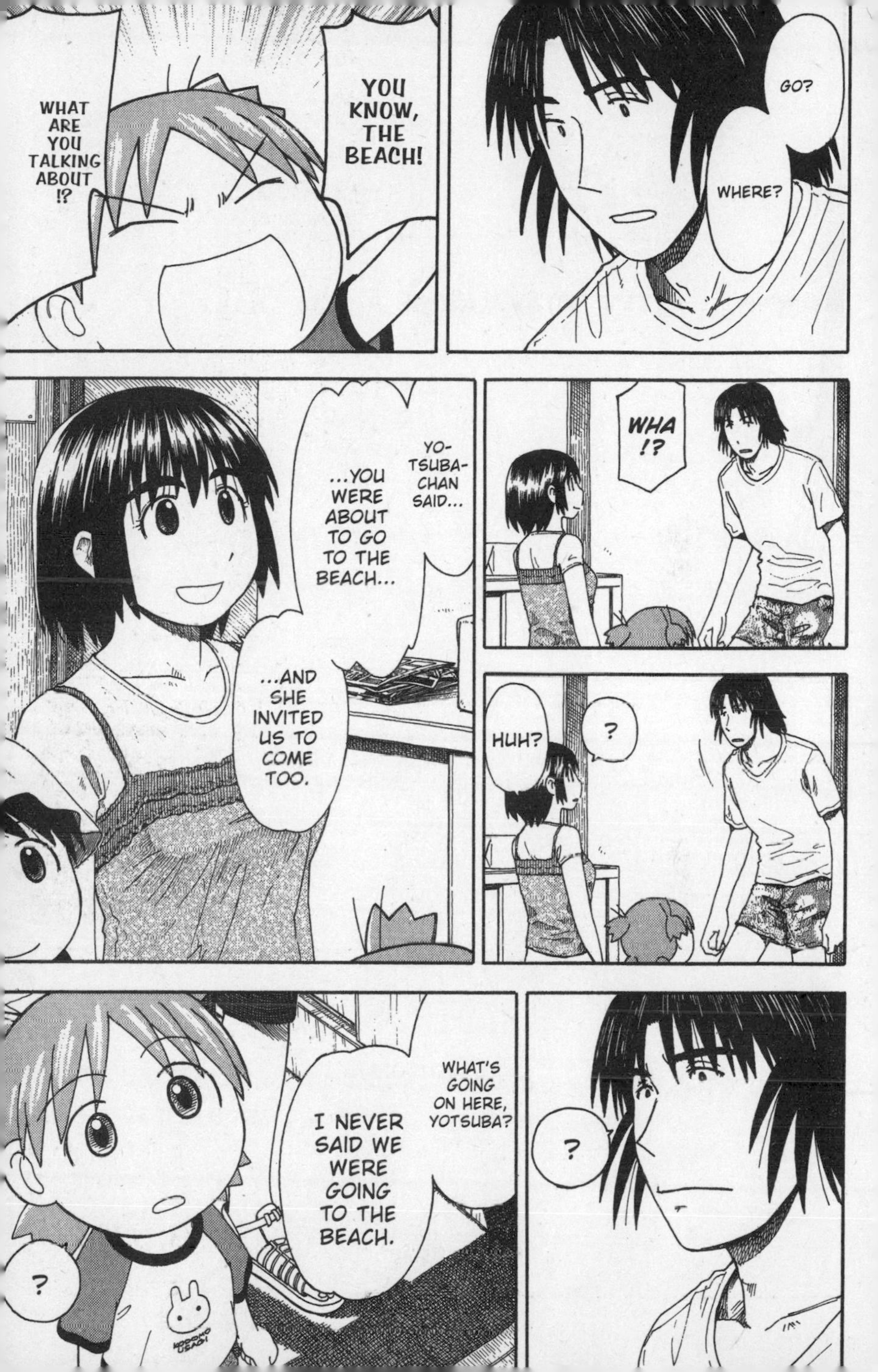
GO?
WHERE?
YOU KNOW, THE BEACH!
WHAT ARE YOU TALKING ABOUT !?
WHA !?
?
HUH?
YO-TSUBA-CHAN SAID...
...YOU WERE ABOUT TO GO TO THE BEACH...
...AND SHE INVITED US TO COME TOO.
?
WHAT'S GOING ON HERE, YOTSUBA?
I NEVER SAID WE WERE GOING TO THE BEACH.
?

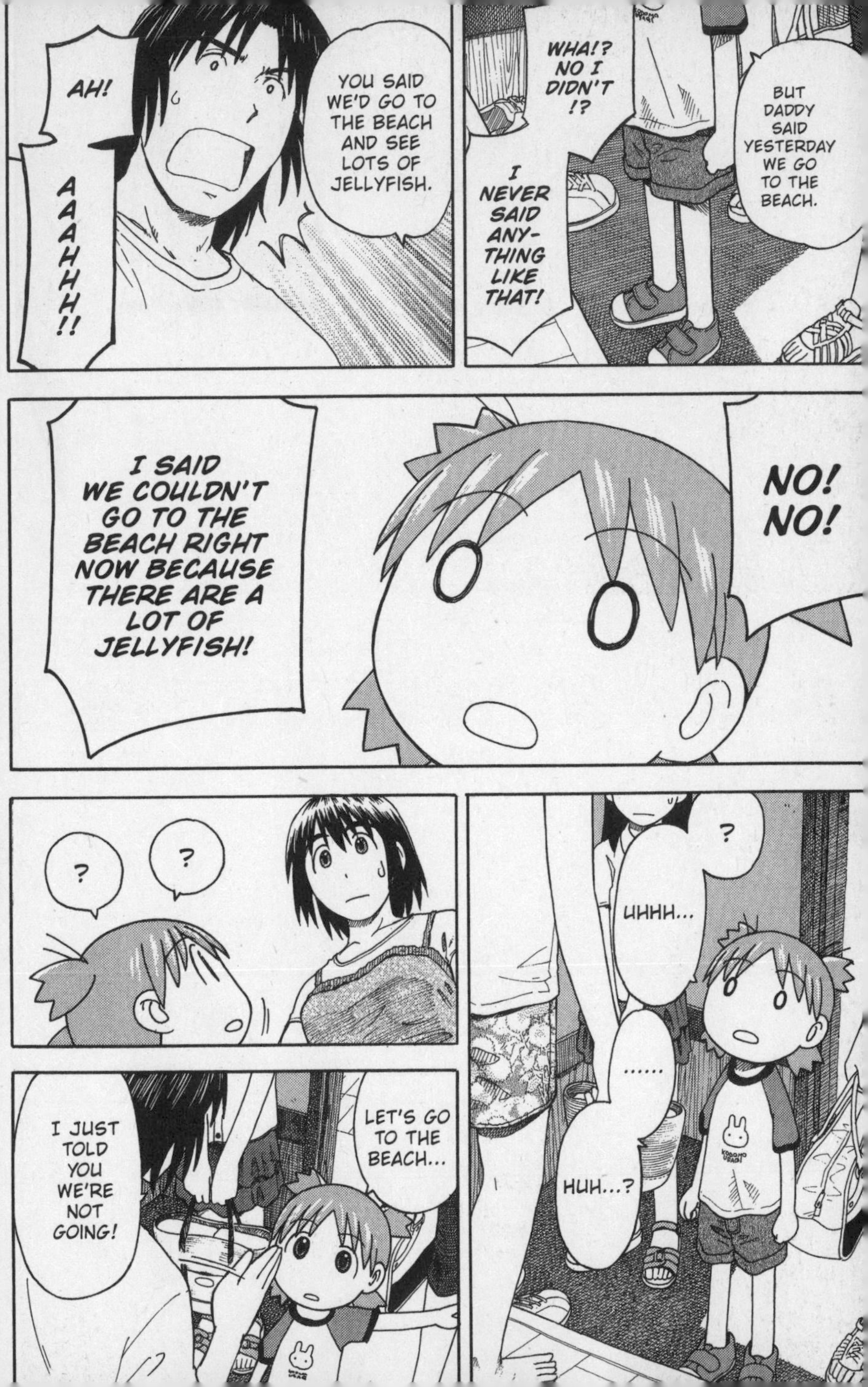
BUT DADDY SAID YESTERDAY WE GO TO THE BEACH.
WHA!? NO I DIDN'T !?
I NEVER SAID ANY-THING LIKE THAT!
YOU SAID WE'D GO TO THE BEACH AND SEE LOTS OF JELLYFISH.
AH!
AAAHHH!!
NO! NO!
I SAID WE COULDN'T GO TO THE BEACH RIGHT NOW BECAUSE THERE ARE A LOT OF JELLYFISH!
?
UHHH...
......
HUH...?
?
?
LET'S GO TO THE BEACH...
I JUST TOLD YOU WE'RE NOT GOING!

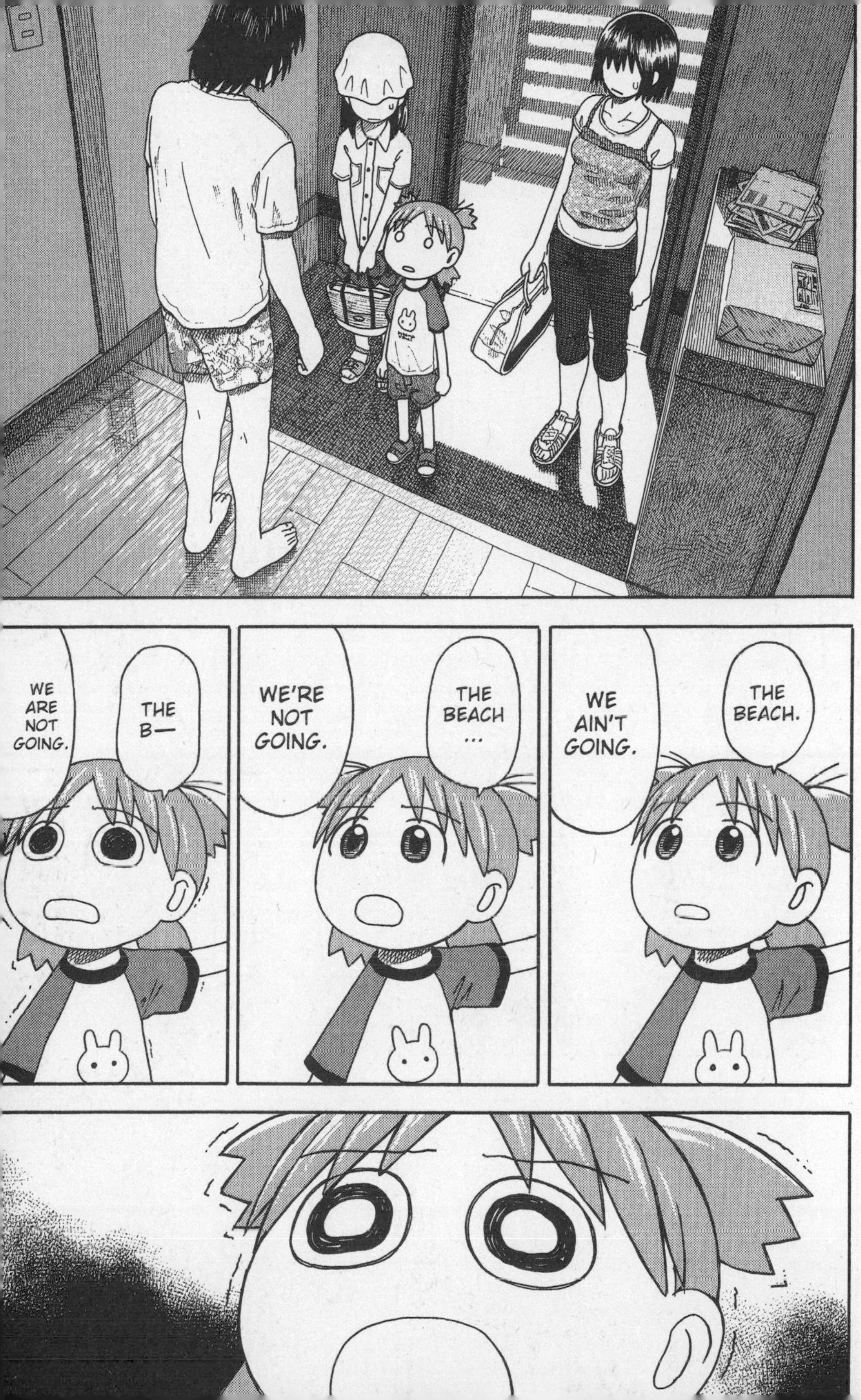
THE BEACH.
WE AIN'T GOING.
THE BEACH ...
WE'RE NOT GOING.
THE B—
WE ARE NOT GOING.

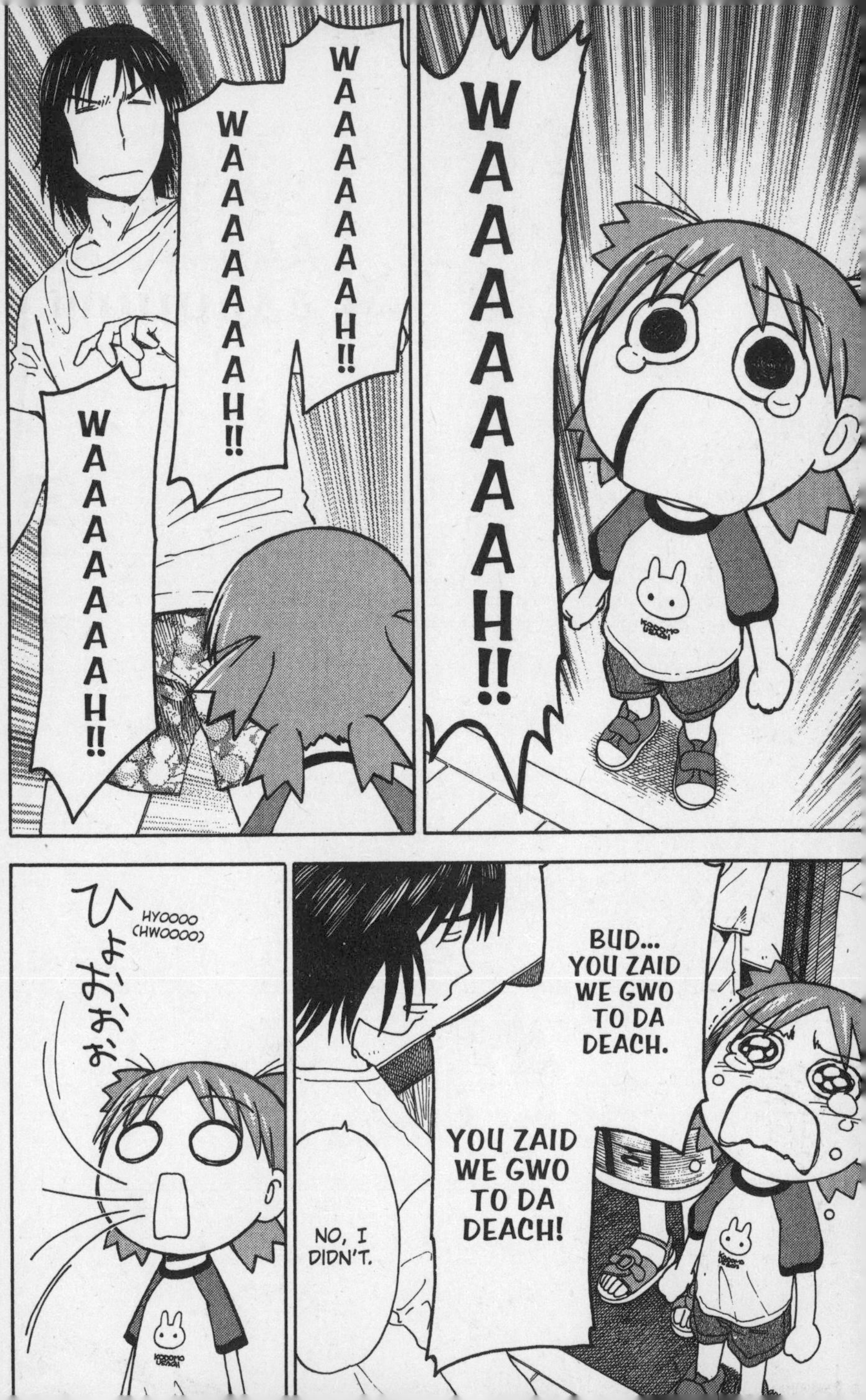
WAAAAAAAH!!
WAAAAAAAH!!
WAAAAAAAH!!
WAAAAAAAH!!
BUD... YOU ZAID WE GWO TO DA DEACH.
YOU ZAID WE GWO TO DA DEACH!
NO, I DIDN'T.
ひょおおお
HYOOOO (HWOOOO)

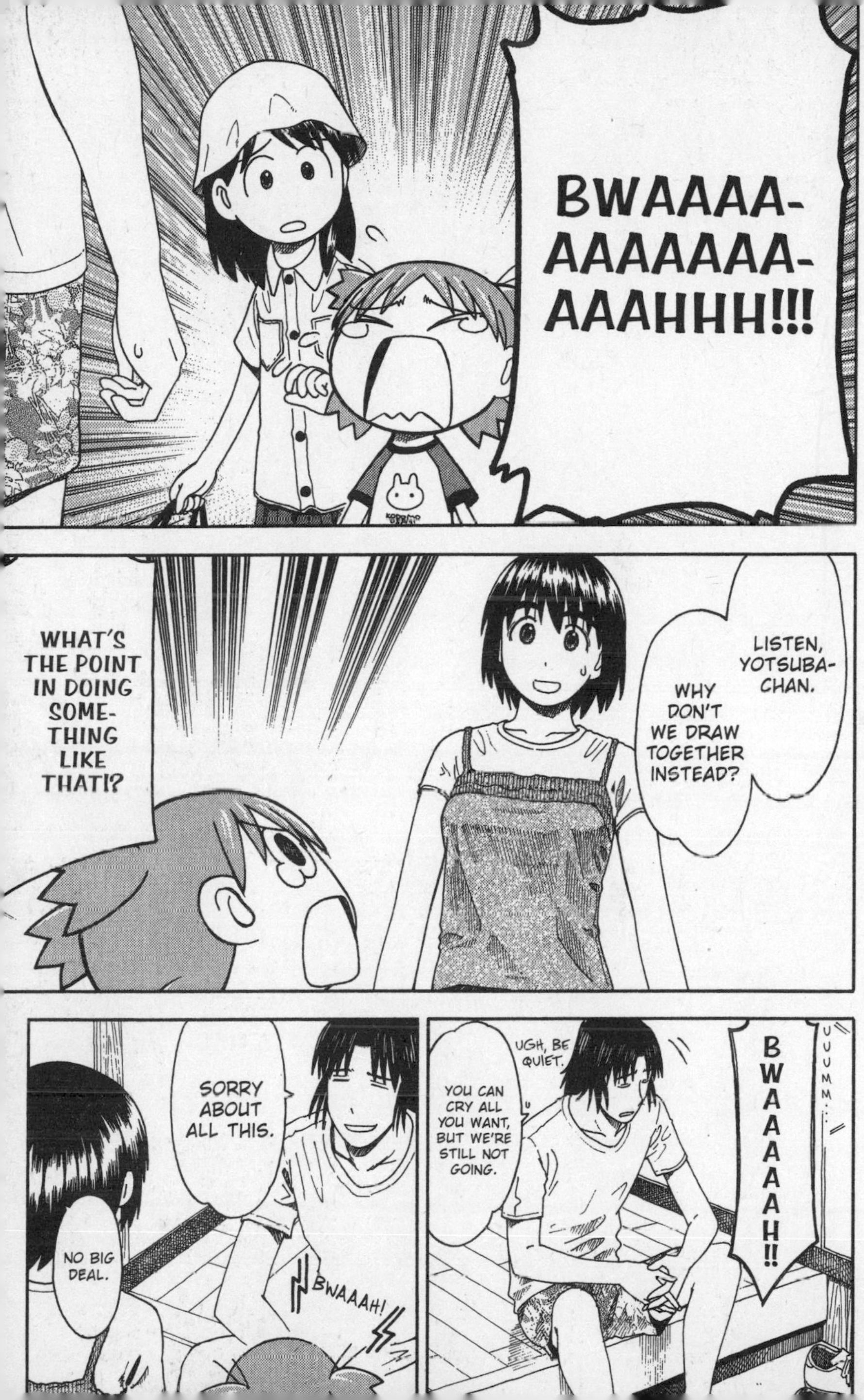
BWAAAA-AAAAAAA-AAAHHH!!!
LISTEN, YOTSUBA-CHAN.
WHY DON'T WE DRAW TOGETHER INSTEAD?
WHAT'S THE POINT IN DOING SOMETHING LIKE THAT!?
BWAAAAAAAH!!
UUUMM...
UGH, BE QUIET.
YOU CAN CRY ALL YOU WANT, BUT WE'RE STILL NOT GOING.
SORRY ABOUT ALL THIS.
BWAAAH!
NO BIG DEAL.

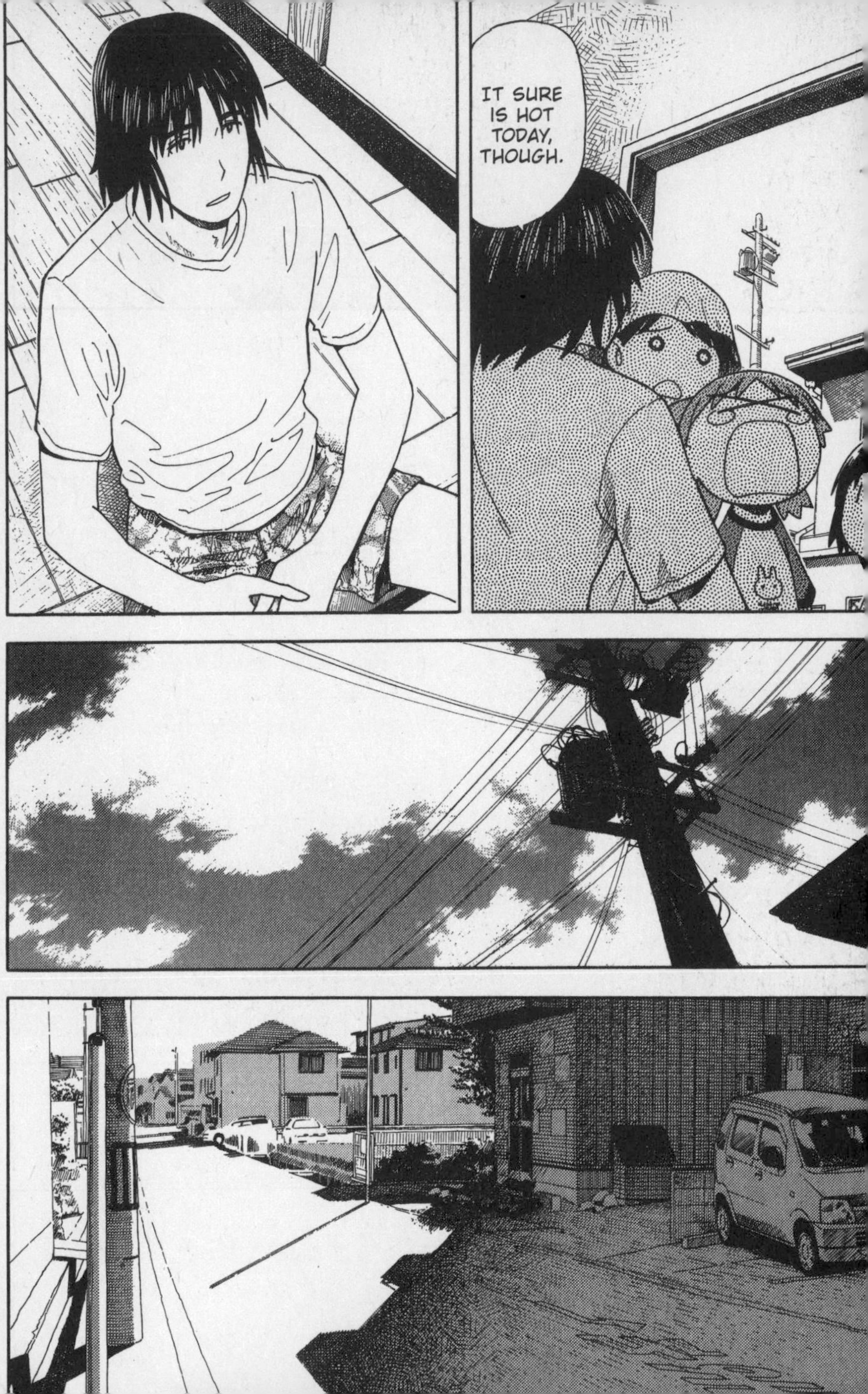
IT SURE IS HOT TODAY, THOUGH.

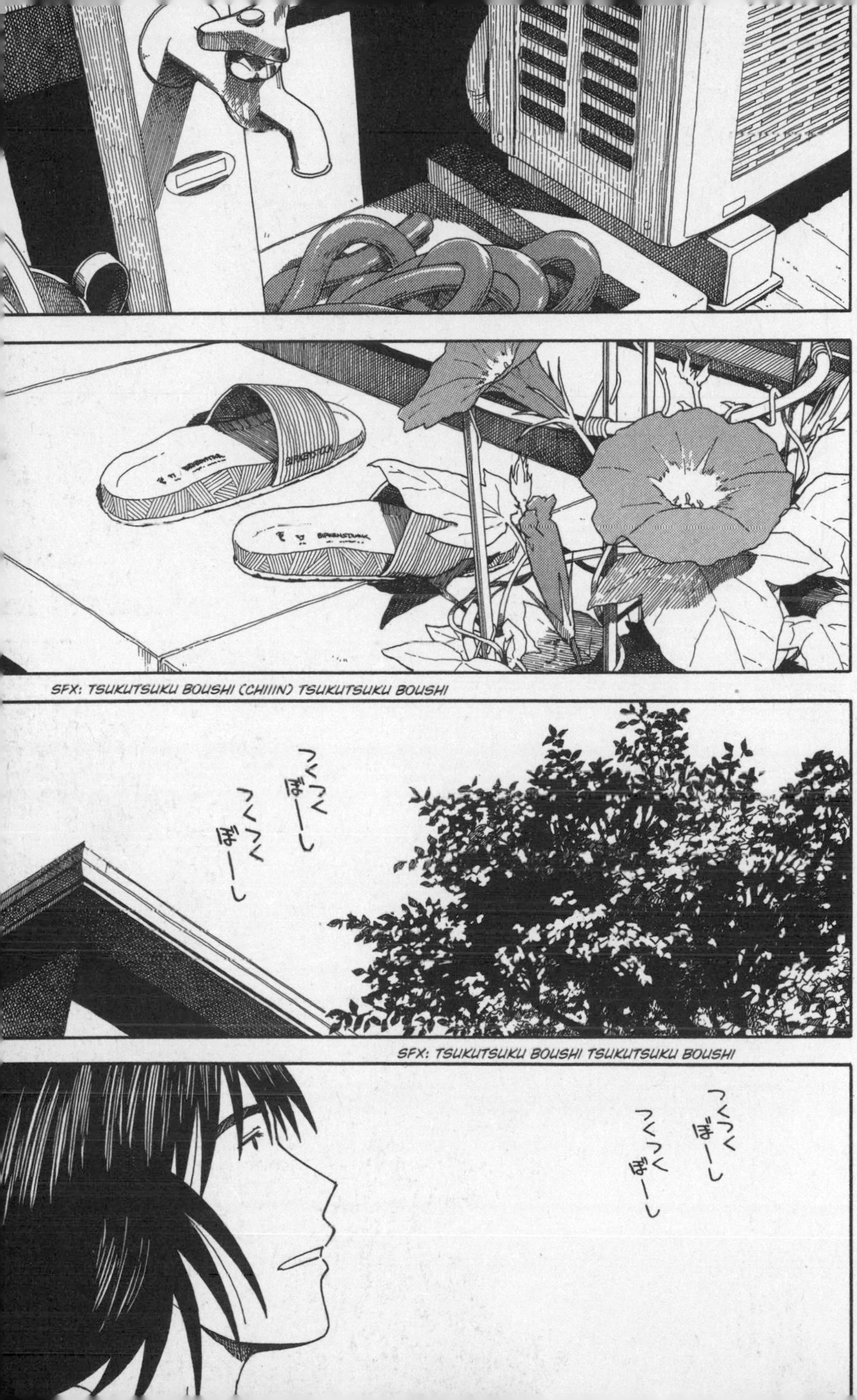
SFX: TSUKUTSUKU BOUSHI (CHIIIN) TSUKUTSUKU BOUSHI
つくつくぼーし
つくつくぼーし
SFX: TSUKUTSUKU BOUSHI TSUKUTSUKU BOUSHI
つくつくぼーし
つくつくぼーし

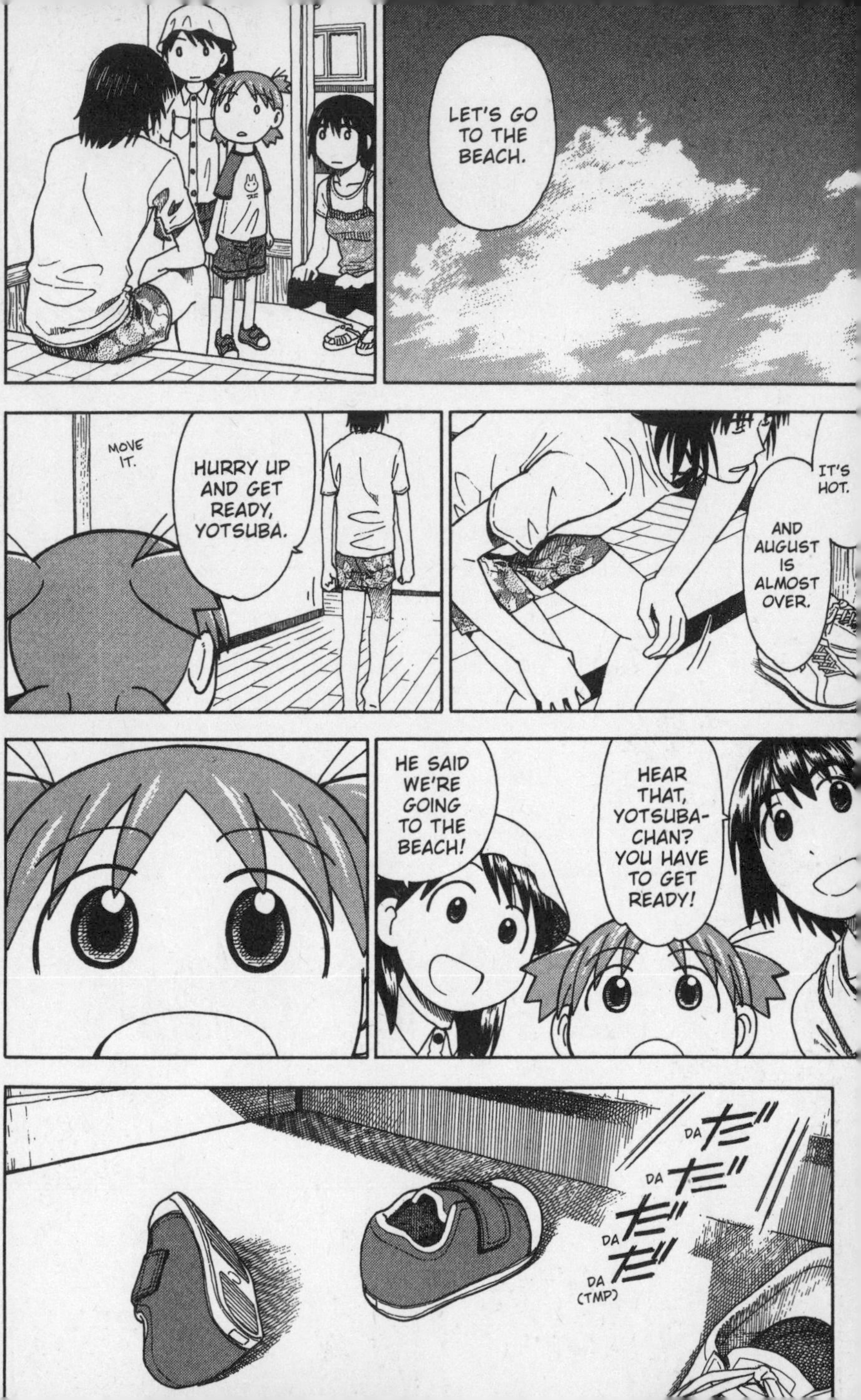
LET'S GO TO THE BEACH.
IT'S HOT.
AND AUGUST IS ALMOST OVER.
HURRY UP AND GET READY, YOTSUBA.
MOVE IT.
HEAR THAT, YOTSUBA-CHAN? YOU HAVE TO GET READY!
HE SAID WE'RE GOING TO THE BEACH!
DA だ
DA だ
DA だ
DA だ
(TMP)

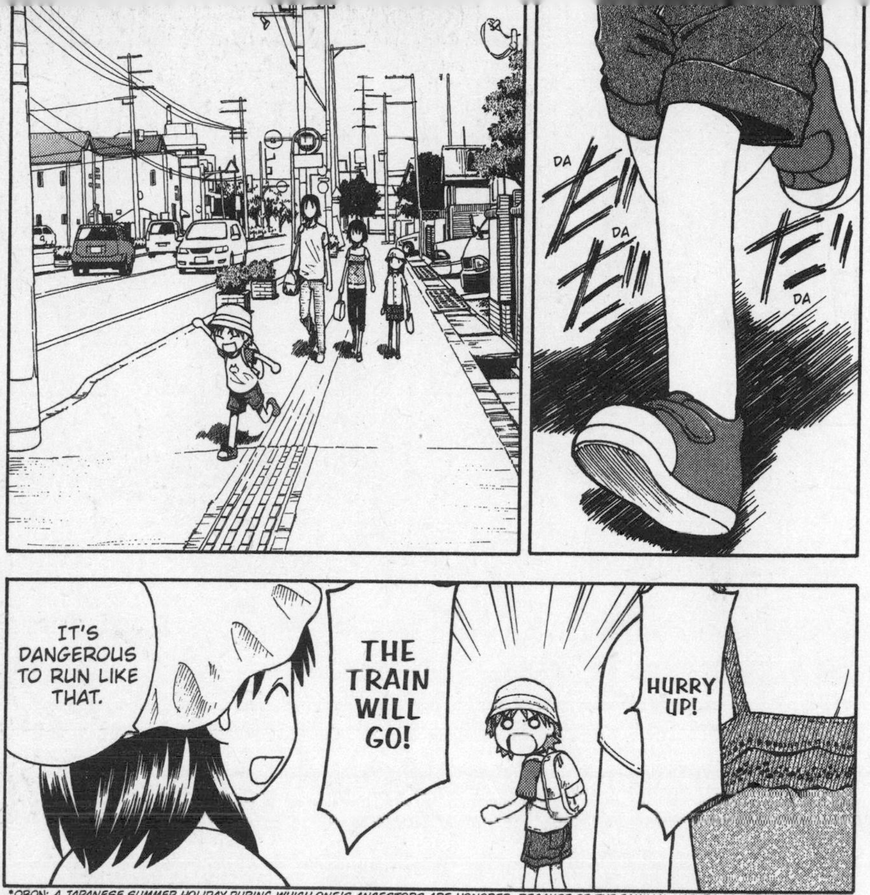
DA
DA
DA
DA
HURRY UP!
THE TRAIN WILL GO!
IT'S DANGEROUS TO RUN LIKE THAT.

*OBON: A JAPANESE SUMMER HOLIDAY DURING WHICH ONE'S ANCESTORS ARE HONORED. BECAUSE OF THE FAMILIAL NATURE OF THE HOLIDAY, IT IS COMMON TO REUNITE WITH EXTENDED FAMILY MEMBERS.

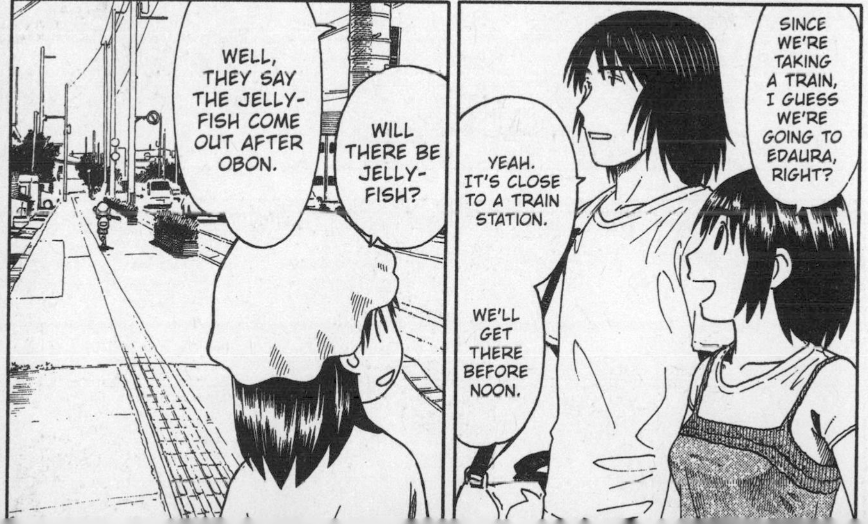
SINCE WE'RE TAKING A TRAIN, I GUESS WE'RE GOING TO EDAURA, RIGHT?
YEAH. IT'S CLOSE TO A TRAIN STATION.
WE'LL GET THERE BEFORE NOON.
WILL THERE BE JELLY-FISH?
WELL, THEY SAY THE JELLY-FISH COME OUT AFTER OBON.

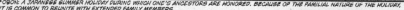

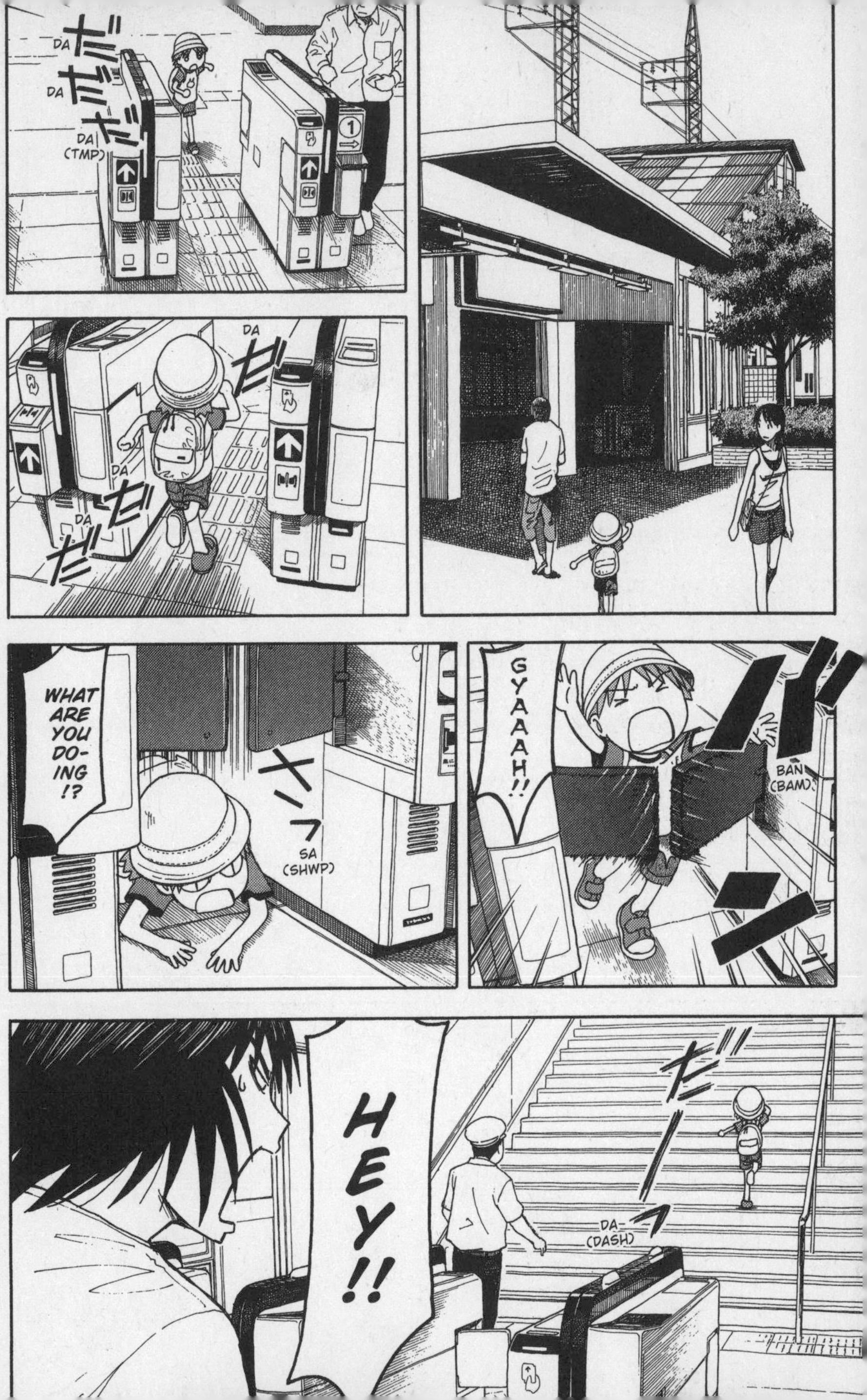
DA
DA
DA (TMP)
DA
DA
DA
GYAAAH!!
BAN (BAM)
WHAT ARE YOU DO-ING!?
SA (SHWP)
DA- (DASH)
HEY!!

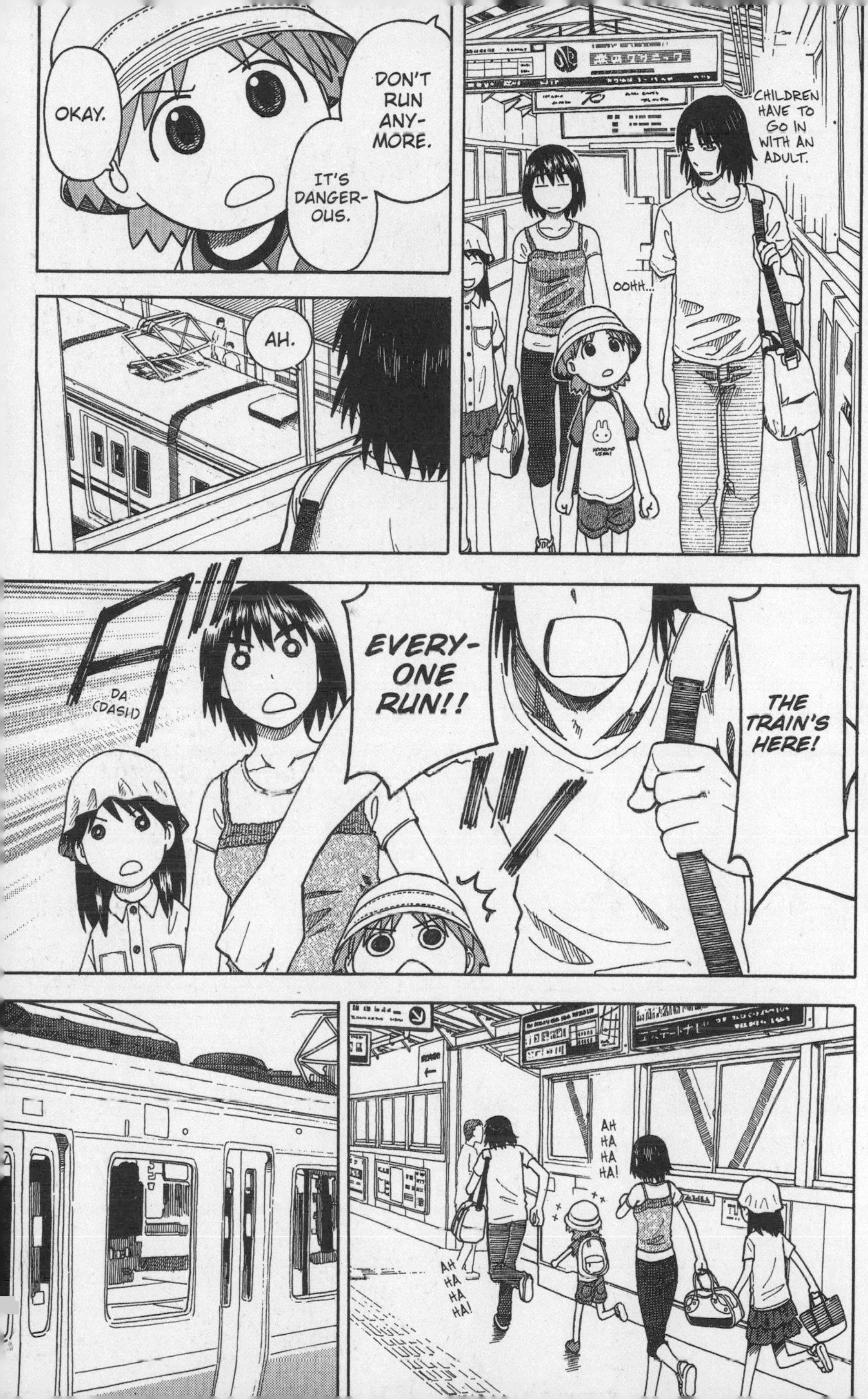
CHILDREN HAVE TO GO IN WITH AN ADULT.
OOHH...
DON'T RUN ANYMORE.
IT'S DANGEROUS.
OKAY.
AH.
THE TRAIN'S HERE!
EVERYONE RUN!!
DA (DASH)
AH HA HA HA!
AH HA HA HA!

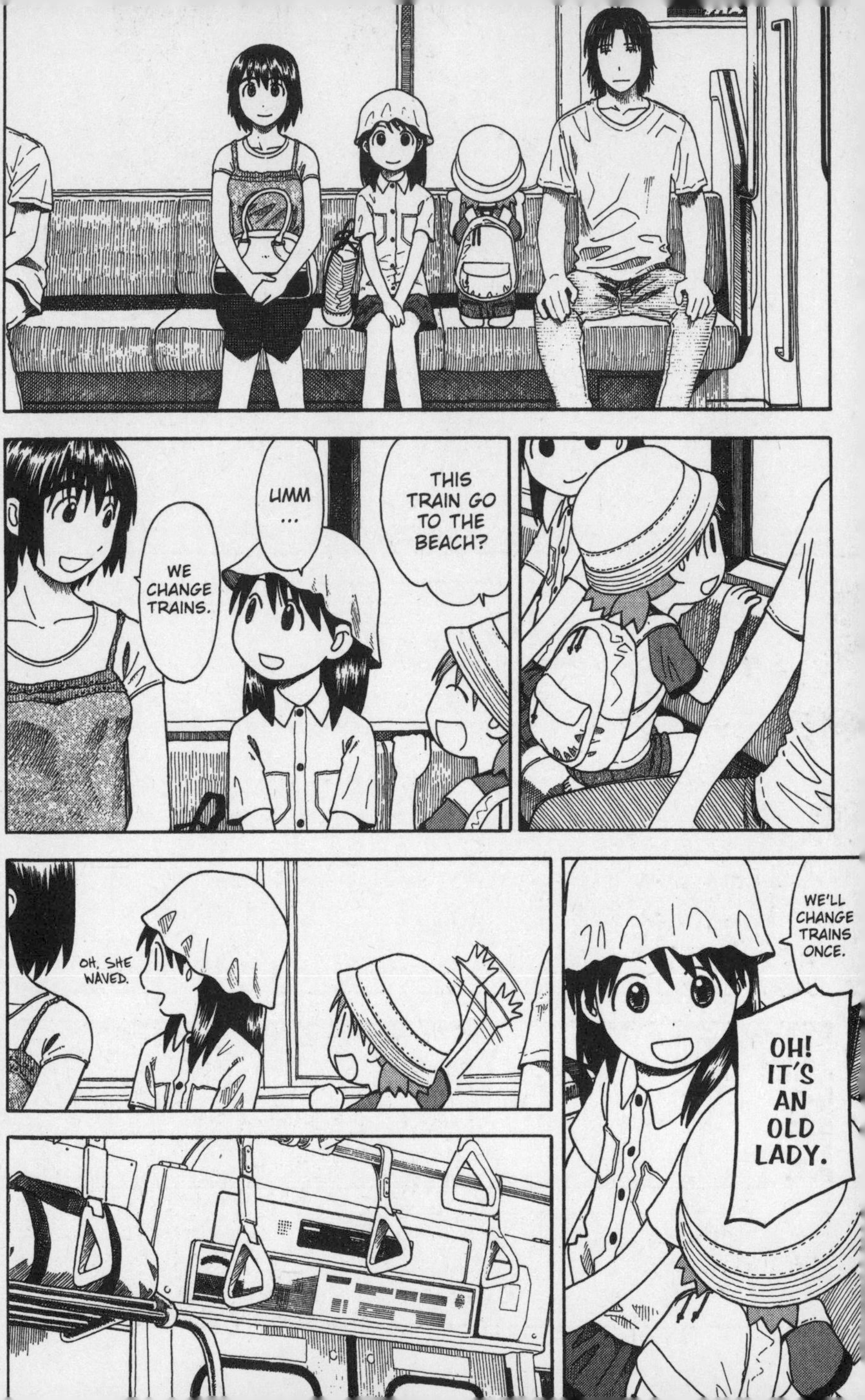
THIS TRAIN GO TO THE BEACH?
UMM ...
WE CHANGE TRAINS.
WE'LL CHANGE TRAINS ONCE.
OH! IT'S AN OLD LADY.
OH, SHE WAVED.

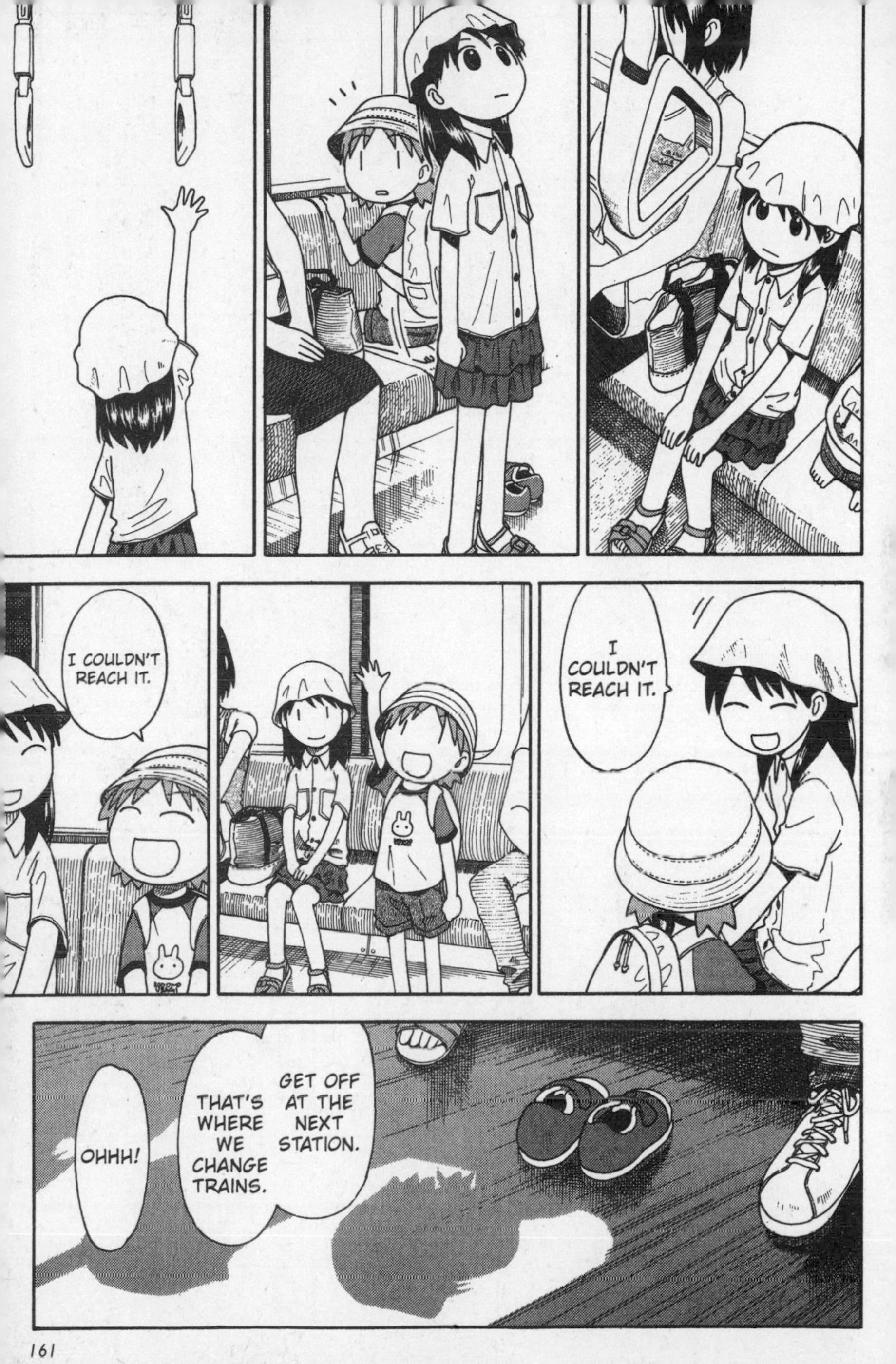
I COULDN'T REACH IT.
I COULDN'T REACH IT.
GET OFF AT THE NEXT STATION.
THAT'S WHERE WE CHANGE TRAINS.
OHHH!

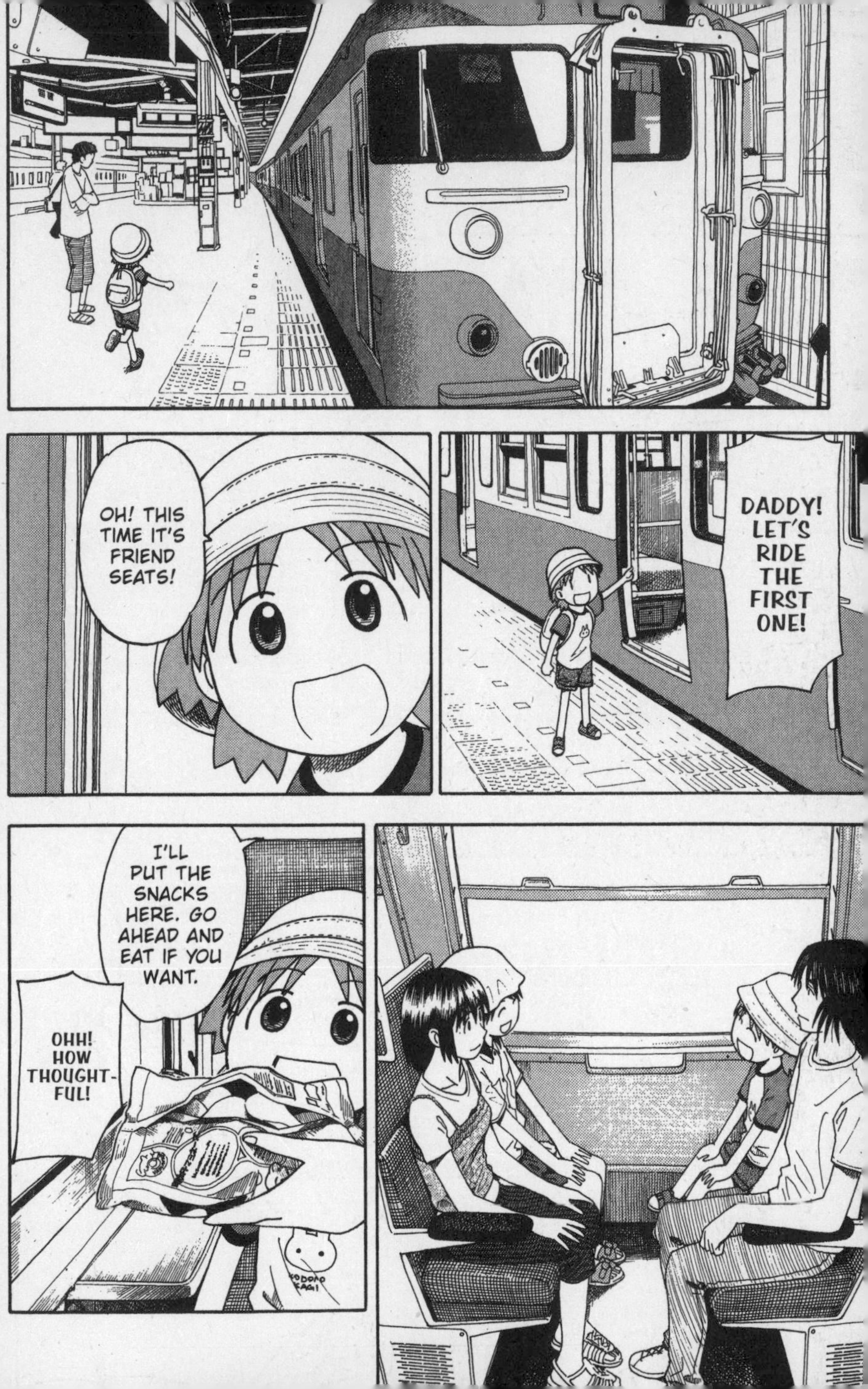
DADDY! LET'S RIDE THE FIRST ONE!
OH! THIS TIME IT'S FRIEND SEATS!
I'LL PUT THE SNACKS HERE. GO AHEAD AND EAT IF YOU WANT.
OHH! HOW THOUGHT-FUL!

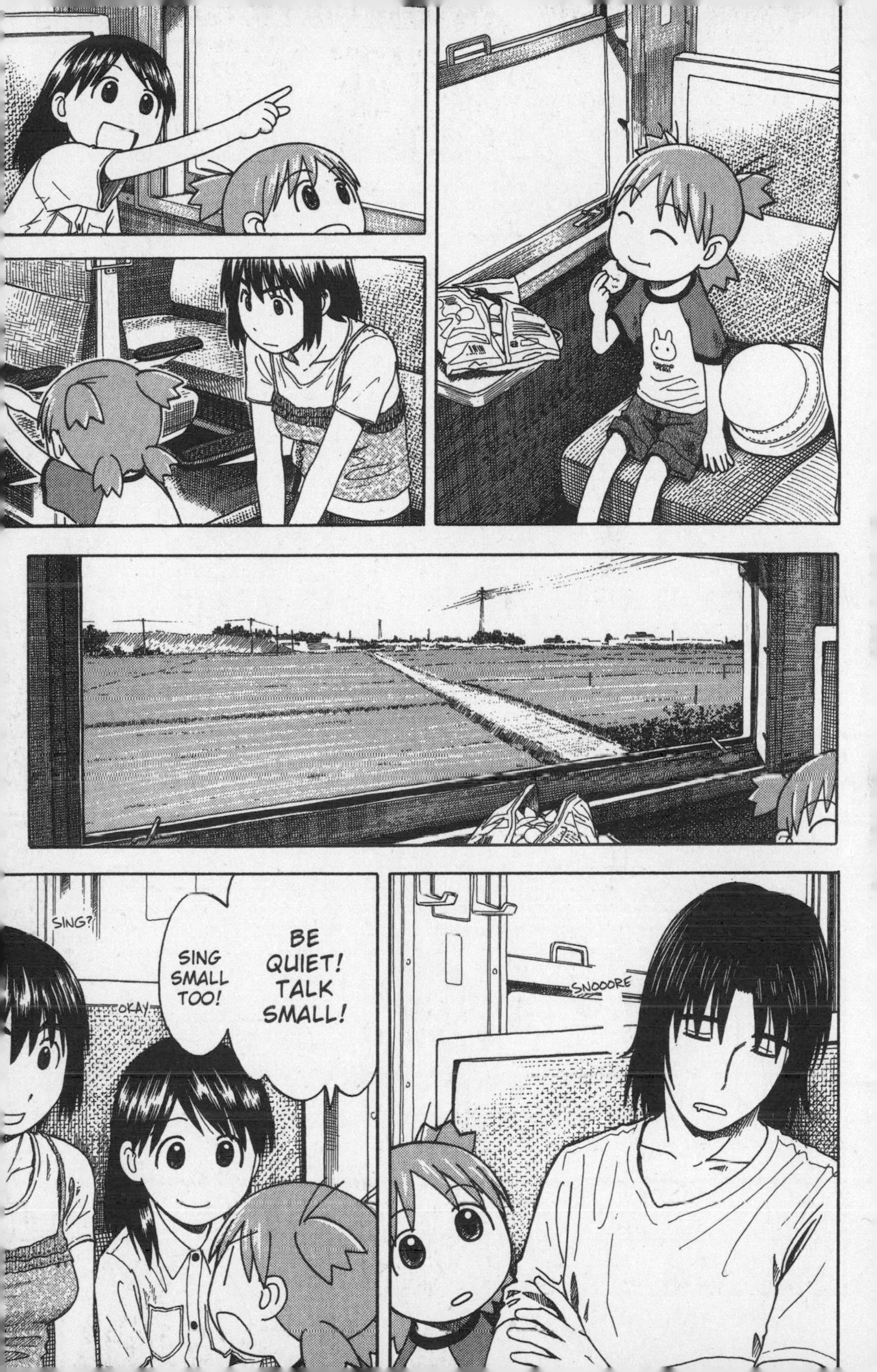
SNOOORE
BE QUIET! TALK SMALL!
SING SMALL TOO!
OKAY
SING?

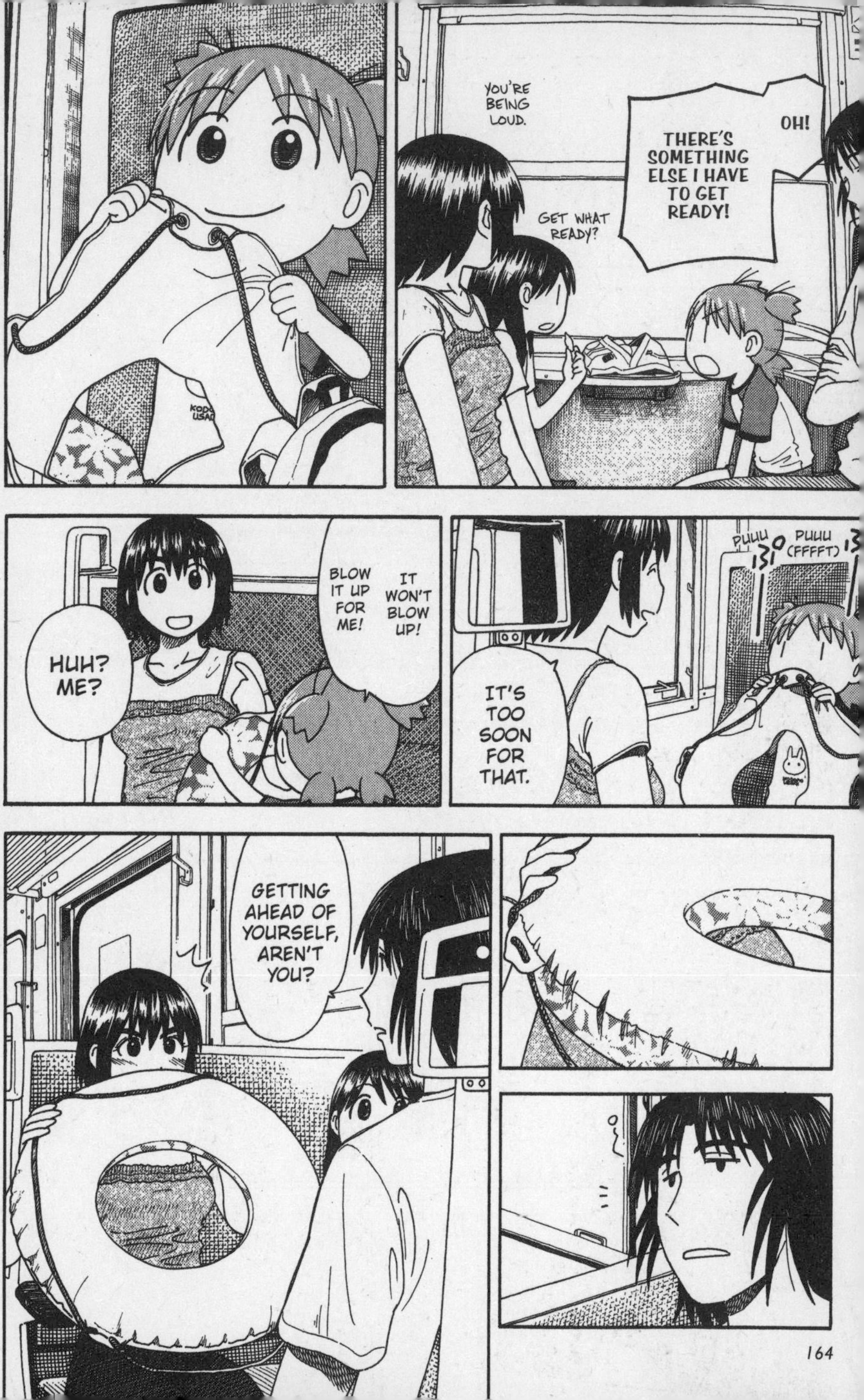
OH!
THERE'S SOMETHING ELSE I HAVE TO GET READY!
YOU'RE BEING LOUD.
GET WHAT READY?
PUUU
PUUU (FFFFT)
IT'S TOO SOON FOR THAT.
IT WON'T BLOW UP!
BLOW IT UP FOR ME!
HUH? ME?
GETTING AHEAD OF YOURSELF, AREN'T YOU?

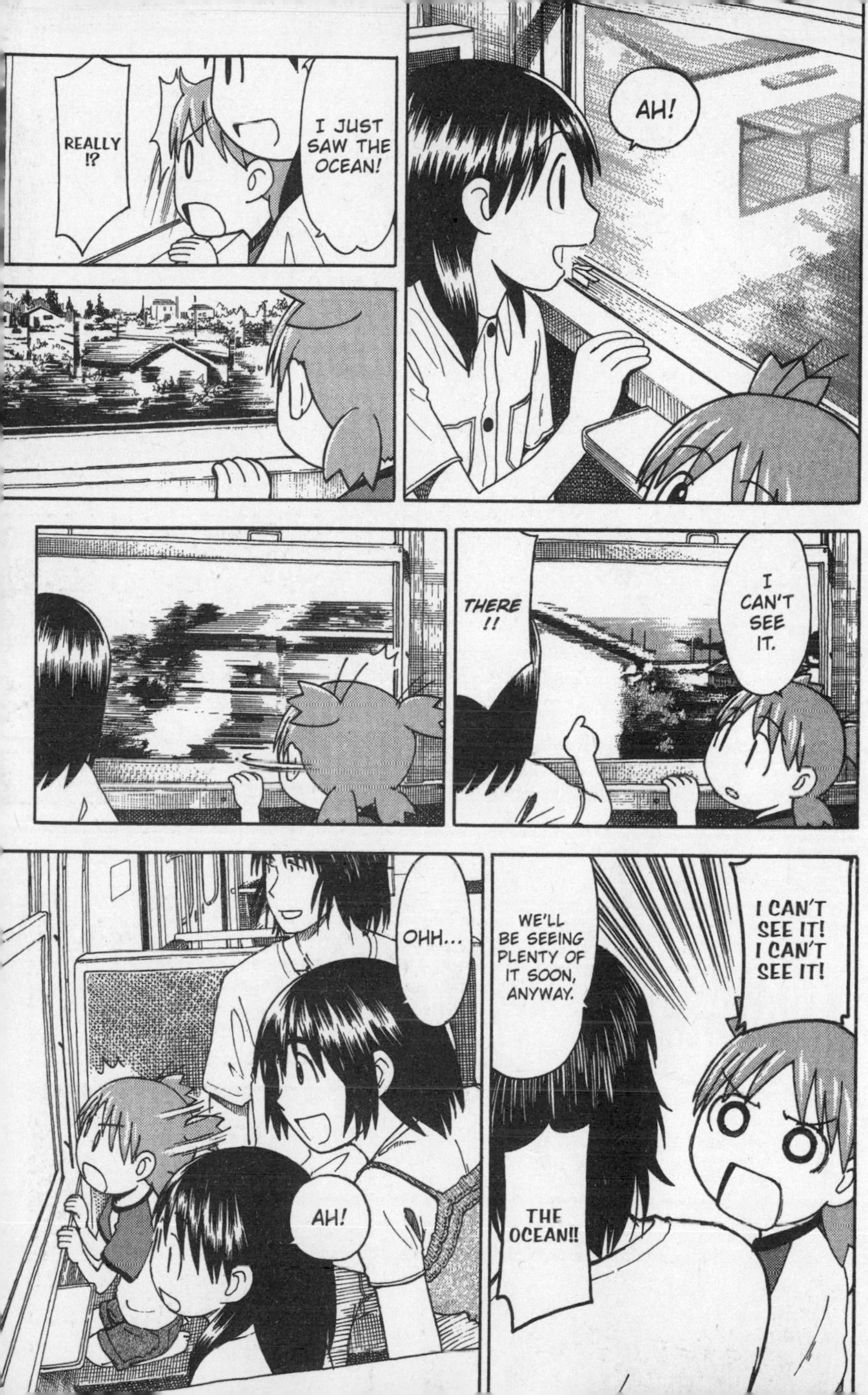
AH!
I JUST SAW THE OCEAN!
REALLY !?
I CAN'T SEE IT.
THERE !!
I CAN'T SEE IT! I CAN'T SEE IT!
WE'LL BE SEEING PLENTY OF IT SOON, ANYWAY.
THE OCEAN!!
OHH...
AH!

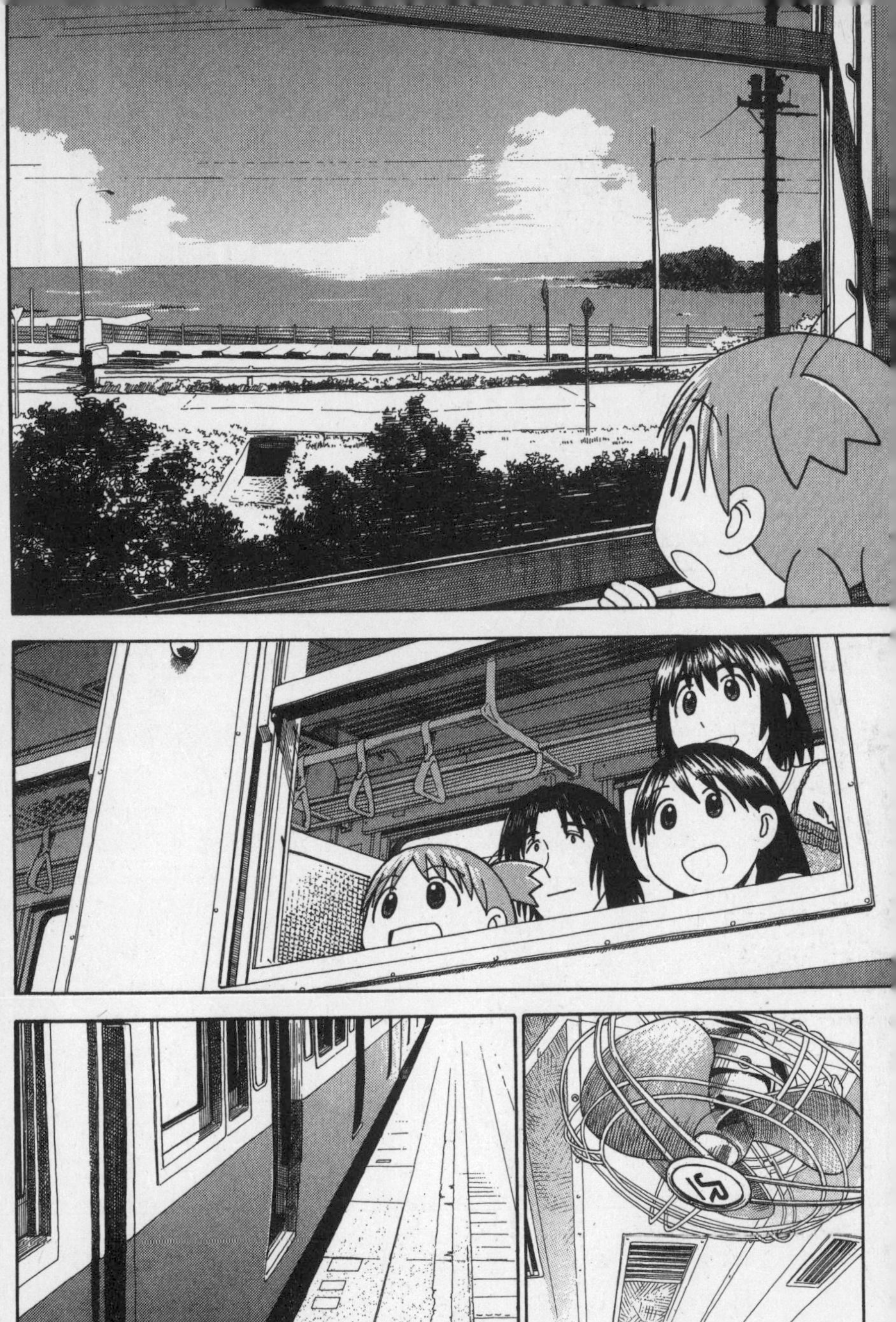

GIVE HIM MY TICKET FOR ME.

OHHH!

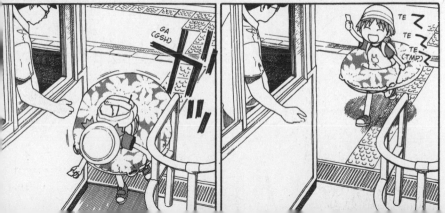

GA (GSH)

TE
TE
TE (TMP)

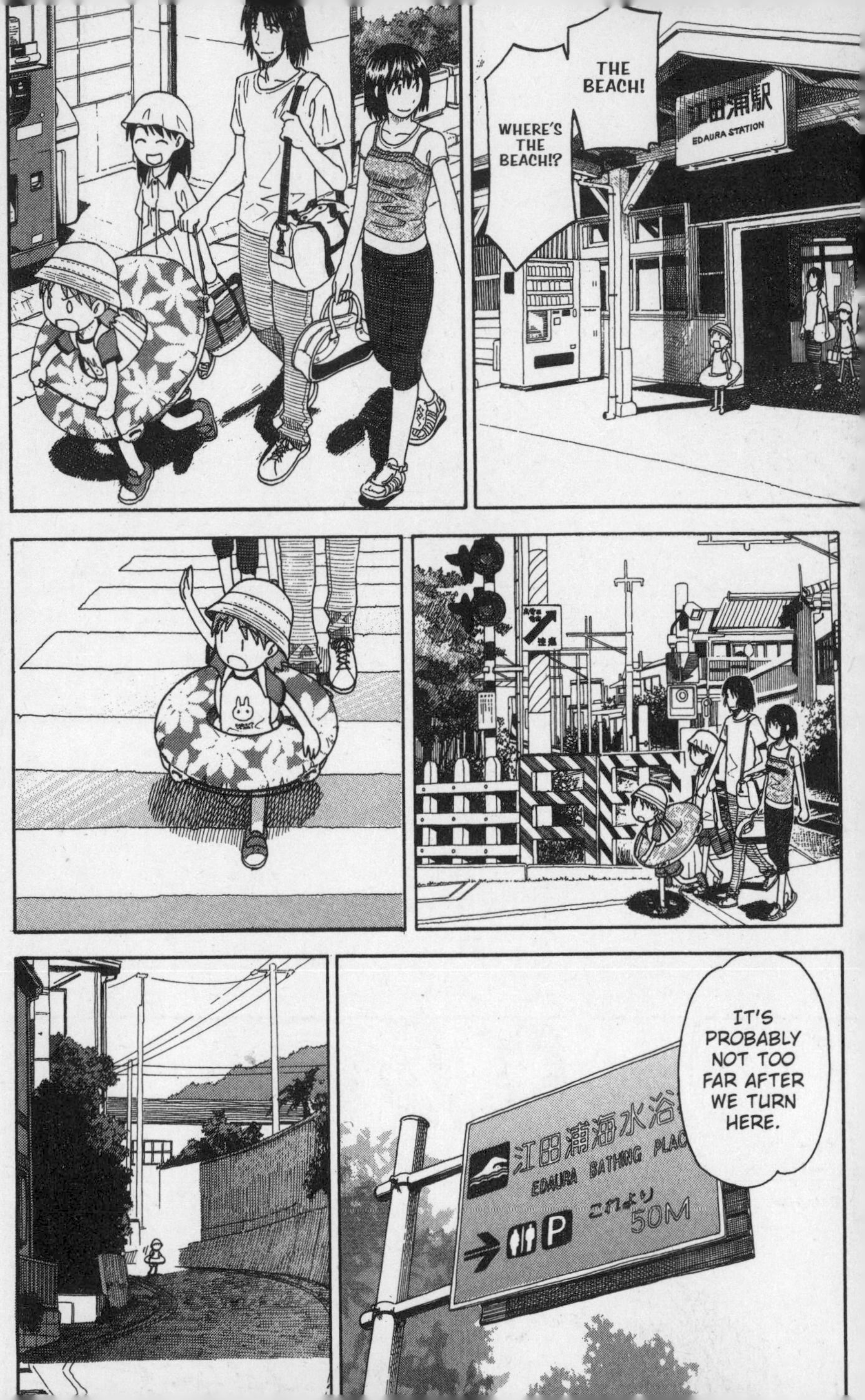
THE BEACH!
WHERE'S THE BEACH!?
江田浦駅
EDAURA STATION
IT'S PROBABLY NOT TOO FAR AFTER WE TURN HERE.
江田浦海水浴
EDAURA BATHING
これより
50M

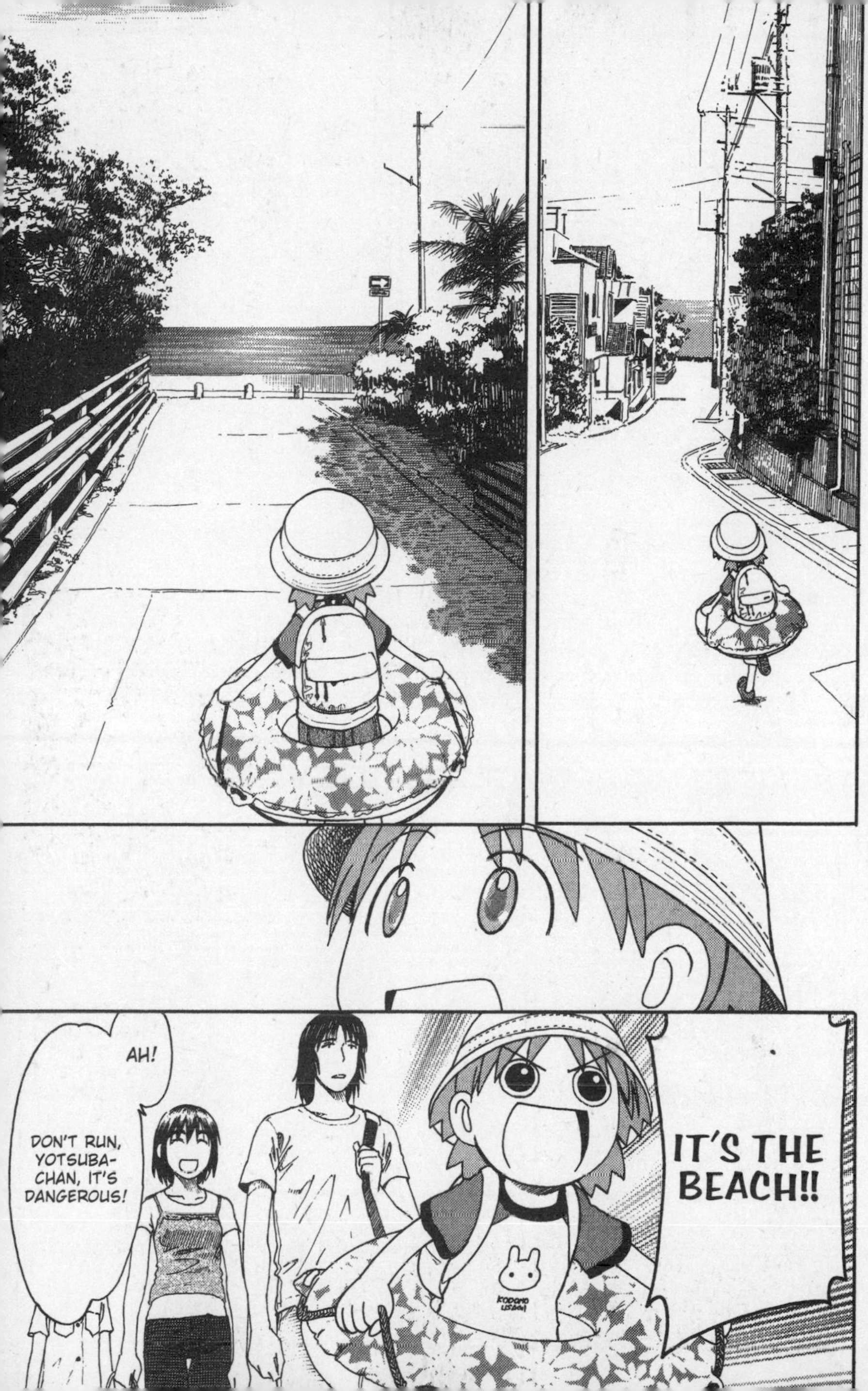
IT'S THE BEACH!!
AH!
DON'T RUN, YOTSUBA-CHAN, IT'S DANGEROUS!

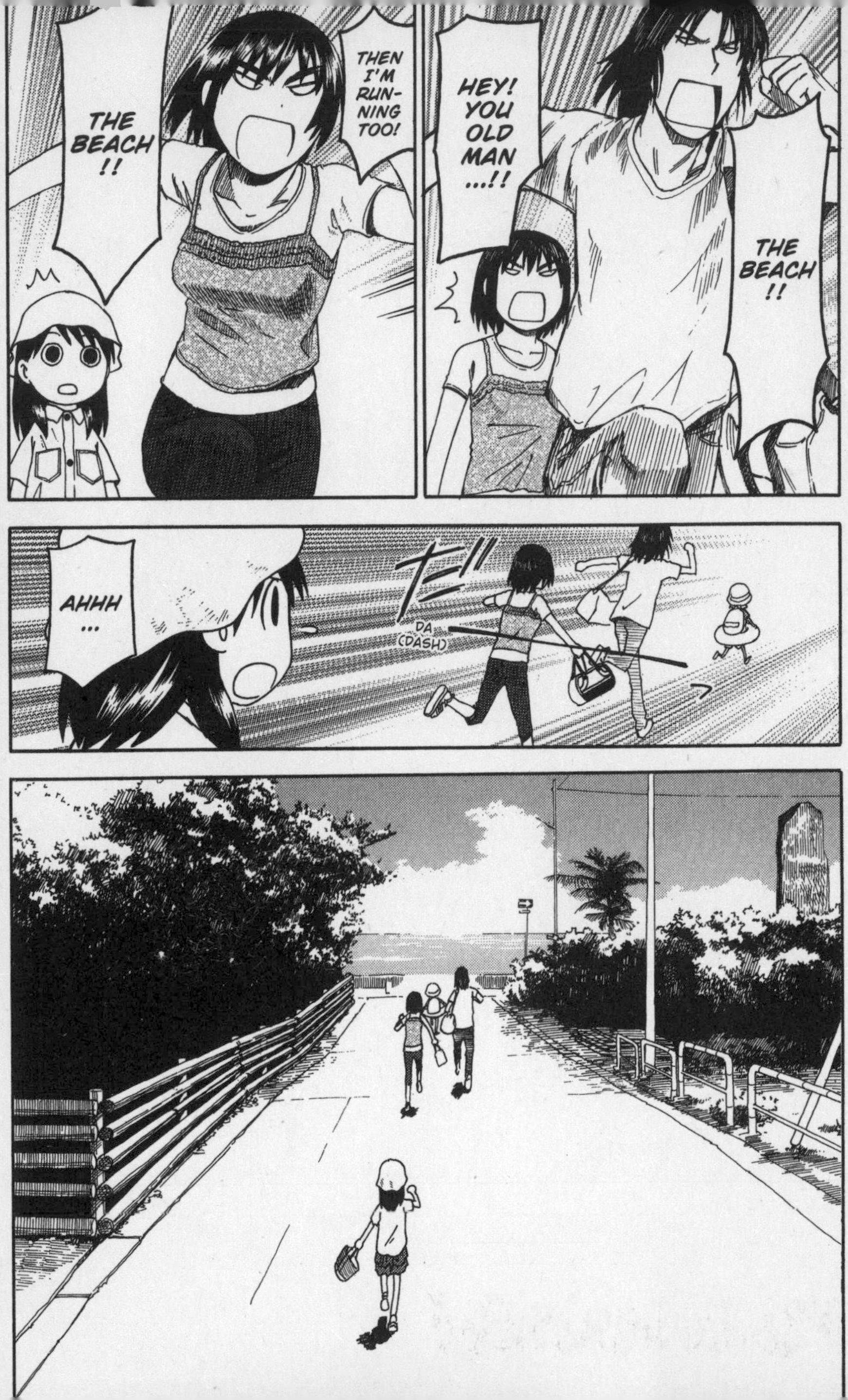
THE BEACH !!
HEY! YOU OLD MAN ...!!
THEN I'M RUN-NING TOO!
THE BEACH !!
DA (DASH)
AHHH ...

YOTSUBA&!

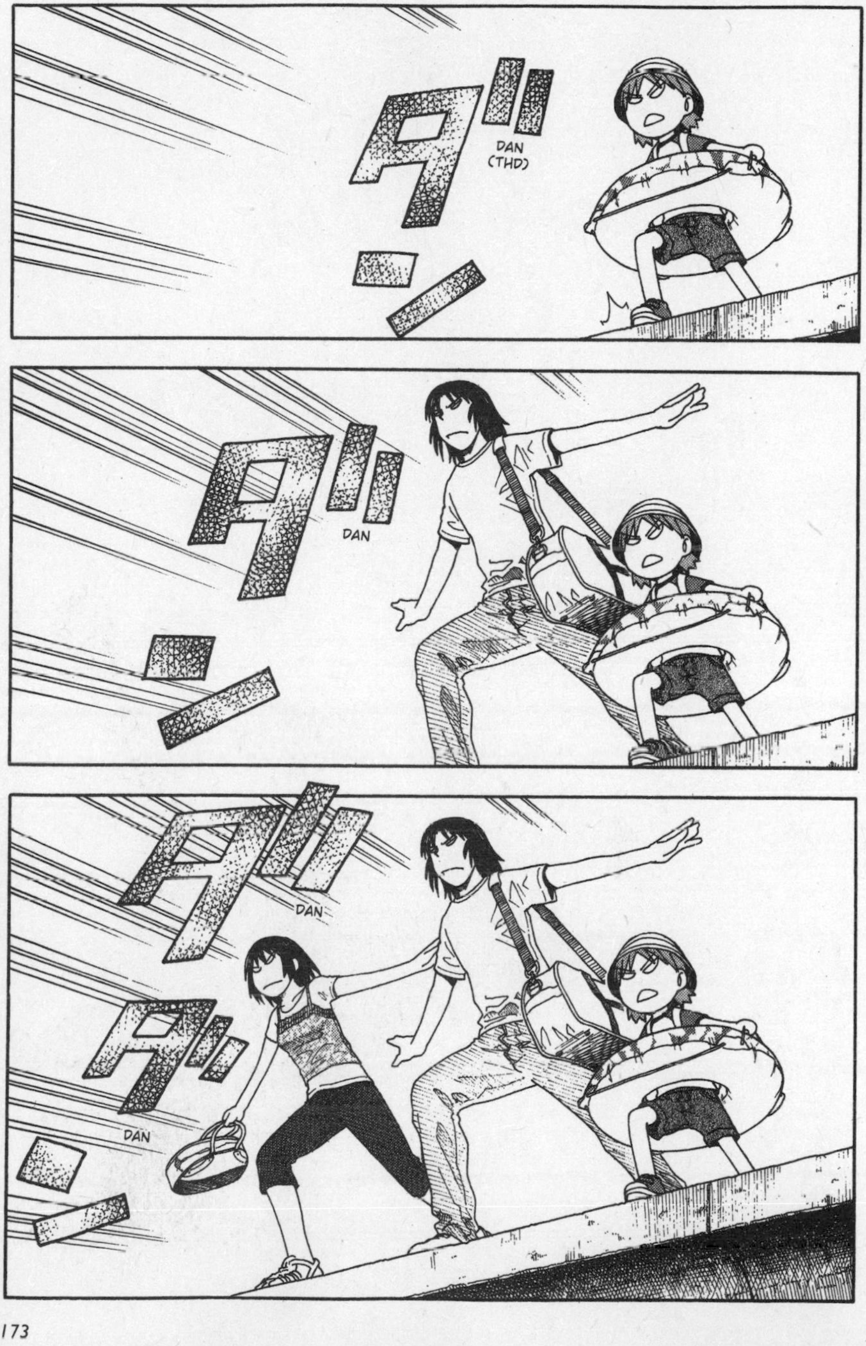

DAN (THD)
DAN
DAN
DAN

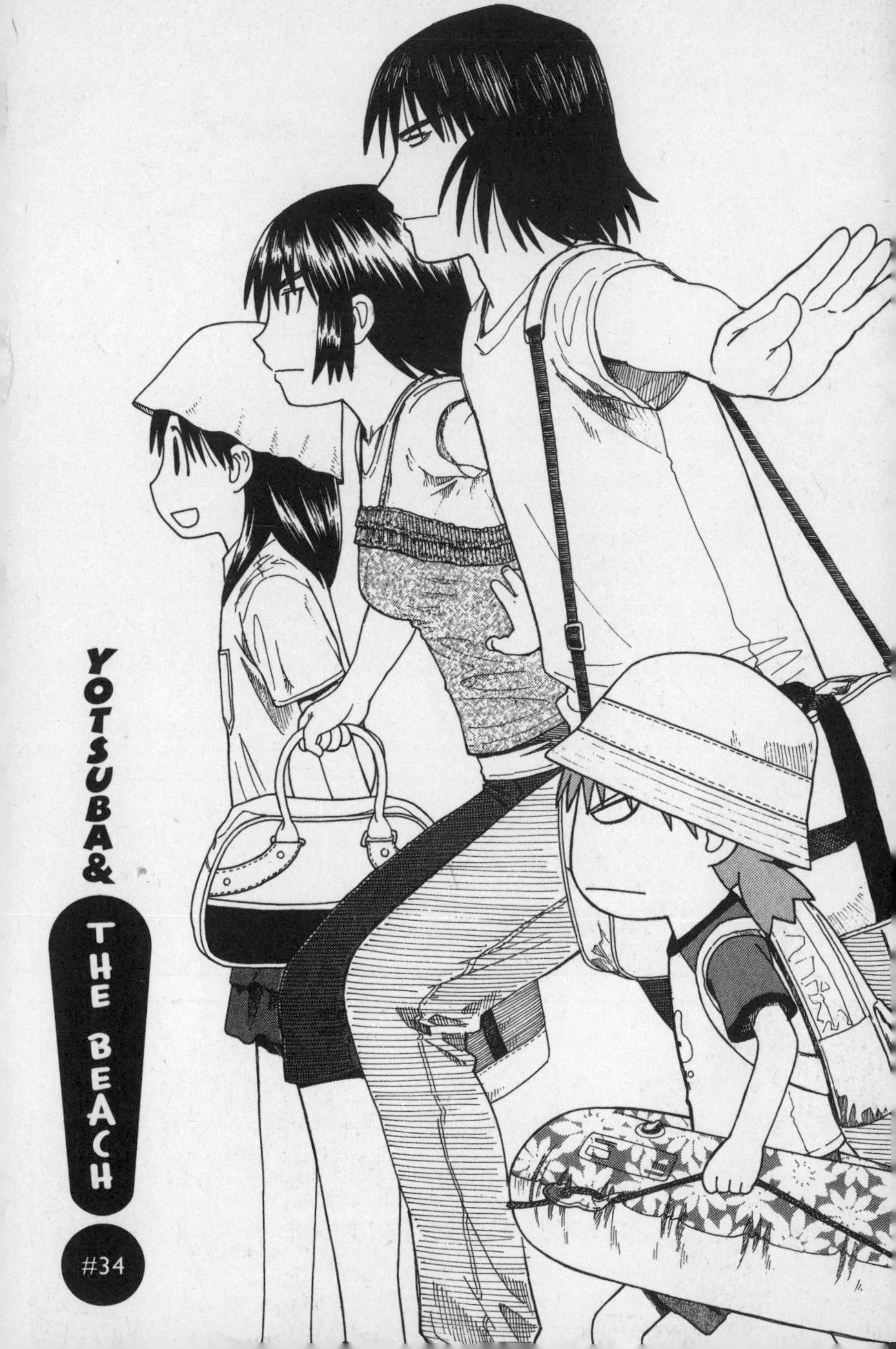
YOTSUBA&
THE BEACH
#34

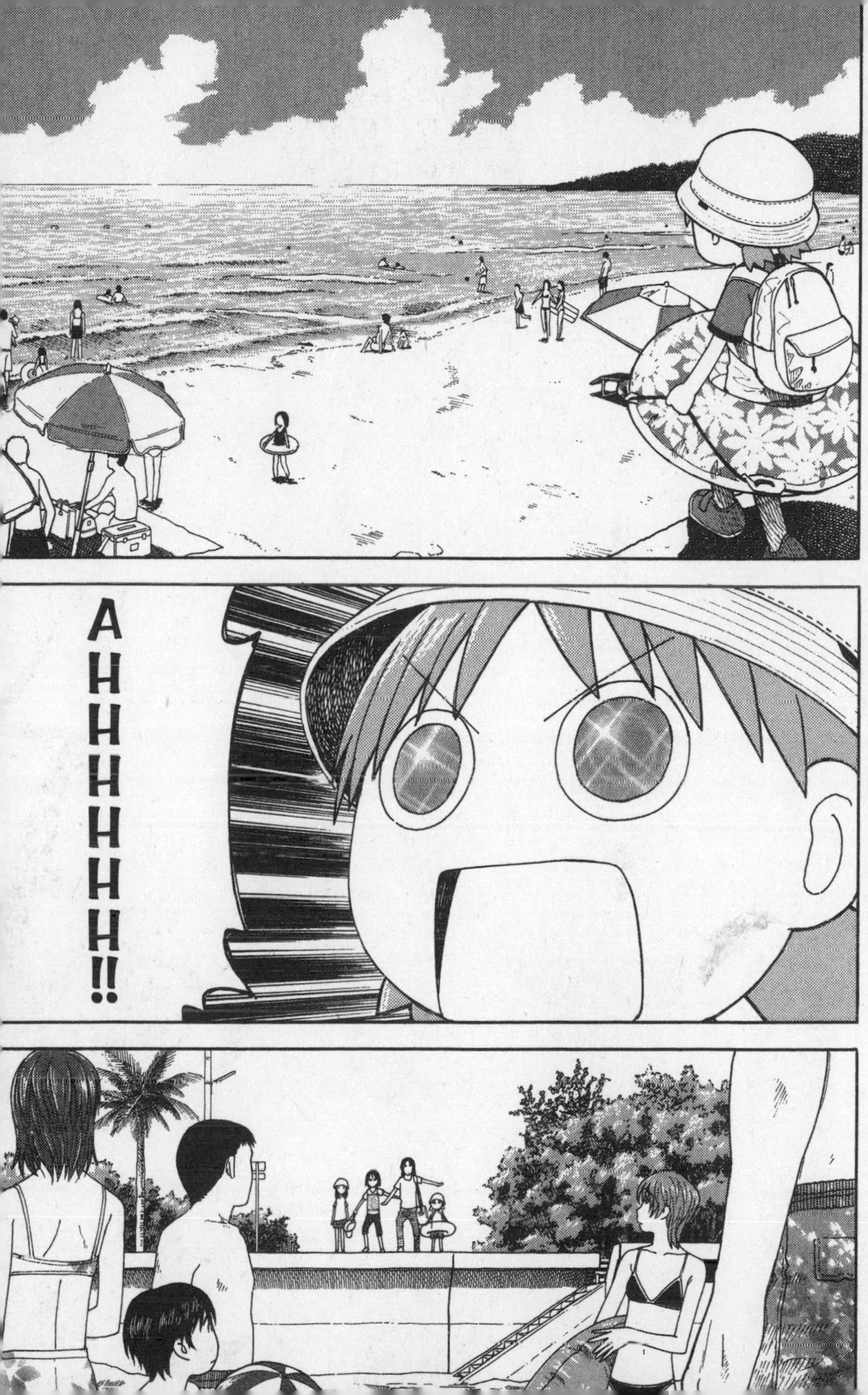
AHHHHHHH!!

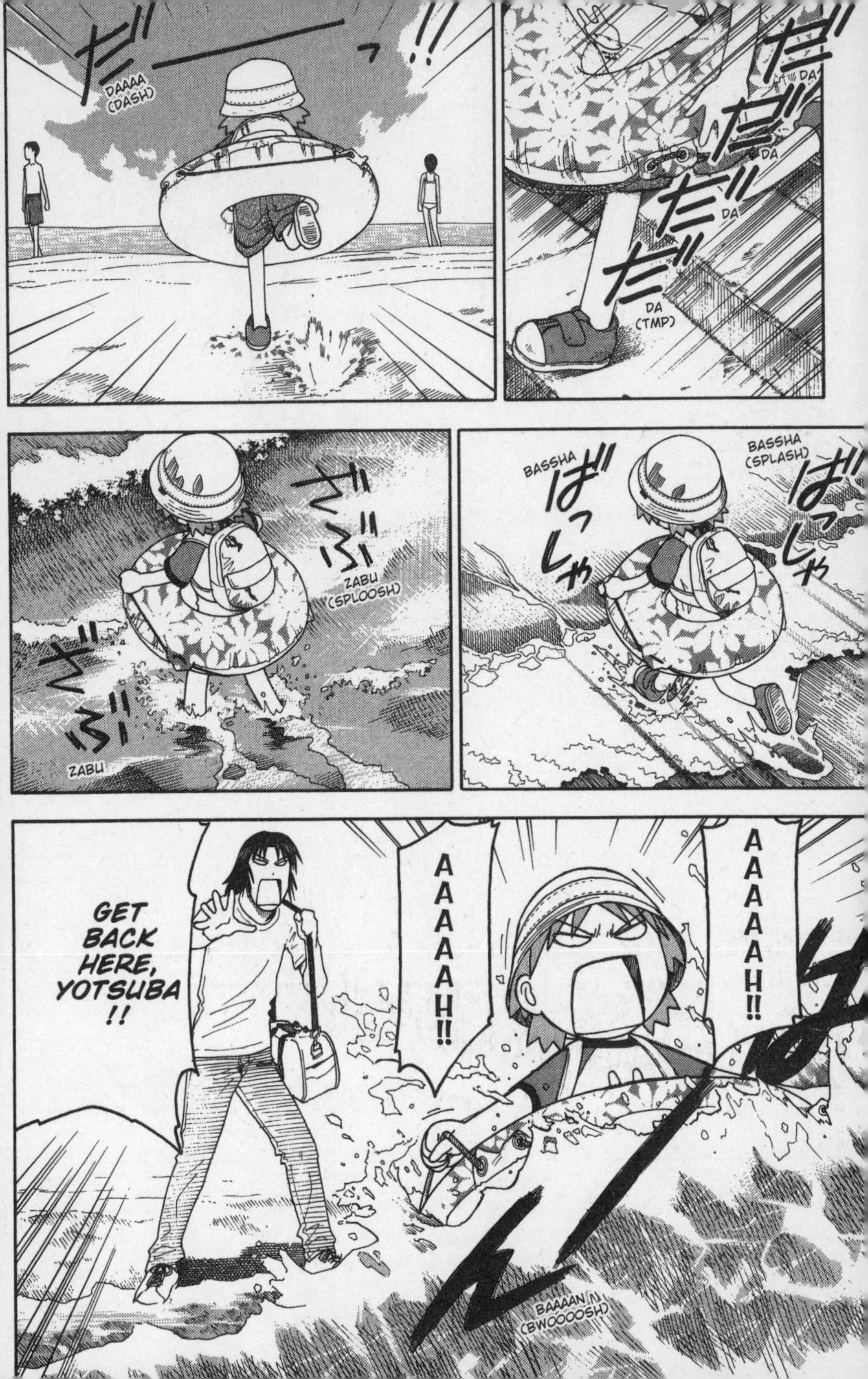

だ
DA
だ
DA
だ
DA
だ
DA
(TMP)
だ
DAAAA
(DASH)
BASSHA
(SPLASH)
ばっしゃ
BASSHA
ばっしゃ
ざぶ
ZABU
(SPLOSH)
ざぶ
ZABU
AAAAAAH!!
AAAAAH!!
GET BACK HERE, YOTSUBA!!
BAAAAN
(BWOOOOSH)

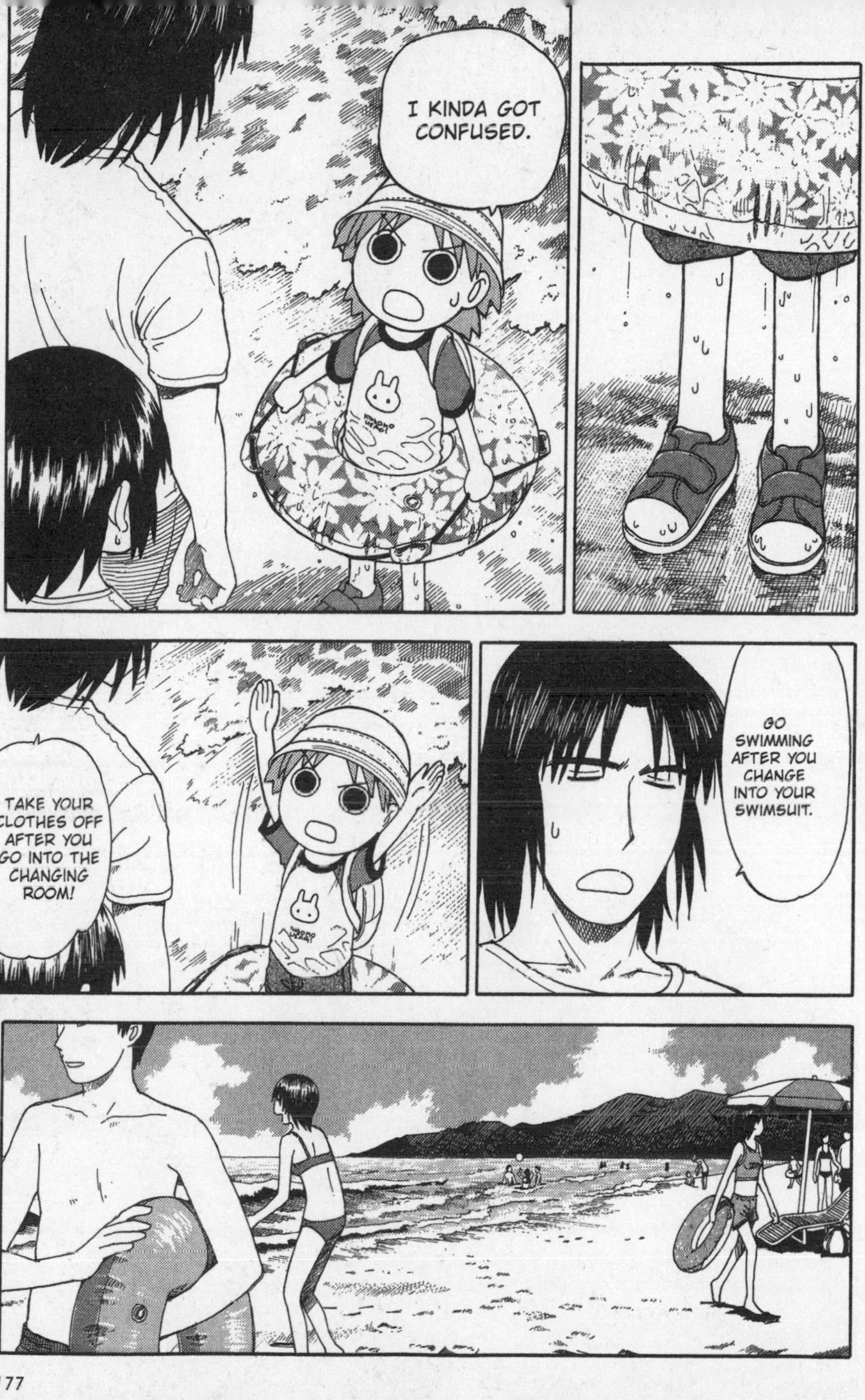
I KINDA GOT CONFUSED.
GO SWIMMING AFTER YOU CHANGE INTO YOUR SWIMSUIT.
TAKE YOUR CLOTHES OFF AFTER YOU GO INTO THE CHANGING ROOM!

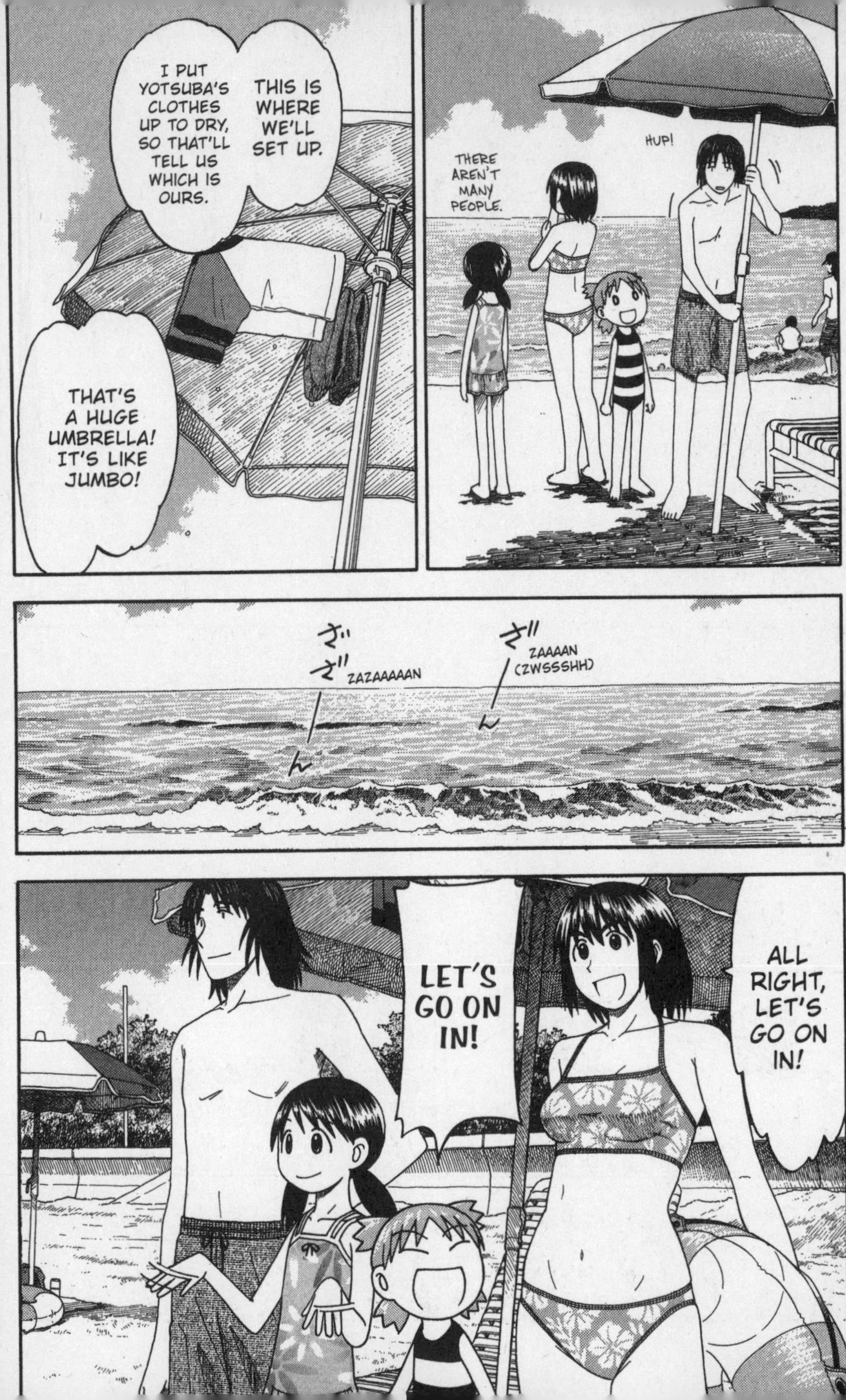
HUP!
THERE AREN'T MANY PEOPLE.
THIS IS WHERE WE'LL SET UP.
I PUT YOTSUBA'S CLOTHES UP TO DRY, SO THAT'LL TELL US WHICH IS OURS.
THAT'S A HUGE UMBRELLA! IT'S LIKE JUMBO!
ざーん
ZAAAAN (ZWSSSHH)
ざざーん
ZAZAAAAAN
ALL RIGHT, LET'S GO ON IN!
LET'S GO ON IN!

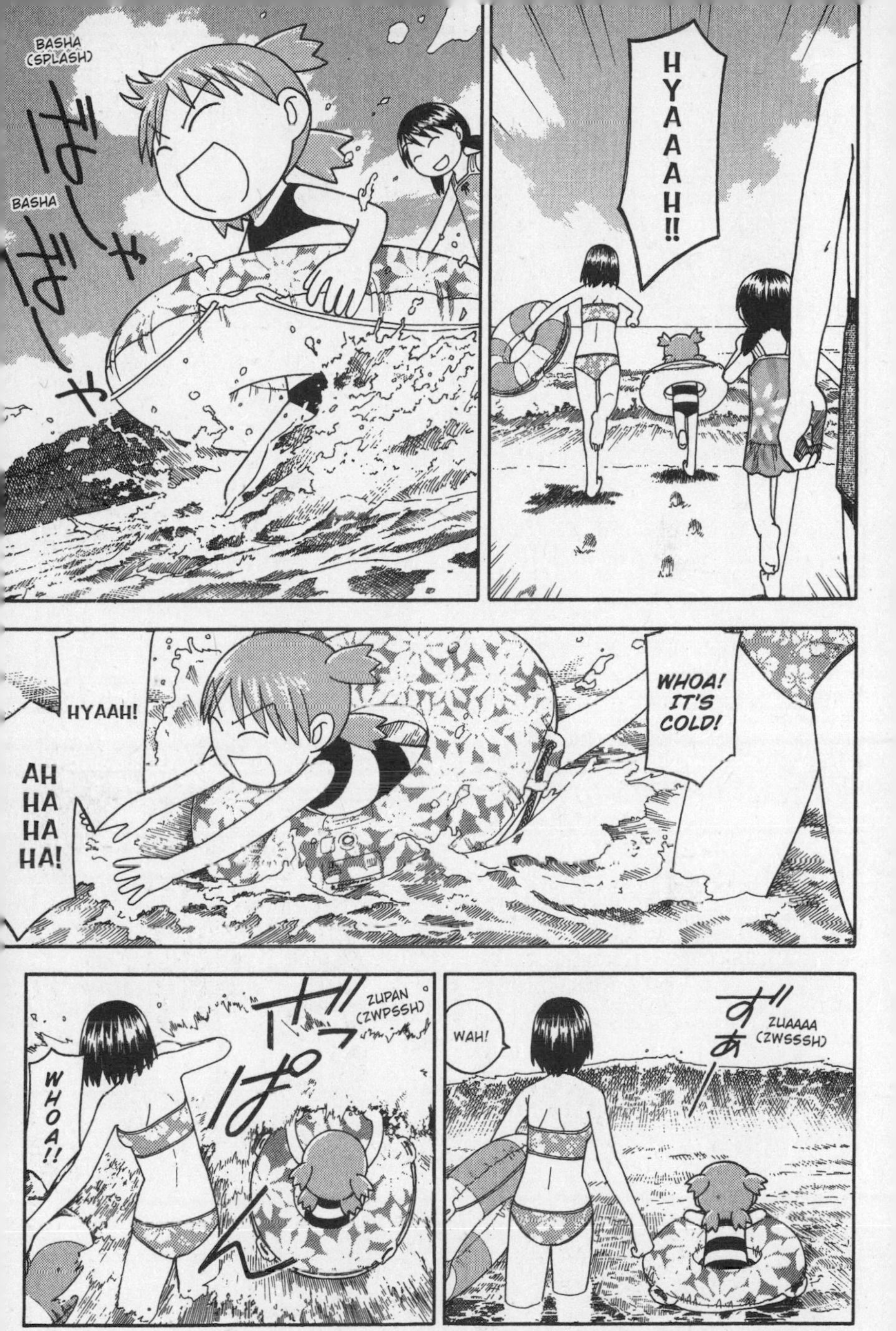
HYAAAAH!!
BASHA (SPLASH)
BASHA
WHOA! IT'S COLD!
HYAAH!
AH HA HA HA!
WAH!
ZUAAAA (ZWSSSH)
ZUPAN (ZWPSSH)
WHOA!!

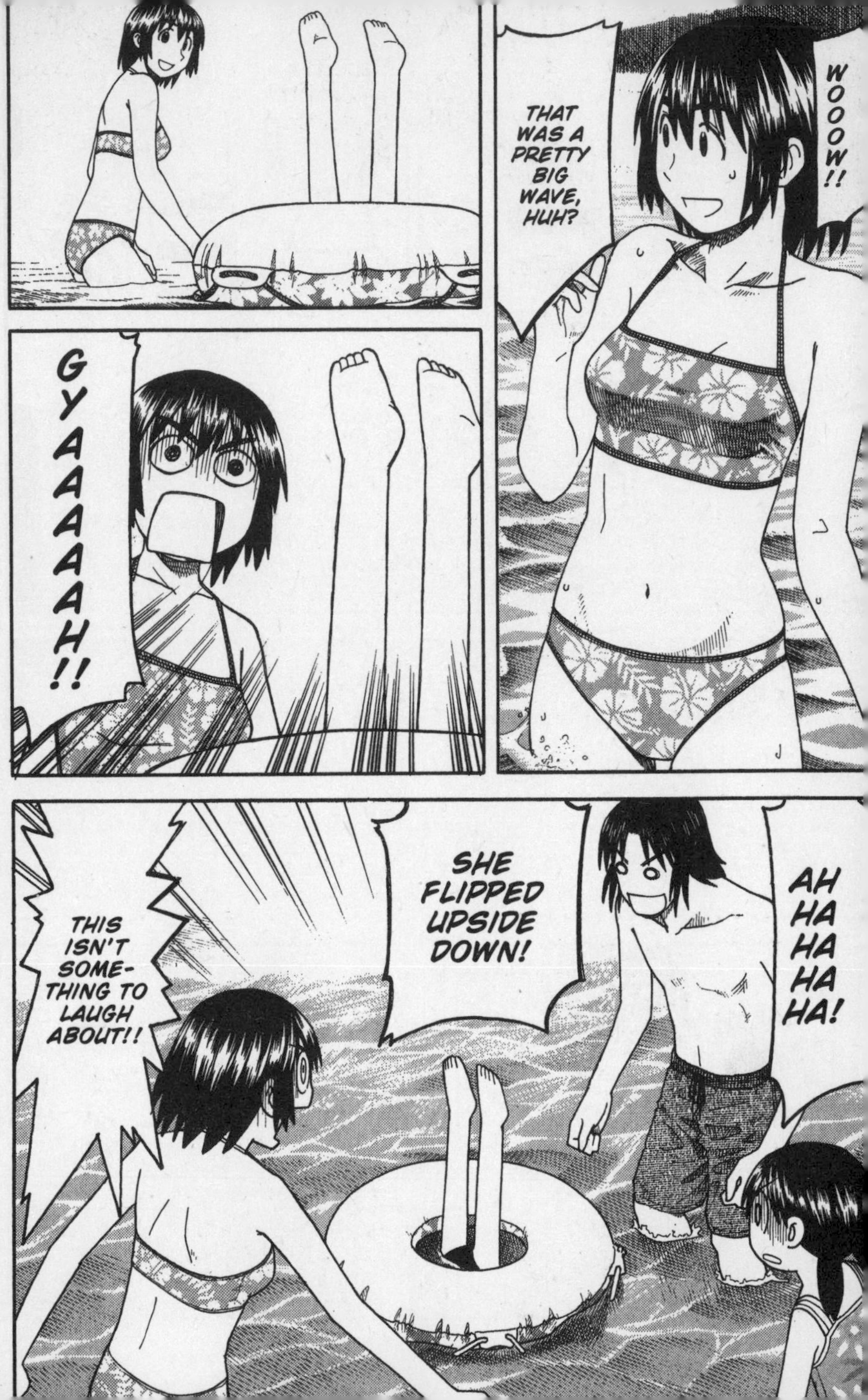
WOOOOW!!
THAT WAS A PRETTY BIG WAVE, HUH?
GYAAAAAAAH!!
AH HA HA HA HA!
SHE FLIPPED UPSIDE DOWN!
THIS ISN'T SOME-THING TO LAUGH ABOUT!!

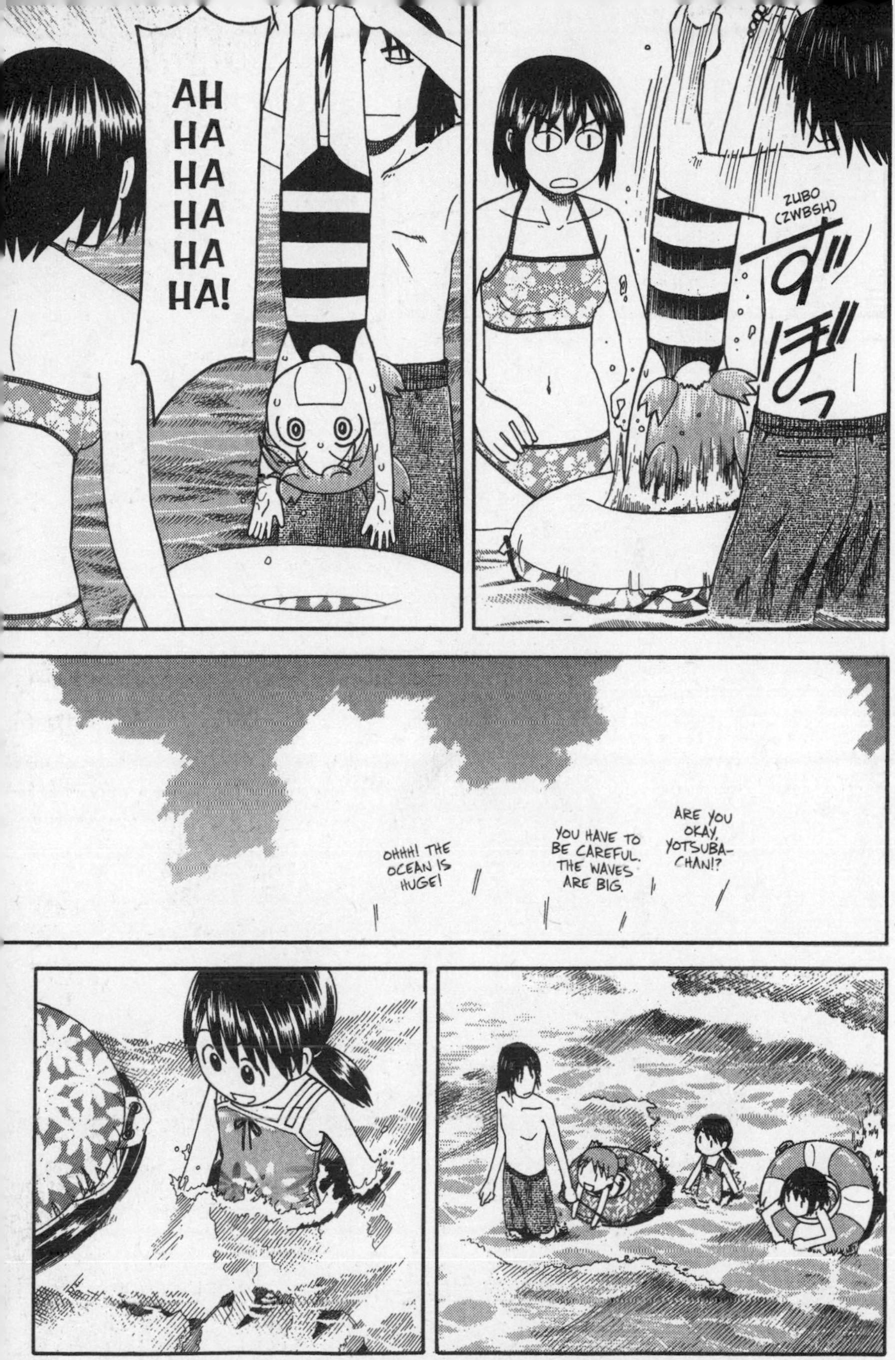
ZUBO (ZWBSH)
ずぼっ
AH HA HA HA HA HA!
ARE YOU OKAY, YOTSUBA-CHAN!?
YOU HAVE TO BE CAREFUL. THE WAVES ARE BIG.
OHHH! THE OCEAN IS HUGE!

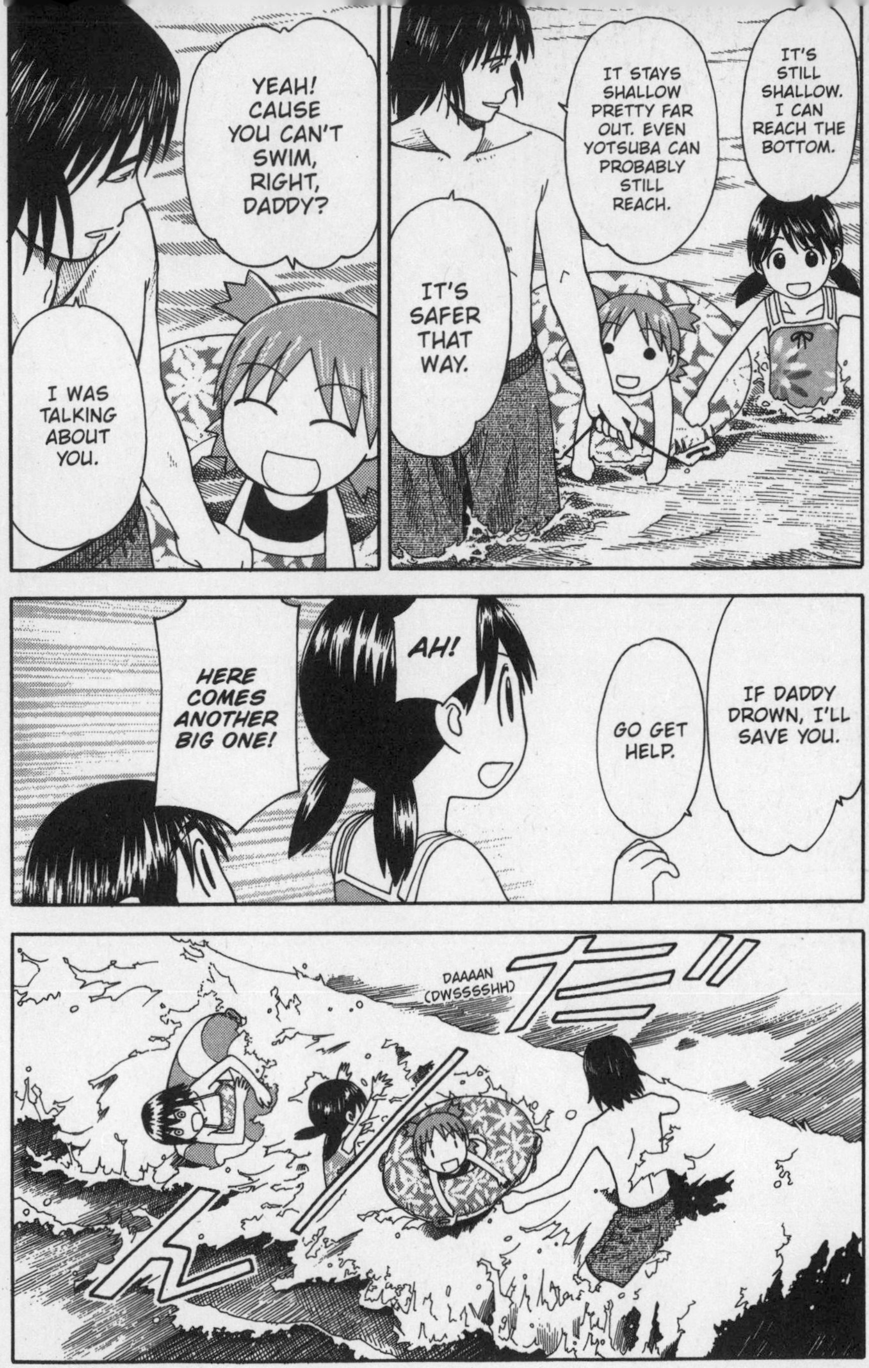
IT'S STILL SHALLOW. I CAN REACH THE BOTTOM.
IT STAYS SHALLOW PRETTY FAR OUT. EVEN YOTSUBA CAN PROBABLY STILL REACH.
IT'S SAFER THAT WAY.
YEAH! CAUSE YOU CAN'T SWIM, RIGHT, DADDY?
I WAS TALKING ABOUT YOU.
IF DADDY DROWN, I'LL SAVE YOU.
GO GET HELP.
AH!
HERE COMES ANOTHER BIG ONE!
DAAAAN (DWSSSSHH)

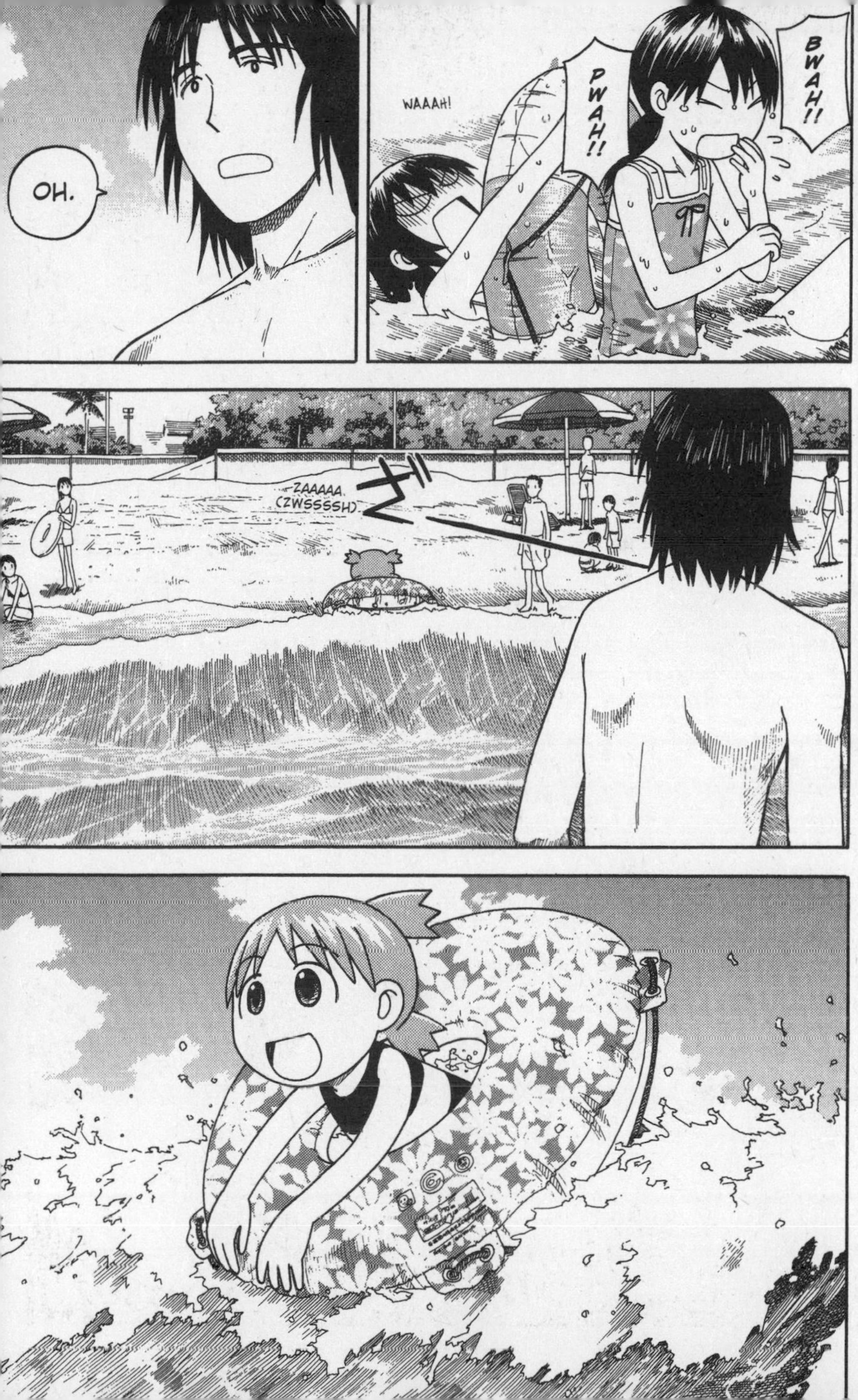
BWAH!!
PWAH!!
WAAAH!
OH.
ザ
ZAAAAA (ZWSSSSH)

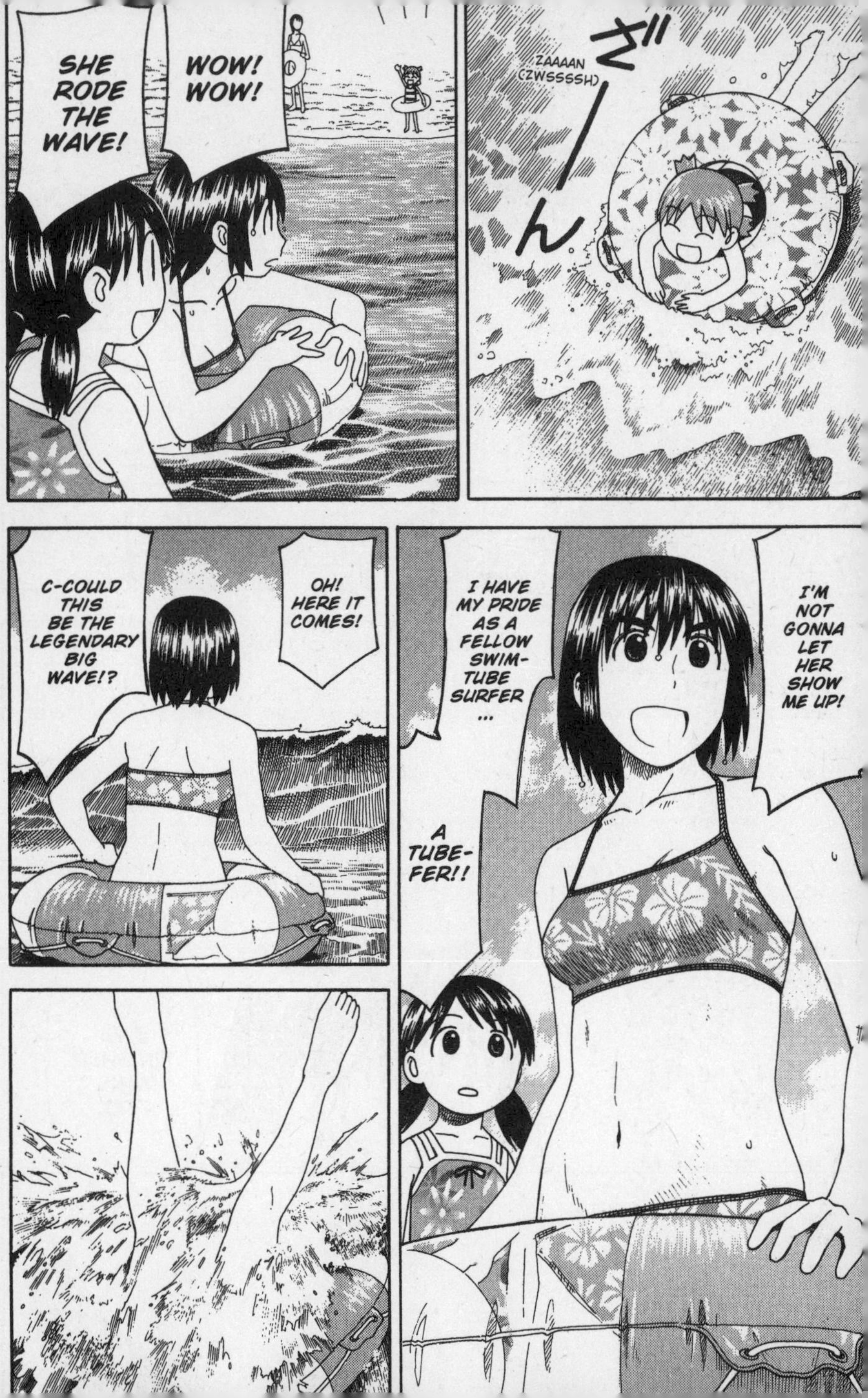
ざーん
ZAAAAN (ZWSSSSH)
WOW! WOW!
SHE RODE THE WAVE!
I'M NOT GONNA LET HER SHOW ME UP!
I HAVE MY PRIDE AS A FELLOW SWIM-TUBE SURFER ...
A TUBE-FER!!
OH! HERE IT COMES!
C-COULD THIS BE THE LEGENDARY BIG WAVE!?

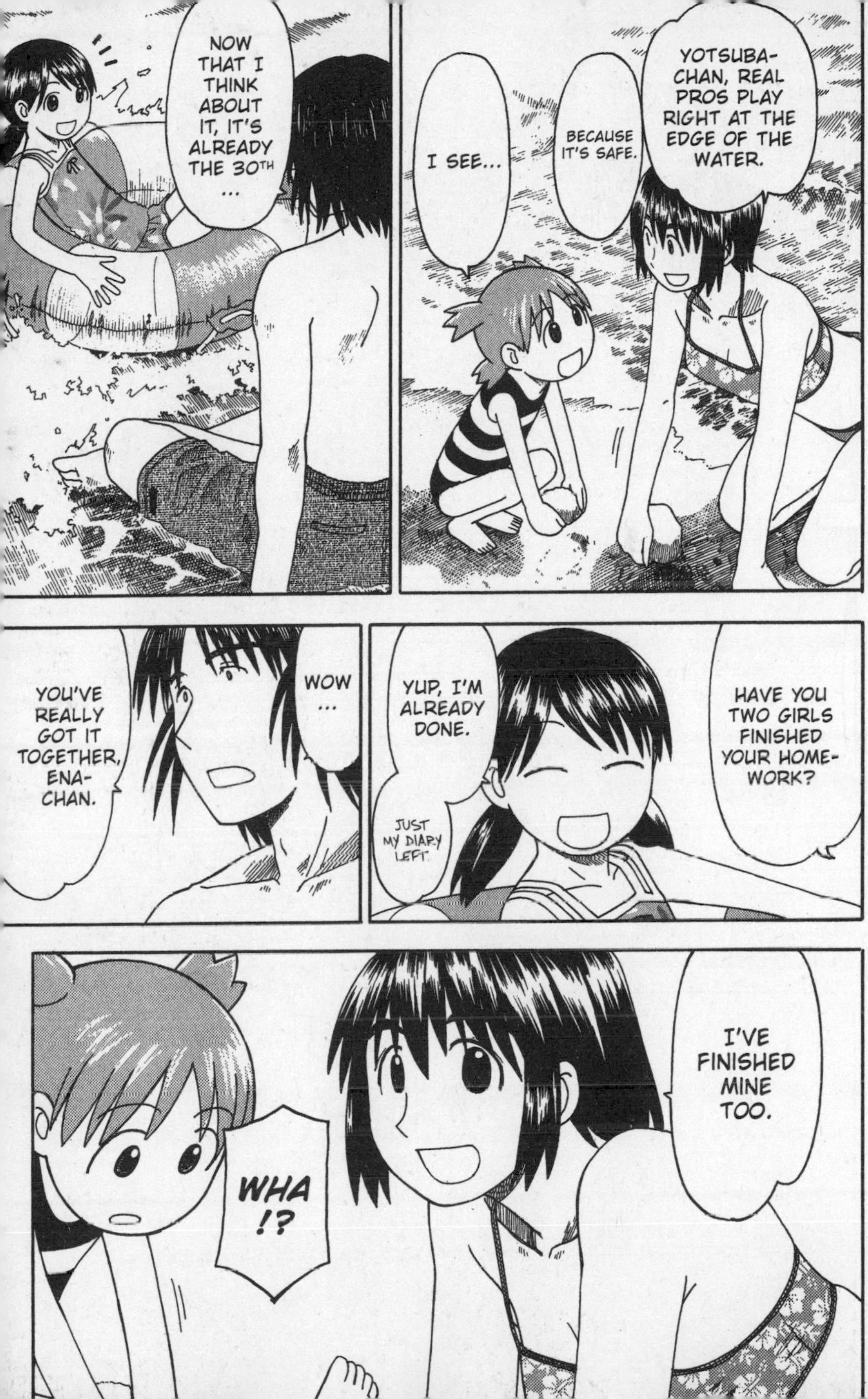
YOTSUBA-CHAN, REAL PROS PLAY RIGHT AT THE EDGE OF THE WATER.
BECAUSE IT'S SAFE.
I SEE...
NOW THAT I THINK ABOUT IT, IT'S ALREADY THE 30TH ...
HAVE YOU TWO GIRLS FINISHED YOUR HOME-WORK?
YUP, I'M ALREADY DONE.
JUST MY DIARY LEFT.
WOW ...
YOU'VE REALLY GOT IT TOGETHER, ENA-CHAN.
I'VE FINISHED MINE TOO.
WHA !?

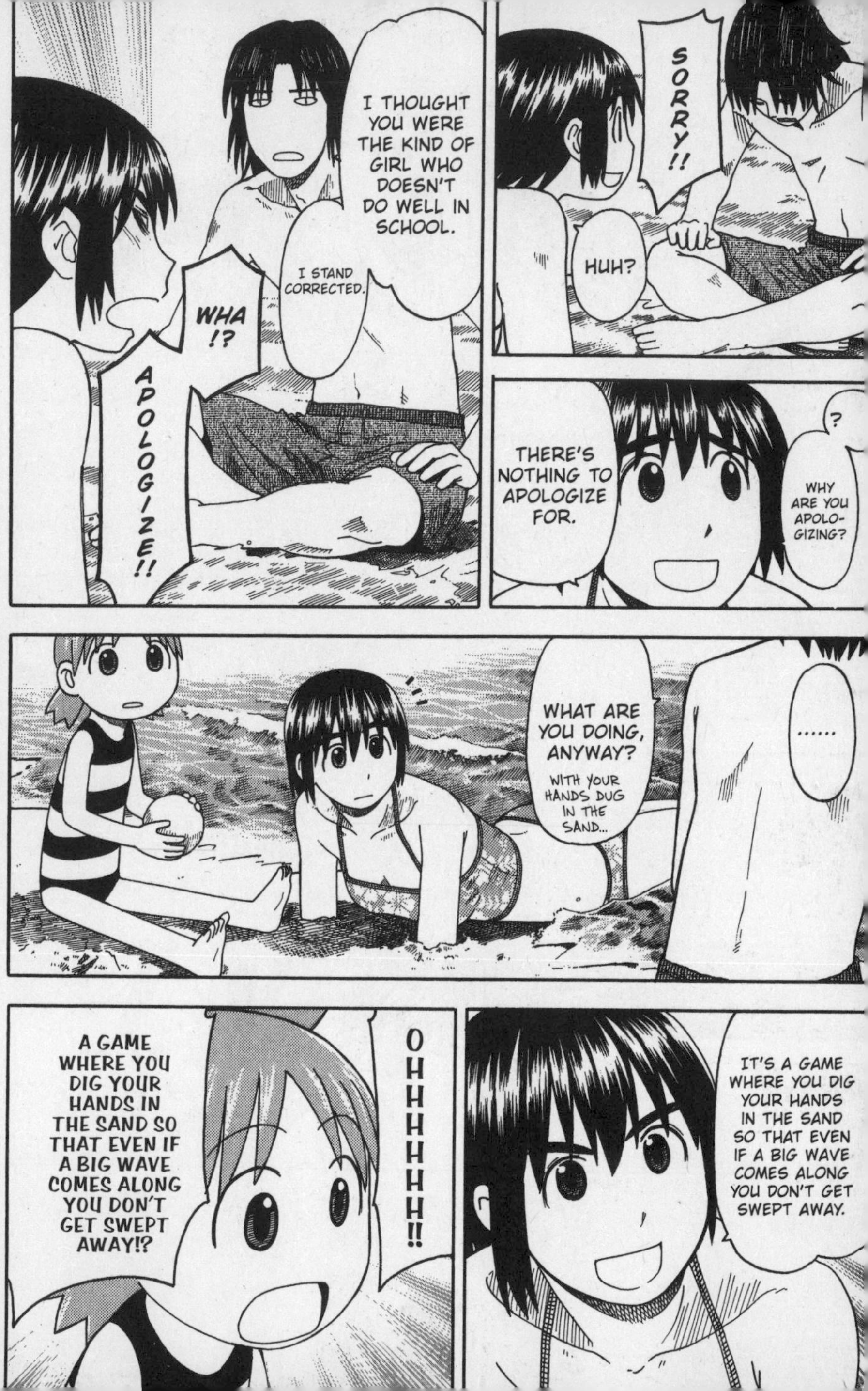

SORRY!!
HUH?
THERE'S NOTHING TO APOLOGIZE FOR.
?
WHY ARE YOU APOLO-GIZING?
I THOUGHT YOU WERE THE KIND OF GIRL WHO DOESN'T DO WELL IN SCHOOL.
I STAND CORRECTED.
WHA !?
APOLOGIZE!!
......
WHAT ARE YOU DOING, ANYWAY?
WITH YOUR HANDS DUG IN THE SAND...
IT'S A GAME WHERE YOU DIG YOUR HANDS IN THE SAND SO THAT EVEN IF A BIG WAVE COMES ALONG YOU DON'T GET SWEPT AWAY.
OHHHHHHH!!
A GAME WHERE YOU DIG YOUR HANDS IN THE SAND SO THAT EVEN IF A BIG WAVE COMES ALONG YOU DON'T GET SWEPT AWAY!?

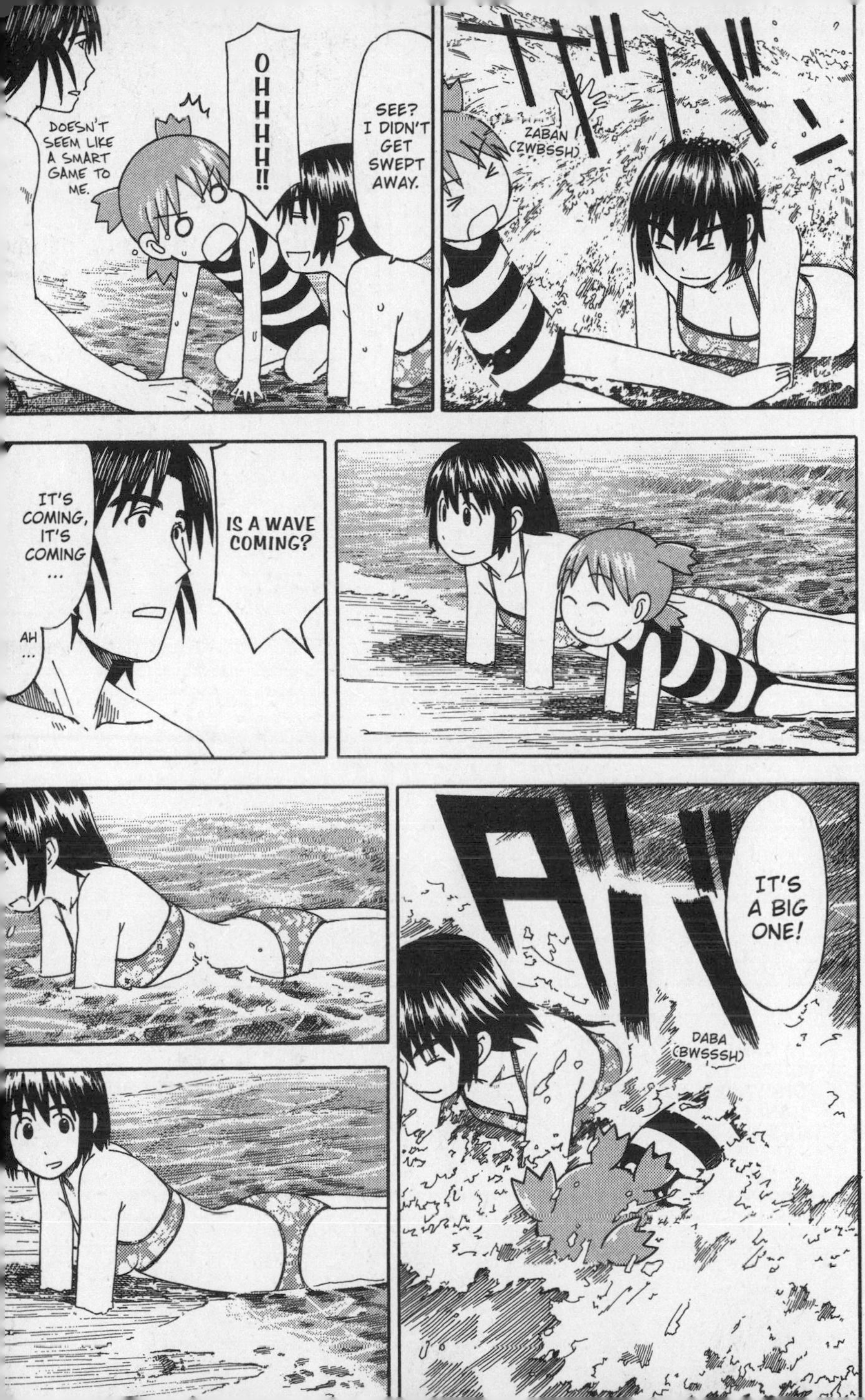
ZABAN (ZWBSSH)
SEE? I DIDN'T GET SWEPT AWAY.
OHHHHH!!
DOESN'T SEEM LIKE A SMART GAME TO ME.
IS A WAVE COMING?
IT'S COMING, IT'S COMING ...
AH ...
IT'S A BIG ONE!
DABA (BWSSSH)

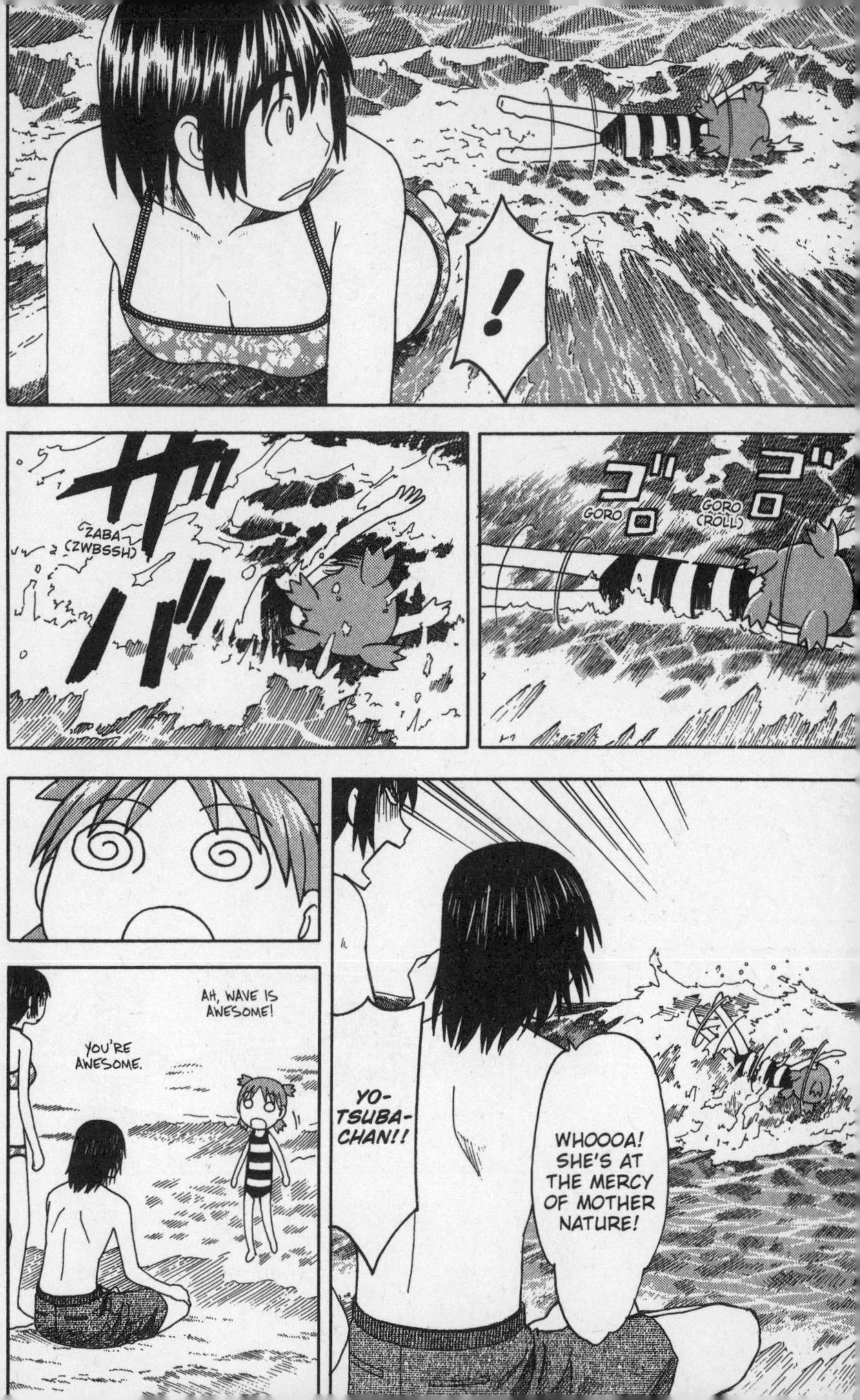
!
GORO (ROLL)
GORO
ZABA (ZWBSSH)
WHOOOA! SHE'S AT THE MERCY OF MOTHER NATURE!
YO-TSUBA-CHAN!!
AH, WAVE IS AWESOME!
YOU'RE AWESOME.

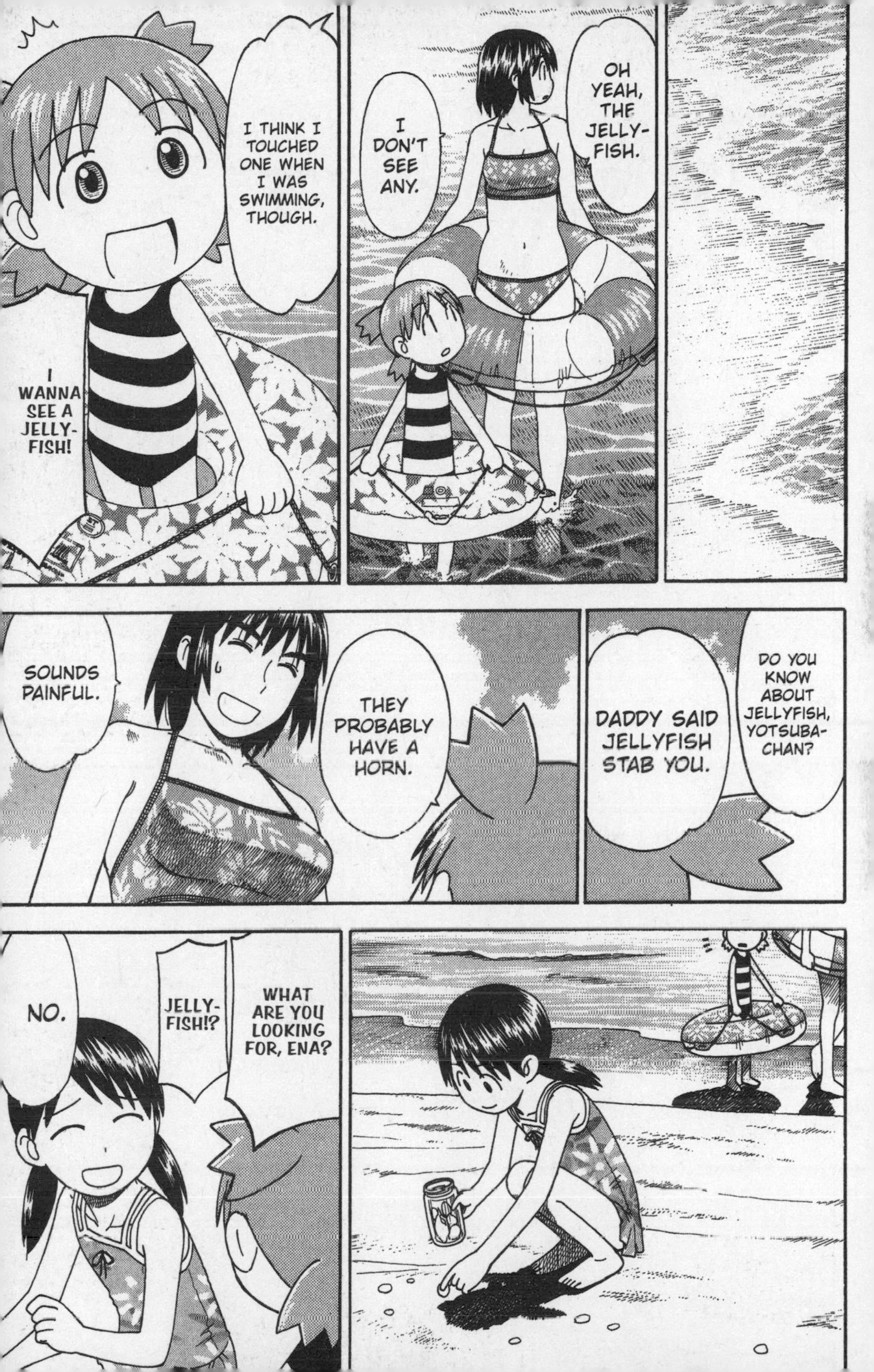
OH YEAH, THE JELLY-FISH.
I DON'T SEE ANY.
I THINK I TOUCHED ONE WHEN I WAS SWIMMING, THOUGH.
I WANNA SEE A JELLY-FISH!
DO YOU KNOW ABOUT JELLYFISH, YOTSUBA-CHAN?
DADDY SAID JELLYFISH STAB YOU.
THEY PROBABLY HAVE A HORN.
SOUNDS PAINFUL.
WHAT ARE YOU LOOKING FOR, ENA?
JELLY-FISH!?
NO.

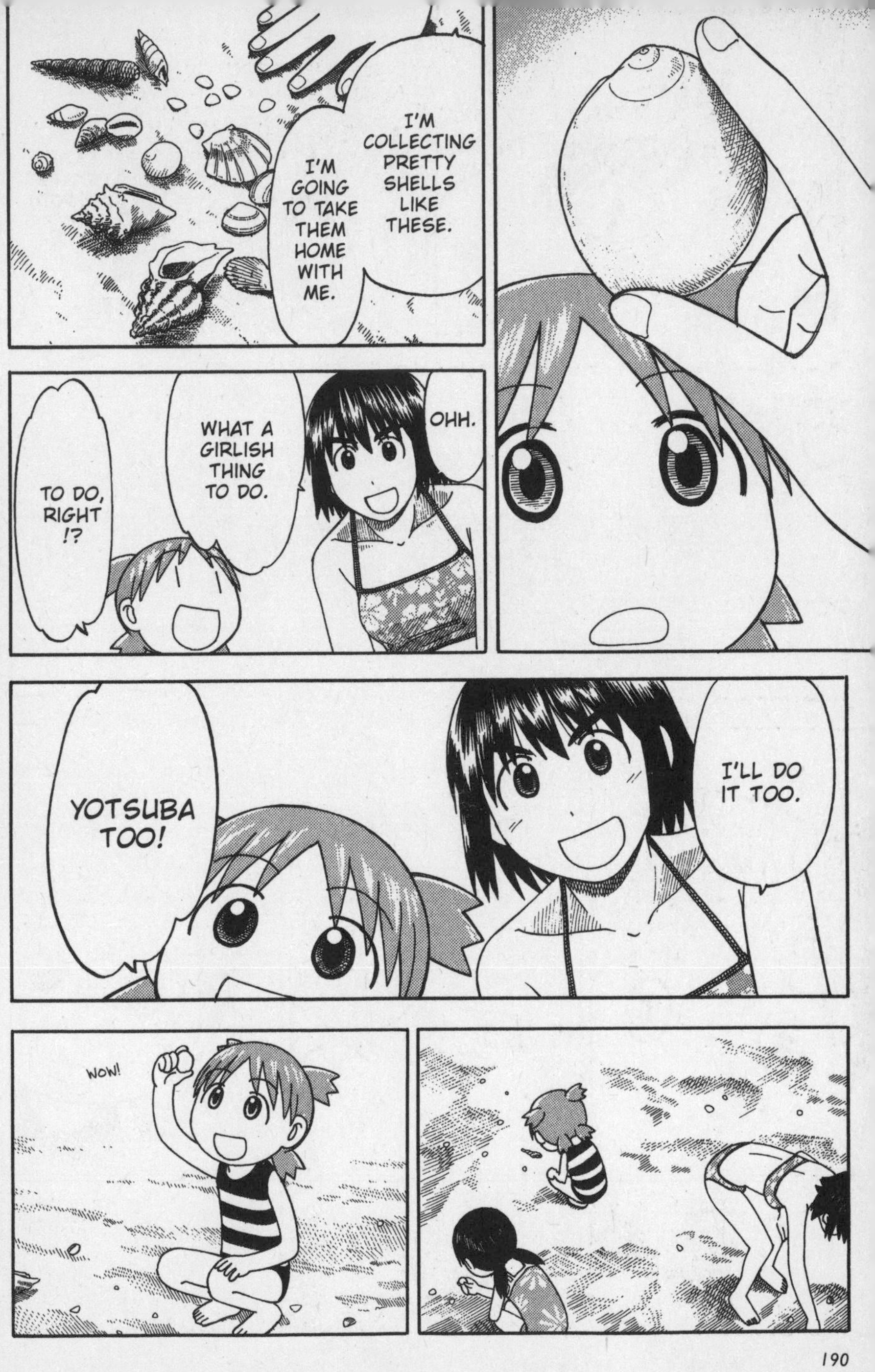
I'M COLLECTING PRETTY SHELLS LIKE THESE.
I'M GOING TO TAKE THEM HOME WITH ME.
OHH.
WHAT A GIRLISH THING TO DO.
TO DO, RIGHT !?
I'LL DO IT TOO.
YOTSUBA TOO!
WOW!

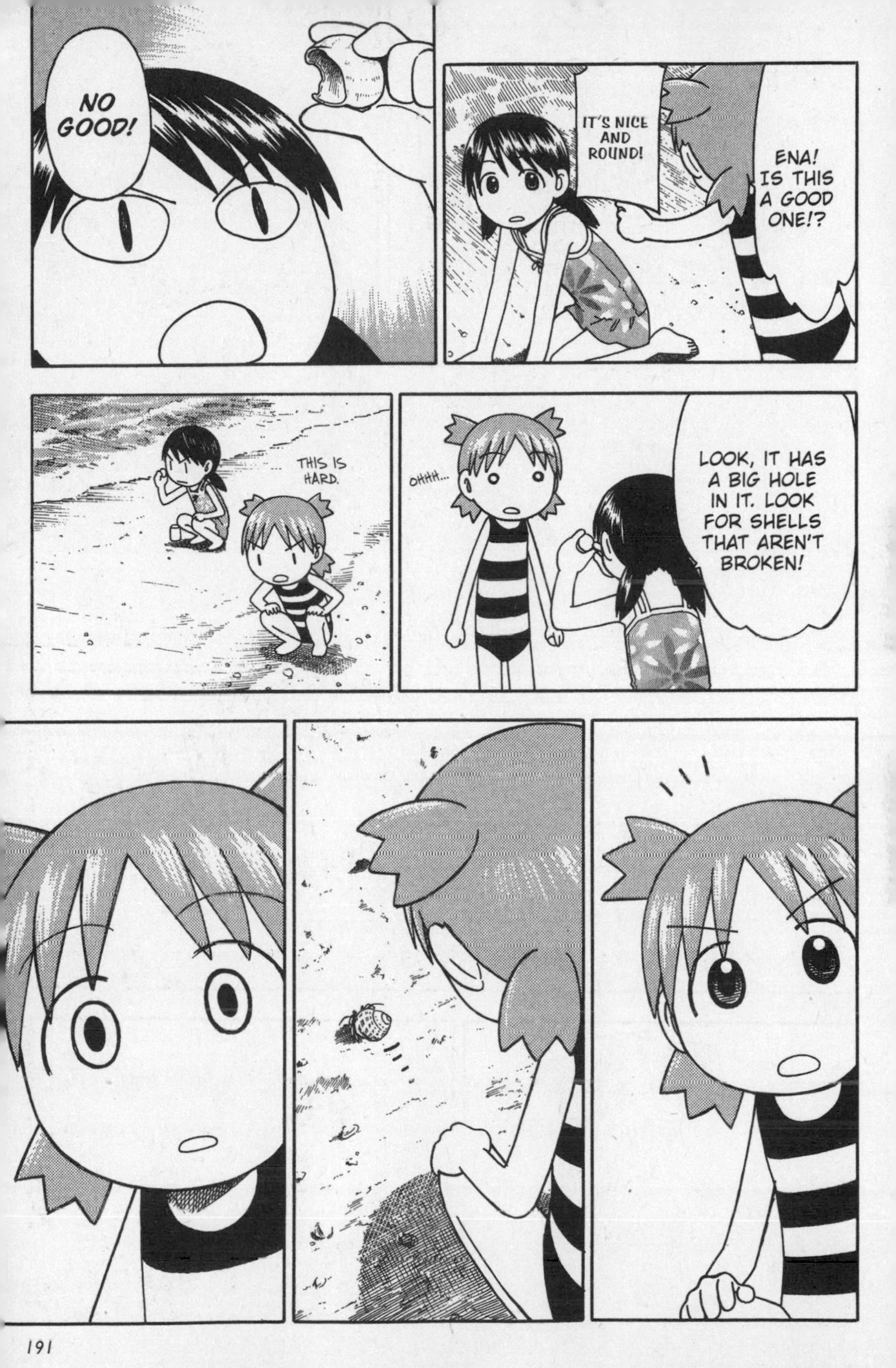
ENA! IS THIS A GOOD ONE!?
IT'S NICE AND ROUND!
NO GOOD!
LOOK, IT HAS A BIG HOLE IN IT. LOOK FOR SHELLS THAT AREN'T BROKEN!
OHHH...
THIS IS HARD.

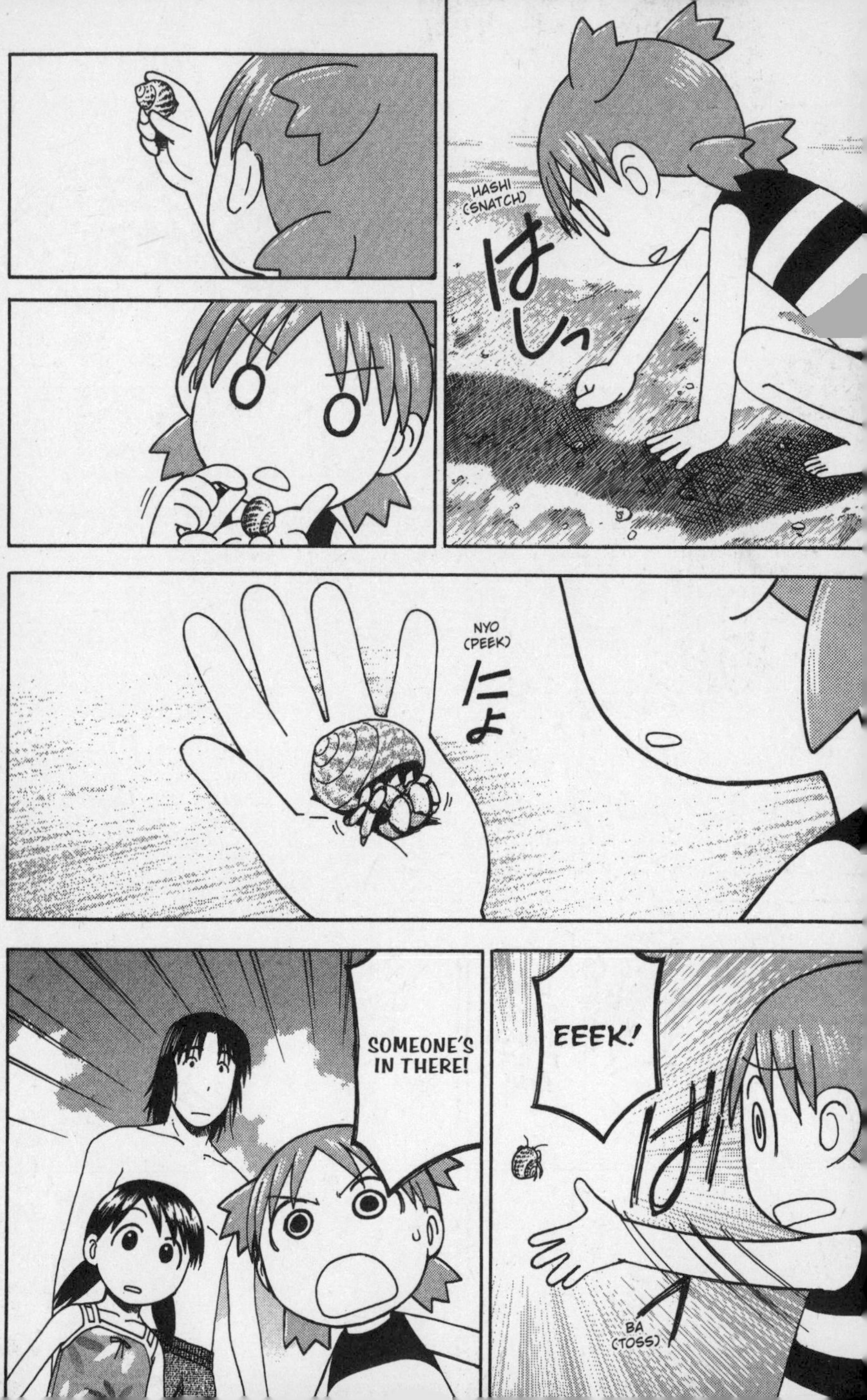
HASHI
(SNATCH)
はしっ
NYO
(PEEK)
にょ
EEEK!
BA
(TOSS)
SOMEONE'S IN THERE!

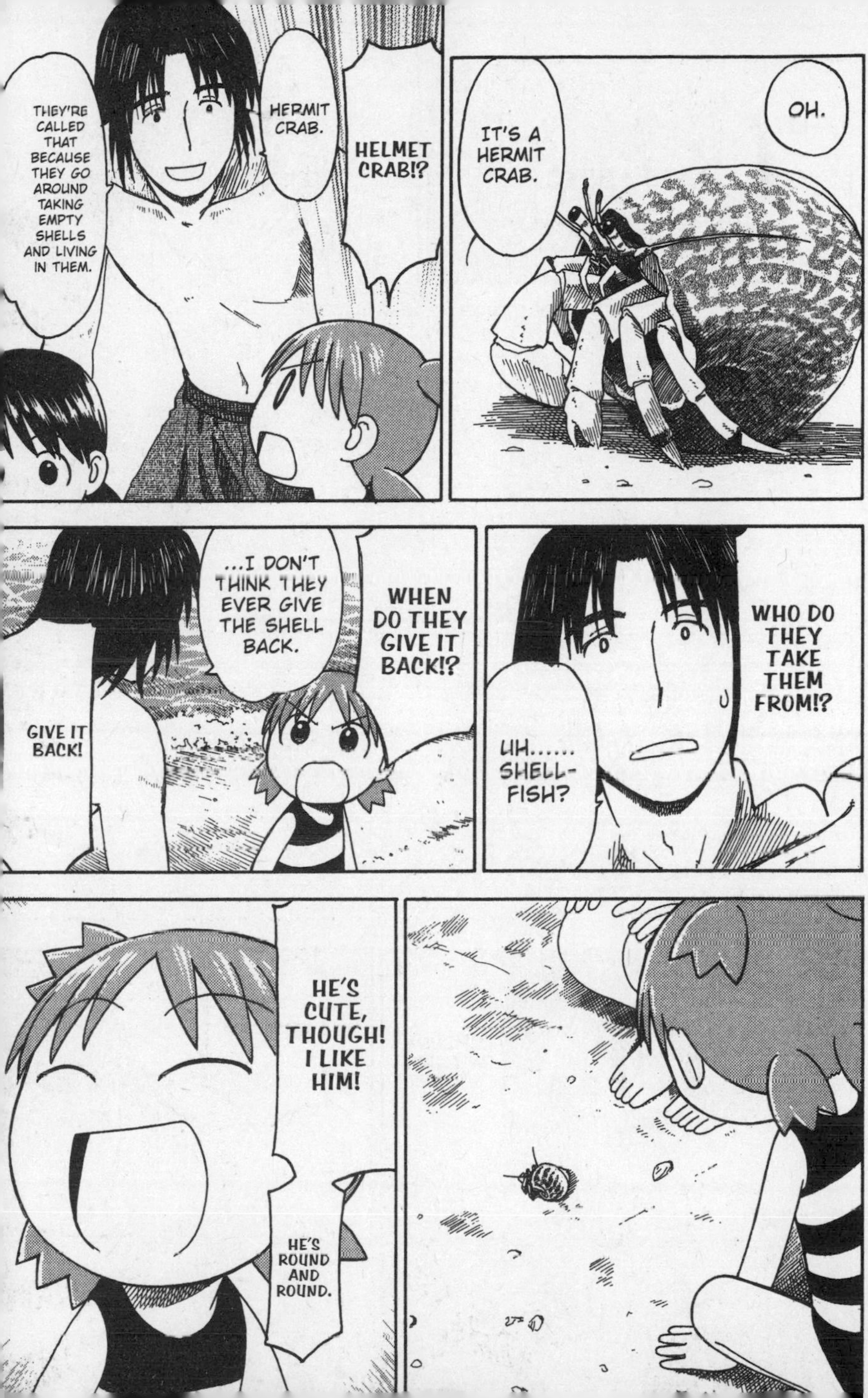
OH.
IT'S A HERMIT CRAB.
HELMET CRAB!?
HERMIT CRAB.
THEY'RE CALLED THAT BECAUSE THEY GO AROUND TAKING EMPTY SHELLS AND LIVING IN THEM.
WHO DO THEY TAKE THEM FROM!?
UH...... SHELL-FISH?
WHEN DO THEY GIVE IT BACK!?
...I DON'T THINK THEY EVER GIVE THE SHELL BACK.
GIVE IT BACK!
HE'S CUTE, THOUGH! I LIKE HIM!
HE'S ROUND AND ROUND.

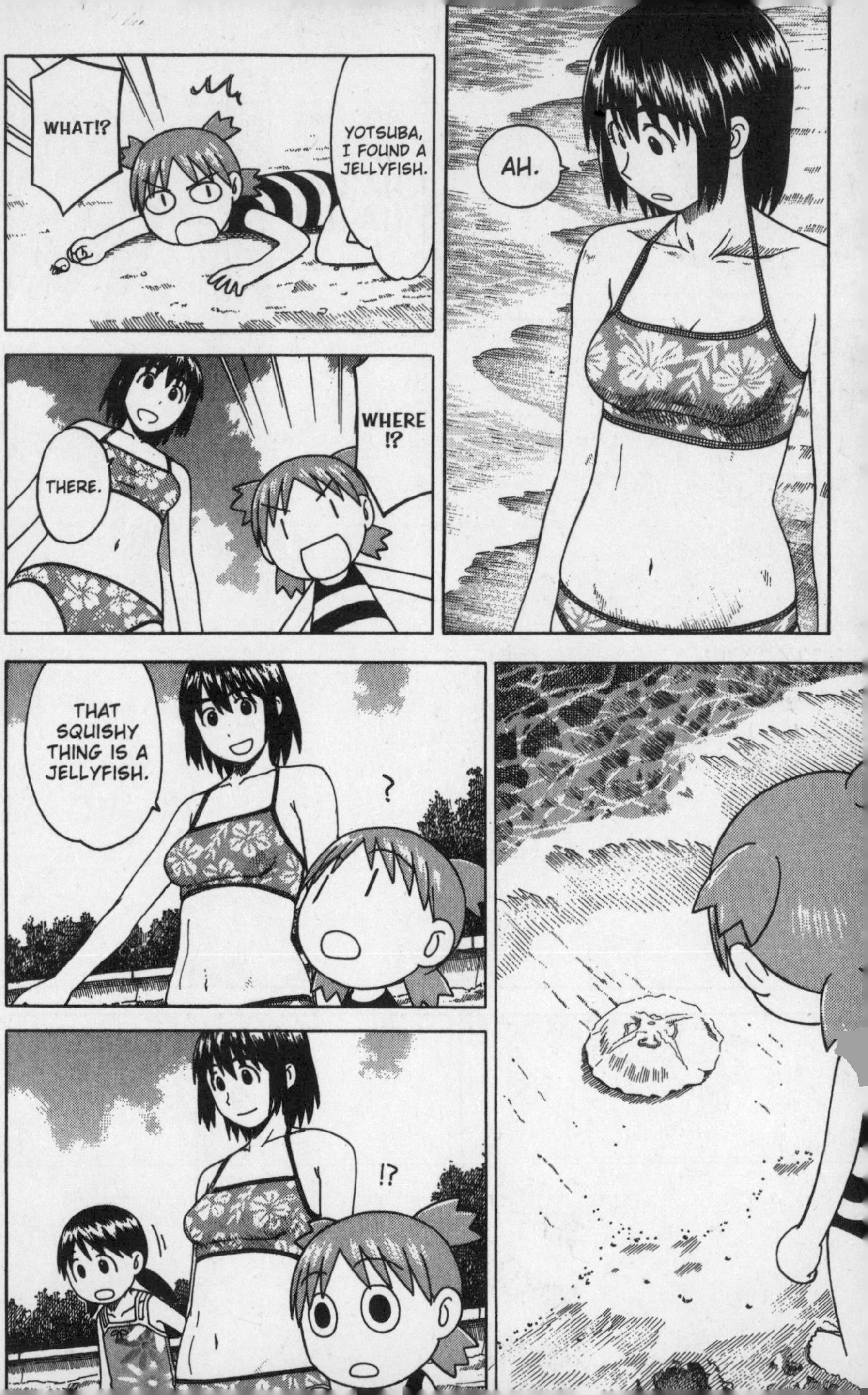
AH.
YOTSUBA, I FOUND A JELLYFISH.
WHAT!?
WHERE !?
THERE.
THAT SQUISHY THING IS A JELLYFISH.
?
!?

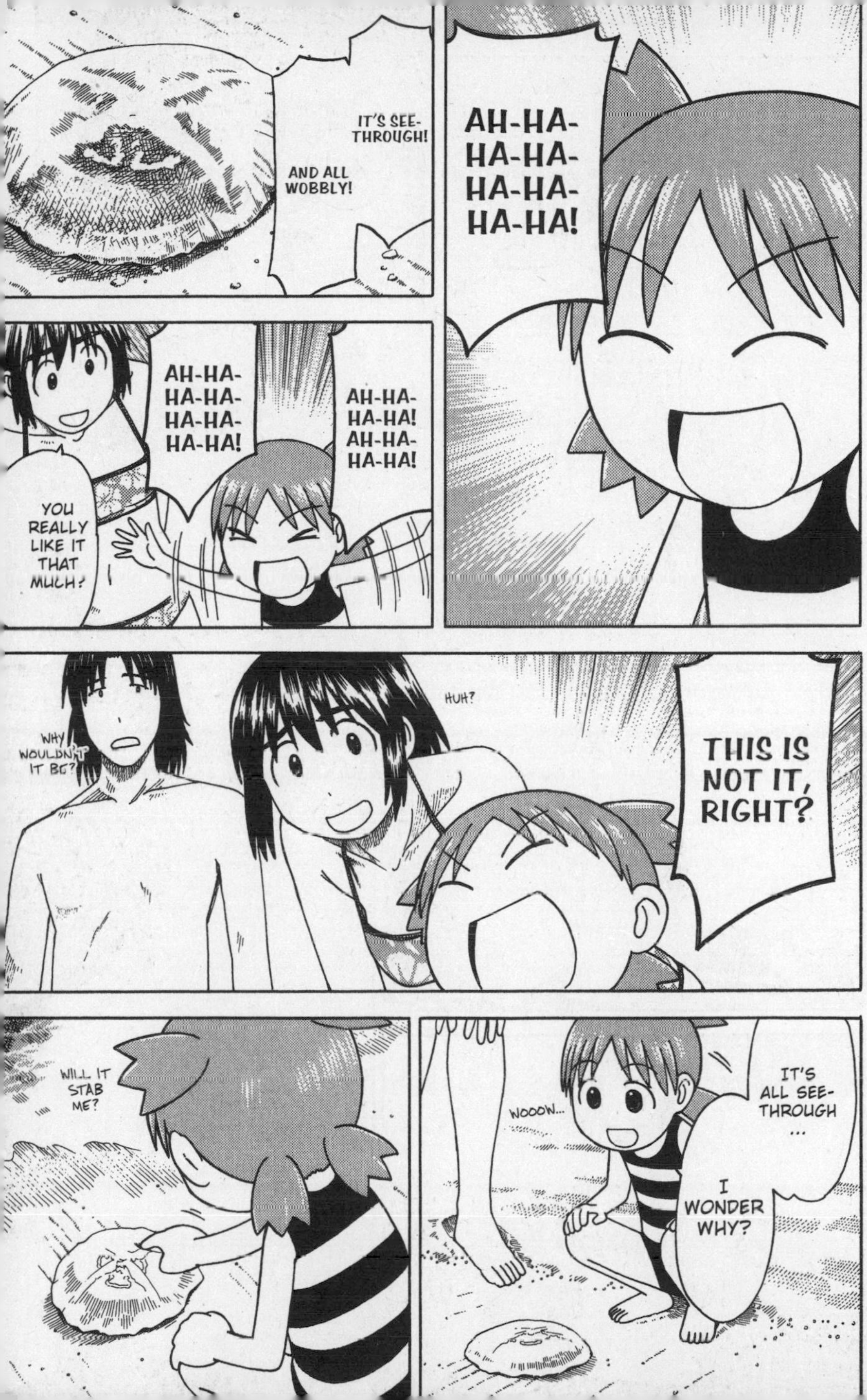
AH-HA-HA-HA-HA-HA-HA-HA!
IT'S SEE-THROUGH!
AND ALL WOBBLY!
AH-HA-HA-HA! AH-HA-HA-HA!
AH-HA-HA-HA-HA-HA-HA-HA!
YOU REALLY LIKE IT THAT MUCH?
THIS IS NOT IT, RIGHT?
HUH?
WHY WOULDN'T IT BE?
IT'S ALL SEE-THROUGH...
I WONDER WHY?
WOOOW...
WILL IT STAB ME?

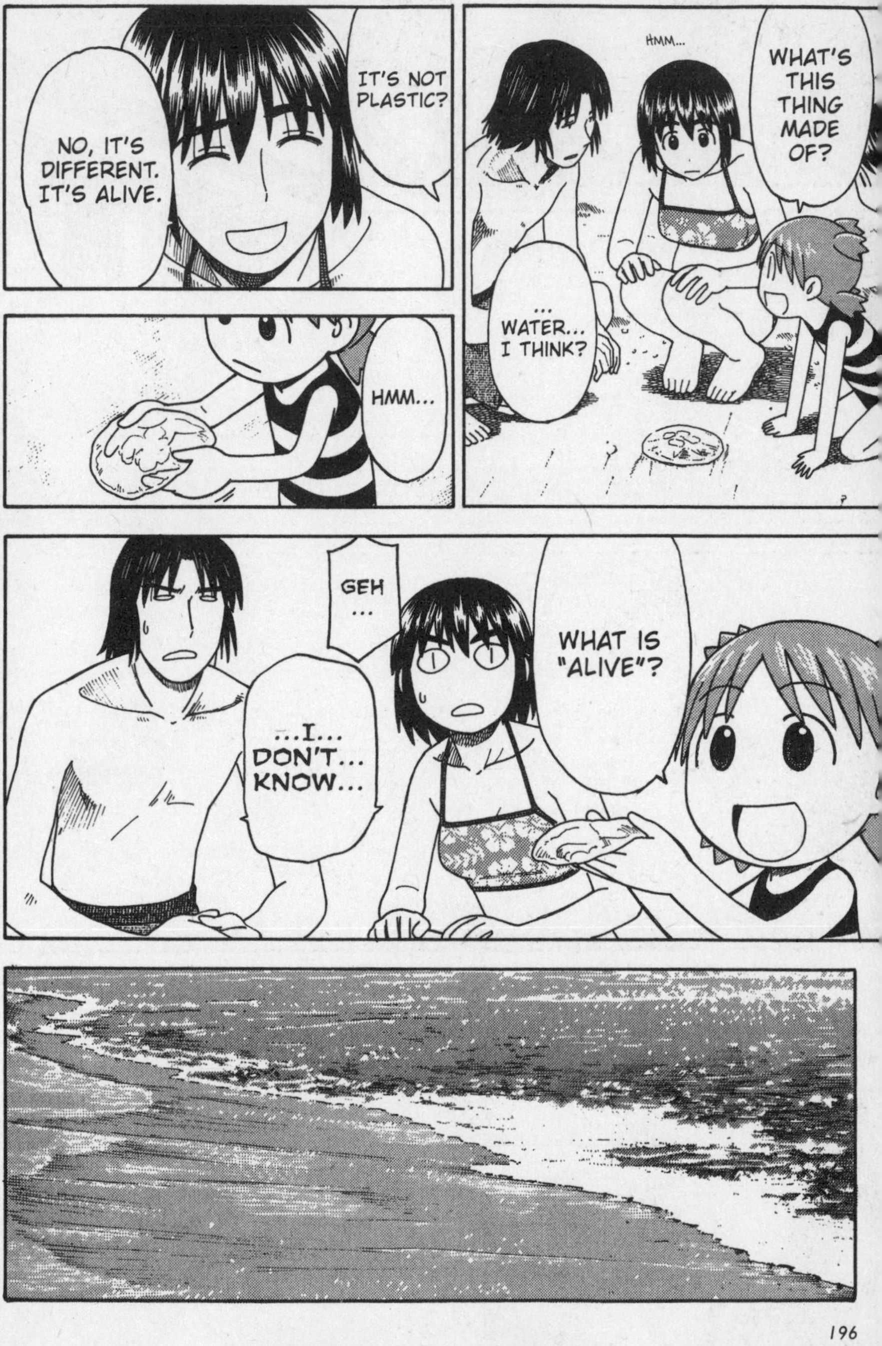
WHAT'S THIS THING MADE OF?
HMM...
... WATER... I THINK?
IT'S NOT PLASTIC?
NO, IT'S DIFFERENT. IT'S ALIVE.
HMM...
WHAT IS "ALIVE"?
GEH ...
...I... DON'T... KNOW...

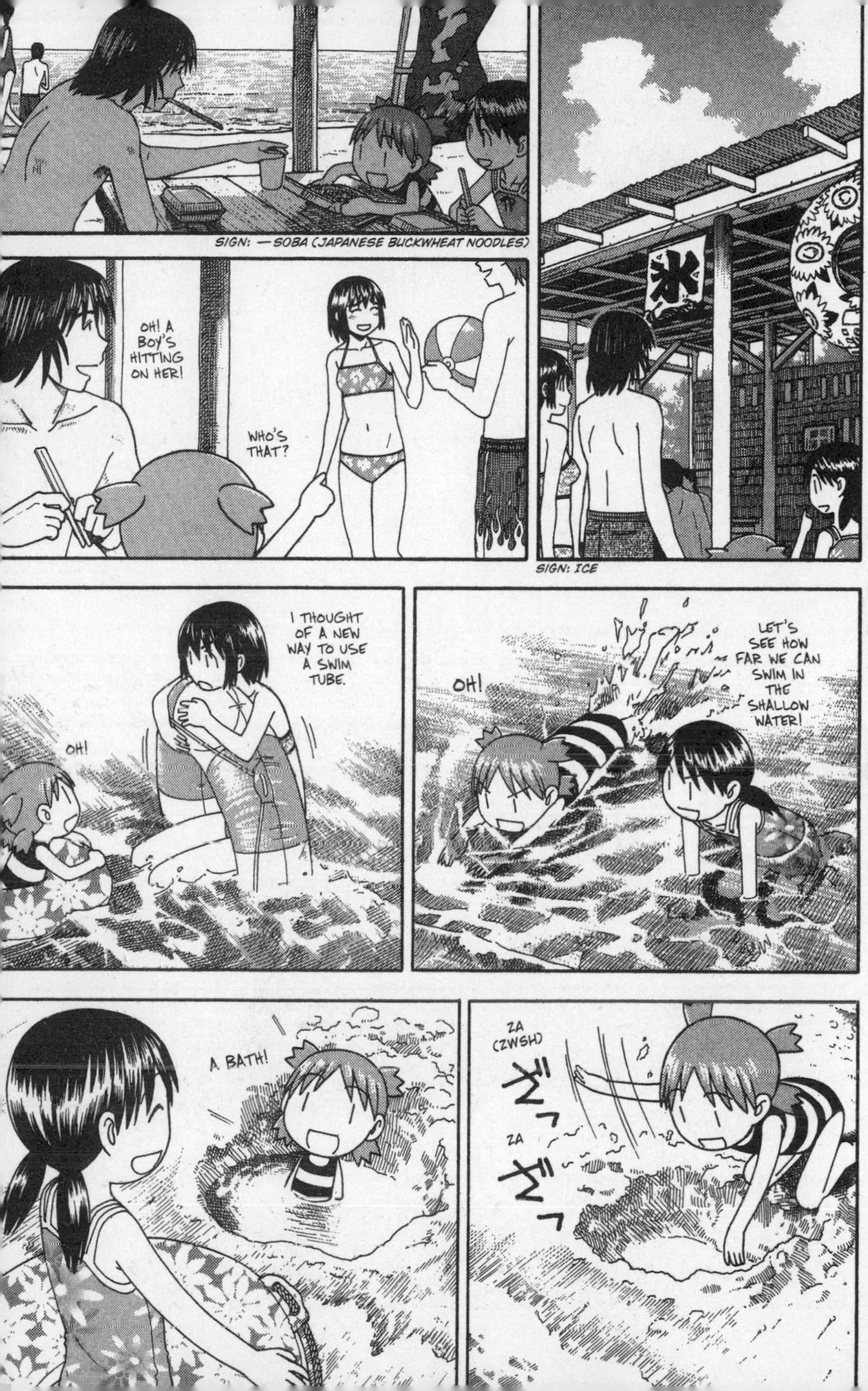
SIGN: ICE
SIGN: —SOBA (JAPANESE BUCKWHEAT NOODLES)
WHO'S THAT?
OH! A BOY'S HITTING ON HER!
LET'S SEE HOW FAR WE CAN SWIM IN THE SHALLOW WATER!
OH!
I THOUGHT OF A NEW WAY TO USE A SWIM TUBE.
OH!
ZA (ZWSH)
ZA
A BATH!

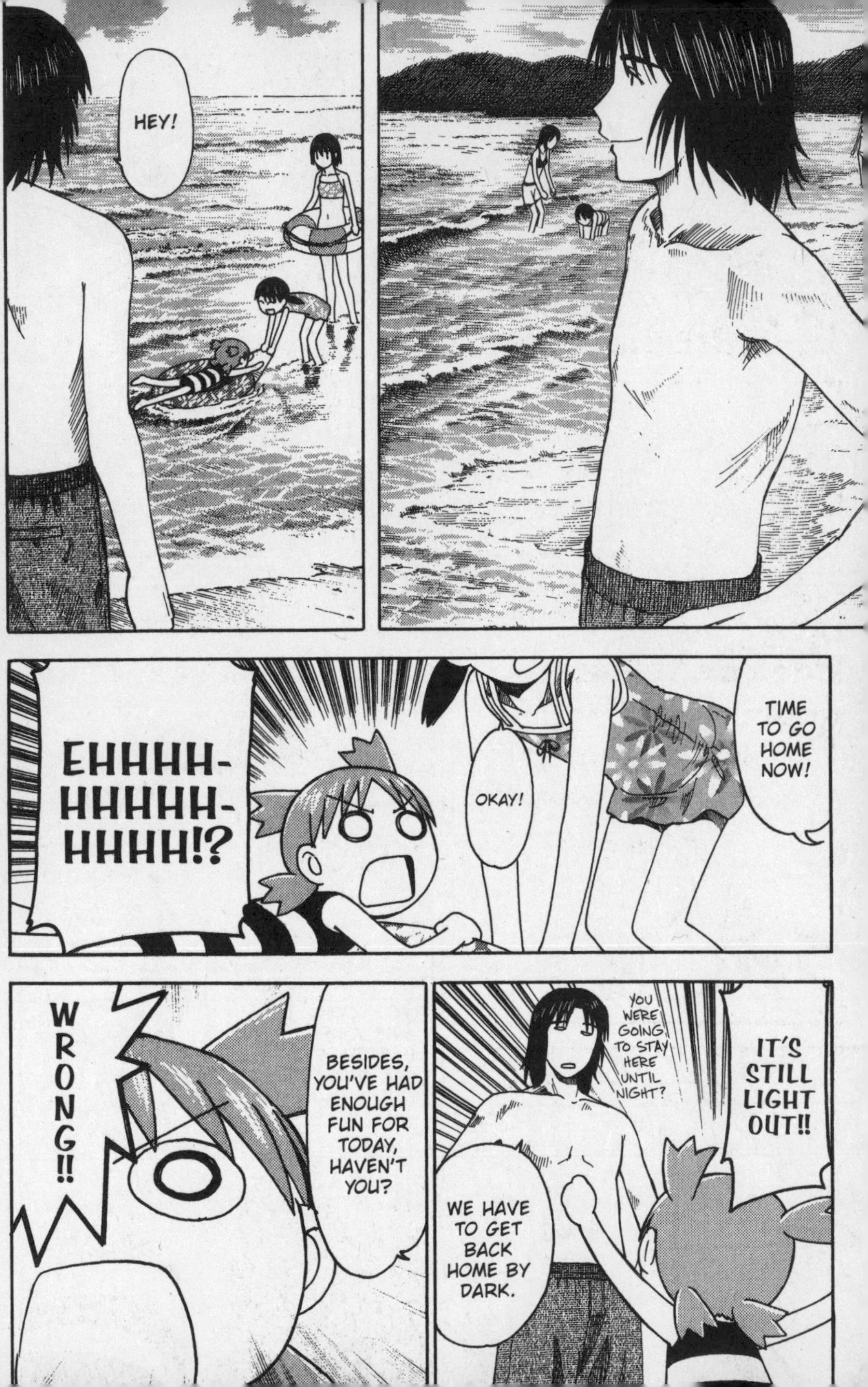
HEY!
TIME TO GO HOME NOW!
OKAY!
EHHHH-HHHHH-HHHH!?
IT'S STILL LIGHT OUT!!
YOU WERE GOING TO STAY HERE UNTIL NIGHT?
WE HAVE TO GET BACK HOME BY DARK.
BESIDES, YOU'VE HAD ENOUGH FUN FOR TODAY, HAVEN'T YOU?
WRONG!!

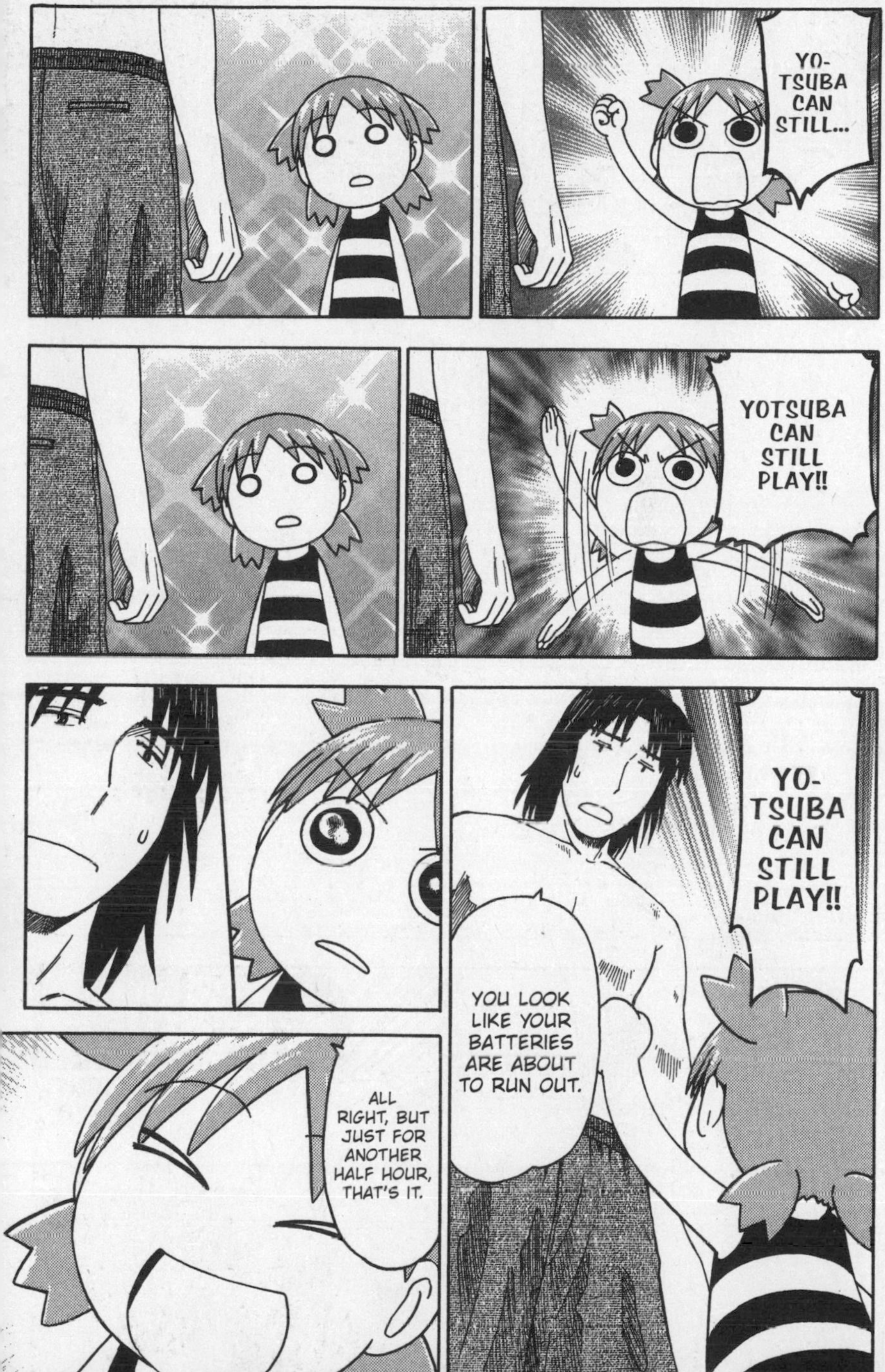
YO-TSUBA CAN STILL...
YOTSUBA CAN STILL PLAY!!
YO-TSUBA CAN STILL PLAY!!
YOU LOOK LIKE YOUR BATTERIES ARE ABOUT TO RUN OUT.
ALL RIGHT, BUT JUST FOR ANOTHER HALF HOUR, THAT'S IT.

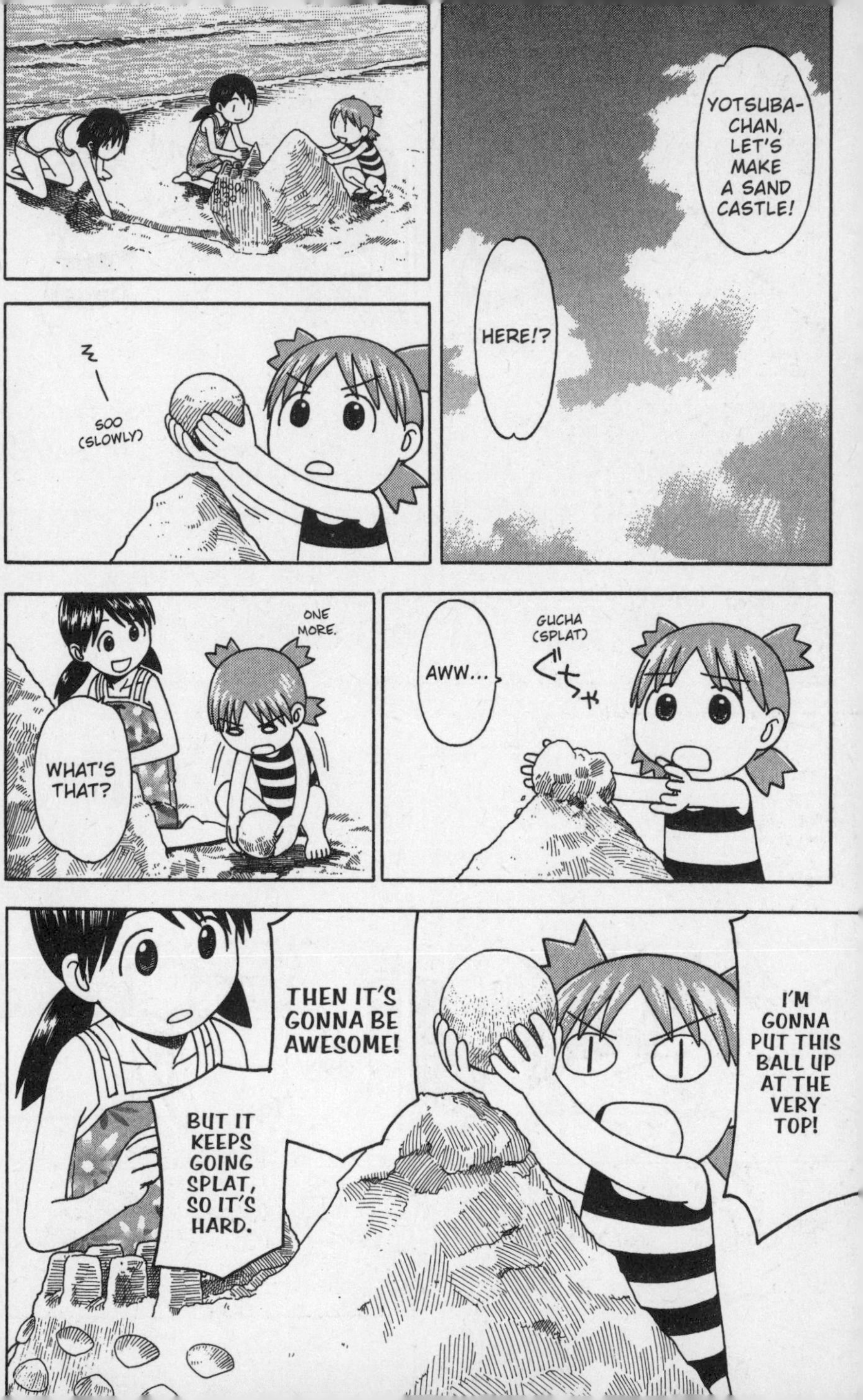
YOTSUBA-CHAN, LET'S MAKE A SAND CASTLE!
HERE!?
SOO (SLOWLY)
GUCHA (SPLAT)
ぐちゃ
AWW...
ONE MORE.
WHAT'S THAT?
I'M GONNA PUT THIS BALL UP AT THE VERY TOP!
THEN IT'S GONNA BE AWESOME!
BUT IT KEEPS GOING SPLAT, SO IT'S HARD.

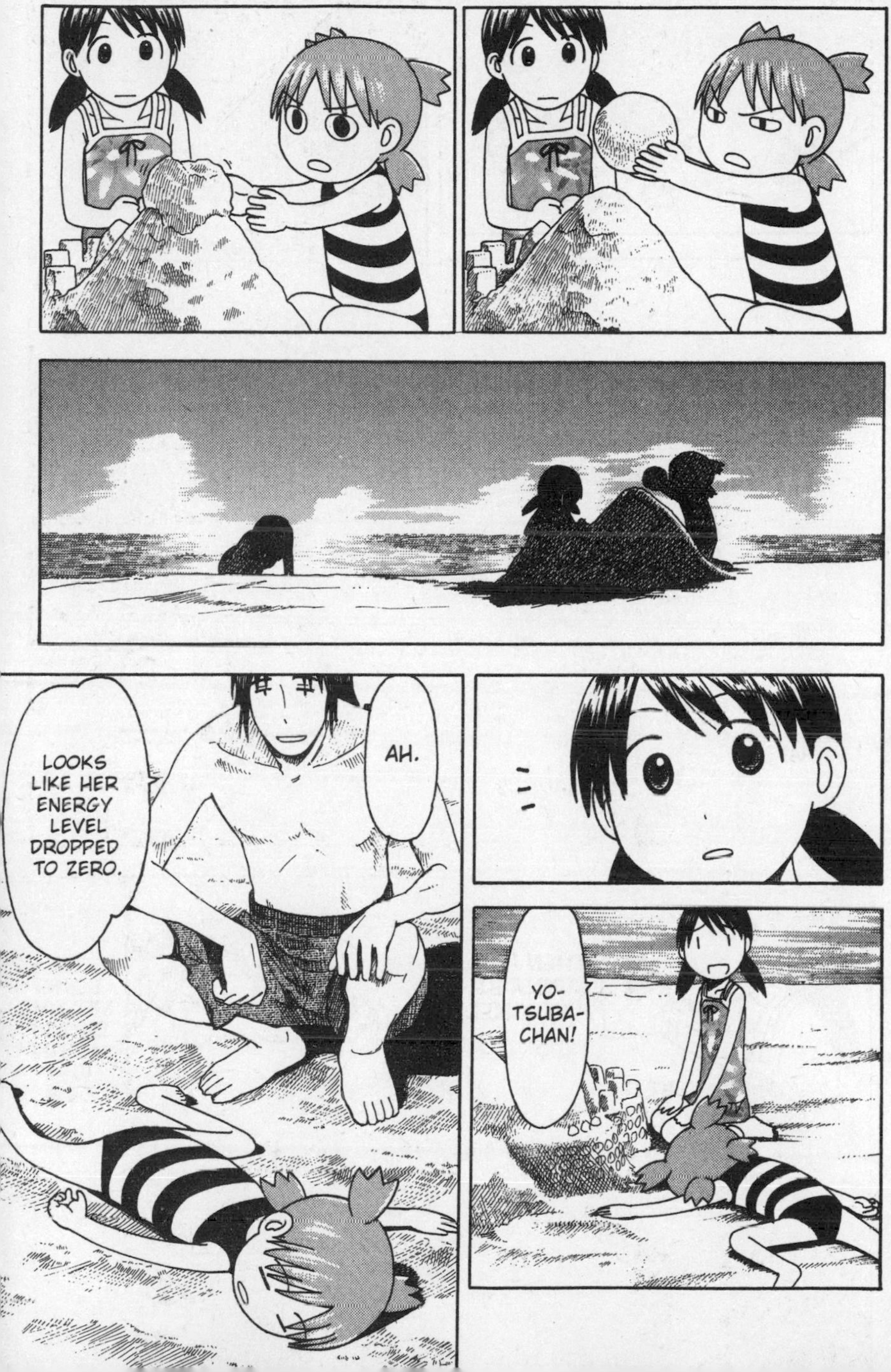
...
YO-TSUBA-CHAN!
AH.
LOOKS LIKE HER ENERGY LEVEL DROPPED TO ZERO.

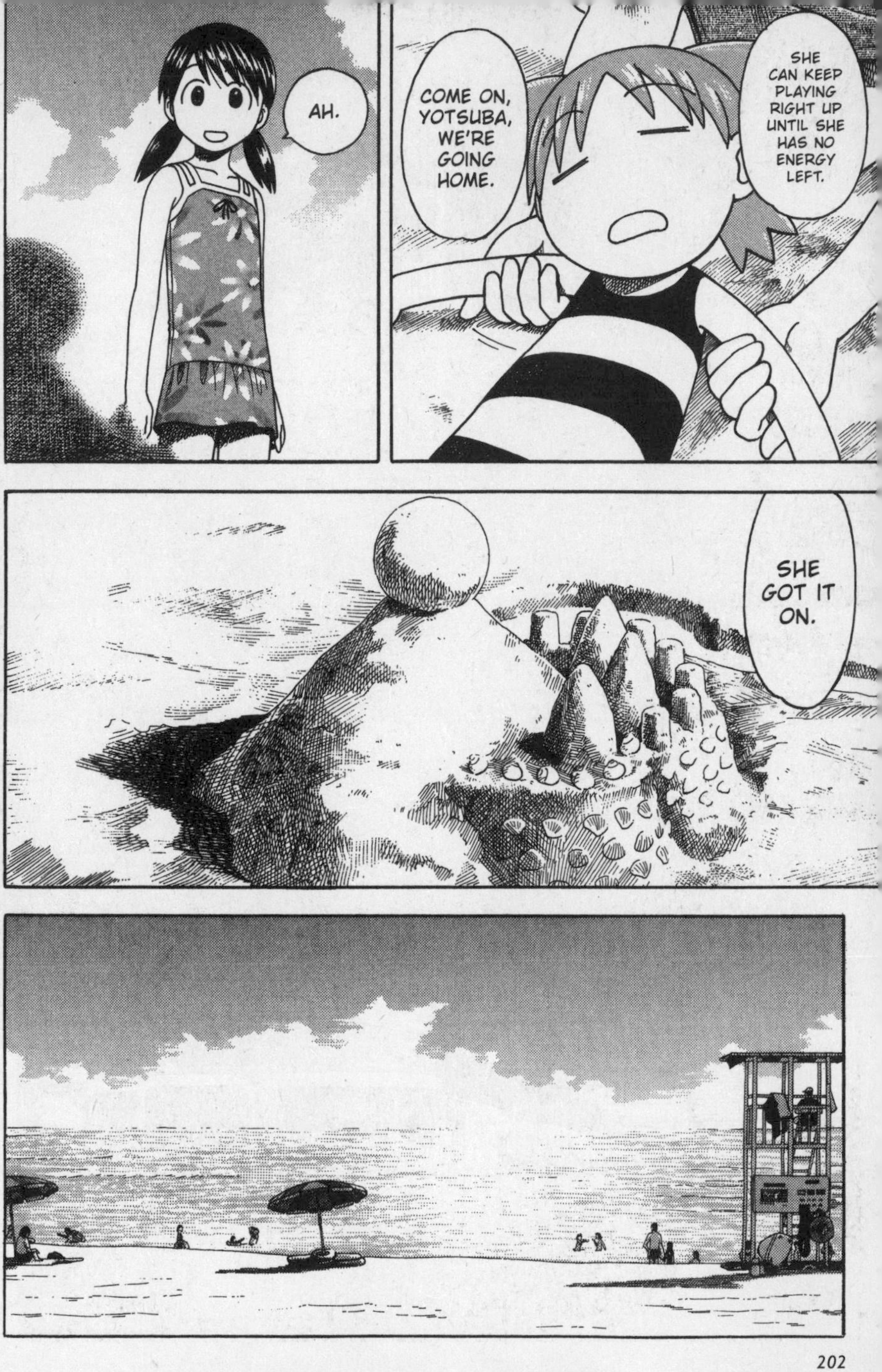
SHE CAN KEEP PLAYING RIGHT UP UNTIL SHE HAS NO ENERGY LEFT.
COME ON, YOTSUBA, WE'RE GOING HOME.
AH.
SHE GOT IT ON.

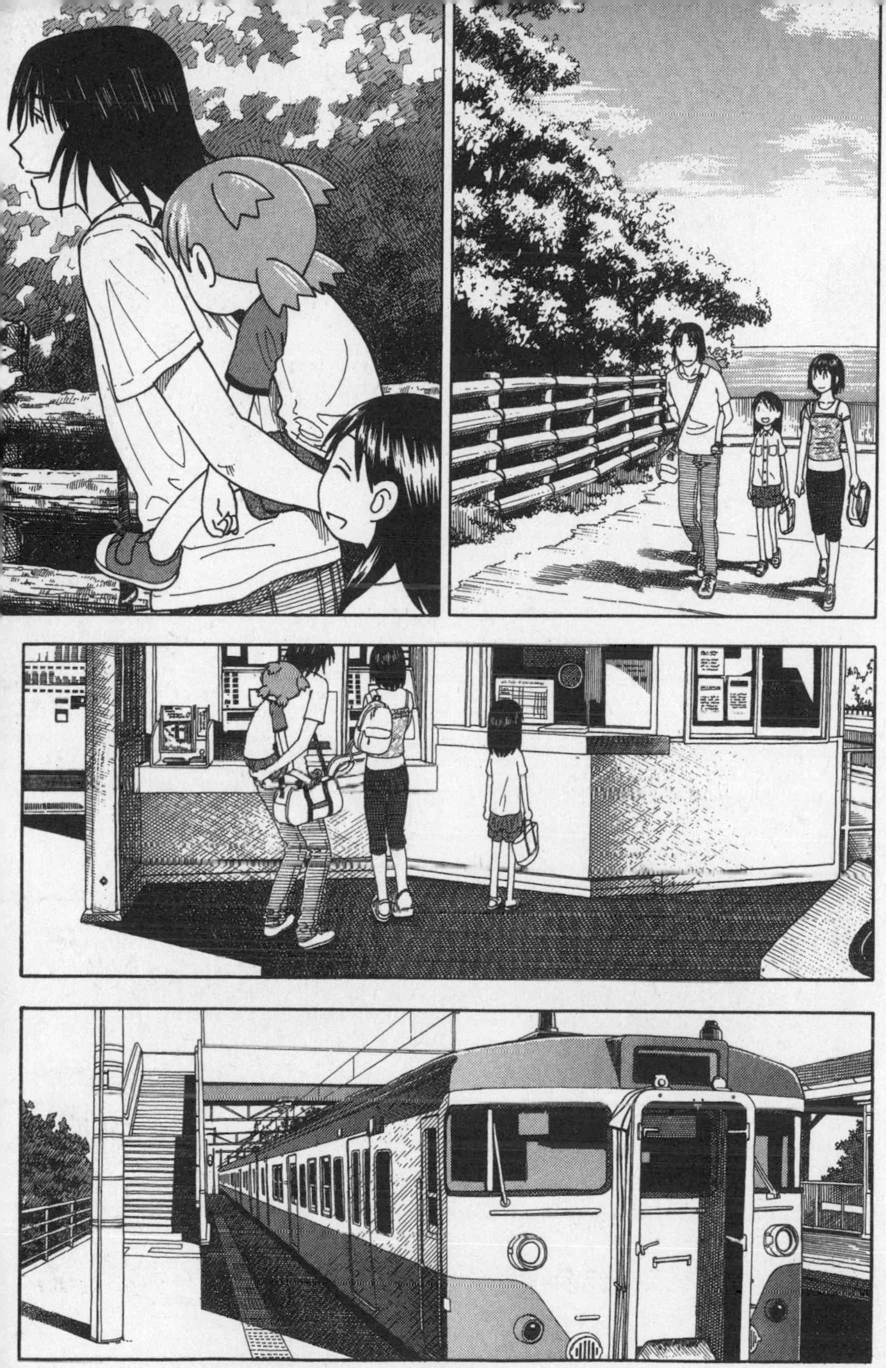

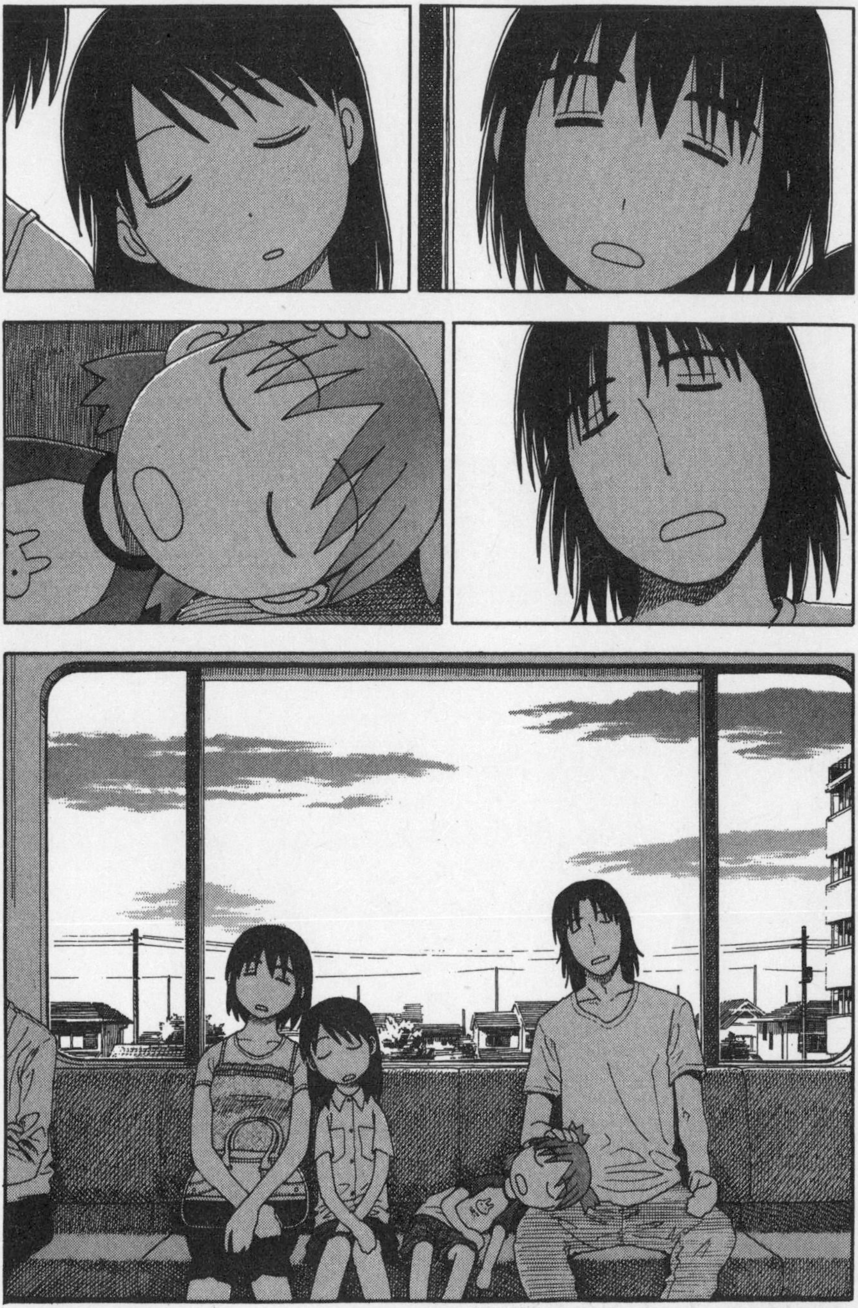

YOTSUBA&!

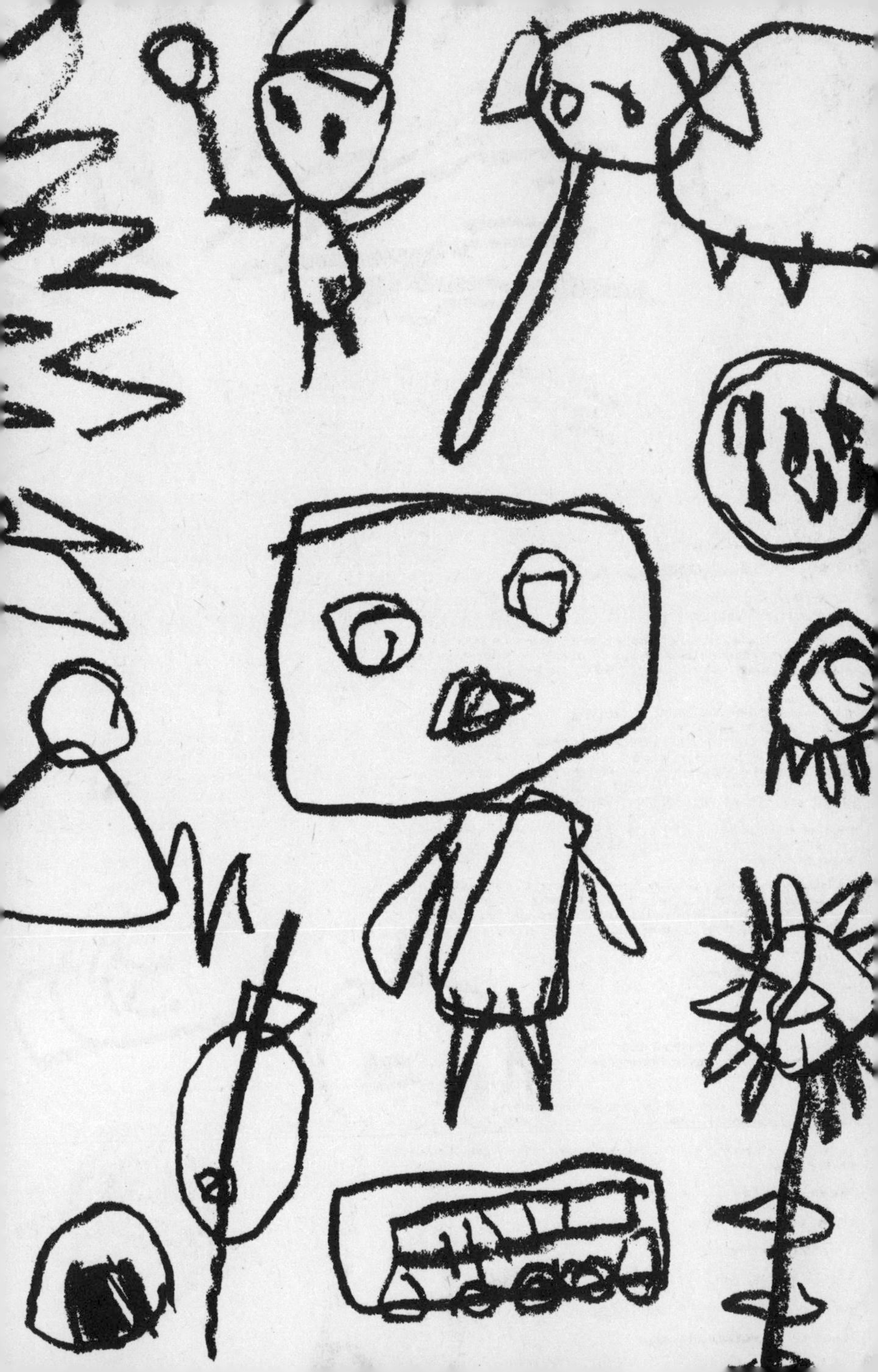

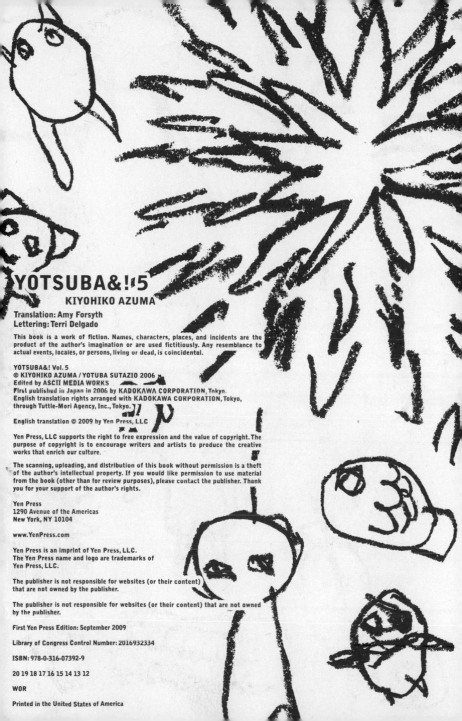

YOTSUBA&! 5
KIYOHIKO AZUMA

Translation: Amy Forsyth
Lettering: Terri Delgado

This book is a work of fiction. Names, characters, places, and incidents are the product of the author's imagination or are used fictitiously. Any resemblance to actual events, locales, or persons, living or dead, is coincidental.

YOTSUBA&! Vol. 5
© KIYOHIKO AZUMA / YOTUBA SUTAZIO 2006
Edited by ASCII MEDIA WORKS
First published in Japan in 2006 by KADOKAWA CORPORATION, Tokyo.
English translation rights arranged with KADOKAWA CORPORATION, Tokyo,
through Tuttle-Mori Agency, Inc., Tokyo.

English translation © 2009 by Yen Press, LLC

Yen Press
1290 Avenue of the Americas
New York, NY 10104

www.YenPress.com

Yen Press is an imprint of Yen Press, LLC.
The Yen Press name and logo are trademarks of
Yen Press, LLC.

The publisher is not responsible for websites (or their content) that are not owned by the publisher.

The publisher is not responsible for websites (or their content) that are not owned by the publisher.

First Yen Press Edition: September 2009

Library of Congress Control Number: 2016932334

ISBN: 978-0-316-07392-9

20 19 18 17 16 15 14 13 12

WOR

Printed in the United States of America

YOTSUBA&!

ENJOY EVERYTHING.

TO BE CONTINUED!